A FOREIGN POLICY RESEARCH INSTITUTE BOOK

8-27

RED STAR ON THE NILE

RED STAR ON THE NILE

*The Soviet-Egyptian Influence
Relationship since the June War*

BY ALVIN Z. RUBINSTEIN

PRINCETON UNIVERSITY PRESS

PRINCETON, NEW JERSEY

TO

FRANKIE RUDA

EXACTING CRITIC
AND GREAT COMPANION

Contents

CONTENTS

CONTENTS

D EFEAT transformed the Soviet-Egyptian relationship. The massive flow of Soviet aid after the June War restored Egypt's military capability and intensified interactions between the two countries on all levels. What previously had been a friendly but limited arrangement became an intimate association that cut across the national, regional, and international interests of each and drew the Soviet Union into the mainstream of Egyptian and Arab politics. Never a partnership or an alliance in the true sense of the term—not even after the Treaty of Friendship and Cooperation of May 27, 1971—the relationship, nonetheless, was of a new type for both parties. For the Soviet Union, it was a pioneering venture in military-political involvement with a non-Communist Third World country. While providing a solid basis for the Soviet strategic presence in the area, it also had serious implications for Soviet relations with the United States. For Egypt,[1] the relationship required a fundamental reversal in Nasir's diplomatic strategy: whereas he had heretofore avoided entanglement with any great power, after June 1967 he made every effort to enmesh a superpower directly in the defense and promotion of Egyptian interests. Politically in difficulty and militarily impotent, Nasir gambled that he could control the actions of the bear while riding it to safety.

The main purpose of this study is to contribute to an understanding of the Soviet-Egyptian influence relationship in the period since the June War: who influenced whom to do what? when? how? and why? Indeed, we must ask, could influence be exerted when wanted by the USSR? by Egypt?

Answers to these questions will provide an understanding not only of the Soviet-Egyptian influence relationship, important in its own right, but also of other Soviet–Third World relationships and of the limits on superpower influence in the Third World. They can contribute to the study of foreign policy in general through the light they shed on the parameters and constraints—

---

[1] The country will generally be referred to as Egypt in this study, even though the official name was the United Arab Republic (UAR) from 1958 to January 1, 1972, when it was changed to the Arab Republic of Egypt (ARE), following the short-lived federation with Syria and Libya.

occasionally intuited but seldom specified—that inhere in relations between a superpower and a nonaligned Third World country; on the contrast between the multidimensionality of influencebuilding and the finiteness of influence; on the linkage between the bilateral relationship and the regional and international politics of each of the parties; and on the interface between domestic politics and foreign policy decisions. What theoretical utility this study may have for foreign policy analysis must emerge from a detailed examination of the actual Soviet-Egyptian influence relationship and from a deliberate effort to understand the phenomenon of influence. The unknowns are considerable. The unavailability of certain crucial data makes divergent interpretations inevitable. But though definitiveness be unattainable, thoroughness is not.

This study seeks to use data and criteria that are as precise and pertinent as possible, and hopes that the hypotheses and approaches used here may help us devise a method for assessing an influence relationship. A few words will define our underlying assumptions. First, every nation engages in influencebuilding—the process whereby a ruling elite seeks by nonmilitary means to advance national aims. This study treats one type of influence relationship, that between a superpower and a nonaligned, developing, non-European country.[2] Even within this category, differences of approach are unavoidable both because of the intrasystemic particularities that distinguish Egypt from non-Arab Third World countries and because it is the USSR and not the United States that is being studied;[3] we assume that variations

[2] Five types of influence relationships may be distinguished: 1) the relationship between a superpower and a nonaligned, developing, non-European country (such as Egypt); 2) the relationship between two countries within one alliance system; 3) the relationship between two countries each of which is the member of a different alliance system; 4) the relationship between two nonaligned countries that are not part of the same alliance system; and 5) the relationship between one country or group of countries interacting with another country or group of countries within the framework of international or regional organizations. The manifestations of influence and the criteria by which they are evaluated would differ from one typology to another.

[3] It was my original intention to attempt a comparative study of the Soviet-Egyptian and Soviet-Indian influence relationships, but once into the research I came to the conclusion that, given the many differences between Egypt and India, a truly cross-national and cross-regional paradigm for assessing influence was beyond reach. The best that can be hoped for at present is a workable approach that will have applicability to societies of similar socio-political

in political systems produce differences in the manifestation and exercise of influence. Second, to be useful operationally, the concept of influence should be used in as limited a sense as possible, in the context of normal diplomatic transactions. Statements such as "Soviet influence in Egypt is growing" will be avoided because they are too general to treat empirically or analytically. The study of Soviet influence on Egyptian policy is quite different from speculation about Soviet goals or objectives, which remain unknown and unknowable, however much "guesstimates" may abound. Though such speculation is essential, the fact is that we have no way of knowing what Soviet aims in Egypt are at any given time—Soviet leaders do not say. We assume a multiplicity of goals, whose order of priority may vary over time and with circumstances. The best that can be done is to infer aims from behavior. Third, changes in Soviet or Egyptian behavior or attitudes, however slight, are the stuff of which assessments of the influence relationship are made, and the place to look for them is in the interaction of the two parties within the developing country that is the target. Thus Soviet influence in Egypt must be sought primarily in Egypt's political system and diplomatic behavior. Fourth, foreign policy is a function of domestic determinants. Any influence that may be exercised by the Soviet Union should be evident from an examination of the "issue areas,"[4] which reveal the concrete policy divergences that are manifested at some point in Egypt's interaction with the Soviet Union. Fifth, there are relatively few instances of influence that can be positively identified as such, because the number of issue areas is, in reality, quite limited. Sixth, the Soviet Union will not press attempts at influencebuilding to the extent of seriously compromising Egypt's sovereignty or undermining the essential internal political base of Egypt's ruling elite, for fear that this would occasion a counterreaction detrimental to the attainment of the Soviet goals that originally motivated the support. Conversely,

---

backgrounds within a particular geographic and cultural area. Hence this study should prove especially germane for those dealing with Soviet relations with Arab countries.

[4] James Rosenau, "Pre-Theories and Theories of Foreign Policy," in R. Barry Farrell (ed.), *Approaches to Comparative and International Politics* (Evanston, Illinois: Northwestern University Press, 1966), pp. 60-92. Rosenau's notion of "issue areas" is useful, but his conceptual framework and proposed model is unwieldy and impossible to operationalize using the data that are available to a researcher concerned with Soviet foreign policy.

Egypt's rulers will not make concessions that would jeopardize their domestic political control. Seventh, the donor is not unaffected by his courtship of the donee; there is a feedback that appertains to all influence relationships. Finally, the Soviet-Egyptian influence relationship is not constant and is never a mere reflection of disparities in power. In the present international system, power-in-being has less utility for influence-building in nonwar situations than at any time in history. Soviet inputs into Egypt do not automatically bring increments in influence. They are the materials used in the hope of building influence. But the building blocks must not be confused with the completed design.

Our aim is to identify and understand influence, not to predict it: we want to know when it exists and how it can be assessed. As a working definition we may use the following: influence is manifested when A (the Soviet leadership) affects, through non-military means, directly or indirectly, the behavior of B (Egypt's rulers) so that it redounds to the policy advantage of A. Definition immediately raises a semantic problem because the phenomenon of influence is both a process and a product. As defined here, influence is a process; yet what is in fact observed and assessed is the net result or outcome of the process. No wording can completely free us of this problem. However, we hope our use of either of the two meanings is sufficiently precise to make our intent clear.

Influence may be considered to have a number of characteristics:

a) it is a relational concept involving "the transferral of a pattern (of preferences) from a source (the controlling actor) to a destination (the responding actor), in such a way that the outcome pattern corresponds to the original preference pattern";[5]

b) it is issue-specific and situation-specific: the duration of influence is restricted to the life of the issue or the situation

---

[5] Jack H. Nagel, *The Descriptive Analysis of Power* (New Haven: Yale University Press, 1975), p. 33. Nagel uses the terms *power* and *influence* interchangeably. Though he does not operationalize his own definition of power, which he describes in terms of preferences among variables rather than overt behavior of individuals or groups, he provides a lucid assessment of the difficulties entailed in measuring and evaluating power, i.e. influence.

within which it appeared, and when these change so does the influence relationship;

    c) it is a short-lived phenomenon;

    d) it is an asymmetrical interaction process;

    e) it has no fixed pattern of achievement costs; and

    f) it is multidimensional, manifesting itself in different spheres.

Several possible criteria for identifying instances of influence may be considered. First, we can try to isolate the concrete instances in which Egypt modifies its position or behavior in a manner congenial to the Soviet Union. From the degree, frequency, and implications of such modifications, inferences can be made concerning Soviet influence. It is important, however, to be aware that what seems to be influence often turns out instead to be joint interests of the two parties: there are in practice only a few issues of importance to both parties on which one of them adapts to the preferences of the other. Minimal adaptations are part of the overall influence relationship; they are the "payoffs" for services rendered or requested and are usually made since the costs are negligible. The problem of distinguishing between important and less important issues can be knotty, but in the case of Soviet-Egyptian relations it is not insuperable. The critical instances become apparent to the close observer; and agreement on them, though perhaps not always on their significance, should not be difficult to reach. What may not always be readily apparent, however, is who influenced whom.

A second criterion of influence is a sharp improvement in Soviet ability to carry out transactions in Egypt. However, it is difficult to know when quantitative increments connote qualitative changes. Sergei Vinogradov, the overbearing Soviet ambassador in Cairo from September 1967 to late 1970, frequently bragged of his ability to see Nasir any time he wanted. Even if he had more entrée than any other ambassador, how significant was the content of the discussions? Was Nasir more responsive to his views than to those of other ambassadors whom he saw less frequently? Again, we know that Soviet advisers are at different times more or less active in many important areas of the Egyptian economy, but how does that correlate with their influence on the leadership's development strategy and priorities?

Third, any sudden and marked increase in the quantity, quality, and variety of resources committed by the USSR to Egypt suggests a change in the influence relationship. But whereas a major change in Soviet security commitments, for example, may result in greater influence, it may also represent a response to Egypt's enhanced bargaining position, an effort to maintain and consolidate the previous relationship at even greater cost. The final determination of who is the influencer and who the influencee must await examination of specific issues arising during the course of subsequent interactions.

A fourth and very important criterion is the extent to which the Soviet Union's strategic position improves. Obtaining tangible short-term advantages within the framework of the Soviet-Egyptian relationship may not always be the Soviets' main purpose. The success or failure of their influencebuilding also needs to be evaluated in terms of the consequences discernible within the broader context of the regional and global benefits the Soviets hope will redound to them as a result of enabling Egypt to follow its policy preferences. A donor may have a number of objectives in mind; the desire for immediate return may be present but not pressing. By way of illustration, the Soviet Union gave Egypt extensive aid after the June War. It quickly received strategic dividends: naval facilities at Alexandria and the use of airfields for reconnoitering the U.S. Sixth Fleet. These capital gains were virtually wiped out after July 17, 1972, when President Anwar Sadat ousted most of the Soviet military personnel. One might therefore argue that the Soviet Union made a poor investment, and, if the argument relates primarily to the immediate payoff, the case is convincing. But this would overlook or minimize what may well have been the most important consideration for Soviet leaders: to keep Egypt from negotiating a settlement of the Arab-Israeli conflict lest this eliminate from the Middle East the festering problem that helped the Soviet Union intrude itself into the politics of the region. Gauging influence in terms of consequences external to the Soviet-Egyptian relationship itself is clearly open to the criticism of being highly judgmental and of complicating rather than clarifying the concept of influence. Yet this criterion does serve an explanatory function that provides an additional, perhaps crucial, dimension to our analysis.

The utility of the concept of influence for policy-oriented analysts depends on the extent to which it can be operationalized.

The determination of influence in the relationship between Egypt and the Soviet Union demands a method and data appropriate to that milieu. It may be likened to building a house: certain essentials govern the building of any house, but adaptations in design, materials, and methods will be necessary in light of the particular conditions attending in Egypt. Just as we know in advance the limitations imposed by the landscape and make appropriate allowances in the blueprints, so, too, do we know and allow for the data limitations inherent in studying Soviet-Egyptian relations. In both cases a useful end-product is possible nonetheless.

The task of identifying data that are relevant, that lend themselves to comparative analysis, and that can be set in a conceptual framework is formidable. The body of data available for the study of Soviet-Egyptian relations may be organized into five broad categories: 1) measures of direct interaction; 2) measures of perceptual and attitudinal change; 3) measures of attributed influence; 4) case studies; and 5) impressionistic and idiosyncratic commentary. Each of these categories has definite limitations.

First, the measures of direct interaction bring into play the entire range of quantitative and aggregate data, such as trade, aid, U.N. voting patterns, and exchanges of missions. Though readily available and abundant, these data turn out to have a low substantive yield: certainly, as generally compiled and used they provide us with little that can flesh out an influence relationship. Studies based on Soviet-Egyptian trade and aid flows are apt to make judgments about Soviet influence that are not warranted by the data as presented; they read into economic data political assessments that may be true but that need to be proven not merely postulated. For example, a heavy trade deficit does not necessarily bring the creditor political influence, because it no longer causes fears of "gunboat diplomacy." Military intervention to collect debts or seize valuable natural resources has gone out of style. Trade data could be useful if we knew more about the terms of trade, the prices that Egypt pays for Soviet imports and receives for its exports to the USSR relative to world market prices. Not surprisingly, these are closely guarded commercial and political secrets, but the Egyptians say the USSR drives a hard bargain, something not likely to foster sentiment in Cairo about the disinterested nature of the relationship.

Similar shortcomings attend the use of data on economic aid.

More pertinent than the totals of Soviet credits would be the amounts actually utilized by the Egyptians. Instead of dwelling on the projects to which the credits were applied, analyses are needed to tell us what individuals or groups benefited from the economic aid; what ministries and sectors of the economy were strengthened, and how the power of specific elites was enhanced as a consequence; in what ways, if any, Soviet inputs facilitated Soviet penetration of economic or non-economic institutions. Certainly the Aswan High Dam is a monumental example of Soviet assistance, and the Soviets can be justifiably proud of their role in its construction; but has it made Cairo more receptive to Soviet wishes? One is reminded of the congressman who was campaigning for reelection and asked a farmer how he intended to vote. On receiving a noncommittal response, the congressman indignantly recalled all that he had done for his constituent: "Six years ago I saved you from bankruptcy with a government loan; four years ago I arranged for power and telephone lines to be extended to your farm at no cost; and two years ago I had your government subsidy payments doubled."

"That's true," drawled the farmer, "but what have you done for me lately?"

One type of aggregate data that has virtually no value for evaluating influence, at least not as presently compiled, is U.N. voting statistics. They do not tell us who influenced whom: whether Egypt voted with the Soviet Union because of Soviet pressure, because it independently opted for the same outcome as the USSR, or because it wanted to be on the winning side on a popular issue; or whether it was the other way round, and the Soviet Union voted for the resolution out of a desire to align itself with Egypt. Voting studies examine end-products, not processes. They do not consider the political dynamics that are responsible for modifying the antecedent resolutions on which, after intensive corridor lobbying, the final resolution is drafted and acted upon. By using roll call votes as the basis for attributing influence, they divorce the outcome from the reality that produced it, with the frequent result that the outcome itself is misinterpreted. Only by comparing all the draft resolutions introduced by the various national delegations on a given issue with the resolution finally voted on would it be possible to make meaningful inferences concerning the extent of Soviet influence. It may also be important to know the dynamics within individual delegations, the degree to which nondecisions play a role in the General Assembly, and the ways in which decisions are reached without voting.

For our purposes one potentially useful type of aggregate data is the exchange of visits. Those who use these data view them as "communications flows" whose patterns throw light on influence relationships, on the assumption that "the nation *receiving* the preponderant number of visits will be considered the nation exercising asymmetrical influence over the other," and that in the long run "the nation which is visited, when it boosts its 'credit' with the nation seeking support, tends to exercise continuing direction over that nation's foreign policy."[6] While highly innovative, this approach treats all visits as equally important and ignores their significant differences. Thus, in addition to tallying the number of visits, it is essential to examine their composition, to compare their apparent purposes with the results achieved, and to evaluate the treatment accorded them in the media before, during, and after the visits. Exchanges of missions are meaningful only when evaluated contextually. The measures of direct interaction used in this study have been adapted to meet some of the caveats noted above, and they will be linked to specific issue areas.

A second category of data is measures of perceptual and attitudinal change, which include thematic content analysis of joint communiqués and evaluations of editorials and articles in key newspapers and journals, official speeches and statements, and radio broadcasts. Of these, joint communiqués and key newspaper editorials are especially valuable. Strict quantitative content analysis was not applied to the joint communiqués and editorials because preliminary research revealed that this technique did not yield any additional substantive insights into the influence relationship itself. Thus, the use of thematic content analysis is deliberate.

The examination of joint communiqués as a method of ascertaining the condition of relations between states has been neglected. Little has been written on this pulse-taking procedure.[7]

6 Steven J. Brams, "The Structure of Influence Relationships in the International System," in James N. Rosenau (ed.), *International Politics and Foreign Policy*, rev. ed. (New York: The Free Press, 1969), pp. 585, 595.

7 For example, there is no discussion of joint communiqués in Robert C. North, et al., *Content Analysis* (Evanston, Illinois: Northwestern University Press, 1963), which treats the more voluminous types of diplomatic documents,

Communiqués are generally published at the conclusion of visits by high-ranking delegations. The usual procedure is for each party to prepare a draft before the actual talks begin. Working groups of the two parties negotiate to determine what will appear in the final communiqué, while the leaders exchange views and go sight-seeing—an interlude for allowing loose ends to be tied together and for public relations.

In communiqués issued after meetings between representatives of the Soviet government and Third World governments, a preponderance of Soviet formulations (whose style and content are readily identifiable) indicates that the final draft is basically the one provided by the Soviet delegation. The more formal the visit, the more commitments the Soviet Union is apt to make and the longer the communiqué it is likely to request, leading to the inclusion of issues broached by the USSR and of interest primarily to it.

As the path of least trouble, Third World leaders often accept the Soviet draft on issues extraneous to their immediate concerns. Since Egyptian leaders care little about developments outside of the Middle East, the inclusion of issues such as disarmament, European security, Berlin, or SALT (strategic arms limitation talks) is a sop for some service. But on matters of consequence to them, Third World leaders are quite capable of looking out for their own interests. The Egyptians, especially, have a reputation for Jesuitical skill in drafting communiqués, hence it is to be assumed that these instrumental expressions of position say precisely what their drafters intend.

The particular language of communiqués that the Soviet Union signs with Third World countries is a rough measure of the degree of agreement. For example, we take the words "frank" or "candid" to mean that differences were aired but remained unresolved. The term "the Soviet Union appreciates" indicates that the USSR understands the Third World country's policy dilemma but does not agree with its proposed course of action. A "similarity of views" signifies some disagreement; in cases of agreement "identical views" is the preferred term. Other examples will be developed in the analysis of specific communiqués. The terms, unfortunately, are on occasion used in ways that

in its effort to link the content and flow of messages to perceptions of hostility.

confound easy standardization. Also, each party relies on the version put out in its own language, a situation that can give rise to a difference in emphasis. Finally, as the Arabologists argue persuasively, communiqués have an ephemeral significance for the Egyptians. Once issued, once the obeisance and commentaries are made, they are quickly forgotten and rarely referred to again.

Sovietologists and Arabologists disagree on the precise weight to be assigned to communiqués: the former regard them as important, the latter as merely suggestive, their main use being propaganda for domestic consumption. Sovietologists scrutinize each phrase; Arabologists are less concerned with identifying key words and focus on the explicit and on the context. Both look for departures from the norm, for variations from preceding communiqués. The absence of a communiqué may not be significant, but if a high-ranking official is involved, the presumption usually is that the visit was a failure, that substantive disagreements proved irreconcilable. Refusal to sign even a pro forma statement of principles, as was the case during Boumedienne's visit to Moscow in June 1967, means that the Third World country is completely at odds with the Soviet position unless the mission or visit has been secret. However one approaches them, communiqués offer an important barometer of the ups and downs of the Soviet-Egyptian influence relationship.

Those using the data outlined here will, I believe, find them appropriate for an elucidation of changes of attitude and tensions between national positions. They are particularly useful in studying the foreign policies of authoritarian and closed societies. (Although Egypt is a more relaxed society than the Soviet Union, it is in some ways even more difficult to obtain political information from, because of the paucity of serious journals expressing official views. The accessibility of Egyptians to foreigners and the richness of rumors give the illusion that more information is available than really is.)

Third, measures of attributed influence entail polling the experts, on the assumption that consensus among the leading specialists will provide an authoritative answer. While useful as a control on the work of the individual researcher, polling is no substitute for the effort undertaken in this study; it merely begs the central questions about influence raised earlier. No matter what the specialists say about the Soviet-Egyptian influence relationship, the problem remains of evaluating the assumptions, data, and criteria on which their analyses are based.

Fourth, case studies offer an opportunity to trace the unfolding of influence on significant issues and to bring varieties of data to bear on a particular problem. Heavy reliance will be placed on them, though with the realization that key information may be unavailable. This problem, of course, faces anyone studying contemporary affairs.

Finally, where appropriate, impressionistic and idiosyncratic material will be used to supplement "hard" data and to reinforce speculative interpretations. Though their printed matter may repeat basic facts and lack depth, the journalists, privy to declassified NATO intelligence reports and leaks from friendly embassies, are privately an important source of information. A well-informed journalist in Cairo, for example, often knows a great deal about the constraints on Moscow's ability to operate in Egypt. He knows about the day-to-day relationship between Egyptian officials and their Soviet counterparts and the kinds of preferential treatment accorded to Soviet diplomats in Cairo. Lebanese commentaries are particularly informative on Egyptian politics and Egypt's relations with the Arab world. Interviews are also useful: knowledgeable officials, in a communicative mood, can fill in some gaps in the published record.

A chronological approach has been adopted for several reasons. The manifestations of influence that emerge will do so within discrete historical time frames. They need to be identified, examined, traced, and compared over time. Chronological scrutiny lessens the possibility that anything important will be overlooked and increases the likelihood of identifying the variables that lend themselves to analysis and comparison. Like ballet, an influence relationship can be properly understood only if the moves of the performers are watched closely and each action is taken to have a meaning that enhances understanding of the whole. Such an approach also lends itself to the exploration of issue areas, to seeing foreign policy as an integral function of domestic politics. Finally, it sensitizes the analyst to the concatenation of pressures, attitudes, and options.

A number of hypotheses that seek to establish correlations between Soviet inputs and Soviet influence will be tested, utilizing the relevant data that are available.

1. The greater the economic, military, and cultural interaction

between the USSR (*A*) and Egypt (*B*), the greater will be Soviet influence. (Rationale: A stepped-up flow of goods and services from *A* to *B* creates a measure of dependency, which, in turn, fosters expectations in *A* that *B* will become more amenable to *A*'s preferences.)

2. The greater the presence of *A* in *B*, the more likely *A* is to exercise influence over *B*. (Rationale: Access is held to be the key to influence: the more that *A* channels aid into *B*'s domestic system, the more will be its dealings with *B*'s decision-makers; the more that *A* has access to *B*'s decision-makers, the greater will be its influence.)

3. The larger the relative number of *B*'s missions to *A*, the greater will be *A*'s influence. (Rationale: The influencer will be the one who receives the disproportionate share of visits.)

4. The treatment in *B*'s media of visits by *A*'s officials (or the converse) reveals more about the *A-B* influence relationship than does any asymmetry in the number of visits exchanged. (Rationale: Interactions assessed as aggregates miss much of the continuing ebb and flow that characterizes influence relationships. To identify influence, which is time-specific, interactions must be evaluated within fairly limited time periods.)

5. The political use of aid diminishes over time. (Rationale: Aid is useful primarily in establishing a presence; its utility in bringing influence wanes with regularization; and its diminution entails costs to *A*.)

6. The more sophisticated the weaponry sent by *A* to *B*, the more likely *A* is to have influence. (Rationale: The quality of weaponry greatly affects *B*'s dependence on *A* for spare parts and sustained deliveries of equipment and ammunition, since it makes replacement from other sources more difficult, and hence makes *B* more compliant to *A*'s preferences.)

The moment has come to proceed, even though the tools and materials are imperfect. Surgeons, even with the impressive advances in medicine must, I am told, often operate on the basis of suggestive symptoms, lacking a surer way of knowing what really is the problem. Only by venturing can they hope to learn. And so with us.

A few words of appreciation: many would not be inappropriate. This project has led me into interesting byways and blind alleys. It could not have been completed without the encouragement and support of a number of institutions, to whom I most gratefully acknowledge my deep appreciation. The Barra Foundation and the National Science Foundation helped in the initial stage. The American Philosophical Society supported a month of research in Cairo. The Earhart Foundation and the Joint Committee on Soviet Studies of the American Council of Learned Societies and the Social Science Research Council made possible a year of uninterrupted research to complete the study. The chapters began to take form during a month's stay as a Resident Scholar at the Rockefeller Foundation's Bellagio Study and Conference Center in September 1974. The first draft was completed during the 1974–1975 academic year at Cambridge University, where I was a Visiting Fellow at Clare Hall and the Center for International Studies. Professor F. H. Hinsley of St. John's College was most helpful in making my stay in Cambridge productive and pleasant. The Foreign Policy Research Institute provided a summer to complete the writing. Officials, scholars, and journalists in Washington, Cairo, Jerusalem, London, and Belgrade were generous with information.

The study has benefited from the critical analysis and helpful comments of a number of individuals who read all of the manuscript, and I acknowledge their assistance with pleasure and appreciation: Richard H. Dekmejian of the State University of New York at Binghamton; William B. Quandt of the University of Pennsylvania; and Oles M. Smolansky of Lehigh University. Ibrahim M. Gheiadi ably assisted with the Arabic translations. Mrs. Katherine Wainright and Miss Jo Ellen Milkovits of the Foreign Policy Research Institute typed the manuscript. As always, Princeton University Press was a delight to work with, and I especially wish to thank Sanford G. Thatcher and Mrs. Gail Filion.

Alvin Z. Rubinstein

Bryn Mawr, Pennsylvania
May 30, 1976

RED STAR ON THE NILE

THE Soviet Union and Egypt discovered one another after 1953 in the changed domestic, regional, and international circumstances that followed the death of Iosif V. Stalin and the emergence of Gamal 'Abd al-Nasir as the dominant personality in the Revolutionary Command Council, which had deposed King Faruq in July 1952. Soviet interest in Egypt, like its policy toward the Arab world in general, matured only after World War II. From 1917 to 1945 Soviet strategy in the Middle East had centered on geographically contiguous Turkey and Iran. Through treaties and correct diplomatic relations, Moscow had sought to ensure that these countries would not become part of any prospective hostile capitalist coalition and that Soviet access to the eastern Mediterranean through the Bosphorus and the Dardanelles would be assured. In 1945–1946 Stalin tried to acquire a trusteeship over either Libya, Eritrea, or Italian Somalia, but was rebuffed by the Western powers, already suspicious of Soviet imperial ambitions as manifested in pressure on Turkey for a return of the area of Kars and Ardahan in eastern Anatolia, the granting of a military base in Turkish Thrace, and the attempted incorporation of Persian Azerbaijan into the Soviet Union. Stymied in these expansionist thrusts, Soviet policy, with the exception of the intercession on behalf of the partition of Palestine and the creation of the state of Israel, had no effect on developments in the Arab East.

But decolonization, domestic upheavals in Syria and Egypt, and the Western fixation with military pacts, whose consequence was the polarization of regional rivalries and loyalties, transformed the Middle East environment and paved the way for Soviet penetration. After seizing power in Egypt, Nasir moved to end the residual British presence in the Suez Canal zone. He refused to join any Western-sponsored military pact and opposed the U.S. and British policy of containing Soviet expansion through a network of interlocking alliances with the countries of the Middle East and Southern Asia. Further, angered at the flow of arms to Iraq, Egypt's main rival in the Arab world, which was reaping its reward for participating in the Western security system, and pressed by his military to end the weakness that they perceived Egypt to be in vis-à-vis Israel, Nasir turned to Moscow. The timing was felicitous, the convergence of interests was to prove momentous.

One of the objectives of the post-Stalin Soviet leadership was to crack the chrysalis of containment. Starting in the United Nations in the summer of 1953, the USSR evinced new interest in the Third World. It ended the Soviet bloc's unwillingness to contribute to U.N. economic programs for developing countries, extended economic and military credits to Afghanistan, concluded a mini-arms deal with Syria in late 1954, and agreed in February 1955 to construct the Bokaro steel plant in India. Underlying this incipient, far-ranging foreign aid program was a determination to undermine and destroy, if possible, the Western system of regional alliances and the military threat that it posed to the exposed southern underbelly of the Soviet Union.

On April 16, 1955, the USSR Ministry of Foreign Affairs issued a statement signifying Moscow's intention to pursue an active policy in the Arab world and counter the newly created Baghdad Pact. It attacked the Western countries for drawing the nations of the Middle East into military groupings linked to the North Atlantic Treaty Organization (NATO) and asserted that "the Soviet Union cannot remain indifferent to the situation arising in the region of the Near and Middle East, since the formation of these blocs and the establishment of foreign military bases on the territory of the countries of the Near and Middle East have a direct bearing on the security of the USSR." Coming less than a month after Moscow had publicly declared its readiness to help Syria defend its independence, the statement put the Western powers on notice that continued Turkish and Iraqi pressure on Syria would bring full Soviet support to Damascus to uphold the Syrian government's policy of nonalignment. If it were to weaken the West's grip on the area, the USSR had to make alternative policy options feasible for the regional actors. The ideological sanction for this "forward policy" in the Third World was proclaimed at the Twentieth Congress of the Communist Party of the Soviet Union (CPSU) in February 1956, when Khrushchev emphasized the political-strategic importance of the Afro-Asian world, noting that "a vast 'zone of peace,' including both socialist and non-socialist peace-loving states in Europe and Asia has emerged in the world arena."

4

Nasir's aims paralleled Moscow's. Accordingly, the Soviet government, perceiving the disruptive potential of Egypt's nationalist and anti-Western position, responded to Cairo's request for weapons and in so doing escalated the Middle East arms race. In late September 1955, Nasir announced a major arms agreement between Egypt and Czechoslovakia (the USSR's temporary surrogate). While it enabled him to circumvent the Western arms embargo, this commercial transaction had fateful consequences: it further alienated the United States and Britain, heightened Israel's fears, and strengthened Nasir's confidence, leading both to his recognition of the People's Republic of China in May 1956, a move that, in turn, impelled Secretary of State John Foster Dulles to drop support for America's financing of the Aswan High Dam, and to his nationalization of the Suez Canal Company in July 1956, thus triggering the chain of events that prompted Israel, France, and Britain to attack Egypt at the end of October 1956.

Notwithstanding Moscow's professions of full support for Egypt in the weeks preceding the Suez War, the USSR behaved with the utmost caution during the eight critical days of October 29 to November 5, when the fighting and maneuvering of the interested parties were at their peak and when Nasir seemed defeated. The unexpected intervention of the United States saved him. True, the Soviet Union was absorbed with unrest and revolt in Poland and Hungary, but it did not really have the military power to challenge the tripartite invasion. Khrushchev blustered and threatened only after America's stand had obviated the need for any direct action.

In the years that followed, the full implications of the arms deal materialized. Moscow established strong links to Egypt, thus facilitating the expansion of its relations with Syria, Lebanon, and Yemen; and the arms race it set off was to have enormous significance for the future of Soviet-Egyptian relations: from mere arms merchant, the Soviet Union was to become, in time, the ultimate guarantor of Nasir's rulership. Moscow's commitments to Egypt expanded; in October 1958, it agreed to finance the construction of the Aswan High Dam. Trade increased, as did interaction in the political and cultural spheres. Soviet support underpinned Egypt's independent line in Middle East affairs, and it showed what friendship with the Soviet Union could bring.

However, successes also brought underlying conflicts of interest to the fore. The toppling in July 1958 of the pro-Western leaders in Iraq and that country's formal withdrawal from the Baghdad Pact the following March were hailed by Moscow and Cairo. Yet during the 1959–1961 period this major turnabout in Arab politics contributed to the serious strains that were besetting the Soviet-Egyptian relationship. These were engendered by a number of developments: by differences over the treatment of Egyptian Communists; by Khrushchev's stress on the struggle against imperialism (i.e. the West) at a time when Nasir was making an effort to balance good relations with the Soviet Union with an improvement in ties to the Western powers; by the struggle between the Nasirites and the Communists in the United Arab Republic, which had been created by the union of Egypt and Syria in February 1958; by the deterioration in relations between Cairo and Baghdad, which adversely affected Soviet-Egyptian relations because of Moscow's interest in promoting ties with the Iraqi military regime of General 'Abd al-Karim Qasim, who was more tolerant of local Communists; and by discordant public exchanges over the merits of Arab socialism versus the Soviet version—scientific socialism.

If in the 1950s the Soviet Union had courted Egypt with political aims in mind—to strengthen Nasir's resistance to Western pressure, to provide him with the wherewithal to make nonalignment a viable option and thus thwart the American plan of linking Egypt to NATO, and to allay anxieties elsewhere in the Arab world over the supposed dangers of improved relations with the USSR—in the 1960s it was motivated, in addition, by a growing desire for military privileges. The Sino-Soviet rift cost Moscow its naval base in Albania and whetted its strategic interest in Egypt. The Soviet Union's pro-Yugoslav policy led Tirana to side with Peking in the widening Sino-Soviet rift and in May 1961 to evict the Soviet navy from the base at Vlone that it had been operating since 1945. This military setback coincided with the USSR's increasing concern over its vulnerability to America's nuclear strike force: not only did the United States have intermediate range ballistic missiles (IRBM's) deployed in Italy, Greece, and Turkey and attack aircraft carriers in the Mediterranean that could launch planes capable of reaching key Soviet targets, but it was also on the verge of deploying Polaris submarines. These SSBN's (fleet ballistic missile nuclear-powered submarines) greatly expanded American strike capabilities against the Soviet Union. The Soviet military establishment acted to offset these advantages.

Moscow proceeded on several fronts: diplomatically, it proposed that the Mediterranean be declared a nuclear-free zone; militarily, it gave the go-ahead for a permanent naval presence in the Mediterranean, with all that was required to expand the Soviet navy; politically, it brought increasing pressure to bear on Egypt and other friendly Arab states for naval and air facilities and played up the threat to them all from imperialism. Military considerations persuaded Khrushchev to tone down his on-again off-again dispute with Nasir.

For reasons of his own, Nasir did not want the quarrel with Khrushchev to jeopardize the Soviet-Egyptian relationship. As a gesture, he amnestied all political prisoners (mostly Communists) on the eve of the Soviet leader's visit in May 1964 and allowed them to resume political activity within Egypt's one-party structure. Soviet naval ships were permitted to make visits, but Nasir carefully side-stepped any permanent arrangements.

After Khrushchev was deposed in October 1964, his successors, urged on by the Soviet military, signified their intention of promoting closer ties between the Soviet Union and Egypt. Economic aid was increased (though this had been one of the grievances the other members of the Politburo had held against Khrushchev); high-ranking officials exchanged visits more frequently (for example, Nasir visited the USSR in August 1965 and Premier Aleksei N. Kosygin made his first trip to Egypt in May 1966); major arms agreements were concluded in November 1964 and again a year later. Moscow increased the size of its military and economic package to Egypt and tried to persuade Nasir to grant the Soviet navy full and automatic access to Egyptian ports and permanent naval facilities. However, there is no evidence that they succeeded in this until after June 1967. Soviet assistance in 1965 and 1966 helped alleviate Nasir's economic difficulties. Also, he was dependent on Soviet military support to sustain his intervention in the Yemeni civil war, which started in October 1962; and since Moscow, too, had a stake in the survival of the pro-Nasir Yemeni Arab Republic and in the fanning of unrest in that region, the flow of weapons remained largely unaffected by the periodic tensions that beset their overall relationship.

In broad political terms, the Soviet Union had, through its

assistance to Nasir, helped to nurture a diplomatic environment in the Arab world that was far more congenial to Soviet interests in the spring of 1967 than it had been twelve years earlier. Relations between Moscow and Cairo were good, but far from intimate. It took a catastrophe to alter this relationship and to bring the Soviets the military dividends they coveted.

Chapter One

TRANSFIGURATION

T HE Middle East war of June 1967 was a watershed in Soviet-Egyptian relations. In the ensuing months, Moscow assumed commitments far greater than any it had previously undertaken in quest of imperial objectives in the Third World: the arms deal of September 1955 and the building of the Aswan High Dam in the 1960s were by comparison low-risk, uncomplicated initiatives whose dramatic impact overshadowed their actual strategic significance. After the June War, the Soviet Union became Egypt's benefactor, munificent but calculating, supportive but ambitious and sometimes overbearing. This ever-changing relationship acquired global importance, affecting as it did issues of war and peace and the superpower détente.

In the following pages the historical background is presented with the purpose of delineating the relationships and outlooks that serve as the starting point for our study of the Soviet-Egyptian influence relationship.

DEFEAT

Shortly after the outbreak of fighting in the early hours of June 5, 1967, the Kremlin activated the "hot line" to Washington for the first time.[1] Premier Aleksei N. Kosygin "expressed Soviet concern over the fighting," called on the United States to make Israel desist from its attack against Egypt, Syria, and Jordan, and stated Moscow's intention to seek a cease-fire through the United Nations.[2] Later in the day, the Soviet government denounced the Israeli "aggression" in a statement that criticized the encouragement given by the "covert and overt actions of certain imperialist circles." It affirmed the "resolute support" of the USSR for the

[1] The "hot line," which was an outgrowth of the superpower experience during the Cuban missile crisis of October 1962, was installed on August 30, 1963, to provide instantaneous teletype communications between Moscow and Washington in times of crisis.

[2] Lyndon Baines Johnson, *The Vantage Point: Perspectives of the Presidency, 1963–1969* (New York: Holt, Rinehart and Winston, 1971), pp. 287, 298.

Arab governments and peoples, demanded that Israel "stop immediately and unconditionally its military actions . . . and pull back its troops beyond the truce line," and ended on the ominous note: "The Soviet Government reserves the right to take all steps that may be necessitated by the situation."[3] In the United Nations, the Soviet delegation proposed a resolution calling for an immediate cease-fire, condemnation of Israel, and a full Israeli withdrawal. Egypt (and the other Arab states), however, opposed any cease-fire because in Cairo Gamal 'Abd al-Nasir was still being told by his Military Operations Command that an Egyptian counterattack was imminent and that the campaign was far from lost.

On the morning of June 6, Cairo and Damascus broke off diplomatic relations with the United States and Great Britain, accusing them of collusion with Israel, of "taking part in the Israeli military aggression insofar as the air operations are concerned."[4] In Moscow, Egyptian Ambassador Muhammad Murad Ghaleb met with Premier Kosygin and urged prompt Soviet support. Kosygin again exchanged views with President Lyndon B. Johnson via the hot line and was informed—indeed, he probably already knew on the basis of his own intelligence reports—that Cairo's allegations were false: American aircraft were not involved, nor had they been at any time. A meeting of the Politburo of the Communist Party of the Soviet Union (CPSU) was held on the morning of June 6 to discuss the situation. It is evident that the Politburo realized the inaccurate and reckless nature of the Arab charges of American participation in the Israeli attack

[3] BBC Summary of World Broadcasts: The U.S.S.R. (hereafter referred to as BBC/SU). BBC/SU/2484/A4/1 (June 7, 1967).

[4] BBC Summary of World Broadcasts: The Middle East (hereafter referred to as BBC/ME). BBC/ME/2484/A/18 (June 7, 1967). On June 8, 1967, Israeli authorities issued the text of a monitored radio telephone conversation that had taken place on Tuesday, June 6, at 0450 hours between Nasir and King Husayn. The conversation reveals the fabrication by Nasir and Husayn of the lie that American and British planes were flying with Israeli forces. Nasir is quoted as saying: "I say it would be better for us to issue a statement. I will issue a statement and you will issue a statement. We will also let the Syrians issue a statement that there are American and English aircraft acting against us from aircraft carriers. We will issue a statement and thus make the subject more emphatic, I mean." BBC/ME/2487/A/12 (June 10, 1967).

Not until October 20, 1967, were the Egyptian people officially told, albeit elliptically, that the air attacks had been carried out solely by Israeli planes flying low over the sea: "The enemy did not fly in from the West as we had previously thought, but rather followed the natural course of approach—the gap between Port Said and the Lake of Burullus." The *New York Times* (hereafter referred to as *NYT*), October 21, 1967.

for the Soviet press ignored them. Moscow had no desire to be dragged into a war with the United States just to pull Arab chestnuts out of the fire. The same evening the Soviet delegation at the United Nations dropped its previous demand for the condemnation of Israel and announced its readiness to accept a resolution calling for an immediate cease-fire, without the precondition of a withdrawal to the June 4 lines. This resolution, which the Americans had proposed from the very beginning, was unanimously adopted by all fifteen members of the Security Council. But of the Arab states, only Jordan accepted on the following day, Egypt insisting on a full Israeli withdrawal. Israel agreed to a cease-fire, but only on the condition that it was accepted by all the Arab states.

The June 6 issue of *Pravda* carried, in addition to the text of the Soviet government's declaration of June 5 condemning Israel, an article by Igor' Beliaev, a well-known analyst of Middle East affairs, in which he went beyond a mere reaffirmation of Soviet support for the Arab nations and emphasized that "Nobody can doubt this for a single minute."[5] The target of his remark was not clear, though it was probably intended for Washington and not Cairo, since the situation early on June 6 may still have appeared fluid in Moscow, given the claims of intense fighting and counter-attacks emanating from Arab sources; and Moscow was putting Washington on notice that it would not stand idly by and accept an American intervention to help defeat Egypt and Syria.

Twenty-four hours later Moscow no longer had any doubts about the truth: Egypt, Syria, and Jordan had been decisively defeated, and by Israel alone. Surprised by the dismal showing of Arab forces and unable to prevent the unfolding disaster on the battlefield, the Soviet Union mustered diplomatic support for the Arabs. The Soviet government "warned" the Israeli government that if it did not "comply immediately" with the demand for a cease-fire expressed in the Security Council's resolution, "the Soviet Union will reconsider its attitude towards Israel and decide whether to continue to maintain diplomatic relations with Israel."[6] In the United Nations, Soviet Ambassador Nikolai Fedorenko pressed for immediate implementation of the cease-fire resolution, but his efforts foundered on Egypt's continued insistence that this also entail a full Israeli withdrawal, an interpre-

5 *Pravda*, June 6, 1967.
6 BBC/SU/2486/A4/1 (June 9, 1967).

tation of the Security Council's resolution with which not even the USSR could agree.[7] On the afternoon of June 8 Cairo submitted to the inevitable: Egypt's catastrophic defeat in Sinai was finally realized by Nasir. When it was no longer possible to ignore the evidence of collapse, Foreign Minister Mahmud Riyad hurriedly telephoned Ambassador Muhammad al-Quni at the United Nations "just a few seconds before he was due to address the Council. The instructions this time were completely different from those given a few hours before." Riyad said, "the picture has changed. Go back to the meeting and announce acceptance of the ceasefire."[8] Once Egypt had agreed to the cease-fire, the Soviet delegate pushed for new resolutions condemning Israel as an aggressor and demanding its full withdrawal.[9]

Syria agreed to the cease-fire on June 9, but the fighting continued, each side accusing the other of violations. It was clear that Israel was making an all-out effort to capture the Golan Heights before the cease-fire took hold. On June 10 Moscow again activated the hot line. Kosygin impressed upon President Johnson the urgency of forcing Israel to stop further military operations, or else the Soviet Union would take "necessary actions, including military."[10] Johnson responded to the implicit threat in Kosygin's message by ordering the U.S. Sixth Fleet closer to the Syrian coast, but he also pressured Israel to abide by the cease-fire, which it did on June 10, having achieved its objective—the capture of the Golan Heights.

For the moment there was nothing the Soviet government could do for the Arabs, other than mount a major diplomatic campaign in the United Nations. Beyond that, Moscow was faced with the question, how far should it go to help Egypt and Syria. The answer came quickly.[11]

[7] Arthur Lall, *The UN and the Middle East Crisis, 1967* (New York: Columbia University Press, 1968), p. 61.

[8] This account was given by Muhammad Hasanayn Haykal in his weekly column in *Al-Ahram* on May 30, 1969. See BBC/ME/3088/A/8 (June 2, 1969).

[9] Lall, *The UN*, p. 66. Soviet media accused Israel of ignoring the Security Council resolutions calling for a cease-fire; they made no mention of Israel's conditional acceptance of June 6 and suppressed all information concerning the nonacceptance by Egypt until June 8 and by Syria until June 9.

[10] Johnson, *Vantage Point*, pp. 301-303.

[11] The Soviet decision not to trim its commitments in the Middle East was a surprise to many in the U.S. government. State Department experts were divided between those who thought Moscow would not allow its stake in the area to go by default and those who saw a Soviet disengagement as inevitable.

DECISION IN MOSCOW

On June 9 Moscow mobilized the East European Communist countries on behalf of the Arab states. The leaders of Bulgaria, Czechoslovakia, East Germany, Hungary, Poland, Romania, and Yugoslavia attended a conference in Moscow and issued a Declaration condemning Israel and pledging to "do everything necessary to help the peoples of Arab countries to give a firm rebuff to the aggressor, to protect their lawful rights, and to eliminate the hotbed of war in the Middle East and to restore peace in that area."[12] The Declaration was the first of the Soviet steps taken to entrench Moscow's position in the area and to stiffen Cairo's resolve not to settle with Israel. On June 10 the Soviet Union broke diplomatic relations with Israel. The East European countries followed suit, with the exception of Romania, which had also not signed the Declaration. *Pravda* repeated the USSR's intention of providing "all necessary material assistance" to the Arabs, and on June 12 the Soviet government sent a squadron of TU-16 bombers to show the flag and bolster Egyptian morale.

A massive Soviet airlift of military equipment began on or about June 12, the day Algeria's leader, Premier Houari Boumedienne, unceremoniously arrived in Moscow to assess Soviet intentions. His visit was an irritant as much to Moscow as to Cairo, which resented his unsolicited advice on how to fight a guerrilla war and his high-handed offer of Algerian troops.[13] The arrival

---

One high-ranking official, an acknowledged specialist on Soviet affairs, was quoted as saying, "The Soviets are finished in the Middle East."

Veteran Washington correspondents reported the lack of consensus. Max Frankel quoted American officials who thought that "Soviet leaders would need several weeks or months to reassess their Middle Eastern policies. They are expected to try to press their traditional campaign to exploit the Arab cause against Western interests in the region and to conserve the huge amounts of military and economic aid that encouraged the Arabs to provoke war but did nothing to avert a humiliating defeat," *NYT*, June 11, 1967; and John W. Finney reported that State Department officials were skeptical of Israeli reports of a major Soviet resupply effort and doubted that "the Kremlin has yet made a new decision to send military aid to the Cairo Government," *NYT*, June 15, 1967.

12 BBC/SU/2488/A4/2 (June 12, 1967).

13 The absence of a communiqué at the time of Boumedienne's departure on June 13 suggests his continued skepticism of Soviet policy, notwithstanding the start of the Soviet airlift. Boumedienne's attitude was reflected in Algeria's newspapers, which questioned whether the Soviet bloc, in its promotion of peaceful coexistence between the socialist and capitalist blocs, was

of "significant quantities of Soviet military assistance" in Egypt was reported on June 15 by Tanyug (the Yugoslav News Agency), quoting the Cairo correspondent of *Oslobodjenje*, a Sarajevo newspaper, to the effect that "for the past three days large Soviet army transports have been arriving in the UAR with MiG's as the first urgent assistance to the Egyptian Army," about one hundred MiGs having already been delivered.[14] For the next few weeks Antonov-12s landed at about the rate of one every fifteen minutes. This air bridge, which facilitated the rapid rebuilding of the Egyptian army and air defense system, was made possible by Tito's immediate accession to Nasir's request that the Soviet transports be allowed to refuel in Yugoslavia.[15] No mention of the airlift or of the magnitude of Arab losses and Soviet replacements appeared in the Soviet press. The resupply effort continued at an intensive pace throughout most of the summer.

While reprovisioning the Arab armies, the USSR simultaneously moved on the diplomatic front. Since all the Soviet resolutions in the Security Council had been overwhelmingly rejected, it looked to the General Assembly for vindication of its position and that of the Arab states. On June 13 Soviet Foreign Minister Andrei A. Gromyko formally requested the U.N. secretary-general to convoke an emergency special session of the General As-

---

prepared to relegate its support for national-liberation movements to second place. BBC/ME/2490/A/6 (June 14, 1967).

It is alleged that Boumedienne asked, "Where is the line at which peaceful coexistence ends?" to which Brezhnev retorted, "What's your opinion of nuclear war?" *Egyptian Mail*, August 26, 1967.

[14] Radio Belgrade, June 15, 1967. Yugoslav correspondents in Cairo reported heavy traffic of Soviet transport airplanes continuing "almost without interruption." *Bor'ba*, June 26, 1967.

[15] On the occasion of Tito's 80th birthday, *Al-Ahram*'s editor Muhammad Hasanayn Haykal, revealed the following: "When Egypt had lost her arms in the battles of the six day war and the Egyptian Ambassador in Moscow went to see Soviet Premier Alexei Kosygin with a message conveying Egypt's needs, Kosygin replied that while the Soviet Union was prepared to rush the arms Egypt needed, Yugoslavia, maintaining her policy of nonalignment, denied any facilities to military traffic across her territory. Abdel Nasser referred the Soviet reply to Tito, who immediately replied that Yugoslavia's territory was open for the free passage of anything dispatched from the Soviet Union to Egypt and that he had given instructions to all authorities concerned for the prompt execution of the order. The whole arrangement took only three hours which was the time spent in deciphering the coded messages from Moscow to Cairo to Belgrade and back to Cairo. Immediately afterwards an airlift began between the Soviet Union and Egypt via Yugoslavia." *Cairo Press Review* (hereafter referred to as CPR), no. 5598, May 19, 1972.

sembly, in accordance with Article 11 of the Charter. Gromyko's letter asking that the General Assembly consider the situation and "adopt a decision designed to bring about the liquidation of the consequences of aggression and the immediate withdrawal of Israeli forces behind the armistice lines" was unusual in that it implied the Security Council was failing in its assigned Charter responsibilities regarding the Middle East, even though there were a number of resolutions still awaiting its consideration.[16] The United States did not agree with the Soviet view that a stalemate existed in the Security Council, but "was not disposed to be too strict" and insist that all the resolutions before the Council be considered first, as would have been proper procedure.[17]

As a result, the Fifth Emergency Special Session of the General Assembly convened briefly on June 17 and started its substantive deliberations on June 19 with a major statement by the Soviet premier. Kosygin blamed Israel for "unleashing" the war, condemned it as the aggressor, demanded its withdrawal from all occupied territory, and insisted on restitution for the damage inflicted on the Arab countries. While extolling the United Nations and calling upon it to "use all its influence and all its prestige in order to put an end to aggression," he also said the USSR "will undertake all measures within its power both in the United Nations and outside this organization in order to achieve the elimination of aggression, and promote the establishment of a lasting peace in the region."[18] Besides general criticisms of Israel, Kosygin made three specific points, whose intent was to dispel the shadow from Soviet policy and ingratiate Moscow with the Arab nations. First, clearly sensitive to Arab criticism over the lack of timely Soviet support, Kosygin tried to vindicate Soviet behavior by claiming that several weeks prior to the outbreak of fighting "the Soviet government, *and I believe others, too,* began receiving information to the effect that the Israeli government had chosen the end of May for a swift strike at Syria in order to crush it and then carry the fighting over into the territory of the United Arab Republic" (emphasis added). He thus implicated

[16] Lall, *The UN*, pp. 118-121.

[17] *Ibid.*, p. 122. The former Indian ambassador to the United Nations presents a clear analysis of the manner in which the General Assembly, with the tacit agreement of the permanent members of the Security Council, modified through practice the legal provisions of the U.N. Charter pertaining to the 1950 Uniting for Peace Resolution.

[18] U.N. General Assembly Document, A/PV.1526.

the Egyptian government and apportioned to it some responsibility for what had happened. Yet it was the Soviet Union alone that had passed on to Cairo and Damascus the faulty intelligence information that an attack was impending.[19] Indeed, Moscow had apparently given Nasir assurances, which he had erroneously interpreted as a promise of full support in the event of war.[20] Second, Kosygin likened Israeli actions to those of the Gauleiters of Hitler's Germany, thus initiating a virulent propaganda campaign whose blatant anti-Semitism had not been witnessed internationally since the latter years of the Stalin era. By linking Zionism and Hitlerism, he tried to tarnish Israel's achievement and case and to curry favor with the Arabs. Third, Kosygin maintained that the policy of the Soviet Union and the other anti-imperialist forces in the world had succeeded in frustrating Israel's attempt to topple the progressive regimes in Egypt and Syria.

[19] According to Lt. General Salah al-Din Hadidi, chief of Egyptian Intelligence during the Six-Day War, Egypt was dissuaded by Moscow from attacking Israel on May 27 [1967]; he confirms that the Soviets misled Egypt into believing that Israel was about to attack Syria. As quoted in *The Jerusalem Post Weekly*, August 29, 1972. See also, Mohamed Heikal, *Nasser: The Cairo Documents* (London: New English Library, 1972), p. 217.

In a speech in Cairo on September 28, 1975, President Anwar al-Sadat related that, when he was in the Soviet Union in early May 1967 as the head of a delegation from the National Assembly, the Soviet leaders had officially told him that "Israel was massing 10 or 11 brigades against Syria. . . . What they told me was also communicated to 'Abd an-Nasir." Foreign Broadcast Information Service, *Daily Report: Middle East and Africa: Egypt* (hereafter referred to as FBIS/Egypt), September 29, 1975, p. D 28. (FBIS will be used with other countries as well.) Sadat also revealed that a committee under Vice-President Husni Mubarak was conducting an investigation into the causes of the 1967 Six-Day War and would make its findings public.

[20] On May 29, 1967, in a speech to members of the National Assembly, Nasir, discussing Egypt's military build up in Sinai and the tense situation, had said: "After my statements yesterday I met with the War Minister Shams Badran and learned from him what took place in Moscow. I wish to tell you today that the Soviet Union is a friendly Power and stands by us as a friend. . . . Last year we asked for wheat and they sent it to us. When I also asked for all kinds of arms they gave them to us. When I met Shams Badran yesterday he handed me a message from the Soviet Premier Kosygin saying that the USSR supported us in this battle and would not allow any power to intervene until matters were restored to what they were in 1956." BBC/ME/2478/A/15 (May 31, 1967).

According to Haykal, Badran apparently had reported the Soviet position incorrectly. Accordingly, after Nasir finished the above-mentioned speech, an Egyptian official who had taken minutes of the meeting between Badran and Kosygin sent the minutes to Nasir, requesting that he read them. The implication is that Nasir read them and then moderated his position, only to be deceived by the Americans. Heikal, *Nasser*, pp. 219-222.

On June 20, less than twenty-four hours after Kosygin's U.N. speech, Radio Cairo announced that Soviet President Nikolai V. Podgornyi would arrive the following day with a high-ranking military mission headed by the Chief of the General Staff, Marshal Matvei V. Zakharov. On June 21, a plenum of the CPSU Central Committee passed a resolution fully approving "the political policy and the practical activity of the Politburo of the Central Committee,"[21] and giving formal party sanction to Kosygin's efforts and to the Politburo's decision to resupply the Egyptian and Syrian armies; and, most important, it reaffirmed the objective of taking whatever measures were necessary to restore and strengthen the Soviet position in the Arab world.[22]

Podgornyi's visit (June 21–24) served several purposes: symbolically, it demonstrated Soviet solidarity with Egypt; it bolstered Nasir's position and weakened the case for a negotiated

[21] *Pravda*, June 22, 1967.

[22] There were undoubtedly differences among the Soviet leaders over what course to follow on so important an issue, though as usual evidence is scanty about intraparty debates on foreign policy. One indication was the dismissal of Nikolai G. Egorychev, First Secretary of the Moscow City Committee of the CPSU, a week after the Central Committee Plenum. Since November 1962 Egorychev had held the key post to which he had been advanced, presumably by Khrushchev, shortly after the Cuban missile crisis. Egorychev headed a CPSU delegation to Egypt (April 11–24, 1967) after Foreign Minister Gromyko's sudden visit in late March, and he may have been implicated in Nasir's decision to precipitate a crisis with Israel, supposedly to forestall a planned Israeli attack against Syria. Egorychev may have been critical of the Politburo's handling of the Middle East war, which would have placed him at odds with the Brezhnev faction, a rivalry already rooted in differences over how to implement economic reforms and how to treat the liberal intelligentsia. For searching discussions see Christian Duevel, "The Political Credo of N. G. Yegorychev," Radio Liberty Research Paper (No. 17, 1967), and his "Soviet Party Press Attacks Left Opposition," Radio Liberty Dispatch (August 25, 1967).

The promotion of Iurii V. Andropov, head of the KGB, to candidate member of the Politburo by the June Plenum strengthens this interpretation, since Andropov's patron has been Brezhnev. Andropov was made a full member of the Politburo in April 1973, at a time when Brezhnev was gathering support for his policy of improving relations with the United States.

John R. Thomas argues that Egorychev "apparently advocated direct involvement" in the June War and tries to glean something of the line-up in the Soviet leadership between the political and military leaders, and within the military; "Soviet Foreign Policy and the Military," *Survey*, 17, No. 3 (Summer 1971), 147-153.

Though I have no corroborating evidence, a leading Israeli Communist party official, who visited Moscow in the summer of 1967, told me that the Politburo decision to resupply Nasir quickly and massively had been decided by a vote of 6 to 5.

settlement that some within the Egyptian leadership advocated; it served as an antidote for the anti-Soviet fever cropping out in various Arab countries; it provided Podgornyi with an opportunity to assess Nasir's determination to resist and his readiness to carry out internal reforms of the army, party, and economy, which Moscow deemed essential; and it impressed upon Nasir the need for political struggle. According to the Yugoslav party newspaper, *Bor'ba*, "well-informed circles" [presumably Soviet diplomats] indicated that Podgornyi strongly urged Nasir to seek a political solution: "There is no other way of liquidating the territorial gains of the aggressor except negotiations and even some crucial concessions with respect to navigation and the recognition of the fact of the existence of the Israeli state in the Middle East."[23] But there was no Soviet statement or any hint by Soviet officials to support this sanguine Yugoslav assessment of Soviet policy. The Podgornyi-Nasir communiqué of June 24 did not provide anything explicit to go on. Commenting that the meeting had been held "in a spirit of fraternal mutual understanding and traditional friendship," it said:

> In the course of the discussions, questions were considered, relating to the situation in the Middle East in connection with the aggression of Israel against the UAR and other Arab governments, and to the measures which need to be undertaken for the liquidation of the consequences of this aggression.[24]

The visit, however, was crucial for Nasir. Moscow's assurance of massive aid put Egypt in a position to refuse the kind of compromise settlement that Israel might have been prepared to accept. Moscow thus gave Nasir the option he most desired, namely, the chance to continue the struggle against Israel by political means, meanwhile playing for time, rebuilding his army, showing outward flexibility but preparing himself internally for a prolonged conflict. For the moment, Nasir willingly went along with Moscow's preference of ruling out military means. Completely dependent on the Soviet Union for military assistance and protection—he had even asked Podgornyi to take charge of Egypt's air defense under Soviet commanders but was turned down[25]—and acutely aware of Egypt's vulnerability and need to

23 *Bor'ba*'s commentary was reported in *NYT*, June 22, 1967.
24 *Pravda*, June 25, 1967.
25 This disclosure was made by Sadat on April 25, 1974. CPR, No. 5772,

rebuild its armed forces from the ground up, Nasir jockeyed for time. He welcomed the USSR's attempt to effect a voluntary pullback of Israeli forces and the statement made by CPSU leader Leonid I. Brezhnev on July 5 in a speech in the Kremlin at the annual reception for graduates of the Soviet military academies. There Brezhnev announced that "at this new *political* stage of struggle against the aggression and for the removal of its aftermath," the Soviet Union was giving "every assistance" and attached great importance to visits such as Podgornyi's, and it sought to strengthen relations and coordinate "joint actions in the *political* struggle in defense of the rights of the interests of the UAR, Syria and other Arab countries" (emphasis added).[26] An experienced diplomatic intriguer, Nasir was not without a capacity, even in weakness, to use the Soviet commitment to his advantage.

DISSONANCES

Anti-Soviet sentiment surfaced in Egypt and elsewhere in the Arab world in the wake of the June War. Open criticism occurred mostly in those Arab countries (especially Algeria, Iraq, and Libya) not directly involved in fighting, because their leaders were not dependent on Soviet aid and goodwill. A Libyan newspaper commented that the Soviet severing of diplomatic relations with Israel "adds nothing new to the battle and the current conflict"; and Radio Algiers called on the Communist countries to "give practical assistance." Nasir himself contributed to Arab ire against the Soviet Union: in his "resignation" speech of June 9, he said that Egypt's defeat was in part due to its heeding Moscow's urgent request not to start a war. But calculation quickly superseded condemnation, and *Al-Ahram*, the semi-official Egyptian newspaper often used by Nasir to convey policy positions, put a damper on anti-Soviet outbursts. On June 13 an editorial entitled "The Arabs and the Soviet Union" stressed the "colossal economic and military aid" extended by the USSR to the Arabs and warned that in the critical period through which "the Arab nation is now passing" it "should think and act carefully. The last

---

April 25, 1974. Sadat held that at first Podgornyi agreed, "but later, at an urgent meeting the next day, informed President Abdel Nasser that the Soviet Union regretted it could not meet the request."

[26] *Soviet News*, No. 5394 (July 11, 1967), p. 19.

thing it can afford to do now is to become emotional."[27] This article set the stage in Egypt for favorable commentary on the Soviet role in the Middle East crisis.

Evgenii Primakov, *Pravda*'s man in Cairo, blamed the anti-Soviet outcries on "the enemies of the Egyptian people," on "reactionaries" who, exploiting Egypt's current plight, are "making feverish efforts to try all possible means of sowing in the minds of the Egyptian people defeatist sentiments, a lack of faith in their own strength, and of scattering seeds of doubt regarding the support which the Arab countries receive in their just struggle from other peoples, including the socialist camp." He lumped the Chinese officials in Egypt among this group, accusing them of "spreading various anti-Soviet lies"; and he noted that "all that is reactionary in Egypt today gladly takes up their slanderous fabrications against the Soviet Union and other socialist countries."[28] A few days later he was able to report that the local organizations of the Arab Socialist Union (ASU), Egypt's only legal party and mass political organization, were carrying out a "large-scale effort" to inform the Egyptian people of the significance of Soviet assistance and to counteract the anti-Soviet virus.[29] The Soviet media also widely disseminated the "gratitude and appreciation" for Soviet support expressed by the twelve Arab diplomatic missions in Moscow.

The attention of Soviet leaders to the incidence of anti-Sovietism after the June War needs a word of explanation. In Egypt anti-Soviet feelings took various forms. Of least concern to Moscow politically is an emotional antipathy shared by Egypt's political, technocratic, and social elites, and rooted in their suspicion of the reserve, secretiveness, and social distance maintained by

[27] BBC/ME/2491/A/1 (June 15, 1967). One British diplomat told me that on June 9 while the staff was in the Canadian Embassy, which was safeguarding British interests and which was ringed by police, the Egyptians called the embassy and said that the police could no longer be kept there because they were needed to protect the Soviet Embassy from mobs.

[28] *Pravda*, June 13, 1967. A pamphlet intended for a Soviet audience acknowledged that in the days after the war "reactionary elements attempted to create mistrust among the Arabs toward the Soviet Union, expatiating on the ineffectiveness of its assistance. . . . Why didn't the Soviet army come? they whispered in the shops of Cairo and Beirut." The author did not give a direct answer. P. Demchenko, *Arabskii vostok i chas ispytanii* (The Arab East and the Hour of Trial) (Moscow: Politizdat, 1967), p. 73. E. Primakov commented on this period in "Cairo Conspiracy Trial," *New Times*, No. 7 (February 21, 1968), 15-16.

[29] Radio Moscow, June 16, 1967.

Soviet officials. The gregarious and pleasure-seeking Egyptians frankly do not understand the Soviets, whose contacts with them tend to be restricted to official functions. However, this socio-cultural antipathy (the Soviets, conversely, find little in Egyptian society that is attractive to them) seldom adversely affects government-to-government relations. Moscow has long learned to live with this phenomenon, for nowhere in the Third World does the indigenous elite look to Soviet society, culture, or mores as a model. Only Communists and their camp followers see the Soviet developmental experience as having relevance for Egypt.

The second variety of anti-Sovietism is more troublesome. It engenders anxiety in Moscow that Egyptian leaders might prefer to look to Washington for assistance in reaching a settlement, and thereby lessen their need for the USSR. To forestall this, Moscow seeks to institutionalize Egypt's dependency without imposing onerous conditions. This type of anti-Sovietism, linked as it is to realpolitik and tangible national goals, keeps Moscow active, accommodating, businesslike.

The third variety is seen in the repressive policy of the Egyptian government toward its internal Communists. The Sino-Soviet rivalry and the competition for the allegiance of Communist and "progressive" movements puts pressure on the USSR not to support regimes that persecute their Communists. Yet practical considerations transcend ideological categorizations: in any conflict between Soviet state interests and Soviet ambitions to dominate the international Communist constellation of parties, groups, and organizations, the former takes precedence over the latter. But Moscow is aware of the value of an international constituency and fears the intrusion of a Communist rival.

As the dominant Communist power, the USSR is bedeviled by a need to explain to Communist "outgroups" why it strengthens regimes that refuse to legalize the Communist Party or allow it to function openly. Georgii I. Mirskii, a highly respected Soviet scholar on Arab and African affairs, gave a reasoned defense of the Soviet position.[30] Revolutions cannot be exported. A Communist movement must grow out of objective internal conditions. In most Arab countries "the conditions are not ripe for the creation of strong Communist Parties" because their class structure is such "that there are no strong classes either of capitalists or of the working class." Nonetheless, "some forces [the military] in

30 BBC/SU/2511/A4/1 (July 8, 1967).

the revolutionary democratic governments" in Egypt, Syria, and Algeria have emerged and taken the lead in moving "these countries along on the path of noncapitalist development." These regimes have the support of Communists, who are too weak themselves to play a leading role at present. In Egypt, for example, the Communists have not been banned since 1965; rather, it is they who dissolved their party and joined the ASU and are in this way propagating the ideals of socialism; "it is wrong to believe that the Communist Parties are banned, or that the regimes which the Soviet Union is supporting are anticommunist regimes." Mirskii's ratiocination may be accepted by pro-Soviet groups, but it assuredly is not by pro-Chinese.

Besides being uneasy over the anti-Soviet manifestations, Moscow viewed Egypt's internal situation with disquiet: What was to prevent another defeat, and with it a blow to Soviet arms and credibility? It recognized a need not only for the rebuilding of Egypt's army but also for extensive political, economic, and military reforms. Egyptian society needed overhaul. But how far dare Moscow go in pushing for it?

A foreshadowing of the Soviet prescription for change was first heard on June 13 in a broadcast entitled "Reasons for the Arab Defeat."[31] It attributed the collapse of Egypt's army to a backward social structure. Observing that the social base of the Israeli military was a well-trained army of educated men knowledgeable in the use of modern weapons, the program contrasted them with the fundamentally peasant composition of Arab armies, "most of them with faulty education, not always able to make the best of modern weapons, not always understanding the significance of the social and economic transformations taking place in their country. . . . This was the difference that proved decisive in the first grave period of the war." The Arabs were backward ideologically and organizationally. Their weaknesses reflected the basic weaknesses of their societies. By contrast, in Korea, Cuba, Algeria, and Vietnam, the masses were able "to stand up to the brutal armed onslaught of imperialism" because there "a real people's war" was organized in which the masses were made

[31] Radio Moscow, Peace and Progress in English to Asia, June 13, 1967, as given in BBC/SU/2491/A4/5-7 (June 15, 1967). For an astute assessment of the socio-psychological factors accounting for the Arab defeat, written by an Israeli scholar and former Chief of Intelligence, see Y. Harkabi, "Basic Factors in the Arab Collapse During the Six-Day War," *Orbis*, 11, No. 3 (Fall 1967), 677-691.

strong "by their organization, conscientiousness, and ability to comprehend the tasks confronting their nation." Finally, the Soviet commentator criticized the Arabs' propensity for militant sloganizing that demands revenge:

> Imperialism will not be vanquished by the heroism of individuals or groups; nor will it be vanquished by revolutionary phrases, meetings, and resolutions. What is needed now is heroism, patience, organization, stamina, skillful politics, and skill in diplomacy. . . . Israel . . . is after all not a paper tiger. It will not be overcome just by meetings and resolutions, which in themselves weigh no more than the UN Security Council resolutions.

Moscow counseled extensive change.

Soviet analysts viewed "the dismissal of certain top military leaders," especially in the air force, as the beginning of "a reconstruction process" and much-needed shake-up of the "military bourgeoisie."[32] They placed heavy responsibility for the defeat on "certain generals and senior officers, who inwardly did not accept the revolution" and who therefore opposed any political work among the soldiers and noncommissioned officers that would strengthen the government's policy of social transformation.[33] The air force, traditionally the most privileged of the services, was singled out as having consistently sabotaged efforts to democratize the National Assembly, openly threatening not to allow "radish and lettuce sellers" to sit side by side with "respected politicians." All too often, argued the Soviet analysts, the government saw fit to utilize military cadres in economic sectors, with the result that "there appeared a type of officer-businessman who was more concerned with business than with the combat training

---

[32] Evgeny Primakov, "Hour of Ordeal," *New Times*, No. 26 (June 28, 1967), 8. See also, I. Belyaev and Y. Primakov, "Lessons of the 1967 Middle East Crisis," *International Affairs*, No. 3 (March 1968), 40-44.

[33] Igor' Beliaev and Evgenii Primakov, "Kogda voina stoit u poroga" (When War is at the Threshold), *Za rubezhom*, No. 27 (June 30–July 6, 1967), 7. These veteran journalists wrote the most devastating critique of the Egyptian military caste that appeared in the Soviet press in the period immediately following the June War.

For a later serious Soviet evaluation of the shortcomings of Egypt's military, see G. I. Mirskii, *Armiia i politika v stranakh Azii i Afriki* (The Army and Politics in the Countries of Asia and Africa) (Moscow: Nauka, 1970), pp. 87-95; for a shortened version, see G. I. Mirskii, "The 'New' Revolution in the U.A.R.," *The African Communist*, No. 41 (Second Quarter, 1970), 21-40.

of soldiers and noncommissioned officers."[34] They commended Nasir's cashiering of hundreds of such officers from the army and his strengthening of organized political activity among the masses as twin developments that would destroy the "old state machine" and restore Egypt's commitment to socialism. Nasir's Cabinet shakeup of June 19 and the announcement of extensive changes in the composition and character of the government, party, and military bureaucracies were viewed as "the beginning of a new stage in the Egyptian revolution." Noting that the Egyptians quite naturally considered their main problem was to bring about the withdrawal of Israeli forces from Sinai, Moscow stressed that for this to happen "it is necessary in the first place to have internal unity in the UAR."[35]

THE DIPLOMATIC FRONT

During his U.N. visit Kosygin met with President Johnson in Glassboro, New Jersey, on June 23 and 25. Unwilling to talk about specific proposals, he was intent mainly on impressing Johnson with Soviet determination to render the Arabs whatever support was necessary to effect an Israeli withdrawal. In early July, the vote on the Soviet resolution before the special session of the General Assembly was 53 in favor to 46 opposed, thus falling short of the required two-thirds majority needed for adoption. By the end of the month, after the failure of the bilateral Soviet-American effort to find a formula acceptable to both sides, the General Assembly finally acknowledged its inability to deal with the problem and turned it back to the Security Council. However, the setback to the Egyptian-Arab position was by no means a complete defeat: the session showed that the Arabs could unfailingly count on a core of at least fifty states to support them on any resolution; and this partisan international base led Cairo to include a heavy U.N. component in its diplomacy.

The closest Nasir may have come to accepting a compromise settlement was in the third week of July. On July 11, Soviet Deputy Foreign Minister Iakov I. Malik arrived in Cairo for discussions with Nasir and Riyad. On July 16, the heads of state of Egypt, Algeria, Syria, Iraq and the Sudan, meeting in Cairo, agreed on the need for effective action "to eliminate the conse-

---

[34] Beliaev and Primakov, "Kogda voina stoit u poroga," p. 8.
[35] *Pravda*, June 21, 1967.

quences of the Israeli aggression" and called for an Arab foreign ministers' meeting in Khartoum in late July to discuss the steps to be taken. The next day, Presidents Boumedienne of Algeria and Aref of Iraq flew to Moscow. The communiqué issued after their meeting with Soviet leaders made no reference to the superpower talks and took an uncompromising stand. Malik, meanwhile, prolonged his stay and met twice with Nasir on July 18 to discuss the substance of intensive Soviet-American talks in New York, which had resulted in a proposal that drew heavily on a text originally drafted by a group of Latin American countries and that the superpowers thought might satisfy both sides and assure "the substance of peace and the renunciation of all acts of war."[36] The formula linked an Israeli withdrawal from Arab territories with immediate Arab acknowledgment of Israel's right to an independent national state of its own and its right to live in peace in the area, without threats and claims against its sovereignty. On July 19 Malik again delayed his departure. Though interested, Nasir was finally constrained from acceptance of the compromise by considerations of his position within the Arab world. At odds with Saudi Arabia and the other conservative Arab regimes, Nasir was unwilling to jeopardize his links to the radical Arab states by agreeing to a solution that entailed an end to the state of belligerency vis-à-vis Israel and acceptance of its statehood. As long as they were opposed, he felt it obligatory to stay in step. Ambitious, proud, and shaken by the disaster he had sowed, Nasir knew that recognition of Israel, however masked, at a time of his abject defeat would end his unique position of leadership among the Arab masses; it would elicit contempt from the conservatives and denunciation from the radicals.

On July 20, in a lengthy discussion with Gromyko, Algeria's Foreign Minister Boutefika reportedly said that acceptance of the Soviet-American proposal "would amount to total betrayal of the Arab cause."[37] Several weeks later, in an interview on August 16 in *Le Monde*, he stated with characteristic bluntness:

> We were not opposed *a priori* to a Soviet-American agreement, for we know well that nothing can be effected in the

---

[36] Lall, *The UN*, p. 211. A respected Yugoslav journalist, Aleksandar Nenadović, reported that the U.S.-Soviet discussions were on the threshold of an important breakthrough. *Politika*, July 21 and July 22, 1967.

[37] Daniel Dishon (ed.), *Middle East Record, Volume Three: 1967* (Jerusalem: Israel Universities Press, 1971), 83.

Middle East without the agreement and action of Washington. But the proposed text could under no circumstances be signed by the Arabs. We do not deny the Soviets the right to remain faithful to their line, which is based on the recognition of the State of Israel. But both our doctrines and our interests are different. We cannot approve a text which would link rigorously the return to the frontiers of 5 June, the Arab objective, to the recognition of the Jewish state.[38]

On July 20–21 the Arab states caucused at the United Nations and rejected the Soviet-American compromise resolution. By their intransigence the radical Arab leaders deprived Nasir of a rare opportunity to create a possible rift between the United States and Israel. A former senior adviser to the permanent U.S. representative to the United Nations from 1967 to 1971 has written that it was Israel, not Egypt, that objected to the draft resolution produced by Soviet Ambassador to the United States Anatolii Dobrynin and U.S. Ambassador to the United Nations Arthur Goldberg:

> The Dobrynin-Goldberg negotiations proceeded very well in New York; a draft resolution was worked out that was acceptable to the U.A.R., Jordan, the Soviets and the U.S.—but not to Israel. The U.S. was nevertheless ready to go forward with it; however, when violent opposition from Algeria and Iraq caused the U.A.R. to draw back, the Soviets—with evident reluctance and discomfort—abandoned the endeavor, much to the relief of Israel.[39]

Thus it was Nasir who had to reject the draft resolution, because of intra-Arab politics.

[38] *Ibid.*, pp. 83-84.

[39] Seymour M. Finger, "The Arab-Israeli Problem and the United Nations," *Middle East Information Series*, 17 (February 1972), 6-7. According to Israel's permanent representative to the United Nations at the time, so strong was the American desire "to reach with the Soviet Union a parliamentary understanding in the United Nations" that the State Department moved very close to the Soviet position, which did not call for a lasting peace or an end to the state of belligerency in return for a full Israeli withdrawal. The Israeli delegation was shown the text of the American-Soviet draft resolution, but was not consulted at any stage. No doubt Israel would have opposed it had the matter come before the Emergency General Assembly for consideration. However, the occasion never arose because the negative stand of Syria and Algeria "doomed the Soviet-American initiative and relieved Israel from Big Power diplomatic encirclement." Gideon Rafael, "UN Resolution 242: A Common Denominator," *New Middle East*, No. 57 (June 1973), 28-29.

In any event, the Goldberg-Dobrynin talks may well have lacked real significance. They were conducted at too low a level for serious negotiations—U.S. policy was fashioned in the White House, not in U.N. corridors, and Goldberg was no intimate of Johnson. While the State Department may have been ready to pressure Israel to concede Arab demands, there is no evidence that the White House would have agreed. Johnson was not unhappy over the turn of affairs in the Middle East. Indeed, given the poor relations between the United States and the Soviet Union and his growing preoccupation with Vietnam, he was pleased by the blow to Soviet prestige in the Middle East and by the blockage of the Suez Canal, which complicated the Soviet supply problem to North Vietnam. However, he also felt that it was dangerous for a superpower to be humiliated by a small power like Israel, so he refrained from further exploiting their setback in the Middle East.

A crucial unanswered question is how hard did Moscow really push? True, observers reported that Soviet diplomats were counseling the Egyptians in private to reach a settlement. But one searches Soviet speeches and commentaries in vain for any intimation that the Arabs' refusal to accept the existence of the state of Israel was largely responsible for the failure of the UN special session. The Soviet (and Arab) media never mentioned the behind-the-scenes Soviet-American discussions at the United Nations, and they were silent on Malik's visit to Cairo, which is unusual since the pattern is to mention such visits; and Soviet scholarly writings have never referred to the superpowers' initiative. On July 21 TASS blasted Israel for its repeated flouting of Security Council resolutions and accused the United States of using Israel as a weapon with which to cow the Arabs into submission and using the occupation of their territories "to prepare for the pillaging of their natural wealth."[40] Moscow did not want another war, but neither did it want a full settlement of the Arab-Israeli conflict, certainly not to the point of bringing strong pressure to bear on its newly dependent client. In the hierarchy of Soviet regional and global objectives, a political settlement in the Middle East ranked very low.

At times, Moscow incurred Arab ire for exchanging views with the United States on the principles of a possible Middle East settlement. On one occasion the sniping was so serious that Mos-

[40] *Pravda*, July 21, 1967.

cow, perturbed by its tarnished image in the Arab world and smarting from Chinese charges of pusillanimity, had to deny publicly rumors of a "Soviet-American initiative," inveighing against allusions to "some kind of mythical 'coincidence of interests' between the Soviet Union and the United States" in the Middle East.[41] Yet such periodic superpower exchanges continued, for each was acutely aware of the dangers another war posed to its interests in the area. The USSR was kept active by its desire to counter American initiatives and deliver some victories to the Arabs without war.

The Soviet bloc countries reaffirmed their support for the Arabs at a conference held in Budapest on July 11 and 12. The East European countries promised economic assistance, but the actual burden of providing both economic and military assistance was shouldered by the USSR, though the final communiqué was silent on the military aspect of the aid.[42]

Soviet and Egyptian strategies dovetailed: the focus was on political struggle set within a framework of military buildup. Moscow welcomed a statement by Nasir on July 23 to the effect that Egypt would fight by political and economic, as well as military, means to defeat Israel and would intensify the social revolution in Egypt. It noted with approval that Egypt "believes that political means are preferable in the circumstances," there being "hardly any point in giving the Tel-Aviv 'hawks' a pretext for extending the aggression."[43] One writer deplored "leftist" irresponsible proposals and praised Nasir for being "wiser than the statesmen who failed to make a deep analysis of the cause of the

[41] *Pravda*, September 8, 1967.

[42] *Pravda*, July 13, 1967: "The participants . . . confirmed again their support . . . for the liquidation of the consequences of Israel's aggression . . . they . . . exchanged information on the political support to be rendered to the Arabs . . . and on economic aid."

Soviet coyness about publicly acknowledging its military assistance did not last indefinitely. One writer, reporting that representatives of the socialist countries of Europe met in June, July, September, and December 1967 to discuss the situation in the Middle East, noted: "The socialist governments resolutely declared their full support for the victims of aggression and planned concrete steps for rendering them political, economic, and *military* assistance" (emphasis added). G. Starchenkov, "Agressiia Izrailia protiv arabskikh stran" (The Aggression of Israel Against the Arab Countries), *Mezhdunarodnyi ezhegodnik: politika i ekonomika, 1968* (Moscow: Politizdat, 1968), p. 206.

[43] Igor Belyaev and Evgeny Primakov, "The Situation in the Arab World," *New Times*, No. 39 (September 27, 1967), 8.

crisis and the real relation of forces" in the region and who "called upon the Arabs to hurl themselves headlong into a second round of war."[44] The Khartoum meetings—in early August of the Arab foreign ministers and a month later of the Arab heads of state—satisfied Soviet interest in a united Arab front that could be converted into an anti-imperialist (anti-American) coalition and that, incidentally, might facilitate the extension of diplomatic recognition to East Germany, a persistent Soviet objective.[45]

ARMS[46]

Though political struggle was the order of the day because of Moscow's preference and Egypt's crippled capability, the military recovery proceeded apace. The Soviet resupply effort began almost immediately after the June War ended. Egypt's material losses were estimated at approximately two billion dollars. However, these Western cost estimates can be seriously misleading: based on prices prevailing in Western markets, they give no real clue to the production cost to the USSR or the purchase price for Egypt. By the end of June, the USSR had replaced 200 MiGs; by October, an additional 100 MiG-21s, 50 MiG-19s, 50 to 60 Sukhoi-7s, and 20 Ilyushin-28s. By late fall 80 percent of the aircraft, tanks and artillery that Egypt had lost in June were replaced.[47] In consideration of Egypt's already heavy financial indebtedness and in any event committed for political and strategic reasons to restoring Egypt's military strength, the Soviet government resupplied on terms that amounted to a virtual gift, as Nasir acknowledged on July 23, 1968: "We have so far paid not one millieme for the arms we obtained from the Soviet Union. We have no money to buy arms. . . . Had it not been for the Soviet Union and its agreement to supply us with arms, we should now

---

[44] V. Kudryavtsev, "The Middle East Knot," *International Affairs*, No. 9 (September 1967), 32.

[45] For example, *Pravda*, July 22, 1967.

[46] Neither the USSR nor Egypt gives any details of Soviet military assistance. Most of the information that appears in the Western press on the subject comes from declassified briefings by Western officials; other sources are Israeli officials and commentaries, and occasional details appearing in the Lebanese press. The International Institute of Strategic Studies (IISS) in London publishes an annual, *The Military Balance*, that is the best single source available.

[47] For example, *NYT*, October 12, 1967; and *Strategic Survey 1967* (London: IISS, 1968), p. 37.

be in a position similar to our position a year ago. We should have no weapons and should be compelled to accept Israel's conditions under its threat."[48]

The arrival in Cairo on June 21 of Chief of Staff Zakharov (with Podgornyi) confirmed Moscow's decision to rebuild Egypt's army. Zakharov's twenty-four-man military delegation remained until July 1. Two weeks later, Egypt's Chief of Staff General Muhammad Abd al-Mon'im Riyad went to the USSR for further talks (July 14–29). All the while, Soviet military advisers poured in. The estimates by American military analysts that the rebuilding effort would take two years proved accurate:[49] it was in the late summer of 1969 that Nasir was able to carry on his "war of attrition" in earnest. On July 10, 1967, to underscore the Soviet commitment to Nasir and shield Egypt from further Israeli attacks, Moscow sent units of its Mediterranean fleet to Alexandria and Port Said for a week's visit. The Soviet navy was to be a frequent visitor in the months ahead.

The military relationship between the USSR and Egypt altered dramatically after the June War. From approximately 500 Soviet military advisers before the war, the number jumped to several thousand; from a purely advisory role relating primarily to the technical operation of weapons, Soviet advisers moved into all phases of training, planning, and air defense; and from advising mostly at the divisional level, Soviet personnel were assigned to all levels of the Egyptian armed forces. The magnitude of the Soviet commitment was unprecedented, surpassing in both quantity and quality the aid given to North Vietnam and exceeding the rate at which aid had hitherto been given to allied or friendly countries.

The rapid Soviet resupply dispelled any lingering doubts Nasir may have had.[50] That it slowed down by late August stemmed from Egypt's limited absorptive capacity and not from Soviet restraints or second thoughts. Bringing the air force up to the levels of June 4 was relatively easy, since most of the planes had been destroyed on the ground and few pilots had been lost (in his speech on November 23, 1967, Nasir gave the figure of forty

[48] BBC/ME/2830/A/9 (July 25, 1968).

[49] *NYT*, August 21, 1967.

[50] To help wipe the slate clean, Moscow, on August 28, 1967, announced the replacement of Dmitrii Pozhidaev as ambassador in Cairo. Sergei Vinogradov, deputy foreign minister (formerly ambassador to France), took up his new post in late September.

pilots lost in the June fighting). Israeli sources estimated that it would take about three years to restore Egypt's tank units; prior to the war, the USSR had supplied Egypt with about 100 tanks annually.[51] The Soviet weapons were consistently modern, among the best in the Soviet arsenal. Somewhat overlooked as a result of the overwhelming Israeli victory, this was recalled on October 21, when Soviet Styx missiles sank the Israeli destroyer, *Eilat*. A ship-to-ship subsonic missile capable of carrying a 1,000-pound high explosive warhead and having a range of twenty to twenty-five miles, the Styx had first been given to the Egyptian navy in 1962 (Cuba was also given the missile at this time).[52] Western analysts were wrong in assuming that the Soviet Union would "take more care about giving its clients the latest weapons."[53] This was not the last time they were so to underestimate Moscow's readiness to provide advanced weaponry. For its part, once committed to a full restoration of Egypt's military capability, the USSR lost whatever interest it may have once had in arms control proposals for the Middle East. Kosygin rejected Johnson's suggestion that the two superpowers cooperate to limit the arms race by publicly reporting all arms shipments to the area; other such American overtures met the same fate. The USSR had once held a contrary position, but that was a decade earlier in vastly different circumstances.[54]

The military assistance programs tightened the political links between Moscow and Cairo: they strengthened the Nasir regime and gave Nasirite elements in the Arab world a new lease on life;

[51] BBC/ME/2556/A/12 (August 31, 1967). According to Israeli sources, the Soviet Union had replaced over 60 percent of Egyptian aircraft losses, as well as approximately 40 percent of the weapons lost in Sinai: "Egypt's main difficulties lie in restoring its armored forces. According to estimates, the Egyptians lost about 700 tanks in the Sinai peninsula. Taking into consideration that the training of tank personnel takes 20 months the restoration of Egyptian tank units will take at least three years."

[52] An Egyptian general captured in Sinai said that the Soviet Union was in the process of delivering ground-to-ground missiles, of the Luna-1 type, with a range of 43 to 49 miles, when the June War broke out; agreement on the delivery of the missiles had been reached in Moscow during a visit in November 1966 by Field Marshal 'Abd al-Hakim Amir. *NYT*, July 1, 1967.

Washington worried that the missiles would be given to North Vietnam, fearing they could exact a heavy toll on the Seventh Fleet, but Moscow never made them available to Hanoi.

[53] For example, C. L. Sulzberger, *NYT*, July 5, 1967.

[54] "Report by USSR Foreign Minister D. T. Shepilov to the Sixth Session of the USSR Supreme Soviet," *New Times*, No. 8 (February 21, 1957), Documents Supplement, p. 17.

they expanded the Soviet presence in Egypt and enhanced the USSR's status as a major Mediterranean power; and they raised the ante in open challenge to two decades of American dominance in the region.

PLUS ÇA CHANGE...

Moscow expected Egypt's humiliating defeat to give rise to sweeping reforms that would make Cairo more receptive to the USSR's experience and thus bring the USSR a more intimate role in the restructuring of Egypt and concomitantly an increase in Soviet influence. But Nasir's antennae were pointed in another direction.

Strains between Cairo and Moscow surfaced in late summer and early fall. On August 25, Muhammad Hasanayn Haykal, the editor of *Al-Ahram* and a confidant of Nasir, discussed Soviet-Egyptian relations at length for the first time since the June War.[55] He welcomed the Arab Marxist Left to the anti-imperialist nationalist front, provided that it not try to dominate the nationalist movement, "not claim for itself more than its natural size is capable [of]." The Arab world, he observed, does not deal with the Soviet Union through the Arab Marxist Left; on the contrary, its dealings with the USSR had begun, even flourished, at a time when the Marxists were outlawed or in fetters because of their inability to understand "the national, patriotic, and religious factors" that have shaped Arab political life and struggles. Haykal lauded Arab-Soviet friendship, which "has created a comradeship in arms between the Arab revolution and the international revolution against imperialism" and which "has enabled the Arab nation to conduct its struggle more effectively in the international arena." But he warned that the Soviet Union is a global power with interests of its own and cannot be expected to act always in ways that meet with Arab approval, any more than Egypt's plans, which are dictated by its independent stand and national interests, can necessarily always harmonize with the Soviet Union's. Moscow has reason, Haykal said, to avoid confrontation with the United States because of the danger of nuclear war and its difficulties with China. Yet, despite a desire for improved relations with the United States,

[55] *Egyptian Mail*, August 26, 1967.

the USSR will nevertheless continue to support Egypt in the future for several reasons. First, "friendship with the Arab nation was the most important achievement of Soviet foreign policy." Second, as long as the Arab national revolutionary movement remains dominant in the area, it "prevents the Middle East from becoming a springboard for stabbing the USSR in the back." Third, if the revolutionary Arab regimes were liquidated, the USSR would stand to be a prime loser in the Third World and the United States would achieve "crushing strategic supremacy." Finally, it would also give China "an inestimable revolutionary advantage to emerge as the unchallenged leader of the anti-imperialist world."

This assessment, while selective—for example, not mentioning Moscow's interest in penetrating the Arab world in order to encourage nonaligned propensities among the countries of NATO's southern flank—neatly sized up the tangible considerations underlying Soviet imperial and interventionist policy in the area. Haykal put the Soviets on notice that Egypt's dependency should not be construed as a license for unbridled Soviet interference. He also set out with remarkable clarity Cairo's view that the basis of Soviet-Egyptian friendship was convergent national interests, and nothing more. Haykal cautioned the Soviets against seeking too bold a role for local Communists, who had been tolerated, but barely, in journalism and the arts and even in a few economic ministries since 1965. They were always suspect, carefully watched, and kept on the periphery of political activity.

Egypt sought to avoid polarizing the Arab-Israeli conflict into one between the USSR and the United States. As a nonaligned country, it realized that excessive identification with the Soviet Union would limit its efforts to gain support internationally, among countries such as those in Latin America who were put off by Egypt's friendship with the USSR and its client, Cuba.[56]

To revitalize Egyptian political life Moscow considered it necessary that there be "a reorganization of the A.S.U. assuring direct contact between the authorities and the broad masses everywhere."[57] No popular and socialist revolution or reform could succeed without weeding out those in the government and party who were still rooted in feudalism and privilege.

[56] Radio Cairo, September 22, 1967.
[57] BBC/SU/2507/A4/3 (July 4, 1967).

The Israeli aggression . . . made obvious the necessity of support by the popular masses, by the working sector of the population, the necessity for the development and broadening of democracy. The Arab community understands quite well that in this way one can most quickly and effectively heal the damage of war and strengthen the economic potential and social base of progressive regimes.[58]

It is possible to trace the essence of a "debate" in the Egyptian press on the question of whether fundamental internal changes were necessary to remove "the traces of aggression"; and if so, what they should be.[59] But by late November the debate ran its course when Nasir signalled the end, asserting that no right or left "wings" existed in Egypt.[60]

Personnel were shifted, and extensive leadership changes were expected. Even a permanent constitution for Egypt was promised.[61] Some Western scholars saw this and the later reforms and "democratization" that followed the March 30, 1968 Declaration as a genuine attempt at self renewal.[62] Soviet commentators, also,

[58] D. Volskii, "Istoki i uroki izrail'skoi agressii" (The Sources and Lessons of the Israeli Aggression), *Mirovaia ekonomika i mezhdunarodnye otnosheniia*, No. 8 (1967), 26.

[59] Dishon, *Middle East Record*, pp. 562-570. The debate focused on four general issues: 1) national unity—was it Egyptian and all-Arab or did it also have a class character? 2) democracy—was it rule of law, safeguards for individual freedom, curbs on bureaucratic "centers of power," or vigilance against the return of the "feudalists and capitalists"? 3) the future of the ASU—was it to be a mass party or a "socialist avant-garde" party? and 4) foreign policy—should it rest on adherence to nonalignment or on closer ties to the Soviet Union? Each theme had a number of variations, and much of the discourse was Aesopian in its expression.

Haykal wrote a series of articles in which he analyzed many Egyptian mistakes. See *Al-Ahram*, October 6, October 13, and October 20, 1967. For an absorbing account of a searing critique by an Egyptian exiled to Beirut because of his condemnation of Nasirism and espousal of Islamic populism, see Elie Kedourie, "Anti-Marxism in Egypt," in M. Confino and S. Shamir (eds.), *The U.S.S.R. and the Middle East* (New York: John Wiley and Sons, 1973), pp. 321-334.

[60] Dishon, *Middle East Record*, p. 563.

[61] BBC/ME/2653/A/7 (December 21, 1967). The chairman of the National Assembly committee to look into the matter was Anwar Sadat.

[62] For example, see R. Hrair Dekmejian, *Egypt Under Nasir: A Study in Political Dynamics* (Albany, New York: State University of New York Press, 1971), pp. 253-286. However, in the aftermath of Sadat's purges of May 1971, Haykal and others revealed how the ASU actually functioned during the post-1967 Nasir period and showed Nasir's reforms to have been ineffectual and even calculatedly superficial. Far from undergoing any revolutionary

pointed out the influx of new faces in the ASU committees, the political activity among "the vast popular masses," and the public dissemination of information about Soviet efforts to aid Arab countries. Like some of their Western counterparts, they saw in the "more meticulous" recruitment process signs of the emergence of progressive forces, able to bring about essential reforms. However, their analyses proved overly optimistic. It was a British journalist who put his finger squarely on the pulse of the immediate post-June frenetic reformism:

> Since the war ended Nasser has done some shuffling of ministers. There is not too much significance in this, the men merely having been moved up or down the scale of Nasser's personal friendships. He has dumped a few deadheads, promoted some likely lads, but the new Cabinet is permitted only to administrate. Policy decisions are Nasser's alone. And of course the Cabinet is content for things to go this way. Only a fool would bid for power at present, with Egypt in such a mess and Nasser's stature higher than ever. But in Arab politics there is always time to call for another cup of coffee and wait.[63]

When hundreds of officers, including dozens of generals, were cashiered in the year following the June War, Moscow welcomed the purge of the "military bourgeoisie"—the privileged, influential elite that dominated Egypt's political and economic, as well as military, life and opposed rapid change and closer ties with the Soviet camp.

Bedfellows make strange politics. Soviet cooperation with military regimes was largely responsible for its advances in the Middle East. Policy considerations transcended ideological antipathies. It remained for Soviet theorists to grapple with the task of reconciling the unproletarian class base and outlook of the military regimes in the Arab world with their generally "progressive" role in deposing reactionary monarchical rulers, implementing needed economic and social reforms, severely limiting foreign private investment activity, and pursuing an anti-imperialist (i.e. anti-

---

transformation, the ASU was deliberately kept bureaucratic and inept at mass mobilization, politicization of the masses, or economic surveillance. An institution whose elections were rigged in classical dictatorial style, it entrenched conservatism instead of pushing progressivism.

[63] Anthony Carthew, "Double-Think, Egyptian Style," *NYT Magazine* (August 20, 1967).

Western) foreign policy. As always, ideology proved infinitely malleable.

Moscow's immediate dilemma was how to blame the military bourgeoisie for the June defeat without undermining Nasir. Mirskii praised the bravery of the soldiers, but censured the behavior of "a significant portion of the officers, especially the senior ones":

> Poor preparations for the war, the absence of a clearcut organization, groundless self-confidence, a mood of victory quickly changing to confusion—all these features, which were typical of the officer corps, influenced the course of the war in pernicious ways. Analysis of the deep causes of the failure showed that the causes were surely not only military, not only professional shortcomings, oversights, lack of preparedness, and so on.
>
> The fact of the matter is that a certain part of the upper echelon of the officer corps did not share the revolutionary ideas of the UAR leadership and even wished secretly for the replacement of this leadership. The reason for these views is the transformation of part of the officer corps into a privileged caste, a military-bureaucratic stratum, so to speak, which is not interested in marching the country toward socialism.[64]

The arrest, on August 25, 1967, of former Field Marshal 'Abd al-Hakim Amir, who had resigned his posts of first vice-president and deputy commander-in-chief of the armed forces on June 10, conveniently enabled Moscow to distinguish between military reactionaries, such as Amir, and military progressives, such as Nasir. A friend of Nasir for almost thirty years, Amir was accused of forming a cabal to seize power. He and Nasir had fallen out over the issues of responsibility for the defeat and the subsequent course to be followed. Openly critical of the Soviet Union, Amir's views on foreign policy were burrs in Moscow's flank, constant reminders of its part in Egypt's defeat:

> Amer's views on foreign policy stressed that the USSR was to be blamed for taking part in a "conspiracy" [which had dragged the UAR into the war] . . . Amer and the ousted high-ranking officers held that the USSR had . . . held up the de-

<hr>

[64] G. Mirskii, "Ob'edinennaia arabskaia respublika v god tiazhelykh ispytanii" (The United Arab Republic in a Year of Severe Trials), *Mezhdunarodnyi ezhegodnik . . . 1968*, p. 222.

livery of the arms shipments agreed on during Badran's [Minister of War] visit to Moscow in May [1967]. Furthermore, they held that the USSR had not kept what they regarded as an undertaking to intervene in the event of war. They believed, in consequence, that the UAR ought to come to an agreement with the U.S. and effect the withdrawal of Israel through U.S. influence.[65]

Although Moscow did urge reforms and was undoubtedly pleased by the removal of known critics of the USSR and the assignment of additional responsibilities to officials considered friendly, like Ali Sabri,[66] nevertheless, Nasir's shake-up of the military was mandated by his own need for a strong army, and not by the Soviet Union. Nasir proceeded in his own way, talking boldly, but acting cautiously and calculatedly. Like the proverbial Italian driver, who, having banged into another, gesticulates furiously and appeals to onlookers for support but avoids contact with his adversary lest he be drawn into a fight neither wants, so Nasir talked belligerently and sought assistance abroad, but, fully cognizant of his weakness and complete dependence on the Soviet Union, eschewed provoking the Israelis.

THE UNITED NATIONS AND RESOLUTION 242

Notwithstanding the failure of the Soviet-American initiative in July and the termination of the special emergency session of the General Assembly, diplomatic activity continued. In early August, Yugoslav President Tito, then seventy-five years of age, braved the Middle East heat, traveling to Cairo, Damascus, and Baghdad with his five-point plan, which met with Nasir's approval, but was rejected by Israel. Tito labored hard to mobilize effective support for Nasir among the nonaligned nations[67] and,

[65] Dishon, *Middle East Record*, p. 560.

[66] Ali Sabri, the Deputy Prime Minister, was appointed minister resident in the Suez Canal zone, giving him responsibility for civilian affairs in this key battle area. *Egyptian Gazette*, October 1, 1967. However, he proved inadequate to the task and was "promoted" to a less demanding operational assignment.

[67] For an account of their special relationship, see Alvin Z. Rubinstein, *Yugoslavia and the Nonaligned World* (Princeton: Princeton University Press, 1970), Chapter VII. See also Anthony Nutting, *Nasser* (New York: E. P. Dutton and Company, 1972), p. 433; Robert Stephens, *Nasser: A Political Biography* (New York: Simon and Schuster, 1971), *passim*; and Mohamed Heikal, *Nasser*, Chapter 8.

to quote one veteran American Arabologist, helped get him "off the war kick" and onto the diplomatic track.

At Khartoum (August 29–September 1) the participating Arab heads of state (Syria and Algeria had refused to attend because of their insistence on "armed struggle") agreed to a policy of "no recognition, no negotiation, no peace" toward Israel. They pledged cooperation, but were unable to establish machinery or procedures for implementing their policy, prompting one Arab official to note that incantations would not bring Israel down. However, two important decisions relating to inter-Arab affairs were made: first, oil-rich Saudi Arabia, Kuwait, and Libya agreed to subsidize Egypt (as well as Syria and Jordan) to the amount of $266 million a year, payable quarterly, for the loss of revenue stemming from the closing of the Suez Canal, the drop in tourism, and the loss of the Sinai oil fields; second, Nasir acknowledged failure by pulling Egyptian troops out of Yemen, thus assuring King Faysal of no serious opposition in the Arabian peninsula and ending the five years of bitter fighting that had pitted Egypt against Saudi Arabia in the civil war between the republican and royalist Yemeni factions, respectively, and had polarized Arab world politics. This was a trying decision, but Nasir had no real choice. In early September, Foreign Minister Riyad twice exchanged views in Moscow; during his second visit on September 11 (which had crystallized in the course of talks in Belgrade) he met with Brezhnev himself.

The sinking of the Israeli destroyer on October 21 and Israel's retaliatory shelling and destruction of Egyptian oil refineries at Port Suez on October 24 inflamed the situation and dominated the General Assembly's fall session. The Security Council reconvened hurriedly on October 25, condemned both incidents, and called for observance of the cease-fire. Spurred on by fears of renewed hostilities, the permanent and nonpermanent members tried to devise a formula acceptable to the Arabs and Israelis, while "behind the scenes the United Arab Republic was urging its friends to accelerate their efforts to find a solution."[68] Nasir badly needed a political booster, as was evident when the Egyptian delegation unexpectedly called a meeting of the Security Council on November 7 to push for the passage of a favorable resolution.

[68] Lall, *The UN*, p. 236.

Several weeks of intensive corridor diplomacy ensued. Much of the tactical infighting centered on the wording of a few key phrases whose political significance was clearly understood. One in particular merits attention. The compromise resolution proffered by British Ambassador Lord Caradon and adopted unanimously by the Security Council on November 22, 1967, affirms that the establishment of a just and lasting peace in the Middle East should include "withdrawal of Israeli armed forces from territories occupied in the recent conflict."[69] On November 20, in an attempt to stave off its adoption, the Soviet delegation had tabled a draft resolution that called, inter alia, for an Israeli withdrawal "from *all* the territories" (emphasis added).[70] Kosygin himself had tried to convince President Johnson to agree to this new wording in return for the Soviet approval of the British resolution; failing in this, he offered a compromise: "Instead of 'withdrawal from *all* the territories,' he was willing to accept the wording, 'from *the* territories occupied.' "[71] Johnson refused.

After Security Council Resolution 242 of November 22, 1967, was adopted, the Arab states, the USSR, and their adherents maintained that it meant "all territories" because, they claimed, the French and Russian versions assumed the word "the" preceded "territories." However, the approved draft was written in English. Neither the French, Russian, nor Arabic versions are equally authoritative. Cairo was well aware of Lord Caradon's refusal to include the word "the," lest the intended balance and integrality of the resolution be disrupted and thereby disap-

[69] UN Security Council Resolution 242 also affirmed the necessity for ending all claims or states of belligerency and the right of every State in the area "to live in peace within secure and recognized boundaries free from threats or acts of force"; for guaranteeing "freedom of navigation through international waterways in the area; for achieving a just settlement of the refugee problem; for guaranteeing the territorial inviolability and political independence of every State in the area, through measures including the establishment of demilitarized zones." It requested the secretary-general "to designate a Special Representative to establish and maintain contacts with the States concerned in order to promote agreement . . ." and to report to the Security Council on the progress of his efforts. Gunnar Jarring, Sweden's ambassador to the USSR and formerly his country's permanent representative at the United Nations, was appointed on November 23, 1967, by the U.N. secretary-general as special representative to the Middle East charged with exploring the possibilities of a settlement in accordance with the provisions of Resolution 242.

[70] S/PV. 1381, p. 1.
[71] Rafael, "UN Resolution 242," p. 32.

proved.[72] On November 18 Arab delegations had met three times to discuss the matter.[73] In all probability Nasir decided to accept the British draft resolution at a meeting with his Cabinet on the evening of November 19.[74] He accepted it because he needed some symbol of accomplishment: a flawed resolution was better than none at all. Cairo had maintained an uncompromising position publicly, as long as there was a possibility that Moscow could persuade Washington to agree to a change in phrasing.[75] In the end, however, after close consultation with the Soviet government, Cairo instructed the Egyptian delegation to drop its objection and persuaded most of the Arab states to go along, arguing that the essential Arab demands for an Israeli withdrawal and the inadmissibility of acquiring territory by war were integral in Resolution 242. Once accepted, the resolution was interpreted in the light of Egypt's aims; and the lobbying for international acceptance of this interpretation began.

That the resolution did not call for withdrawal from *all* the territories or even from *the* territories was deliberate. The ambiguity of the wording was the price the Egyptians and the Soviets had to pay in order to obtain any resolution at all. The evidence of diplomats involved in the negotiations indicates that the resolution would have been rejected by the United States had the Soviets insisted on inclusion of the word "all" or "the." According to one U.S. diplomat, "the resolution would not have been accepted by a substantial number of members of the Security Council and certainly not by Israel if the word 'all' had appeared," a view substantiated by others.[76]

In the Security Council, as soon as the resolution had been approved, Egypt's foreign minister studiedly ignored it in his comments, demanding instead a full Israeli withdrawal and full rights for "the people of Palestine." He gave no indication of the conciliatory spirit implicit in Resolution 242. His truculence

---

[72] *Al-Ahram*, November 19 and 21, 1967.

[73] *Al-Ahram*, November 19, 1967, p. 1.

[74] BBC/ME/2626/A/17 (November 21, 1967).

[75] *Al-Ahram*, November 21, 1967. The lead article noted: "The United Arab Republic sees that the British resolution, without the modification that it had suggested, can not be considered sufficient for a solution of the crisis."

[76] Finger, "Arab-Israeli Problem," p. 8. See also the repeated explanations by Lord Caradon, for example, in *The Jerusalem Post Weekly*, February 13, 1973, and in an interview with the Lebanese press, as quoted in *Journal of Palestine Studies*, 4, No. 1 (Autumn 1974), 198-199; and Eugene V. Rostow, *NYT*, October 14, 1973.

came as a surprise, but as was soon evident, it could not be attributed solely to the personal animus of Riyad, who shortly thereafter did acquire a reputation for uncompromising hostility to
U.S. mediatory efforts. In Cairo, too, the campaign started to
bend Resolution 242 to Egyptian desires. "The Indian delegation," wrote *Al-Ahram*, "understands this to mean withdrawal
of Israel from all the Arab territories."[77] Subsequent articles
lengthened the list of supporters. In an address to Egypt's National Assembly on November 23, Nasir termed the resolution
"inadequate" and declared that there were two points on which
Egypt would "accept no give and take":

> The first is full withdrawal from all Arab territory, from
> every inch of Arab land occupied in the June battles whether
> in the UAR or the Hashemite kingdom of Jordan or the Syrian
> Arab Republic. This point to us is not subject to any bargain-
> ing and the second point is that we shall never allow Israel,
> whatever the cost, to pass through the Suez Canal.[78]

Indeed, Nasir disclaimed any particular interest in the resolution: "In fact we were not eager for any resolution by the UN
whether in the Security Council or the General Assembly."
Though untrue, this suited the emotional temper of his audience.
Whether out of disappointment or design, domestic politics or
inter-Arab considerations, or all of these factors, Nasir took pains
not to be labeled a waverer or to be outradicalized by the extremists; he slighted the United Nations' effort and fell back on
the Khartoum formula—no recognition, no negotiation, no
peace, and no agreement on the Palestinians without their full
consent. In time a pattern evolved: 242 was used for non-Arab
audiences, the Khartoum position for Arab ones.

By contrast, the Soviet reaction was favorable: "This resolution
bears the obvious stamp of compromise. Nevertheless, in the
present dangerous situation its approval by the Security Council
is a step forward."[79] The resolution was viewed as a "diplomatic
defeat" for Israel and as a step toward a political solution. Soviet
media, reporting on Nasir's speech, hailed his intention of exploring all political means for a settlement, but omitted refer-

[77] *Al-Ahram*, November 23, 1967.
[78] BBC/ME/2630/A/16 (November 25, 1967).
[79] D. Volsky, "A Diplomatic Defeat," *New Times*, No. 49 (December 6, 1967), 13.

ence to his prohibition against Israeli ships ever using the Suez Canal.[80] They also criticized those "hotheads" in some Arab capitals who "issue hasty utterances," thereby "providing a windfall to Western propaganda hostile to the Arabs."[81] Their targets were not just the extremists, but also those like Haykal who held that the task assigned to Gunnar Jarring (the Swedish diplomat appointed by the secretary-general as his special representative for the Middle East) was "almost foredoomed."

Haykal's views, presumed to reflect Nasir's thinking, were often irritating to Moscow. Regarding Resolution 242, Haykal disagreed with Moscow's positive assessment but exercised restraint, saying "we cannot behave with the irresponsibility of rejecting the principle of the political solution, even though chances of this solution may appear as far removed as a miracle."[82] Whereas the Soviets castigated Israel for ignoring this opportunity to break the cycle of tension and war, noting "that most Arab countries link the withdrawal of Israeli troops with a stop to the nineteen year state of war with Israel,"[83] the gist of Haykal's commentaries in the following weeks was that Egypt must play for time, build itself up, then resume fighting, and aim not just for the retaking of the territory lost in the June War but for a return to the original borders set out by the United Nations in 1947. However, the disagreements over ultimate objectives that were rooted in the divergent Soviet and Egyptian outlooks were kept in the background, as both parties turned to the immediate tasks at hand.

WAITING FOR BREZHNEV

The timing of Brezhnev's visit to Cairo was propitious. It had been first announced in Moscow on November 11 and blazoned in the Egyptian press.[84] The invitation was extended on behalf of President Nasir by Ali Sabri, who headed the Egyptian delegation to the Soviet Union's golden anniversary celebration

[80] *NYT*, November 25, 1967.

[81] *Pravda*, November 27, 1967, as translated in *Current Digest of the Soviet Press* (hereafter referred to as CDSP), 19, No. 48 (December 20, 1967), 21.

[82] CPR, No. 4521, December 15, 1967.

[83] *Pravda*, December 7, 1967.

[84] See, for example, *Al-Ahram*, November 12, 1967; and the long article on Egyptian-Soviet friendship by the Egyptian Marxist Loutfi al-Kholi, *Al-Ahram*, November 13, 1967.

of the Bolshevik Revolution. Brezhnev "accepted with gratitude" and agreed to visit Egypt early in 1968.[85] Cairo's newspapers were elated at the announcement. *Al-Akhbar* said that the Egyptian-Soviet communiqué issued at the end of Sabri's visit "confirms the identity of views of the UAR and the USSR on the Middle East crisis and on ways to settle it"; and *Al-Ahram* considered that "Leonid Brezhnev's anticipated visit to Cairo at the beginning of next year . . . is an expression of the spirit of mutual amity, fraternity and respect prevailing in relations between the two friendly countries. . . . It is therefore sure to bear the best of fruit."[86]

Cairo readied a regal welcome in appreciation and expectation of further amity.

[85] BBC/SU/2620/A4/1 (November 14, 1967).
[86] BBC/ME/2621/A/6 (November 15, 1967).

Chapter Two

THE ILLUSORY CONSENSUS

THE change in an influence relationship and its impact on the parties can be observed and analyzed, though the causes are invisible. We can only infer causes, and must do so within a framework that consists of continuity of substantive concerns whose parameters are always in flux in response to domestic politics and the international situation; that includes concerns susceptible to ambiguous interpretation, partly because priorities are unknown; and that is structured on evaluations of policy outcomes that were made by people using differing sets of assumptions. These are the elements that we have to work with.

Part of any influence relationship is not only dependence but ambition. Openness to influence—vulnerability to enticement—does not exclude reactive resistance, whether defensive or competitive in origin. This is taken into consideration in any would-be influencer's calculations, as it must be by those trying to understand an influencee's responses. In international politics the weaker member of an influence relationship is rarely quiescent for long. After the June War, Egypt was helpless, bereft of effective capability, yet it possessed tangibles with which to bargain because of the strategic position it held in Soviet thinking. The more assistance Moscow extended, the more chips Nasir accumulated not only for use against Israel and his Arab rivals but for his dealings with the Soviet Union as well. The game stayed in constant session, the pace and stakes varied, and Nasir did not always use his chips in the way that his backer anticipated.

THE MAZUROV VISIT

On January 1, 1968, the Soviet embassy in Cairo confirmed that Leonid Brezhnev would not head the Soviet delegation coming to mark the eighth anniversary of the start of work on the Aswan High Dam and the tenth anniversary of the first Soviet-Egyptian economic agreement.[1] The Cairo press passed over the

---

[1] *Arab Report and Record* (hereafter referred to as ARR), No. 1 (January 1-15, 1968), p. 10; BBC/ME/2661/i (January 5, 1968).

incident without comment. The Soviet delegation was led by Kirill T. Mazurov, First Deputy Chairman of the USSR Council of Ministers and a member of the CPSU Politburo. An unknown figure to Nasir, Mazurov was given a correct but cool reception. His arrival on January 7 was mentioned in a small news item in *Al-Ahram*; his departure on January 13 received little attention. Cairo's disappointment with the visit may be gleaned from the perfunctory attention it received in the press.

The communiqué issuing from the meeting suggested serious differences.[2] It was short and dealt only with Soviet-Egyptian bilateral relations. There was no mention of any of the global issues so favored by the Soviets. Mazurov and Nasir held "detailed, friendly discussions," but it was not said that agreement on key issues was produced. The talks were "particularly concerned with the problems of the liquidation of the effects of the Israeli aggression, especially the withdrawal of the Israeli troops from all the occupied Arab territory back to the lines of June 5, 1967," but they did not invoke Resolution 242 as the justification for this demand, even though both parties had pressed for its adoption the previous November. The omission was clearly the preference of Nasir, whose public statements had continually slighted the resolution, which for Moscow symbolized its professed desire for a political settlement. That the two sides merely "exchanged views on the development and strengthening" of their cooperation suggests that there were important areas in which this was yet to be realized. There was no expression of gratitude by Egypt for Soviet aid—a striking omission, considering the massive assistance it had received in the previous six months—signifying Egyptian dissatisfaction with the level of Soviet commitments. There was no mention of "imperialism," i.e. the United States, thus reflecting either disagreement over strategy of dealing with the United States or tacit recognition that by minimal public criticism the United States would be encouraged to pressure Israel to withdraw. Nor did the communiqué mention the Palestinians, who had not yet become a serious factor in Nasir's calculations. The level of contact was government-to-government; party-to-party relationships were conspicuous by their absence, though the communiqué kept the prospect open by raising "the possibilities of increasing cooperation in all

2 *Egyptian Gazette*, January 14, 1968; FBIS/United Arab Republic, January 15, 1968, p. B1.

fields." The visit revealed differences between Cairo and Moscow, but no interruption of the military and economic relationship that had broadened since the June War.

The most likely explanation for the sending of a surrogate was Brezhnev's preoccupation with bloc affairs: the leadership crisis in Czechoslovakia and the consultative meeting of Communist parties, scheduled to take place in Budapest in February, required Brezhnev's personal attention. In light of the pressures for liberalization in Czechoslovakia, the minor ceremonial chores at Aswan were something to be handled with minimal diplomatic inconvenience. Also, given the gap between Egyptian and Soviet assessments of the Middle East situation, the Kremlin may have seen little that could be gained from a personal visit by Brezhnev; whereas his failure to go, albeit for reasons not pertaining to Soviet-Egyptian relations, put Nasir on notice that some concessions to the Soviet position were in order. Egypt was, after all, still vulnerable and completely dependent on the Soviet Union. Finally, by sending Mazurov, Brezhnev conveyed to the United States a low-keyed Soviet interest in Egypt. A small move in the global power game, it suggested that the USSR wanted to keep the Middle East quiet. The result was that the United States remained riveted to its costly preoccupation with Vietnam, while the USSR talked settlement but expanded its presence in Egypt without unduly alarming the Americans.

Whatever Brezhnev's reasoning, and whether by coincidence or calculation, Nasir did take two steps in the next few weeks that pleased Moscow: he granted the Soviet navy support facilities at Port Said and Alexandria, and on January 24 he appointed Ali Sabri to the post of ASU secretary-general.

PAYOFFS OR COME-ONS?

The granting of port facilities, which entailed jurisdictional control by Soviet personnel over the repair shops and warehouses needed for the maintenance, repair, and provisioning of the Soviet fleet, was extended de facto in January 1968 and formalized in a secret five-year agreement in April 1968, at which time Soviet TU-16 reconnaissance aircraft were also deployed in Egypt for surveillance of the U.S. Sixth Fleet and Israeli positions. This development flowed logically from the deterrent role that had been assumed by the Soviet navy since July 1967. To forestall

Israeli attacks, several ships were kept in Egyptian ports on a fairly regular basis. At the time, Foreign Minister Mahmud Riyad told a diplomat, "We are delighted to have Soviet ships in Alexandria and Port Said; they keep the Israelis away." The Soviets moved discreetly, careful to avoid the onus of having acquired a base (the distinction between a "facility" and a "base" has become important in the post-colonial era, the latter signifying an inequality and surrender of sovereignty that is unacceptable to nationalistic nonaligned regimes). Commenting soon afterward on the permanent Soviet naval presence in Egyptian ports, Haykal argued that one could not expect Soviet naval units to protect arms deliveries to Egypt without enabling them to replenish their "drinking water";[3] furthermore, "at least under present circumstances," they were a counterbalance to the U.S. Sixth Fleet. The formalization of the military arrangement was a logical consequence of a convergence of basic Egyptian and Soviet interests. Nasir was granting privileges that redounded to his advantage, and that also could not fail to delight Soviet planners. Ever since 1961, Commander-in-Chief of the Soviet navy, Admiral Sergei G. Gorshkov, had impressed on the political leadership "the need for the fleet to develop its sea-keeping and all-weather combat capabilities" and to undertake a forward deployment in order to augment the navy's effectiveness as an instrument for projecting Soviet national power.[4] Nasir gave the Soviets their first tangible local return on the massive post-June inputs.[5] The Soviet military finally obtained the facilities it had coveted since 1961.

Nasir's promotion of Ali Sabri to secretary-general of the ASU

[3] BBC/ME/2687/A/3 (February 5, 1968).

[4] Michael MccGwire (ed.), *Soviet Naval Developments: Capability and Context* (New York: Praeger Publishers, 1973), pp. 191-193. The Soviet Union benefited strategically from the increased naval activity by acquiring "progressively extended use of Egyptian facilities, including airfields. The average length of individual deployment almost doubled, and for the first time a naval presence was maintained over the winter months. Numbers on station rose sharply and throughout most of 1968, included 6 to 9 submarines and 8 to 12 surface combatants" (p. 346).

[5] One minor instance of Soviet influence occurred several months earlier. Shortly after the June War the Ministry of Foreign Affairs let it be known among the diplomatic community in Cairo that in view of the existing crisis no national holidays would be celebrated, to cut down on meaningless protocol and valuable resources. However, as November 7, 1967 approached and the Soviet Union was preparing to celebrate its fiftieth anniversary, Moscow pressed Nasir to permit it to hold an appropriate reception. Nasir relented and personally attended. This led other countries to make similar requests, and the practice quickly revived.

was reported in the Soviet press,[6] and was widely interpreted by foreign analysts as another gesture to the Soviets. Much of the attention lavished on Sabri stemmed from the assumption that Nasir's shuffling of personnel had significance for foreign policy, especially when it involved Ali Sabri. However, these administrative reorganizations were frequently intended primarily to prevent the possible coalescing of cabals.

Nevertheless, the fluctuations in Sabri's fortunes were very often used as a gauge of the Soviet-Egyptian influence relationship. A member of the Free Officers group that overthrew Faruq in July 1952, Ali Sabri had held many high positions, including the posts of minister for presidential affairs (1957–1962) and prime minister (1964–1965), but he was no intimate of Nasir. Of upper class background, he, more than any other influential Egyptian official, became identified with a pro-Soviet outlook and a "leftist" ideological disposition, possibly because he had helped to negotiate the 1955 arms deal and had visited the USSR on a number of occasions, generally to represent Egypt at some official Soviet function calling for a "comradely" delegation, such as the 1967 celebration of the Bolshevik Revolution. Also, from the mid-1960s he had maneuvered "to concentrate power in his own hands, through the development of a vigorous force within the ASU. . . . The line he presented was identical in many respects with that of the Marxists (i.e. liquidating the 'feudal' elements in the villages and the bourgeoisie and 'New Class' in the towns, relying on a vanguard cadre-system in the ASU, etc.), but basically he did not overstep the boundaries of Nasserism."[7] As ASU secretary-general he acquired a new potential for influence and was returned to the position he had held at the time of the June War, after which Nasir had taken over the post himself. But Sabri's tenure was brief. In March he lost his ministerial position, and in May, when new ASU elections were being prepared, his party post as well. His removal may have been due not only to his close ties with the USSR but to Nasir's distrust of his effort to establish a secret and personal cadre network within the ASU *apparat* and of the provocative role his henchmen were alleged to have played in the February workers' demonstration in Hel-

---

[6] *Izvestiia*, January 26, 1968.

[7] Shimon Shamir, "The Marxists in Egypt: The 'Licensed Infiltration': Doctrine in Practice," in M. Confino and S. Shamir (eds.), *The U.S.S.R. and The Middle East* (Jerusalem: Israel Universities Press, 1973), p. 310.

wan. Moreover, he was also reputed to be fiercely at odds "with Heikal and his liberal version of 'change.' "[8]

There is no firm evidence that Sabri was Moscow's man in Cairo. Western assessments are based mainly on gossip bandied about in the Cairo social circuit or on information from Egyptian informants and Soviet defectors.[9] Yet Moscow acted as if it were basically true; and Nasir chose, when it suited his purposes, to use this perception of Sabri to communicate policy turns to the USSR and to the West. There was just enough significance behind the juggling of Sabri to merit the attention of foreign analysts, but not enough to provide a sound basis for evaluating Nasir's policy intentions.

THE PROMISES OF MARCH 30

The first commandment of nondemocratic politics is "Thou shall stay in power," for once out there is rarely a road back. This demands an infinite capacity for manipulation and chameleonlike responses to the vagaries of the masses, whose emotions can be exploited but not always programmed.

On February 21 demonstrations unexpectedly broke out in the iron and steel center of Helwan, seventeen miles outside of Cairo, in protest against the leniency of the sentences meted out the

[8] Daniel Dishon (ed.), *Middle East Record: Volume Four 1968* (New York: John Wiley and Sons, 1973), p. 781.

[9] Analysts dealing primarily with Soviet affairs tend to be firmest in describing Ali Sabri as "procommunist." See John Barron, *KGB* (New York: Reader's Digest Press, 1974), p. 52: Most of his information came from a Soviet defector, an intelligence agent based in the Middle East. That Moscow's hopes for a move to the left in Egypt were centered on Ali Sabri is argued by another analyst who finds support for him especially strong in *Trud* (the trade union newspaper), which more than *Pravda* appeared to have been concerned with actual rather than supposed moves toward socialism. See, Ilana Dimant-Kass, "*Pravda* and *Trud*: Divergent Soviet Attitudes Towards the Middle East," *Soviet Union*, 1, Part 1 (1974), 11-14.

This assessment was also shared by many Western journalists covering the Middle East. One, who interpreted the shift of editors on *Akhbar al-Yawm* as signifying a victory for Sabri and an attempt to offset the less enthusiastically pro-Soviet attitude of Haykal and *Al-Ahram*, also noted: "Ali Sabri may not be Moscow's man but that is what many Egyptians believe him to be. Hitherto, President Nasser has managed to preserve a balance between the Left and the Right wings of his regime, but now, as the conflict intensifies, he risks either becoming a prisoner of one or other faction or falling between two stools and losing the support of both." David Hirst, "Left-Wing Threat to Nasser," *The Guardian* (March 1, 1968).

previous day to the officers on trial for their behavior during the June War. The unrest spread to the students at Cairo University. Nasir was placatory and politic. He eschewed force and ordered retrials. On March 3, speaking to the workers at Helwan, he deplored the "misunderstanding" that had led to clashes between the workers and the police and expressed sympathy for the emotional reaction to the verdicts handed down by the court.[10] However, he also denounced the "strange slogans" that had mysteriously appeared demanding the abolition of the ASU and the National Assembly and calling for democracy and freedom. He defended the institutions, arguing that they represented all strata of the people and promoted the ideals of the revolution and of an "open society." Implying the existence of an internal opposition, Nasir vowed to crush it, whether it stemmed from the "extreme Right, or the extreme, radical Left." A few days later, counselling patience during the period of military preparation for renewing the struggle against Israel, he addressed the troops stationed along the Suez Canal, seeking to allay their anxieties over the reports of unrest and to dispel the incipient mood of defeatism.

Nasir had spoken often of the need to cleanse the revolution "of all blemishes," to rid it of those who had betrayed its ideals. At a conference of Arab journalists in mid-February 1968, during the trials of the air force officers, he dwelt on this theme.[11] On March 15 Haykal said that " 'the power group' in the system" had been "bypassed by events and had become a burden to the revolution, although it ruled in its name," and was in need of change.[12] On March 20 a new and enlarged Cabinet was announced, notable for the absence of Zakariya Muhyi al-Din and Ali Sabri, the symbols of the Right and Left, respectively, within the power structure. Like the monkey in the Krylov fable who tried to make the barnyard orchestra play sweet music by constantly changing the instruments around, Nasir sought to give his government a new image by giving new assignments to familiar hands and by bringing in some newcomers who lacked experience and any power base within the bureaucracies. To cap his movement, he presented an elaborate "Program of Action" on March 30—the Muslim New Year's Day in 1968.[13] It was not a serious proposal for reform but a masterful improvisation, which

10 BBC/ME/2712/A2-A5 (March 5, 1968).
11 BBC/ME/2698/A/4 (February 17, 1968).
12 *Egyptian Mail*, March 16, 1968.   13 *Egyptian Gazette*, March 31, 1968.

left the power where it had always been, with Nasir and the palace clique around him. A joke that made the rounds in Cairo after Nasir's death exemplifies his political style. Sadat, it seems, was riding in an automobile driven by Nasir's former chauffeur when they came to a crossroads. Sadat, not knowing which way to go, told the driver to do what Nasir would have done. The driver pressed the turn signal to indicate a left turn, put out his hand to indicate a right turn, and drove straight ahead.

The March 30 Action Program called for the moral and technological regeneration of the armed forces, for the overhaul and democratization of the ASU, and for greater attention to economic problems and the home front.[14] Civil rights were to be guaranteed. The "people" were to be "supreme" and consulted. "Work" was to be the only criterion for human values, and presumably the basis for economic reward. The ASU was to be rebuilt from top to bottom through elections not appointments. In a speech on April 18, Nasir asked rhetorically: "But who are the members of the ASU? The Socialists. It is they who represent the people's forces—workers, peasants, intellectuals, soldiers, and national capitalists."[15] His appeal was to socialism. A referendum held on May 2 duly approved the Program by a predictable 99.989 percent, and ASU elections were held in June and July. However, these were merely exercises in mass participation and manipulation. Both the candidates and the issues were carefully controlled. One Middle East specialist said of the elaborate election procedures for "democratizing" the ASU: "It was all very complicated, very absorbing for the politically minded, and quite meaningless."[16]

The reforms of March 30, 1968, and the domestic problems they mirrored, occupied Nasir throughout the spring and early summer. While very limited in scope, they did result in a freer press, a reduced level of military and police interference in society, and a considerable reform in the army, particularly in personnel and indoctrination, which was to result in the army's improved performance in the October 1973 War. They consoli-

14 BBC/ME/2750/A/1 (April 22, 1968).
15 BBC/ME/2749/A/9 (April 20, 1968). On March 14, 1976, President Anwar al-Sadat described it thusly: "The 30 March Manifesto was issued but not implemented. . . . It consisted of words of gold, but it did not see the light of day at all." FBIS/Egypt, March 16, 1976, p. D7.
16 Malcolm H. Kerr, "Nasser Unloved But Unchallenged," *Los Angeles Times*, July 28, 1968, p. 7.

dated Nasir's power and served also to gratify the Soviet Union.

Soviet analysts were optimistic. They said that the students arrested during the February demonstrations had been released because they supported "the socialist line of policy of the country";[17] and that the demonstrations strengthened the "progressive regime" and foiled those who had tried to exploit them. The behavior of the workers and fellaheen, the constructive response of the government, and the debate in the National Assembly had proved "the futility of the reactionaries to play the role of 'Trojan Horse'."[18] Special importance was attributed to Nasir's new awareness of the need for mass support embracing all "progressive forces" and to his reorganization of the ASU "as the 'socialist vanguard'" for effectively fighting "the bureaucratic bourgeoisie," democratizing social and political life, and creating the material and ideological bases for the transition to socialism.[19] Nasir's March 30 Program was seen as the germination of a policy of transforming the army, strengthening the government, expanding the public sector, and activating "the role of the masses in the political life of the country."[20]

Moscow anticipated a welcome ideological harvest. The "military bourgeoisie" had been seriously weakened; the ASU reforms were promising, even to the extent of a greater role for "progressives" (i.e. Communists, or "Marxists" as they were generally called in Egypt); and Nasir's reorganization of the economy along "noncapitalist" lines was clear.[21] All of this must have made it easier to persuade any waverers in the Kremlin of the correctness of Soviet policy. Military and economic assistance

[17] *Pravda*, March 7, 1968.   [18] *Izvestiia*, March 6, 1968.

[19] G. Savin, "U.A.R.: Revolution Takes New Steps," *International Affairs*, No. 9 (September 1968), 93; G. Mirskii, "Novaia revolutsiia v OAR" (The New Revolution in the UAR), *Mirovaia ekonomika i mezhdunarodnye otnosheniia*, No. 1 (January 1969), 46-48; E. Primakov, "Cairo Conspiracy Trial," *New Times*, No. 7 (February 21, 1968), 16. Primakov wrote: "It is significant, I think, that hand in hand with the trial of the plotters have gone measures to strengthen the Arab Socialist Union. Back in the post of ASU secretary general is Ali Sabri, who in the past did much to build up the core of the organization. . . . Ali Sabri has declared for the principle of elective leadership at all levels of the organization. It is expected that this principle will be adopted in some measure in the ASU itself. Progressive elements, including some known for their Marxist views, are being enlisted more freely than before in ASU activities."

[20] *Pravda*, April 28, 1968; May 4, 1968.

[21] *Izvestiia*, July 4, 1968. M. Kremnev, "The U.A.R. Referendum," *New Times*, No. 19 (May 14, 1968), 20-21.

poured into Egypt.[22] Nasir's commitment to transform the ASU into "the socialist vanguard,"[23] coupled with other welcome expressions of friendship,[24] may well have heightened Moscow's sense of satisfaction, certainly over Egypt's internal policies.

JARRING'S ODYSSEY

In the months after his appointment Jarring traveled extensively, but to no avail. Flying from capital to capital, he was a frequent visitor in Jerusalem, Cairo, and Amman. In early January 1968 he tried to work out an arrangement for reopening the Suez Canal. Cairo hinted at acceptance of dredging operations and the release of the fifteen ships trapped in the canal provided the work was done under the Egyptian flag and without any requirement to grant access to Israeli ships. Jerusalem balked—agreeing only to open the southern half of the canal, pending signs of an Egyptian willingness to negotiate. Its calculation was that economic deprivation and Great Power pressure would force Egypt to make political concessions. Some dredging started, only to be suspended in late January. Subsequent indications of Israeli flexibility were considered inadequate by Cairo. By early February the die was cast: the canal was to remain closed. Riyad expressed Nasir's mood when he said, "We will not allow the Israelis to get comfortable. We will not let them swim in our canal."

Economically, the closure of the canal was no burden on Egypt, which received compensation from the Arab states in accordance with the formula worked out at Khartoum; indeed, it was seen as a means of bringing U.S. pressure on Israel. The United States preferred, however, to keep the canal closed, thereby lengthening the Soviet supply line to North Vietnam and reducing the mobil-

[22] A technical and industrial protocol calling for the expansion of the Helwan iron and steel complex was signed in Cairo on May 15, 1968. The second largest project after the High Dam, the Helwan complex was to increase Egypt's steel-making capacity from 300,000 tons annually to 1.3 million tons by 1977. Moscow agreed to provide an additional 200 million dollar credit.

[23] *Egyptian Gazette*, May 10, 1968.

[24] On June 20, 1968, the Soviet Cultural Center in Cairo was allowed to open a library with a reading room for more than 100 people. Provided with thousands of volumes, it was intended to popularize Soviet achievements among students and intellectuals and encourage the study of the Russian language. In addition, in May 1968, Cairo Radio inaugurated a program beamed to the Soviet Union.

ity of the Soviet navy, which was starting to show the flag in the Persian Gulf and Indian Ocean. Nasir's troubles at home stiffened his reluctance to appear to be wavering in his opposition to Israel. As events turned out, Israel was the main loser. By insisting on political conditions that Nasir could not accept, it eased his economic decision to write off the canal cities, already damaged and largely evacuated, and impelled him that much closer to "the war of attrition."

On March 30 U Thant gave the Security Council a discouraging report from Jarring, whose mission had foundered on the incompatible conditions set by Israel and Egypt:[25] Israel insisted on direct negotiations between the two sides, while Egypt objected, saying that this was not specified in Resolution 242; Egypt demanded Israel's a priori agreement to withdraw from all Arab territories occupied in June 1967, while Israel argued that the resolution did not specify "all" territories and stressed the need to guarantee it "secure and recognized boundaries." Haykal put the dilemma well:

> For the Arabs . . . there are two points on which there can be no argument. The first is insistence on withdrawal from every inch of the Arab territories occupied after June 5, 1967. The second is the absolute and final rejection of peace with Israel. The Security Council resolution clearly provides for withdrawal but does not even hint at peace with Israel. From the Israeli point of view, the situation is more complicated. . . . David Ben Gurion . . . said something striking during an argument with a visitor who talked to him last week in one of the Negev settlements. Ben Gurion said: If we withdraw and there is no peace treaty with the Arabs, what will we have gained from the six-day war? We will only have proved that Moshe Dayan is an efficient general.[26]

The Soviet government upheld Egypt's position. It noted with approval Riyad's letter of May 9, 1968, to Jarring, proposing a timetable for the implementation of Resolution 242:

> Once Israel agreed to carry out fully all its [242] provisions, each side would deposit with the U.N. a declaration concerning

---

[25] Jarring had tried to persuade Israel and the Arab states to send representatives to his headquarters in Nicosia. Israel agreed on February 26, but Egypt's refusal on March 8 killed the proposal.

[26] BBC/ME/2768/A/1 (May 13, 1968).

an end to the state of war, respect for and recognition of sovereignty, territorial integrity and the independence of each government in the given territory and their right to live in peace, in secure and recognized borders; concomitantly, other measures would be discussed for resolving disputed questions.[27]

In the ensuing weeks and months Moscow and Cairo consulted closely on their diplomatic strategy, and Moscow frequently reaffirmed its belief in the possibility of a political settlement.[28] This became a Soviet staple, yet Moscow did not make any specific proposals that could have nudged the discussions off dead center, and Western expectations of a major Soviet push to reopen the Suez Canal proved wrong.

By late May Cairo despaired of Jarring, but it went along with his diplomatic la ronde to improve its image abroad and play for time. Informal discussions droned on at the United Nations in preparation for the fall session of the General Assembly. Nasir was absorbed at home, securing his political power and rehabilitating the armed forces; Israel was content with its new strategic borders; the United States was deeply engaged in Vietnam; and the Soviet Union had problems in Czechoslovakia. The two superpowers kept a wary watch over their clients, while attending to priorities elsewhere.

THE PALESTINIAN RESISTANCE MOVEMENT: FROM SIDE-SHOW TO SYMBOL

The Palestinians had paid heavily for the first Arab-Israeli war (1948–1949), which had been foisted on them by Arab states who were ostensibly committed to preserving the whole of Palestine for the indigenous Arabs but who had actually gone to war for different reasons: Faruq of Egypt to regain some popularity

[27] B. N. Ponomarev, A. A. Gromyko, V. M. Khvostov (eds.), *Istoriia vneshnei politiki SSSR 1945-1970* (The History of USSR Foreign Policy 1945-1970), II (Moscow: Nauka, 1971), 432.

[28] See, for example, *Izvestiia*, June 4, 1968. I. Belyaev, "Ways of Ending the Middle East Crisis," *International Affairs*, No. 10 (October 1968), p. 27. After developing the case for Egypt's exclusion of Israeli ships from the canal pending a full settlement, Belyaev said that, notwithstanding, "the Arab countries are prepared to make substantial concessions, agreeing to the unconditional implementation of the Security Council resolution; I repeat, substantial concessions." And Y. Primakov, "Peace Prospects in the Middle East," *International Affairs*, No. 2 (February 1969), 49-50.

for his venal regime; Abdullah of Jordan to extend the size and resources of his poor kingdom; and Syria to realize her ambitions for a Greater Syria. Victimized by the ineptitude, indifference, and frequent hostility of their fellow Arabs, the Palestinians had been reduced to irrelevancy. War was their salvation. In the months after June 1967 they mounted small-scale terrorist attacks, mainly in Israeli-occupied territory. Their activities were magnified by the Arab press, eager to bolster morale and demonstrate that the fight was not over. At the same time, their militancy, coupled with the search of Arab leaders for a symbol that could unify their efforts to overcome the June 1967 defeat, gave the Palestinians a new status in Arab politics. Though factionalized by ideology and personal rivalries, the various Palestinian groups showed determination to continue the struggle against Israel—and to escalate it.

In so doing, they posed an implicit challenge to the authority and the established state interests of both the Cairo and Amman regimes, especially the latter. But for some of the same reasons that the Arab states had previously found it difficult to turn their backs on the unattainable goal of destroying the Israeli state, so Egypt and Jordan could not now readily disavow the Palestinian resistance groups, especially considering the wide popular acclaim for these groups within each of the Arab states.[29]

The Palestinians were not seen as strategically or militarily significant, but they could not be ignored politically. In late December 1967, the Palestine Liberation Organization (PLO) replaced its chairman, Ahmad ash-Shuqayri, a rabble-rousing, unpopular Palestinian long regarded as Cairo's paid propagandist and an anathema to Amman, with a relative unknown, Yahya Hammuda. The PLO became the umbrella under which the different factions gathered to obtain recognition in Arab councils.[30]

[29] Malcolm H. Kerr, "Regional Arab Politics and the Conflict with Israel" (RAND Corporation Memorandum 5966-FF) (October 1969), p. 44.

[30] The main components of the Palestine resistance movement are *Al Fatah*, led by Yasir Arafat; the Popular Front for the Liberation of Palestine (PFLP), a radical leftist, neo-Marxist group headed by a Palestinian Christian, Dr. George Habash; the Popular Democratic Front for the Liberation of Palestine (PDFLP), a faction that broke off from the PFLP in 1969 under the leadership of Naif Hawatmeh; and Al-Saiqa, a Syrian-based Ba'athist

Cairo publicized the PLO's exaggerated accounts of its exploits. But Nasir knew that its targets rarely had any military value, and for him the Palestinians remained marginal participants in the overall struggle. Haykal maintained that the PLO "cannot achieve—and nobody can ask it to achieve—a decisive result in the struggle."

> Anyone who thinks, for instance, that the Palestinian revolutionary resistance will be able to accomplish the same results as the revolutionary resistance did in Algeria is doing an injustice to the Palestinian situation. . . . The Palestinian resistance in the occupied territory, despite its extreme importance, cannot possibly play a decisive part. In other words, this resistance is not a substitute for a final armed confrontation— army pitted against army, fleet against fleet, air force against air force.[31]

Moscow shared this assessment. Though praising the PLO's aim of liberating the occupied territories, it saw no reason to provide material assistance, notwithstanding Peking's shipments of small arms via Iraq and Syria. This sense of minimal importance was reflected in the Soviet-Egyptian communiqué of January 13, 1968, which ignored the Palestinian issue.

The stock of the Palestinian guerrillas suddenly soared on March 21, 1968, when Israeli forces attacked the Fatah base at Karamah in Jordan and encountered stiff resistance. For the first time, the Fedayeen, fighting alongside Jordanian troops, gave a good account of themselves in an open fight with Israeli troops. Though the Israelis carried the day, the guerrillas emerged with considerable prestige. They began to operate openly in Jordan in increasingly imperious fashion, attracting recruits, exacting tribute, challenging King Husayn's authority, and building up a force that by the end of 1968 "represented a political force parallel to that of the Hashemite monarchy."[32]

---

group. For a useful discussion of the doctrine, organization, personalities, and policies of the different groups see, Dishon, *Middle East Record, Vol. Four*, 397-440; William B. Quandt, Fuad Jabber, Ann M. Lesch, *The Politics of Palestinian Nationalism* (Berkeley: University of California Press, 1973); Walid Kazziha, *Revolutionary Transformation in the Arab World* (London: Charles Knight and Company, 1975).

[31] BBC/ME/2675/A/4 (January 22, 1968).

[32] Malcolm H. Kerr, *The Arab Cold War: Gamal 'Abd al-Nasir and His Rivals 1958-1970*, 3rd ed. (New York: Oxford University Press, 1971), p. 141.

One immediate result was a more forthright championing of the rights of the Palestinians by Nasir, who nevertheless responded cautiously to their efforts to develop an independent political existence and expand military operations. The Karamah battle, said Haykal, had shown the military value of the Palestinians and brought them "an undisputed political status," but it was essential not to be provoked into a war with Israel until the Arabs were ready.[33] Several months later, fearful of just that, he was less enthusiastic about the Palestinian resistance:

> . . . its role is not decisive in the liquidation of the Israeli aggression. Those who think it will be decisive are . . . lazy or ill informed. They are lazy people who want to give the responsibility to others to save themselves the trouble and remain silent, or they do not know the facts about the Arab confrontation with the Israeli enemy in the present circumstances.[34]

Haykal implied that the Palestinians had to acquire a measure of political realism. The struggle in the occupied territory could not be compared to the one in Vietnam because of fundamental differences in terrain, in the function of popular resistance, in the human ratio of "the resistance forces to their enemy," and in the importance of sanctuaries, or their absence.

The Soviet government condemned the Israeli raid into Karamah and reaffirmed its support for the Arabs, but it again called for a "political settlement."[35] Riyad tried futilely to use the incident to pry additional weapons from the Soviet Union, but like Nasir, it shied away from fanning the sparks of Palestinian resistance. In its diplomacy and through Arab Communist parties, the USSR urged the Palestinians to adopt political not military action. In an interview in *Al-Akhbar* on June 5, Soviet Ambassador Vinogradov did not mention the guerrillas, and Soviet journalists refused "invitations of the Palestinians to cover their training and operations."[36] In July, a statement issued by Arab Communist and Workers parties—their first since the June War —criticized "the unrealistic approach" of some Arab nationalist groups to the Palestine problem, which was but a part of the

---

[33] BBC/ME/2756/A/1 (April 29, 1968).

[34] BBC/ME/2851/A/3 (August 18, 1968).

[35] "Soviet Government's Statement [of March 22] on Middle East Situation," *Soviet News*, No. 5430 (March 26, 1968), 158, 168.

[36] John K. Cooley, "Moscow Tries to Ease Tensions in Mideast," *The Christian Science Monitor*, August 22, 1968.

overall Arab national-liberation, anti-imperialist movement: ". . . the call of the exponents of this reckless trend to separate the Palestine issue from the Arab national-liberation movement is entirely incorrect and, consequently, so is the slogan that Palestinians should fight their battle alone on the lame pretext that the Palestinian movements are 'independent' and need no 'patronage.' "[37] Moscow mistrusted eruptions on the Left that fell beyond the pale of its control.

While Cairo and Moscow both preferred to keep the Palestinians on short rations and a tight rein, their policies diverged. By early 1968, the Palestinians, acclaimed a military factor by the Western media and glorified by a generation of Arabs reared on rhetoric and hungry for action, emerged as a potent political force, inducing Nasir to embrace their cause lest the militancy and enthusiasm they evoked deprive him of an important constituency in the Arab world. At its meeting in Cairo on July 18 the Palestine National Assembly, representing all factions, rejected Resolution 242 as a basis for a settlement of the Middle East crisis, on the ground that it would lead to the liquidation of the Palestine issue (Resolution 242, it will be remembered, does not mention the Palestinians as such, but calls only for "a just settlement of the refugee problem"). The movement increasingly took on a dynamic of its own that was quickly reflected in the Soviet-Egyptian relationship. By summer, no speech, no communiqué, no gathering in the Arab world could fail to uphold the rights of the Palestinians, who became the banner around which all Arabs could unite in the struggle against Israel.

NASIR TAKES HIS CASE TO MOSCOW

On June 27, in a foreign policy speech to the Supreme Soviet, Gromyko announced that Nasir would arrive in Moscow on July 4. The presence of Jarring, fresh from talks with Israeli Foreign Minister Abba Eban in The Hague, stimulated expectations of a diplomatic breakthrough that were fed by two further developments. On July 1, on the occasion of the signing of the nonproliferation treaty in Moscow, Kosygin presented a nine-point program for arms control, including the possibility of an

---

[37] Georges Batal, Amjad Rashad, Mohammed Harmel, "Vital Tasks of the Arab National Liberation Movement," *World Marxist Review*, 11, No. 9 (September 1968), 26, 28.

arms freeze in the Middle East, which he linked to an Israeli withdrawal from occupied Arab areas.[38] The immediate purpose seemed designed to encourage the United States to defer a decision—announced nevertheless on July 6—to provide Israel with Hawk missiles and fifty Phantom fighter-bombers (on which Washington did hold off in order to explore the possibility of containing the Middle East arms race). On July 3 Riyad created a diplomatic to-do when he was quoted as saying in a press conference in Copenhagen that "We accept realities, and one of those is Israel. We only want peace now."[39] He seemed to imply that Egypt was prepared to recognize the existence of the state of Israel, once all the provisions of Resolution 242 were implemented, but Cairo quickly issued a denial, alleging that Riyad's remarks had been "distorted." The Soviet-Egyptian communiqué of July 10 also dashed some of the expectations.

This communiqué spanned the spectrum of regional and international issues and revealed as did few others the areas of agreement and disagreement between Moscow and Cairo.[40] It was extremely long, setting out positions not only, as in January, on the Middle East but also on Vietnam, African national liberation movements, general and complete disarmament, the non-proliferation treaty, European security, and East Germany—issues of interest primarily to the Soviet Union, yet befitting a meeting of heads of state. Each party made compromises on issues of importance to the other, but there were still serious disagreements as was suggested by the formulation that "frank views were exchanged" regarding the development of comprehensive cooperation between the Soviet Union and Egypt, the situation in the Middle East, and the "methods of eliminating the consequences of the Israeli-imperialist aggression."

Moscow persuaded Cairo to accept Resolution 242 as the basis for a settlement. In contrast to its refusal in January, Egypt averred its readiness to implement the resolution "as soon as possible" and "to take important and feasible steps" to do so. However, the extent of Egypt's concessions may only be surmised. Moscow said that it "appreciates and supports" Egypt's insistence on the withdrawal of Israeli forces "from Arab territories to the

[38] *Pravda*, July 2, 1968; "The Middle East and Nasser's Visit to Moscow," Radio Liberty Dispatch (July 3, 1968); ARR, No. 13 (July 1–15, 1968), p. 198.
[39] ARR, *ibid.*, p. 197.
[40] FBIS/USSR, July 11, 1968, pp. A9-A13.

positions they held before 5 June 1967," but the communiqué avoided saying *all* the territories, the term that was preferred by the Arabs. The distinction can not lack significance. It may have related to differences in the procedural priorities advocated by Moscow and Cairo; perhaps it was to signal Israel to adopt a more flexible position; perhaps to hint at possible Egyptian concessions. For example, Moscow may have urged consideration of a lengthy period of demilitarization in Sinai and Golan or the exclusion of the Gaza strip from the territory to be returned to Egypt on the assumption that such possibilities would be attractive to Israel (and the United States).

In contrast to the January communiqué, this one identified the United States (and Israel) as the enemy, indicating that Egypt had hardened its public estimate of what could be expected from Washington, and was willing to join in denunciation of "imperialism" and its leading exponent, the United States. This served the Soviet interest in organizing an anti-imperialist front in the Arab world, and it neutralized Arab critics who intimated that Nasir was contemplating a compromise settlement. Whereas, by agreeing to implement Resolution 242, Nasir had conveyed his "reasonableness" abroad, by insisting also that any settlement must take into account "the legitimate rights of the Arab peoples, including the Arab people in Palestine," he protected his rear from attack and stepped to the forefront in espousing what was crystallizing as a common Arab concern.

The Palestinians could no longer be ignored, as they had been in the earlier communiqué, though their importance was still minor. Nasir had secretly brought Yasir Arafat, the leader of the PLO, to Moscow to introduce him to the Soviet leadership and to impress on them the importance of the Palestinian issue.[41] Moscow agreed to the clause concerning the Palestinians to accommodate Nasir, whose future exclusion or inclusion of the issue signaled that he was conveying moderation or intransigency.

[41] This information was made public by Haykal after Nasir's death: "Yasir Arafat was on the aircraft [to Moscow] with us. No one else knew of his presence and no one in the world had yet heard of his name. Jamal Abd an-Nasir took Arafat with him to Moscow to establish a link between the USSR and the Palestine Resistance so that the former would be a source of arms." BBC/ME/3505/A/3 (October 12, 1970).

Arafat was not the unknown figure Haykal reported. On November 14, 1966, *The Daily Telegraph* identified Arafat as the head of Al Fatah, as noted in *Kessing's Contemporary Archives 1967-1968*, xvi, p. 21817.

Egypt's dissatisfaction of January with Soviet aid and arms had in the interim dissipated. Nasir now expressed "deep gratitude" for "the great and true aid which the Soviet Union is extending to the UAR to bolster its economy and its defense potential." He signaled out for particular "thanks" the "massive assistance" given to strengthen Egypt's economy. He did indeed have every reason to be grateful to Moscow for the improved military and economic situation in which his country found itself a little more than a year after its crushing defeat.

The communiqué "welcomed the establishment and development of friendly contacts between the CPSU and the ASU." The party-to-party relationship is prized by the Soviet leadership, to whom it signifies the existence of particularly close ties and whom it presumably helps to justify foreign aid programs for Third World countries in the Kremlin debates on the subject. So, too, is mention of socialism. Both points—party contacts and the commitment to socialism—are generally found in communiqués characterized by a high level of agreement and mutual satisfaction. Many of the "possibilities of increasing cooperation" that were unsaid in January had become realities by July. On the Middle East, the two capitals were largely in agreement, though a difference of views on the terms of a settlement and possibly over weapons is indicated because after Nasir's departure the Egyptian chief of staff stayed behind for additional consultations with the Soviet defense minister, who postponed a scheduled visit to Algeria for several days. Nasir, too, had extended his visit by three more days: the extension was announced on July 6, the day the U.S.-Israeli arms agreement was reported in Washington, thereby strengthening the supposition that Nasir used it, as well as the Israeli shelling of Suez City on July 8, to argue for increased arms deliveries.

Both sides had reason to consider the visit a success. Yet there was an undercurrent of divergent purposes and priorities. Moscow counseled patience, but Nasir needed something tangible to demonstrate activity. He had acceded to Soviet pressure and committed himself to a settlement based on Resolution 242, but his interpretation of what that entailed was qualified by what Haykal described as "the four impossibilities":

Concerning the political solution and its prospects, we are not intransigent and we do not abandon ourselves to the delusion of dictating terms. But there are possibilities and impossibilities: to concede an inch of the occupied Arab territory is impossible and not in my power; to agree on negotiations with Israel is impossible and I do not accept it; to sign a peace treaty with Israel is impossible and I cannot do it; to recognize Israel is impossible and I am unable to extend recognition. This is my attitude. It is on the basis of this attitude that we have offered the opportunity for a political settlement.[42]

These qualifications effectively vitiated much that was intrinsic to Resolution 242. Nonetheless, the Soviets did not expect an outbreak of fighting; indeed, they may even have anticipated a breakthrough on the matter of reopening the canal, judging by their dispatch of dredgers to Port Said in July.[43]

OBSERVATIONS

On July 23, the sixteenth anniversary of the revolution, Nasir addressed the ASU National Congress, and after extolling the centrality of the ASU in Egypt's political life and the success of the elections held in accordance with the March 30 Program he turned to foreign policy.[44] The possibility of a political solution had been accepted after the June defeat for several reasons: because without any armed forces Egypt had no alternative but to talk about a political solution; because it was prepared, as in 1957 when U.S. pressure forced Israel to disgorge the gains of the Anglo-French-Israeli attack on Egypt, to cooperate with efforts to obtain its rights; and because world public opinion had to be considered. However, all efforts had so far failed: "No projects exist now for a peaceful solution, and it does not seem to me that there will be any in the future." Egypt must therefore continue to rebuild its armed forces, "which may be greater than those existing before the battle." When preparations are completed we shall, he promised, assess the prospects of the military and political options, one thing being certain, namely, "the crisis cannot last long."

Nasir was lavish in praise of Soviet assistance and generosity: "We took part of the Soviet weapons as a gift and concluded a

42 BBC/ME/2821/A/2 (July 15, 1968).
43 *The Christian Science Monitor*, July 11, 1968.
44 BBC/ME/2830/A1-A13 (July 25, 1968).

contract for the remainder for which we shall pay in the future in long term installments."[45] During his visit, Nasir related, he had made additional requests for aid; the Soviets had asked for nothing. The Soviet Union had been so generous because it seeks to prevent American domination of the area: "I wish to tell you frankly and clearly that the Soviet Union has never tried, not even in our most crucial times, to dictate conditions to us or to ask anything of us. On the contrary, it has always been we who have asked." To allay the apprehensiveness among his many conservative supporters over the growing Soviet presence, he stressed that the presence of the Soviet navy checked the U.S. Sixth Fleet and was not a threat to Egypt, though he studiedly did not mention the grant of "facilities" at Port Said and Alexandria. Finally, recognizing the prevalence of anti-Soviet sentiments, he warned against falling prey to the enemy's psychological warfare and the bugbear of the dangers of becoming too close to the Soviet Union. His assurance that Egypt's independence and sovereignty were not threatened by the close relationship with the Soviet Union is worth quoting at length because of its bearing on the nature of influence relationships:

> There is a big difference between cooperation and subservience. When we concluded the 1955 arms deal with the Soviet Union they said there was danger in the arms deal because it would drag us into subservience. They cited examples. When we began to conclude the High Dam agreement with the Soviet Union, they said Soviet experts would come to work at the High Dam and that this would lead to some sort of subservience. More than 5,000 Soviet experts came to the High Dam, but none of them interfered in our domestic affairs and none of them tried to convert any of the people of Aswan to communism. Nothing of the sort happened.
>
> Today they are saying the same thing. For example, they say the Soviet experts in the army mean domination of the army and subservience. I have said before that we asked the Soviet Union for these experts and that the Soviet Union was not receptive to giving us experts, saying it would expose us to attack. But in fact, after the 5th June events, anyone with insight who could evaluate things felt that we needed training and that we had a great deal to learn about war. Thus we asked

[45] *Ibid.*, p. A9.

for and got the military experts. They are helping us. We have, in fact, benefited from them; we have benefited from them in all fields. . . .

Brothers, we feel that the entire Arab nation must feel grateful to the Soviet Union. Had it not been for the Soviet Union, . . . we should now find ourselves with no arms in the face of the Israeli militarism, which has been blinded by its victory of June 1967. Egypt's independence—and I say this to all people —is not for sale, is not for anyone to buy and is not for mortgage.[46]

Nasir made it clear that Egypt had no alternative to the Soviet Union.

For its part, the Soviet leaders handled Nasir skillfully. They made no demands, exerted no pressure. True, there was no need: Nasir was behaving admirably from their perspective. He had facilitated their naval operations in the Mediterranean; pressed for an anti-imperialist coalition; legitimized the Soviet role in the Arab national liberation struggle; pruned the military of social "reactionaries"; expanded the Soviet role in Egypt's economy; and revolutionized the role of the ASU (or so they thought; Egyptians were more skeptical).

On July 25 Cairo announced that Nasir was returning to the Soviet Union on the following day for medical treatment to last about two or three weeks (he had suffered for years from a painful arteriosclerosis in the right leg, caused by chronic diabetes). On the eve of his departure Egypt faced serious problems: an invasion of locusts, the worst in fifty years, threatening the cotton crop; a severe shortage of foreign exchange; disunity in the Arab world; strained relations with Jordan and Syria that were a hairline from an open diplomatic break, like the one between Tunisia and Syria in early May; and tension with Saudi Arabia, notwithstanding Egypt's disengagement from the Yemeni civil war. Nasir had many things to ponder in the Georgian spa at Tskhaltubo.

[46] *Ibid.*, p. A12

Chapter Three

TO THE WAR OF ATTRITION

FIFTEEN months after the June defeat Nasir was still groping for a coherent policy. Desperately playing for time, he juggled opponents, wavered between options, and strove in his irresoluteness for a way to retain power, restore his prestige, and force the Israelis to give back Arab lands. Nasir reacted to crises rather than anticipated them, and he had a penchant for straddling several lines simultaneously, for avoiding commitment, even after he had taken a decision. This perennial equivocation had plagued Egypt's developmental programs in the mid-1950s and early 1960s. To the consternation of planners who needed clear-cut decisions and priorities, Nasir bridled at their requests and once even replied, "a politician should not commit himself to any plan or preference" unless he can be sure of success—an understandable political sentiment, but hardly a basis for a strategy of economic development. Nasir's underlying fatalism and the extreme political straits in which he found himself gradually pushed him to a position that strained relations with the Soviet Union and imposed new burdens on an already sorely taxed economy.

The exact beginning of the phase of Egyptian-Israeli relations commonly known as "the war of attrition" is more difficult to pinpoint than the date of its end: it ended with the cease-fire agreement of August 7, 1970; it probably began in earnest on March 8, 1969, though serious fighting had several times erupted earlier only to peter out.

MILITARY JOCKEYING

Egypt stepped up its military assertiveness in the late summer of 1968, initially with sniper fire across the Suez Canal and the laying of mines on the Israeli-held eastern bank of the waterway, and subsequently with periodic artillery and air duels in the canal area during September and October. This escalation was intended to reinforce Egyptian diplomatic maneuvers and pronouncements and create a crisis atmosphere that would force the United Nations and particularly the great powers to demand an Israeli withdrawal. For example, on September 8, the Egyptians laid down their heaviest artillery barrage since the June War.[1] The firing of more than 10,000 shells along the seventy-mile long canal over a four-hour period came just one day before a scheduled meeting of the U.N. Security Council. In the ensuing days, Nasir (recently returned from a period of medical treatment in the USSR) discussed the military situation "on the fighting front" with his Cabinet and at the opening session of the ASU Congress. The Egyptian media warned that "the situation along the front is expected to explode."[2] On September 12 the governor of the Suez governorate (province) announced that the population of Suez (the city at the southern terminus of the canal) would be further reduced from 60,000 to 35,000 to avoid casualties from Israeli shelling (in June 1967 the city had had a population of about 250,000).

Diplomatic activity was increased. On September 25 Egypt called for "positive action" by the U.N. General Assembly to ensure the success of the Jarring mission. The Egyptian press publicized a statement issued by the Soviet foreign ministry on September 25, sharply condemning Israel for its intransigence, warning that it would be held responsible for any provocative actions against Egypt, Syria, or Jordan, and reaffirming Soviet assistance to the Arabs.[3] On September 27, *Al-Ahram* reported on a Soviet peace plan submitted to the United States two weeks earlier, calling for an Israeli pullback to the borders of June 4, 1967, an expanded and revived U.N. presence in areas evacuated by Israel, a guarantee by the great powers against any renewal of fighting, an Arab declaration ending the state of belligerency existing since 1949; and saying "as far as the other problems, such as the refugee problem, that could be discussed later on."[4] On the same day, Haykal wrote: "The Middle East crisis is about

---

[1] *Al-Ahram*, September 9, 1968.   [2] *Al-Ahram*, September 11, 1968.
[3] *Al-Ahram*, September 26, 1968.

[4] *Al-Ahram*, September 27, 1968. One American official was quoted as saying that the Soviet plan coincided with news leaks from the USSR to the effect that Soviet leaders had offered Egypt hundreds of tanks, planes, and pilot instructors. "These are routine Soviet bargaining tactics," the official said. "Outwardly they reassure the Arabs; privately they sound us out on the possibility of a deal. Their private position is not so tough as their public position." *NYT*, September 26, 1968.

to make a decisive and perhaps final appearance in this UN international arena. After this, the race between a political settlement and a military solution—and the political settlement so far has lagged behind in the race—will have ended with the final elimination of the political solution from the race."[5] These remarks were not mere rhetoric. By the fall of 1968 expanded Soviet shipments of arms had restored Egypt's arsenal of tanks, artillery, and aircraft to levels equal to or even exceeding those existing prior to June 1967.[6]

In foreign policy, political agility and timing are all-important. In 1954, Nasir had obtained U.S. assistance in pressuring the British to evacuate the Suez Canal zone; in 1955, he had foiled the Western arms embargo by turning to the Soviets; in July 1956, he had nationalized the Suez Canal Company, thereby transforming the humiliation that stemmed from Washington's reversal of its previous offer to help build the Aswan High Dam into a major political triumph; in October of the same year he had survived the combined Anglo-French-Israeli attack, because of President Eisenhower's moral indignation toward his NATO allies and insistence on a full Israeli withdrawal; and during the 1962–1967 period he had managed to surmount an inconclusive and costly intervention in the Yemeni civil war without losing his preeminence in the Arab world. But in 1968 time and circumstances were no longer with him; Nasir could not produce any sustained response from the great powers, who were then preoccupied with other matters: the United States was in the middle of a presidential election campaign, and the Soviet Union was dealing with the consequences of its August 21 invasion of Czechoslovakia and the September 26 enunciation of the "Brezhnev Doctrine."

[5] Al-Ahram, September 27, 1968.

[6] On October 16, Israeli Defense Minister Moshe Dayan declared that Arab air forces were 50 percent stronger than in June 1967; and Arab armor had regained its prewar force levels. NYT, October 17, 1968. See also Strategic Survey 1967 (London: International Institute for Strategic Studies, 1968), p. 37. On March 1, 1968, Haykal had written: "Today we see that we have a big and strong army—an army prepared and armed but in need of preparedness and more weapons. It is, by any estimate, stronger and more effective than the army we had before the Sinai battles." BBC/ME/2711/A/3 (March 4, 1968). The restoration of Egypt's armed forces was also implied by P. Demchenko, "Blizhnii Vostok mezhdu voinoi i mirom" (The Middle East Between War and Peace), Mirovaia ekonomika i mezhdunarodnye otnosheniia, No. 6 (June 1968), 79.

The Western powers dismissed the new Soviet proposal for a Middle East settlement as merely a ploy to distract attention from Eastern Europe. In general, they interpreted Cairo's silence on Czechoslovakia as a sign of its complete dependence on the Soviet Union, thus strengthening their belief that Nasir would not go to war without Soviet approval, which, given the tense situation in Europe, was considered most improbable.[7] In view of this assessment, they discounted the danger implicit in Egypt's military actions along the canal and the seeming flexibility in national positions suggested in the General Assembly, when on October 8 Gromyko called "for a curb on arms shipments to the Middle East"; on the same day Eban offered a nine-point plan that included a nonaggression treaty between Israel and the Arabs; and on October 10 Riyad proposed that a timetable be established for implementing a peace settlement under Security Council auspices. As it turned out, all this was very much beside the point, for when it came down to specifics, neither side was prepared to give enough to whet the interest of the other.

The Israelis rejected U Thant's plea for indirect talks along the lines of the 1949 Rhodes formula (which had brought an end to the First Arab-Israeli War), and the Egyptians refused to consider direct talks. However, on October 9 Israel did agree to carry on preliminary discussions with Egypt through Jarring. In turn, President Johnson, after the breakdown of talks between Gromyko and Rusk, announced that he had instructed Secretary of State Dean Rusk to "initiate negotiations with the Govern-

[7] Cairo Radio echoed Moscow's views on the necessity for the intervention "following a call by the Czechoslovak Communist Party leaders and the Government of the Czechoslovak Socialist Republic for urgent assistance from the Soviet Union and other allied states" BBC/ME/2855/A/1 (August 23, 1968); it justified the action, stressing "the dangerous and destructive role played by . . . world Zionism, the main agent of colonialism and imperialism" BBC/ME/2858/A/1 (August 27, 1968). Nasir emphasized this point in his speech to the ASU Congress on September 14, 1968.

Only Haykal expressed some personal reservations—one of the reasons the Soviet leaders regarded him as an opponent of closer Soviet-Egyptian relations: "In principle, intervention by any State in the affairs of another is unacceptable. If this intervention takes the form of military action, the matter becomes even more serious, irrespective of the reasons leading to it." Though deploring the intervention on principle, he owned that the Soviet Union had compelling reasons for its action and that "No Arab can easily condemn intervention in Czechoslovakia because the Arab-Israeli crisis was one of the direct causes of the events in Czechoslovakia." BBC/ME/2863/A/5 (September 2, 1968).

ment of Israel" for the purchase of fifty Phantom F-4 jet fighter-bombers (the final arrangements, calling for delivery in late 1969, were concluded at the end of the year, prior to Johnson's leaving office). Three days later "pro-Israeli sources" in Washington reported a major new Soviet arms agreement with Egypt that "is not, and has never been, contingent on a U.S. supply of Phantoms to Israel."[8] The decision to provide Phantoms, however, "was certain to evoke a joint Soviet-Egyptian response, given the level of Soviet entanglement after June 1967 and its thinly disguised use of arms aid as a means of building base facilities on Egyptian territory for the Soviet navy and naval air arm."[9] The Middle East arms race rumbled on.

In the light of Soviet strategic ambitions, the inexorable diffusion of technologically advanced weapons systems to small and middle-level powers, and Washington's deep suspicion of Soviet intentions in the aftermath of Czechoslovakia, Johnson's announcement was clearly not motivated just by partisan electoral considerations, though these undoubtedly prompted the timing of the announcement. (To offset Israel's losses in 1967 and Soviet arms shipments to Egypt, Johnson had promised to provide Israel with fifty Phantom jets during Premier Levi Eshkol's visit to the LBJ ranch in Texas on January 7-8, 1968; in the spring and summer, the State Department and Defense Department tried to pressure Israel to sign the nuclear nonproliferation treaty as a quid pro quo for the Phantoms, but the President finally ordered them to drop the matter in late August.) The influx of Soviet military advisers—about 3,000 by late 1968—and the resupply of some $3 billion in arms since the June War (figured at the cost of equivalent American weapons) convinced the White House that the USSR had no real interest in limiting force levels in the area.[10] (Ever since the Soviet-Egyptian arms deal of 1955, successive American presidents have adhered to a policy of maintaining Israel's military balance vis-à-vis its immediate Arab neighbors.)

In spite of continued air clashes, an intense artillery exchange on October 26, and an Israeli raid on October 31 to destroy a

[8] *NYT*, October 13, 1968.

[9] J. C. Hurewitz, "Weapons Acquisition: Israel and Egypt," in Frank B. Horton, III, Anthony C. Rogerson, and Edward L. Warner, III (eds.), *Comparative Defense Policy* (Baltimore: The Johns Hopkins University Press, 1974), p. 488.

[10] *NYT*, October 22. 1968.

transformer station and two bridges over the Nile, by early November the threat of a major resumption of fighting had receded. On November 6 Nasir briefed the ASU Central Committee. Two days later Riyad returned early from the U.N. General Assembly with the assessment that the Jarring mission was deadlocked and no further purpose was served by his remaining at the United Nations.[11]

MOUNTING PRESSURES

The lull proved short-lived as Nasir found himself under increasing domestic and Arab-world pressures. The reorganization of the ASU, which had been inaugurated with fanfare under the March 30 Program, was capped by a rigged election, the selection of a hand-picked Central Committee, and the establishment on October 20 of an eight-member Higher Executive Committee that included Ali Sabri.[12] Moscow was reassured by these developments. Haykal's discussions of the need for an "open society" and the elimination of "centers of power"[13] sounded the reformist theme Nasir desired to disseminate. On November 14 Nasir dissolved the National Assembly and set new elections for January 8, 1969, stipulating that fifty percent of the new members must be "workers" and "peasants." But this spurious reformism was interrupted with dramatic suddenness during the first days of Ramadan.

On November 20, serious student rioting broke out in Mansurah; it turned violent on November 21 and spread to Alexandria the next day and to Cairo on November 24, leading the government to close all the universities. For the second time in nine months, riots and disorders spread in the major cities; casualties and property damage were heavy. The immediate catalyst was student protest against new school regulations that made it "more difficult to graduate from secondary schools and

11 BBC/ME/2922/A/1 (November 10, 1968).

12 Commenting in May 1971 on the election of the Higher Executive Committee in October 1968, Haykal wrote: "It was clear from all indications that the result had been planned and pre-arranged in favor of a specific, limited group. . . . I can almost swear . . . that had it not been for Abd an-Nasir's concern for things which needed to be preserved at the time, he would have held new elections for the ASU, from the very foundation to the top." BBC/ME/3697/A/1-2 (June 1, 1971).

13 For example, *Egyptian Mail*, November 9 and 16, 1968.

enter college,"[14] a necessary stepping stone to social mobility; nevertheless, it was clear that the slow pace of internal reform was a factor, as was impatience with Nasir's failure to make any progress toward the liberation of Arab lands. The unrest was perceived by the insecure leadership as anti-government, since the demands escalated to calls for more freedom, curbs on the police, and basic societal changes. Nasir hurriedly convened an emergency session of the ASU National Congress and tightened control over the military, among whom there were reports of mounting resentment against the extensive authority granted to Soviet advisers.[15]

In a major speech on December 2 Nasir addressed himself to the roots of the discontent.[16] He spoke of Egypt's recovery from the disaster of June 1967, of the ASU's democratization, of the easing of censorship; he called for understanding by those demanding instant reform and counseled patience, pleading that everything could not be accomplished at once. But above all he tried to explain why the war to recover Egyptian territories and liberate Arab lands was not being pressed. He likened Egypt's situation to that of England after Dunkirk with this difference: "We are neither in a state of war nor of peace—hence the sad atmosphere." Pleading for time to rebuild the armed forces, Nasir asserted that "at the same time we are working for an honorable political settlement," which does not mean surrender, there being "a difference between peaceful settlement and surrender." This was the last time before the outbreak of "the war of attrition" that he spoke of a "political settlement" in so moderate a fashion. It was evident in his speech of January 20, 1969, and interviews the following month with *Newsweek* and the *New York Times*, that domestic pressures had hardened his attitude and impelled him to "the war of attrition."

Firing along the canal predictably intensified in early December, on the eve of visits by Jarring and William Scranton, Presi-

14 *NYT*, November 25, 1968. To upgrade educational standards, especially technological and scientific training, the government issued a decree that prohibited automatic promotion of elementary school students from grade to grade, and restricted students to no more than two efforts to pass their secondary school examinations.

15 *NYT*, December 1, 1968.

16 BBC/ME/2942/A/1-10 (December 4, 1968). In subsequent days Nasir shifted his emphasis, putting the principal blame for the unrest on "Israeli agents" and other "subversive elements." *Egyptian Gazette*, December 4 and 5, 1968.

dent-elect Richard M. Nixon's personal envoy touring the Middle East on a fact-finding mission. Nasir's prestige was lower than at any time since the June debacle. Not only had his image at home been tarnished by the student disorders, and the military—heretofore his bulwark—become increasingly restive, but his leadership in the Arab world was likewise under challenge from the Palestinian guerrilla organizations, whose headline-catching border raids against Israel from Syria, Lebanon, and Jordan and whose terrorist exploits against Israelis abroad and in Israel itself appeared to be the only real resistance to Israel and captured the popular imagination (and presented Israel with a new security problem).

Nasir's forte had always been his diplomatic dexterity, his ability to find a suitable political response to critical challenges. But he was running out of options: his putative democratization was recognized for the sham it was; the army was better equipped and trained than in June 1967, yet it sat immobile along the canal; the economy was kept afloat by a patchwork of expediencies: Arab subsidies, rescheduled debt payments to Western creditors, a smattering of loans from international institutions, and wheat shipments, raw materials, and essential equipment from the Soviet bloc. Peace was unthinkable; the status quo, intolerable; that left war.

FRATERNAL FRICTIONS

When the U.N. session ended without taking any action on the Middle East, Nasir cast about for a new move. Moscow, evidently anxious to avert a new outbreak of war, acted quickly and sent Gromyko to Cairo on December 21 with what Cairo Radio the next day termed "an important message from the Soviet leaders." The message was presumably the "peace plan" presented to Jarring in Moscow on December 22 and formally submitted to the United States, Britain, and France on December 30. According to incomplete reports, this plan called, inter alia, for acceptance of Security Council Resolution 242 by Israel and "those neighboring Arab states willing to participate in implementation" of a plan of action; proposed a timetable and procedure for the phased withdrawal "under UN supervision" of Israeli forces from all territories occupied in 1967; and promised "secure and recognized boundaries," "freedom of navigation in the region's international waterways" [including reopening of the Suez Canal], and "a just solution of the refugee problem."[17]

Gromyko's visit took place at Moscow's urgent request. This was evident from the short notice on which it was arranged and the decision to hold it during the middle of Id al-Fitr, the three-day feast that follows the end of Ramadan and brings a virtual halt to all governmental functions. At the airport Gromyko was cryptic as usual, saying only that he had "come to Cairo to exchange views with U.A.R. leaders on matters of interest to both countries. I not only want to express hope but also confidence that the talks which will take place during my short visit will be beneficial."[18] He was met coolly by Riyad "with a handshake and a goblet of orange juice, but without embraces."[19] The next day Moscow Radio, commenting on Gromyko's discussions with Egyptian leaders, lauded Egypt's general foreign policy orientation and appreciation of Soviet assistance, and lashed out at "the enemies of the Arabs" who continually tried to sabotage Soviet-Arab friendship.[20] Moscow was obviously annoyed with the criticism that it was not doing enough to help the Arabs but was trying to foist a political settlement on them.

The joint communiqué of December 24, 1968, was short and dealt only with Soviet-Egyptian relations and the Middle East situation.[21] Its tone suggested that Cairo had deferred somewhat to Moscow's wishes and was prepared to give Soviet diplomacy an opportunity to produce results. None of the specific proposals contained in the Soviet peace plan was mentioned, but the communiqué did stress the need for a peaceful settlement based on implementation of Resolution 242, and indicated Egypt's readiness to accept such a settlement in principle. A further sign of the

[17] The text of what was reputed to be the Soviet peace plan was published in the Beirut newspaper *Al-Anwar* on January 10, 1969; in *NYT*, January 11; in *Al-Ahram* on January 19 (together with the U.S. reply of two days earlier); and in *Pravda* (in outline form only) on January 25.

[18] Foreign Broadcast Information Service, *Daily Report: USSR International Affairs* (hereafter referred to as FBIS/USSR), December 24, 1968, p. A10.

[19] *NYT*, December 22, 1968.

[20] FBIS/USSR, December 24, 1968, p. A11.

[21] The communiqué was published in *Pravda*, December 25, 1968; translated in *Current Digest of the Soviet Press* (hereafter referred to as CDSP), 20, No. 52 (January 15, 1969), 30; also in FBIS/United Arab Republic, December 24, 1968, pp. G1-G2.

mood of accommodation was the absence of any reference to the problem of the Palestinian refugees (implying that Nasir would not use this thorny issue to block a settlement of the June 1967 "aggression" and that a solution that returned all Arab territories would be satisfactory). Moscow, for its part, agreed to a change from the communiqué issued the previous July during Nasir's visit and fully accepted Egypt's interpretation of Resolution 242 to mean a complete Israeli withdrawal from all Arab territory. There were no denunciations of imperialism, the omission evidently being designed to avoid losing Washington's cooperation in the quest for a settlement and to hold off any comment until President-elect Nixon made known his position on the Middle East.[22] While Gromyko failed to persuade Nasir to make any substantive concessions—if such was one of his aims—according to one report, he did succeed in dissuading him from launching any major attack along the canal for the next three months, though Nasir had warned him: "If I do not do something soon, the people will hang me."[23]

Behind the seeming meeting of minds conveyed in the communiqé, there were still serious differences between the positions of the Soviet Union and Egypt. This was evident in the absence of any of the familiar phrases that connote agreement on key issues. No encomiums to Soviet assistance were included, no new commitments, and no far-ranging global issues. Gromyko's departure was treated in perfunctory fashion—"no applause, embracing or ceremony," and "Egyptian newspapers gave less prominence to his visit than to the moon flight of the American astronauts, and editorialists made no comment on the talks."[24] The Soviet press, which gave the visit cursory treatment, reflected a certain wariness about the extent of Egypt's commitment to a political settlement. There was shortly another indication of mutual Soviet and Egyptian dissatisfaction in the meager attention paid to the ninth anniversary of the start of work on the Aswan Dam: Moscow sent a minor official, the deputy minister of electricity; and Cairo dispensed with the usual displays of Soviet flags, cordiality, and expressions of gratitude. Al-Ahram buried the occasion in a short note on page 5.[25]

[22] In a gesture of goodwill, Nasir cabled Christmas greetings to Nixon, though not to Johnson.
[23] NYT, December 29, 1968.   [24] NYT, December 25, 1968.
[25] Al-Ahram, January 8, 1969.

Soviet statements continued to stress the need for a peaceful settlement,[26] and the Soviet ambassador to the United Nations repeated Nasir's suggestion and that of the French government for an early meeting of the Four Powers (Britain, France, the United States, and the USSR) to forestall a further deterioration of the situation.[27] Unlike the Soviet press, the Egyptian news media stressed the mounting tensions in the Middle East (including sniping incidents along the canal and intense fighting along the Jordanian and Syrian borders with Israel) and tended to reject even the minimal concessions implicit in the Soviet peace plan. Cairo's uncompromising mood was reflected in Haykal's weekly column in *Al-Ahram* of January 3, 1969, in which he wrote:

> A peaceful solution to the Middle East problem is not now feasible . . . even a political solution cannot be achieved or made possible except through some kind of military action. This action alone is capable of changing the present condition of the land, and this action alone can give expression to the terms which eminent diplomats and veteran lawyers are laboring to formulate.

One week later, though ostensibly summarizing the Soviet peace plan, Haykal failed even to mention such key provisions as the phased Israeli withdrawal, Arab guarantees of Israeli sovereignty and territorial security, and the reopening of the Suez Canal once Israel had withdrawn a certain distance in the Sinai.[28]

The discrepancy between the Soviet government's proposal and Haykal's reporting of it suggests that despite the position it had taken in the communiqué of December 24, 1968, Cairo was opposed to even the minimal concessions of the Soviet plan (possibly because Nasir felt domestically insecure). Haykal's analysis sharply diverged from that of Soviet commentators, who though deploring Israel's intransigence and blaming it for the

[26] See, for example, *Pravda*, January 11, 1969.

[27] On December 26, 1968, two members of the PFLP (Popular Front for the Liberation of Palestine) attacked an El Al plane in Athens airport, killing one person and wounding several others; two days later, Israeli commandoes landed from helicopters and destroyed 13 airplanes at Beirut airport in reprisal; on December 31, the Security Council condemned Israel, but not the PFLP, for its attack.

[28] *Al-Ahram*, January 10, 1969.

tense situation in the Middle East nonetheless emphasized the need for a peaceful political settlement.[29]

On January 17, Haykal again looked fatalistically to war. "However ingenious the tactics, however skillful the formulation, however meticulous the arrangement of the words," the Soviet diplomatic effort will inevitably fail; diplomacy alone "will not be able to solve the Middle East crisis" because of the opposition of the Israeli military establishment, which realizes that implementation of Resolution 242 would again expose Israel to its former vulnerability.[30] Israel wants what it cannot achieve: not merely to end the state of war, but also to impose a state of peace on the Arabs, and this is not merely a matter of restoring the 1967 boundaries but of satisfying the Palestinians as well.

It soon became clear that Nasir himself was growing increasingly pessimistic about the chances for a political settlement and hence more belligerent toward Israel. Addressing the new National Assembly on January 20, 1969, the Egyptian president spoke of the strengthening of his country's armed forces over the preceding eighteen months thanks to "the true and sincere cooperation" of the Soviet Union, without whose cooperation "all our plans for the future would have been mere wishes that could not be fulfilled." Though praising Moscow for its help, he pointedly focused on the divergent approaches of the two capitals:

> We must realize that the enemy will not retreat unless we force him to by fighting. As a matter of fact, there is no hope of a political solution unless the enemy realizes that we can force him to withdraw by fighting. In other words, no progress can be made by military or political action unless the military front is the starting point for such progress.[31]

Nasir also spoke of the Palestinian resistance movement, insisting—as he had not in the December 24 communiqué—that no decisions affecting its members would be made without their approval and lauding their "positive role in sapping a part of the

---

[29] *Pravda*, January 25, 1969. *Pravda*, January 11, 1969: Evgenii Primakov wrote that the "Arab countries are advancing along the road of a peaceful political settlement of the Middle East problem." See also, *Izvestiia*, December 27, 1968; and Moscow Radio in Arabic to the Arab world on February 18, cited in FBIS/USSR, February 19, 1969, p. A63.

[30] BBC/ME/2978/A/3-5 (January 19, 1969).

[31] *Al-Ahram*, January 21, 1969.

enemy's energy and blood." His rejection of "any interpretations of the Palestinian refugee question which would confine that question to the framework of charity and humanitarianism" was intended as much for Moscow as for his critics in the Arab world to whom he sought to project an image of inflexible determination and imminent action. Buoyed by President de Gaulle's January 6 embargo on shipments of arms to Israel and by France's urging of Big Four discussions to deal with the Middle East crisis, Nasir had reason to feel the international climate was turning against Israel. Highlighting the growing tensions, Egyptian Minister of War Muhammad Fawzi briefed the Assembly on the military situation in a secret session two days after Nasir's appearance.[32]

Faced with such signs of Egyptian bellicosity, the Soviet leadership made another high-level, if low-key, attempt to deter Nasir from resuming hostilities. It took advantage of a visit to Cairo by CPSU Politburo member Aleksandr N. Shelepin to send an "important letter from Brezhnev to Nasir."[33] In his capacity as chairman of the All-Union Central Council of Trade Unions, Shelepin journeyed to Cairo in late January at the head of the Soviet delegation to the Fourth Congress of the International Confederation of Arab Trade Unions. Publicly addressing the congress, he reaffirmed full Soviet support for "legitimate Arab rights" and declared that an "Israeli withdrawal behind the lines of June 5, 1967, is a necessary condition for any solution."[34] During his visit, however, Shelepin also held a three-hour meeting with Nasir that was described in *Al-Ahram* as "very, very important."[35] The Cairo newspaper claimed that the meeting had indicated "complete agreement that Israel's continued occupation [of its positions in Sinai] will probably create an explosion in the Middle East at any moment." But this was not the message Moscow wanted to communicate. Indeed, Moscow's silence on the subject suggested that there was more to the talk than Cairo was ready to admit. The *Pravda* accounts of Shelepin's trip failed to mention his meeting with Nasir or the messages that Brezhnev and Nasir conveyed through this important envoy. In a word, *Pravda* gave the impression that Shelepin's

[32] *Al-Ahram*, January 29, 1969.
[33] *Al-Ahram*, January 31, 1969. *Pravda*, January 30, 1969, mentioned that Shelepin was in Egypt, but made no reference to any letter for Nasir.
[34] *Al-Ahram*, January 30, 1969.   [35] *Al-Ahram*, February 3, 1969.

only function in Cairo was to represent Soviet trade unions, deliberately ignoring the Middle East aspects of the visit.[36]

The differences in the views of Moscow and Cairo on how best to deal with the crisis were aired in an interview with Nasir published simultaneously in *Newsweek* magazine and *Al-Ahram* on February 4, 1969. Nasir now claimed that he had been pessimistic about the Soviet peace plan from the moment that Gromyko had presented it. He added that, while Israeli acceptance of Resolution 242 might be adequate to liquidate the effects of the 1967 aggression, it "is not adequate for the Palestine problem, *which is the main problem . . .*" (emphasis added). What was particularly noteworthy about the *Newsweek* interview was that "the Arabic version . . . differed from English original in at least 17 places."[37] The deletions and changes in *Al-Ahram* served two apparent purposes: they presented Nasir's position in a tougher light and excised questions that might have cast doubt on the strength of Nasir's internal position. Three weeks later, in an interview with C. L. Sulzberger of the *New York Times*, Nasir spoke openly of Egypt's need to resort to force to achieve its aims.

EGYPT MOVES TOWARD WAR

Throughout February, Egypt stepped up clashes along the canal. These lent a note of urgency to the exploratory Four Power discussions that opened on February 7, and quieted restive elements in Egypt. At the same time, despite Soviet-Egyptian political differences, reports circulated of a large number of Soviet freighters arriving in Egypt with arms.[38] On February 24 a state of emergency was declared in all governorates. The inescapable feeling of impending action was heightened by a headline in *Al-Ahram* on the

[36] See *Pravda*, February 3 and 4, 1969.

[37] ARR, No. 3 (February 1–14, 1969), 66. Two of the changes in *Al-Ahram* may be cited by way of illustration: "Part of a question reading, 'What can you say to convince Israel that both you and the Soviet Union want permanent peace?', was omitted"; and "One of the final questions, 'In 1948, as a young officer embittered by defeat, you resolved to overthrow the regime responsible. If you were a young officer today, wouldn't you be just as bitter and just as determined to overthrow the regime now in power?', became 'How do you describe the feeling of the young officers in the army today? Can this be compared to the feeling they had in 1948?' "

[38] *NYT*, February 19, 1969.

same day that Nasir's interview with Sulzberger was printed: "Fourth Round of Arab-Israeli War is Inevitable."[39]

On March 8, to the accompaniment of broadcasts of martial music, sniper fire, machine-gun exchanges, and periodic mine-laying forays gave way to massive Soviet-style artillery barrages along the southern half of the canal, from Qantarah to Suez, and soon spread along the entire length of the canal.[40] The cease-fires, arranged by U.N. observers, were broken almost as fast as arranged.

In March 1969, as in September 1968, international developments frustrated Egypt's effort to compel great power action, to force the pace of diplomatic deliberations. On March 3, the day *Al-Ahram* featured Nasir's interview with Sulzberger, it carried on the same page under a Moscow dateline a small item reporting a military clash between Soviet and Chinese troops. Sino-Soviet border clashes broke out several times in the middle of March, and for the next six months tensions remained high along the Ussuri River. Moscow was occupied with its China problem, as open war threatened the final rupture of the Communist alliance. The new administration in Washington was absorbed with Vietnam, as it was to be for most of the next four years, and for the moment it chose to follow the general Middle East policy laid down by Johnson. This caused Cairo to level its first critical broadside at Nixon on March 20, when *Al-Ahram* took him to task for training Israeli pilots to fly Phantom jets and "not merely replenishing Israel's military arsenal but also developing Israel's technical know-how."[41] When Golda Meir became prime minister on March 11, after the death of Levi Eshkol, Israel was in no mood for concessions.

The "war of attrition" was Nasir's answer to the humiliating stalemate. It cost heavily: right at the start, on March 9, he lost his best officer, Lt.-General Muhammad Abd al-Mon'im Riyad; the remaining canal economy, already largely destroyed or paralyzed, was sacrificed; additional refugees, the rest of those evacuated from the canal area, had to be absorbed elsewhere. However, Nasir was willing to pay the price.

On March 27, Nasir linked the new hostilities to the Four Power talks scheduled to begin at the United Nations on April

39 *Al-Ahram*, March 3, 1969. The interview took place on February 26.
40 *Al-Ahram*, March 9, 1969.
41 ARR, No. 6 (March 15–31, 1969), p. 127.

3 and suggested that the intensity and scope of the fighting would depend on their outcome. The high level of fighting along the canal was sustained in order to drive his point home to the great powers. He also gave a glowing and unusually detailed description of Moscow's generosity in supplying arms and advisers to help train Egyptian troops, presumably in an attempt to ensure that Moscow would not try to curtail the fighting by restricting the flow of weapons:

> The Soviet Union is supplying us with the arms we need without exerting pressure on our current financial resources, which are bearing the heavy burden of the war. It is enough to tell you that we have not yet paid a single penny. The first consignment of arms we received from the Soviet Union was free. After that, all other arms consignments were paid for with long-term loans . . .
>
> We also asked the Russians to assist us in training, in grasping arms, and in modernizing the various commands—from the supreme to the subordinate commands . . . We have benefited a great deal in the recent months from the Soviet experts and advisers who are with our units.[42]

Nasir's disclosure might also have been motivated by a desire to answer criticisms leveled against the spreading Soviet military presence. He went out of his way to emphasize that "From 1955 to this date, the Soviet Union has neither dictated any political restriction nor made a single condition. It has not made any request which could affect our national prestige."

Although the Soviet Union did not use its muscle, it was anxious to prevent the situation in the Middle East from getting out of hand. Between clashes with the Chinese and putting its Czechoslovak satrapy back in order, Moscow had its hands full. It tried to achieve the nice balance or supporting its Arab partners and at the same time discouraging them from undertaking extreme initiatives. An April 3 commentary in *Izvestiia* illustrated these simultaneous concerns. While blaming Israel for triggering the new fighting, the commentary stated that "the extremists [i.e. the Arabs opposing peaceful settlement of the crisis] have become particularly active now when there have been signs of progress in the search for paths to a political settlement

---

[42] BBC/ME/3037/A/5-6 (March 29, 1969).

of the Near East crisis, when consultations are being held between the representatives of the USSR, the United States, France, and Great Britain on this question."[43] Haykal admitted that the artillery exchanges were not sufficient to inflict a clear defeat on the Israeli army, but he saw merit in escalation, in a battle "in which Arab forces might, for example, destroy two or three Israeli army divisions, annihilate between 10,000 or 20,000 Israeli soldiers, and force the Israeli Army to retreat from the positions it occupies to other positions, even if only a few kilometers back."[44] On April 21, the secretary-general informed the Security Council that the fighting along the Suez Canal had become "a virtual state of active war."[45] Two days later, in a political maneuver calculated to gain maximum attention, the official spokesman for the Egyptian government hinted in a press conference that Egypt might not abide by Resolution 242 indefinitely. The conflict was being waged as bitterly on the political front as along the canal.

In spite of apparent Soviet efforts to curb Egyptian belligerency, the fighting intensified, with Egyptian commando raids on the Israeli-held side of the canal and a fierce air battle on May 22. Nasir was adamant. On May 1, he declared: "Israel must withdraw from the occupied territories or there will be continuous fighting. There is no politics on this subject. We cannot resort to political maneuver on such a subject."[46] And in an interview with *Time* magazine, he said war was necessary, "if, as it appears now, there is no way to get a peaceful settlement," and no settle-

---

[43] *Izvestiia*, April 3, 1969. Soviet disagreement with radical Arab groups over the role of armed force in the Palestinian struggle complicated its efforts to establish closer ties with them and exposed Moscow to criticisms from the Chinese. See "Pravda Charges that Arab Extremists Act as a Shield for Imperialist Agents," Radio Free Europe Research Paper (February 6, 1969). An unsigned editorial in a key Soviet journal linked the "policy of fanning conflicts and of encouraging extremist nationalist groups" to the Maoists in the Third World, where they are trying to increase their influence "on Palestinian organizations that oppose a political settlement of the Middle East conflict." "Politika gruppy Mao Tse-Duna na mezhdunarodnoi arene" (The Policy of Mao Tse-tung's Group in the International Arena), *Kommunist*, No. 5 (March 1969), p. 111.

[44] BBC/ME/3047/A/7 (April 13, 1969). This was the kernel of what was to become the basic Egyptian strategy in the October War.

[45] *NYT*, April 24, 1969.

[46] BBC/ME/3064/A/9 (May 3, 1969). This is the speech in which he claimed that 60 percent of the Bar Lev line—the Israeli network of fortified strongpoints dug deep into the sand on the eastern bank—had been destroyed.

ment was possible without a satisfactory settlement of the Palestinian problem.[47]

An article published in *Pravda* under the title of "Observer," which is used periodically to call attention to authoritative statements of Kremlin policy, blamed the crisis "primarily" (the less than total attribution of culpability is significant) on Israel, for its opposition to the efforts at conciliation being made by the great powers, who "have a special responsibility for maintaining peace . . ."; and it reaffirmed the need for "a political settlement," praising Egypt and Jordan for their readiness to work toward one.[48]

But Moscow was also expressing irritation over Cairo's intransigence. A Soviet note to U Thant on May 8 called for strict adherence to the cease-fire—an implied admonition to Egypt as much as to Israel.[49] More important, a tantalizing glimpse at Soviet ambivalence toward the Egyptian negotiating position and at the countervailing political tugs to which the Soviet leadership felt itself subjected could be gleaned from tentative though quickly hedged expressions of interest in the principle of direct talks. In an article published at the beginning of May and prepared some weeks earlier, *Pravda's* Middle East specialist Igor' Beliaev quietly challenged the genuineness of Egypt's desire for a settlement: "If there is a sincere desire for a settlement, it is not so very important whether the negotiations on a peace settlement are conducted directly between the parties concerned or through a mediator, say, Swedish Ambassador Gunnar Jarring. The most important thing is to come to an agreement, to reach a compromise."[50] This was a departure from the previous fall, when Beliaev had termed the demand for direct talks "a false thesis put forward with the object of frustrating any political settlement in the Middle East."[51] In a domestic radio commentary on May 6, he suggested that "it would be ideal if the [two] sides were to sit down together to discuss the issues which exist between them," but acknowledged that the Arab countries are "categorically opposed to direct talks."[52] However, fearful of

[47] BBC/ME/3074/A/1-3 (May 15, 1969).
[48] *Pravda*, April 30, 1969.   [49] *NYT*, May 9, 1969.
[50] I. Belyaev, "Washington's Asian Boomerang," *International Affairs*, No. 5 (May 1969), 68.
[51] I. Belyaev, "Ways of Ending the Middle East Crisis," *International Affairs*, No. 10 (October 1968), 28.
[52] Moscow domestic radio service, May 6, 1969, cited in FBIS/USSR, May

offending the Arabs, Moscow not only did not broadcast Beliaev's commentary internationally,[53] but it had Beliaev himself denounce, in a *Pravda* article a few days later, the call for direct talks, describing them as "demagogic," as a camouflage of "the real plans of the supporters of a 'Greater Israel!' "[54] Western diplomats reported that in private talks with their Soviet counterparts the latter expressed "little sympathy with the Arab position."[55] Behind the scenes Moscow (and Washington) urged Nasir to desist, arguing that Egyptian military actions were stiffening Israel's resistance to any great power settlement. But despite all of this, Moscow chose to yield rather than exacerbate its differences with Cairo.

While cautioning the Arabs against any "adventurist" action, *Izvestiia* credited Nasir with a "positive attitude" toward the Four Power talks.[56] And while persistent reports emanated from New York about "some progress" in reconciling Soviet and American positions and in putting together a political package, there were also accounts of an increasing Soviet military buildup of Egypt.[57] On June 4, *Al-Ahram* was able to quote, with evident satisfaction, an *Izvestiia* denial of a U.S. report that the Soviet position on Israel was becoming more flexible.[58] Two days later, in a lengthy article by V. Rumiantsev, *Pravda* forcefully reaffirmed Soviet support for Nasir and his "sober, realistic approach" to a solution "by political means," and at the same time lambasted both the Chinese and Haykal: the Chinese were denounced for encouraging Arab extremists (i.e. Palestinian guerrilla groups) to call for a recarving of the map of the Middle East, thereby helping Israel "to frustrate a political settlement, to prolong the occupation of Arab territories, and to continue their attempts to overthrow Arab progressive regimes"; Haykal was taken to task

---

12, 1969, pp. A38-A40. Five weeks earlier, V. Kudriavtsev had gingerly touched on the matter of direct talks. Moscow domestic radio service, March 31, 1969, cited in FBIS/USSR, April 2, 1969, p. A55.

53 *NYT*, May 23, 1969.   54 *Pravda*, May 12, 1969.

55 *NYT*, May 23, 1969.   56 *Izvestiia*, May 25, 1969.

57 ARR, No. 9 (May 1–15, 1969), p. 193; ARR, No. 10 (May 16–31, 1969), pp. 213-214.

58 *Al-Ahram*, June 4, 1969. (*Izvestiia's* correspondent in New York had written that the American press was trying to provoke a deterioration of Arab-Soviet friendship by suggesting that the USSR was revising its point of view on direct Arab-Israeli talks and withdrawal of Israeli forces from all Arab territories. *Izvestiia*, May 31, 1969.)

for extolling the Arab resistance, for saying it "should be outside politics, outside public social struggle," thus ignoring the social basis and socialist content of the struggle against imperialism.[59] Rumiantsev warned that the progressive developments of the past two years were seriously threatened by "nationalist and revanchist attitudes" that "are being kindled among the people and the army" with a view to pushing Egypt on to an adventurist course.

NASIR HAS HIS WAY

The last Soviet effort to avert expanded hostilities along the canal was made on June 10 when, without prior notice, Cairo reported Gromyko's arrival for a "two-day visit."[60] Time was of the essence, witness his having left Moscow in the midst of the world conference of Communist parties. During the next few days Gromyko engaged in an intensive round of discussions with Egyptian leaders, including three meetings with Nasir.

The resulting joint communiqué of June 13 represented a clearcut victory for Cairo's position.[61] It was terse, to the point, and unmistakable in its import. It held that "to find a peaceful settlement in the Middle East requires the implementation of *all parts and provisions* of the 22 November 1967 resolution and the withdrawal of Israeli forces from *all* Arab areas occupied by Israel as a result of the 5 June 1967 aggression" (emphasis added). This wording indicated a hard-line rejection of the various proposals for a phased Israeli withdrawal that were currently circulating. Moreover, it unequivocally linked any peaceful settlement to the solution of the Palestinian problem, further underlining Cairo's resolute stand.

In all probability, Moscow's grudging support of Cairo's uncompromising position[62] was needed to reassure Egypt, which

---

[59] *Pravda*, June 6, 1969.   [60] *Al-Ahram*, June 10, 1969.

[61] FBIS/United Arab Republic, June 16, 1969, p. G1.

[62] Journalistic assessments often oversimplified and misperceived the situation. For example, a resident British journalist in Cairo asserted the USSR "has suffered a severe setback in her relationship with Egypt as a result of what is regarded here as two weeks in which she has outreached herself as a protector and international mentor." In addition, "there has been a measurable Russian slide towards the American viewpoint." Paul Martin, "Disillusionment in Cairo Over Gromyko's Visit," *The Times* (London), June 20, 1969.

had been concerned about press reports of a joint Soviet-U.S. proposal.[63] According to *Al-Ahram*, at their last meeting Nasir made several points with which Gromyko agreed completely: (1) that Israel must withdraw from all occupied Arab lands, the right of the Palestinians to their land is inalienable, and "no outsider has the right to negotiate on their rights"; (2) that the Soviet Union should not, either during the Four Power talks in New York or in the bilateral talks in Washington, agree to anything that the Arabs will not accept; (3) that Soviet-Egyptian ties are considered very important.[64] On his departure Gromyko noted that the talks had been "frank." The day after he left, *Al-Ahram* commented that the communiqué had dispelled the uneasiness aroused by the [United States'] "psychological warfare of the past two weeks," which had insinuated that were differences between Moscow and Cairo; indeed, it noted, "some press reports even went so far as to say that there was an agreement between the United States and the Soviet Union and that Gromyko's visit was intended to ask for Cairo's support."[65] Another Egyptian source added:

> There has been no question of the Soviet Union in any way adopting a less firm attitude than it has done ever since the June aggression. Not that the Soviet attitude was doubted here, but the doubters, or at least the wishful thinkers, abroad . . . needed to be told exactly where the Soviet Union stood.[66]

We may reasonably assume that Gromyko did indeed come to consult about a comprehensive thirteen-point proposal that had been submitted by the United States to the USSR on May 26.[67] But the June 13 communiqué left no doubt that Cairo had turned down the proposal.

The Gromyko visit to Cairo marked the failure of a considerable Soviet diplomatic effort to steer Egypt away from a re-

[63] It was reported that Washington had asked Moscow at least to endorse such principles "as the need for a 'contractual' peace, rather than an imposed settlement; a long-term arrangement, not a temporary armistice; frontiers providing reasonable security for all sides, rather than an automatic return to the armistice lines before the 1967 war." *NYT*, June 8, 1969. For additional details, see *NYT*, October 19, 1969.

[64] *Al-Ahram*, June 13, 1969.   [65] *Al-Ahram*, June 15, 1969.

[66] *Egyptian Gazette*, June 15, 1969.

[67] An outline of the U.S. plan was given by Haykal in his weekly article on June 27. BBC/ME/3112/A/1–4 (June 28, 1969).

newal of the Middle Eastern war. Soviet inputs of military and economic assistance had unquestionably been indispensable to Egypt's recovery from the June 1967 conflict, but they had failed to give Moscow sufficient influence to avert Egypt's return to belligerency in 1969.

Two things stood out in the Soviet-Egyptian relationship in the summer of 1969: Moscow's inability to dissuade Nasir from pursuing a mini-war and its unwillingness to exercise the kinds of pressure that might have given him pause. On close examination, it can be seen that Moscow had little to lose. True, it risked upsetting the exploratory talks with Washington concerning the start of SALT (strategic arms limitation talks), but given Washington's keen interest in having them materialize and the Soviet military's desire to delay any agreement as long as possible in order to close the gap in strategic weapons, the Kremlin stood to obtain the most from either line of approach. True, a crisis in the Middle East might delay Western recognition of the territorial status quo in Europe, but the normalization of East-West relations in Europe was, already by early 1969, proceeding promisingly, unencumbered by the Czechoslovak albatross, which appeared to embarrass rather than disturb the Western powers, who moved with indecent haste to shunt it aside, to act as if it did not exist, in order to facilitate détente with the Soviet Union. True, a Middle East war would be inconvenient if serious fighting developed with the Chinese, but Moscow knew that Egypt's military capability was still limited, notwithstanding the massive influx of Soviet arms and advisers since 1967, and expected the fighting to stay localized; and it was confident of its own ability to handle the Chinese, whose raging "cultural revolution" could not help but impair their military effectiveness. True, a simmering Suez front created problems, but Moscow could afford a gamble to retain its tangible advantages in Egypt. True, Moscow was disappointed by Nasir's affirmative response to Gromyko's question, "Are you of the opinion that we should stop our contacts with the USA on the Middle East once and for all?,"[68] but the Four Power talks were stalemated, and Moscow saw no reason to risk its relationship with Egypt (or Syria).[69] Immediately after

[68] As reported in Haykal's article of June 20. BBC/ME/3106/A/4 (June 22, 1969).

[69] Moscow pledged continued Soviet aid to Syria during a visit by President Nur al-Din al-'Atasi, *NYT*, July 5, 1969.

Gromyko's visit, Soviet analysts toed Nasir's line and no longer alluded to his intransigence or to the search for a compromise solution with the United States.[70]

Meanwhile, Nasir himself kept in close touch with the United States government. However, he dispatched Ali Sabri for a three-week visit with CPSU officials to keep his bridges to the Kremlin in good order and to reassure Soviet leaders about the continued "progressive" character of Egyptian internal developments, on which they put great store, and possibly to wring some additional assistance from them. And on July 10 he agreed to establish full diplomatic relations with East Germany. These were mollifying gestures that cost Nasir little.

The fighting escalated in early July, leading U Thant to inform the Security Council "that throughout the Suez Canal cease-fire sector open warfare has been resumed . . . [and] that since June, 1967, the level of violence in the Middle East has never been higher than it is at present."[71] His report that most of the incidents were started by Egyptian forces had little effect on U.N. discussions.

With dramatic finality Nasir told the ASU National Congress, convened on July 23 to commemorate the 1952 Revolution, that Egypt had risen from the defeat of two years before and was "now embarking on the liberation operation. . . . We are prepared for a long battle to exhaust the enemy. The policy of all Arab states should be to exhaust [Israel] . . . a continuous war between us and Israel exists."[72] He declared the cease-fire no longer operative, criticized the United States, terming its 13-point plan "a replica" of Israel's, and warned of trying times ahead.

Unable to keep Nasir from a new confrontation, the Soviet Union went reluctantly along with Egypt on the road to the war of attrition. It saw no alternative to supporting Egyptian forces. If one judges from the lavish expenditure of artillery shells over the next thirteen months, Moscow did little to restrict supplies, for fear that such blatant pressure would undermine its position in Egypt. The massive use of artillery barrages, a Soviet trademark in World War II, was a technique the Egyptians had

[70] For example, *Pravda*, June 15, 1969; and I. Belyaev, "Dragged-Out Middle East Conflict: Who Stands to Gain?," *International Affairs*, No. 9 (September 1969), 5-6.
[71] *NYT*, July 8, 1969.
[72] BBC/ME/3134/A/7-11 (July 25, 1969).

learned from their ubiquitous Soviet advisers and used well on their own, though it is reasonable to assume that the advisers offered suggestions once the course had been set for war. (The advisers dominated the training programs but were not actually in command; they served in the fire control centers directing Egyptian artillery fire but did not decide when to fire and when to stop.) Moscow's assistance had entrenched its strategic position in the eastern Mediterranean, but this had not brought increased influence over Nasir's policies. Moscow was learning that "dealing with the Arabs was," as one diplomat aptly put the matter, "like swimming in glue."

Chapter Four

MYRMIDONS FROM MOSCOW

THE war that raged along the Suez Canal pitted Israeli planes against Egyptian artillery. Israel used its air supremacy for objectives that were at once punitive and deterrent: to exact a high price for Egyptian artillery and commando attacks and to strike home to Egyptian leaders their inability to provide adequate air cover for any large-scale assault across the canal. Egypt sought to nibble away at Israeli strength, using its limited military capability for tactically and politically appropriate but strategically inconclusive purposes. Both combatants relied on their superpower patrons. Egypt's dependence was the greater, since it had to import virtually all of its arms and supplies and could not do without Soviet advisers.

Each superpower was committed to maintain the security of its protégé. Both the Soviet Union and the United States partially predicated their policies on the premise that any sign of flagging support in this volatile, intense though confined conflict would reflect directly on their regional and global interests. This was particularly true of the White House, which interpreted the escalation along the canal as a Soviet probe of America's imperial will, as a testing of the Nixon Doctrine. First announced on Guam on July 25, 1969, the Nixon Doctrine provided a strategic justification for the planned U.S. military disengagement from Vietnam. It put allies and friends on notice that the United States could no longer police all areas of the world and called on them to assume greater responsibility for their own defense and the preservation of the regional balance of power, with American matériel but not manpower. The effect on the Arab-Israeli conflict was nil, for although the White House was interested in improving relations with Arab countries, it was not willing to do so if this meant a solidification of the Soviet position in the area; and it went to some lengths to demonstrate that the much-heralded "era of negotiations" to supplant the "era of confrontation" with the Soviet Union was not to be ushered in at the sacrifice of American interests in the Middle East.

Nasir, meanwhile, broadened the arena of psycho-political struggle with Israel. During the summer, Egypt began to accuse Israel of using American mercenaries to operate its air force and of augmenting its technical capability with an influx of American Jews.[1] These charges were based on highly exaggerated information about the number of American Jews who had settled in Israel and were serving in the Israeli army (very few as pilots) while retaining their American passports, a constitutionally permissible procedure in the light of various rulings of the U.S. Supreme Court. For Cairo, they served the domestic purpose of explaining Israel's toughness in resisting Egypt's war of attrition and, by implication, the latter's lack of success. They were also used to inveigle the Soviet leadership into providing more military assistance and, in time, to help Kremlin "hawks" justify the case for Soviet military involvement in an operational capacity, i.e. manning missile sites and radar and air defense communications centers, and flying combat missions over Egypt. The timing of these accusations and the growing Soviet role in Egyptian military planning may have been a coincidence, a convergence of circumstances; but, if so, what was originally fortuitous became a ploy, shaping policy and increasing Soviet involvement in the fighting itself.[2]

Nasir also seized on the incident of the fire set by a demented Australian mendicant on August 21 in the revered Al-Aqsa mosque in the old city of Jerusalem to call for a "Holy War" against Israel, for a closing of Arab ranks behind Egypt. He wanted a meeting of Arab heads of state but fell afoul of inter-Arab suspicions and had to settle for the all-encompassing, hence less effective, Islamic gathering, favored by his longtime foe, King Faysal of Saudi Arabia. The resulting meeting in Rabat in late September was a disappointment to Nasir and served mainly to publicize Arab disunity. Contention within the Islamic world

[1] For example, BBC/ME/3128/A/1 (July 18, 1969); BBC/ME/3207/A/1 (October 20, 1969); BBC/ME/3237/A/7 (November 22, 1969).

[2] On August 4, 1969, Israeli Defense Minister Moshe Dayan contended that Soviet advisers had been providing "some operational advice. If in the past they distributed arms and told the Egyptians how to use them, Soviet experts now tell them what to do." *NYT*, August 5, 1969; on October 11, 1969, he charged that they were taking "an active part" in military operations against Israel, directing Egyptian pilots in the air, telling them "to go up and break left and do this and that, all the combinations. . . . They are not flying, not using their hands, but they are in the front lines, and they tell them not only how to use the machines but also what to do." *NYT*, October 12, 1969.

—for example, the bitterness of Pakistan at the seating of an Indian governmental delegation, instead of one representing only members of India's Muslim community; and the opposition of Iran, Turkey, Senegal, and Chad to the militants' demand that all Muslims support the Arabs against Israel[3]—overshadowed the Arab-Israeli conflict; and strain caused by the split between the "progressives" and the "traditionalists" in the Arab world, diverted attention away from Nasir's immediate concerns. The resolution issued at the end of the conference neither expressed solidarity with the Palestinian resistance organizations nor, ironically, mentioned the Al-Aqsa fire.[4] The conference demonstrated that Nasir, who for medical reasons had stayed home and sent Anwar Sadat in his place, was still unable to win over the conservative Arab regimes to full support for Egypt. His diplomacy in the Arab world remained ineffectual, lacking firm ties to any Arab country. The denunciations of Israel in the United Nations continued, as did the efforts to cultivate support among non-Arab nonaligned countries. But these were only filler, hardly the stuff of which power is made.

CRISIS IN CAIRO

A number of discrete but interrelated tremors shook Cairo's political structure in September. First, on September 9, Israeli forces launched a highly successful raid along the Egyptian coast south of Suez: for about ten hours a task force spearheaded by twenty tanks—the Israelis used captured Soviet T-54s to fool the Egyptians—ranged over a thirty-mile strip, destroying SAM-2 missile batteries, radar stations, and manned outposts, and then withdrew by ship across the Gulf of Suez. As disheartening to Nasir as the Egyptian ineptness in opposing the raid were his war minister's denials that anything at all had even occurred.[5] The attack opened a breach in Egyptian air defenses that was systematically widened, so that Israeli planes dominated the sky over Egypt during the coming months. Reports of an impending trip to Moscow by Nasir immediately circulated in Arab newspapers —although not in Soviet papers—only to be denied officially on September 15.[6]

[3] *NYT*, September 25, 1969.   [4] *NYT*, September 28, 1969.
[5] BBC/ME/3697/A/2 (June 1, 1971).
[6] *Egyptian Gazette*, September 16, 1969.

Second, on September 11, Nasir had a serious heart attack.[7] His doctors and Soviet consultants prescribed three to six weeks in bed and total rest. Shortly thereafter, Nasir decided to appoint Sadat as his vice-president, a post Sadat assumed officially on December 20, 1969. On September 18, Moscow sent Dr. Evgenii Chazov, the cardiologist who had directed Nasir's medical treatment in the USSR, to examine his patient and deliver a message from Brezhnev.[8] Whether the message had political content or was merely a condolence is not known. During his last twelve months, Nasir became increasingly cranky, secretive, and arbitrary. He mistrusted those around him, refused to read reports, and was even less willing than before to take advice. He lived with pain and an anguish that was as much of the spirit as of the body.

Third, Ali Sabri was put under house arrest and replaced as chairman of the important ASU Committee on Organizational Affairs by the Minister of Interior, Nasir's trusted Chief of Police, Sha'rawi Gum'ah. His sympathizers on the judiciary and on the board of directors of the Akhbar al-Yawm Publishing House and the editorial board of its ASU-controlled mass circulation newspapers were purged. The top military command was also reshuffled as a consequence of the Israeli raid; the most notable replacement was that of Chief of Staff Ahmad Isma'il Ali (he had taken over in March 1969 after the death of General Abd al-Mon'im Riyad) by General Muhammad Sadiq.

The Sabri affair is interesting for what it reveals about limits of Moscow's involvement in Egyptian domestic politics. It is highly unlikely that Sabri was flexing for a direct thrust for power. Had he been, Nasir would hardly have permitted him to remain a member of the ASU Higher Executive Committee. Nor would Soviet leaders have encouraged him to seize power; not only was it beyond their control to so manipulate Sabri, but they knew that without the Army's support, which he did not enjoy, no takeover could succeed. What seems more probable is that Sabri, an artful bureaucratic intriguer, during his trip to the USSR in late June-early July tried "to exploit the Russians' ideological commitment to the ASU, urging them to help him make it, with himself as its head . . . the real power in the land which it is supposed to be."[9] Nasir, heeding reports of Sabri's coziness

[7] BBC/ME/3697/A/3 (June 1, 1971).
[8] *The Times*, September 26, 1969.
[9] David Hirst, "The People's Man Down But Not Out," *The Guardian,*

with the Russians, on July 19 sent Gum'ah to join him and keep a watchful eye out. As a precautionary measure, on July 16 he replaced the chief of the office of the president, Abd al-Magid Farid, considered an ally of Sabri, with Hasan Tuhami, one of the original "Free Officers" who overthrew the monarchy in 1952.[10] On his return to Cairo, Sabri was kept in virtual isolation, though the matter was not publicly announced until September 21, when *Al-Ahram* reported that the members of his ASU delegation—but not Sabri himself—had been accused of customs irregularities (a common but rarely punished practice in Egypt) on their return from Moscow in late July. By September, Sabri had already been shorn, but Nasir's illness and the purge of Sabri's adherents precipitated the publicizing of his semi-disgrace, in the expectation that his demotion would discourage the creation of other "centers of power." However, Nasir shrewdly kept him in the ASU, presumably for potential usefulness in future dealings with Moscow.

Concerned about Nasir's literal survival and Sabri's fall from favor, Moscow lashed out at the "venal manufacturers of rumors" who insinuated that the Soviet government might be implicated in a plan to topple Nasir; Moscow said the new appointments in Egypt's armed forces, "in the management of a leading publishing house" and in "the leading posts in the Arab Socialist Union . . . were promoted by a desire for a more rational deploy-

---

October 3, 1969. On the occasion of the Soviet-Egyptian Treaty of Friendship and Cooperation in May 1971, and less than a month after Sabri's deposal by Sadat, Ihsan 'Abd al-Quddus, editor of *Akhbar al-Yawm* and a well-connected commentator, attacked Sabri by implication, if not by name. Quddus said the treaty showed that Soviet-Egyptian friendship was "neither attached to nor expressed by one person or group of persons" nor would it "be shaken or changed, if one person or group were ousted." Continuing, he noted: "Certain persons had deliberately used politics to make personal relations between them and Soviet authorities and leaders into centers of power that they believed could be relied upon to attain their ambitions and to gather the internal power in their hands. However, since the time of Jamal 'Abd an-Nasir, these persons have not reached their objective and have been unable to monopolize the Soviet Union's friendship. More frankly, this friendship does not depend on the system of agents. There are no agents of Moscow in Cairo and no agents of Cairo in Moscow." FBIS/United Arab Republic, June 1, 1971, p. G8.

At an even later date, Haykal castigated those (Sabri and others) who "had gone and thrown themselves at the Soviet Union, fawning and thinking out of ignorance that the way to power in Cairo passes through Moscow." BBC/ME/4072/A/2 (August 21, 1972).

[10] ARR, No. 18 (September 16–30, 1969), 395.

ment of personnel inside the country" and were in no way very unusual.[11]

This may have been close to the truth. Nasir's administrative housecleaning was probably determined by internal political considerations, not by fear of a Soviet-sanctioned, much less stage-managed coup. His shifts in the military were the consequence of the Israeli raid, and were unrelated to Sabri, who had no power there.[12] And given his interest in preventing rivals from consolidating their strength in particular bureaucracies, Nasir purged the judiciary and the ASU in order to keep the guardians of these institutions weak and to concentrate power more than ever in the presidency. In the Nasir-Sabri relationship, there was also the residual unpleasantness stemming from disagreements over the pace and extent of some land reforms. On July 23 Nasir had proposed that land reclaimed from the desert with water from the Aswan Dam should be sold or rented by specially established companies, with priorities going to veterans; but the ASU Congress "passed a resolution [supported by Sabri] stating that the entire reclaimed area should become part of the public sector, in other words, State-owned."[13] There is little in the complicated series of domestic events to substantiate a theory of Soviet interference or ability to influence their outcome. Moscow did not possess any sure guide to the by-ways of Cairo's political maze.

PAS DE DEUX

Moscow and Washington held frequent but fruitless discussions on the Middle East. Despite occasional optimistic press reports of a narrowing of differences, they made no progress. There had been a flurry of excitement on September 24, 1969, when Mahmud Riyad had intimated in New York that the "Rhodes formula" might be acceptable, saying "We are doing here exactly the same thing we did in Rhodes. Dr. Jarring is the new Dr. Bunche—the representative of the Secretary General."[14] How-

11 *Pravda*, September 26, 1969.

12 On September 21, 1969, *Al-Ahram* "scorned suggestions that the appointments in the Armed Forces had been related to political intrigues, maintaining that 'the exigencies of war,' not politics, had dictated the changes." As cited in ARR, No. 18 (September 16–30, 1969), 396.

13 *The Observer Foreign News Service* (London), No. 26916 (September 5, 1969).

14 *NYT*, September 28, 1969.

ever, Cairo immediately rejected the notion, tartly insisting that Riyad had been misquoted. Nasir was not ready, or able, to take a step so far out of line with the sentiments of Arab radicals, the Egyptian public, or his constituency in the army and ASU. His opposition led Moscow to withdraw its tentative support for such an approach.[15]

In early October *Pravda* criticized Washington for being inconsistent concerning the Middle East: on the one hand, the United States government entertained Prime Minister Golda Meir and her request for new arms aid and reaffirmed its support of Israel; on the other hand, it pursued talks with Soviet officials, ostensibly to arrange a political settlement.[16] These criticisms, so obviously a mirror image of Soviet behavior, augured ill for an accord.

The proposals under active discussion in Washington[17] by Soviet Ambassador Dobrynin and Assistant Secretary of State Joseph J. Sisco failed to close the gap between the two governments, and the talks finally broke down in late December. Basically, they collapsed because of mutual mistrust and the unwillingness of the United States to pressure Israel more than the Soviet Union would pressure Egypt to make concessions.[18] Moscow rejected the final formulation put forth on October 28 by Secretary of State William P. Rogers and Sisco, whose faith in Soviet cooperation was shown to have been misplaced and whose assessment of the extent of agreement overestimated.[19]

Moscow rudely punctured Washington's lingering hope of producing a workable compromise on October 31, at one of the

[15] Joseph J. Sisco, the Assistant Secretary of State for Near Eastern and South Asian Affairs, said this on July 12, 1970, in an interview on NBC television: "We agreed with the Soviets as late as last September that negotiations ought to be pursued on the basis of the so-called Rhodes model. . . . Unfortunately, the Soviet Union backed off." Cited in *New Middle East*, No. 23 (August 1970), 11.

[16] *Pravda*, October 2, 1969.

[17] Some of the essentials of the two governments' positions were given in *NYT*, October 19, 1969. The Soviets pressed for a comprehensive package, an overall settlement; the Americans, for a piecemeal approach.

[18] Henry Brandon, *The Retreat of American Power* (London: The Bodley Head, 1973), pp. 115-116.

[19] *Ibid.*, p. 117. According to Brandon, Sisco suffered "from a capacity of self-delusion and over-optimism. It has been a persistent strand, even at times when the talks were on the verge of a breakdown." Sisco was reputed to have gone public too soon, and to lack the patience to narrow bargaining positions.

Soviet foreign ministry's infrequent press conferences. Leonid Zamiatin, the head of the press department, deplored the deteriorating situation along the canal, blaming not just Israel but "imperialist circles of the Western powers, and above all those in the United States of America."[20] He charged the U.S. government with encouraging American citizens to serve in the Israeli army by allowing them to retain their citizenship,[21] the first time that the Soviet government officially joined the Arab governments in making this accusation: "By virtue of this measure the U.S. government is offering Israel an opportunity to obtain not only military aircraft but also American pilots and personnel for technical maintenance." He said that in view of the "one-sided attitude" taken by the United States, the USSR proposed a return to the Four Power venue. In the meantime, the Soviet government "will continue to extend comprehensive aid to the Arab states which are struggling to maintain the progressive gains of their peoples against the encroachments of Israel and her imperialist protectors."

The Soviet proposal for the resumption of the Four Power talks encouraged Nasir's belligerency and, concomitantly, his dependence on the Soviet Union. By upholding his policy of limited war, the USSR strengthened its claim to be champion of the Arab cause and facilitated the conduct of Soviet diplomacy with the Sudan, Syria, Iraq, Algeria, and Libya. The proposal also gratified de Gaulle's desire to be a broker in the Middle East negotiations, improved Soviet-French relations, and exacerbated intra-NATO cleavages. From Moscow's perspective the breakdown of the bilateral U.S.-Soviet talks could only redound to its advantage: either the United States would reverse its position and pressure Israel to make greater concessions to the Egyptians—in which case the Soviet Union would share the credit for the shift—or it would find itself the sole support for an Israel increasingly isolated in the international community.

20 "Statement on Situation in the Middle East," *Soviet News*, No. 5515 (November 4, 1969), 61-62.
21 On October 20, 1969, to diplomats of ten Arab countries, the State Department formally denied alleged American combat involvement with Israeli forces and explained the constitutional grounds under which it was possible, against the advice and wishes of the U.S. government, for "some very few Israeli citizens who hold dual Israeli-U.S. citizenship" to serve in the Israeli armed forces. *NYT*, October 21, 1969.

NASIR IN EXTREMIS

The war of attrition was beginning to tell on Egypt. Israeli air power ranged freely over Egyptian positions in the canal area, scornful of the remaining SAM sites and unloading punishment with round-the-clock regularity. The Israelis, now entrenched in well-protected strongpoints in their Bar Lev Line, sat out the Egyptian artillery barrages in relative safety, their losses low. The war had proved to be longer and more costly to Egypt, and less draining on Israel, than Nasir had originally expected; but he had gone too far to turn back.

On November 6, speaking for the first time since his illness two months before, Nasir grimly set out for the National Assembly the dimensions of the "dangerous and difficult time" that Egypt was passing through and warned of the "need to revive ourselves" because there is no longer any possibility of a peaceful settlement, no longer any political half-solution, "no longer any way out except to open our path to what we want by force, over a sea of blood and under a horizon of fire."[22] As usual he spoke of generous Soviet support to the Arabs and of American aid to their enemy. For the first time, he personally leveled the charge, made often in the Egyptian press since the previous summer, that "U.S. military personnel in the Israeli Army are fighting us from behind the guns and in the aircraft which are falsely emblazoned with the Star of David." Like Zamiatin a week earlier, he, in effect, accused the United States of direct military involvement on the side of Israel. The gist of his argument was this: we are having a tough time, even with Soviet assistance, but only because the United States is fighting with Israel; so we face a new situation demanding even greater efforts and sacrifices. He pleaded for a closing of Arab ranks and an end to inter-Arab squabbling, especially to the debilitating fratricide between the Palestinians and Lebanese authorities. To thunderous applause he praised the Palestinian resistance, whose dramatic exploits, though militarily inconsequential, exhilarated Arab audiences:

The Palestine Resistance . . . has come to stay. . . . No one can suppress the Palestine Resistance any longer, not to mention trying to liquidate it. No one can return the refugee problem to its original formula of simply a problem of refugees or mere-

[22] BBC/ME/3224/A/1 (November 8, 1969).

ly a humanitarian case. The issue has become . . . one of a
people who have a homeland. The issue has become . . . also
of a homeland which has a people.[23]

Three days later, *Al-Ahram* advised in a front page article that,
though unhappy with the latest U.S. peace plan [of October 28]
which had been received the day before, "the Egyptian leadership would be gravely disappointed if the United States, vexed
by the negative reactions thus far, dropped its peace efforts."[24]
This was neither the first nor the last time that Nasir went out
of his way to signal his hope that the United States would try to
arrange a settlement.

But it was the Soviet bow that was available for the Egyptian
arrow. On November 12 Cairo Radio reported that a delegation
led by Anwar Sadat, personal representative of the president,
Foreign Minister Riyad, and War Minister Fawzi would shortly
leave for talks in Moscow.[25] The talks, scheduled to begin on
November 18, were delayed until early December, most likely
because Soviet leaders were occupied with preparations for the
meeting of Communist party leaderships in Moscow in late
November. Another factor may have been Moscow's desire to
play down Nasir's "blood and fire" speech of November 6, which
the Soviet press treated cursorily,[26] so as not to alarm Washington or mar the start of the SALT talks in Helsinki, and to ease
the way for the escalation of Soviet arms commitments. In a
statement, issued on November 27, the Communist parties of the
USSR, Bulgaria, Czechoslovakia, the German Democratic Republic, Hungary, and Poland noted that the "dangerously aggravated" tension in the Middle East "requires that urgent measures be adopted" and promised the continued assistance of the
Communist countries.[27]

For a while, the White House ignored repeated suggestions
from American diplomats resident in the Middle East that it try
again to arrange a cease-fire. Sisco, taking umbrage at Soviet in-
flexibility and sweeping rejection of the Two Power talks, argued
in the State Department that nothing more should be done for
the moment, that the Egyptians might become more amenable

23 *Ibid.*, p. A/4.   24 *NYT*, November 10, 1969.
25 BBC/ME/3228/i (November 13, 1969).
26 *Pravda*, November 8, 1969.
27 *Soviet News*, No. 5519 (December 2, 1969), 105.

to U.S. efforts if they took a further clobbering from the Israelis. Nonetheless, Rogers made another attempt. On December 9, the day the Egyptian delegation arrived in Moscow, the Secretary of State announced a detailed peace plan. His speech came a week after the resumption of the Four Power talks and about two weeks after Sisco had told a Senate subcommittee that "the attitude of the Soviet Union in the bilateral talks and its public expressions raise doubts regarding its willingness to play an actively constructive role on behalf of peace in the Middle East."[28] The Rogers Plan was not welcomed by the Israelis or the Egyptians, both of whom found serious faults. The Israelis objected to the prospect of an imposed great power settlement without any direct negotiations between the principals to the dispute; the Egyptians objected to the implied territorial concessions in Golan and on the West Bank and the lack of attention to the Palestinian issue. The Soviets promptly dismissed it: "The United States ruling circles are still sticking to their one-sided and obviously anti-Arab stand."[29]

The Sadat mission had gone to Moscow for help. (Israeli air-power had blasted huge gaps in the air defense system along the entire front from the Mediterranean to the Red Sea, exposing Egypt's heartland and probing more deeply than ever before.) The joint communiqué issued on December 12 suggested success.[30] First, by calling for "urgent and constructive steps" to counter Israeli attacks, it implied that action was taken on the military dimension so vital to the Egyptians. The presence of War Minister Fawzi and the participation of Soviet Defense Minister Andrei A. Grechko in the talks meant the "nuts and bolts" of Soviet-Egyptian military cooperation were under study. The Soviets set in motion the complicated and far-reaching logistical details of organizing, despatching, emplacing, and operationalizing an effective air defense and communications system, which took about three months to implement fully, the new missile systems making their appearance in early March 1970. Though the communiqué did not give details, the Soviets promised hardware and advisers. A dramatic deterioration in the Egyptian position during the next five weeks led to Nasir's secret visit, and may have been the final factor that brought Soviet combat troops in action as well.

[28] *NYT*, November 27, 1969.   [29] *Pravda*, December 14, 1969.
[30] FBIS/USSR, December 15, 1969, pp. A1-A2.

Second, the communiqué openly condemned the United States. Instead of making the usual references to "imperialist aggression," as the December 24, 1968, and July 13, 1969, communiqués had done, it identified the United States as the sinister force behind Israeli aggression. This agreement on the enemy foreshadowed an even greater degree of military cooperation. It may also have meant Egypt had agreed not to float any independent diplomatic trial balloons but to rely on Soviet efforts in the Two Power and Four Power talks. This had been a sore spot with Moscow, which wanted full participation in the political as well as the military decisions; and, aware of the anti-Soviet feeling in Egyptian circles, it interpreted any informal overtures by Cairo to Washington with deep uneasiness.

Third, the communiqué singled out the "leadership of Gamal Abdel Nasser" for praise, thus placing Moscow fully behind his policies and leadership. Moscow did not want any misunderstanding in Cairo about the nature of its interest in the Egyptian Left.

Fourth, by drawing attention to the "party and government" delegation sent by Egypt, the communiqué satisfied Moscow's desire for extensive contacts at the party-to-party level and closer consultations on matters pertaining to Egypt's domestic system. The two sides agreed "on practical steps to further develop this all-round [political, military and ideological] cooperation." In the preceding months, Soviet personnel had appeared in growing numbers in Egypt's communications, internal security, and intelligence services; and Moscow sought to assure its future presence by becoming more deeply involved in other aspects of Egyptian life as well.

Finally, only the Soviet side stated that the USSR would "continue fighting both in and outside the United Nations for a political settlement," thus accepting the fact that Nasir would insist that any settlement give due regard to "the legitimate rights and interests of all Arab peoples, including the Arab people of Palestine." By agreeing that a solution of the Palestine question was "resolutely essential" for any political settlement, the Soviet position actually hardened, leaning toward the extremist Arab position and diminishing the likelihood of a compromise settlement. While Moscow presented herself to the non-Arab world as a party genuinely interested in a political solution, to the Arab world she posed as a vigorous champion of the Palestinians, partly to develop better relations with Al-Fatah and not leave the Chinese an open field. The net thrust of Soviet policy was not negotiation, but polarization. *Al-Ahram* hailed the results of the visit, stressing Moscow's agreement to augment Egypt's military potential and its support for the Palestinian resistance movement.[31]

In contrast to the Moscow meeting, the Arab summit conference at Rabat (December 21–23) was a failure. The proceedings were characterized by indifference to Egypt's plight and inter-Arab wrangling, interspersed with outbursts from Colonel Mu'ammar Qadhdhafi, the pro-Nasir Libyan religious zealot who had overthrown the monarchy on September 7 and was soon to make his mark on Arab and world politics. With the exception of Libya, Algeria, and the Sudan, no one evinced interest in Nasir's call for a mobilization of Arab resources against Israel, and no plan of action was adopted. Nor was financial assistance forthcoming in response to Fawzi's somber appraisal of the military situation, which was that Egyptian forces "were in no way prepared to face a war with Israel at that stage or in the near future" and indeed "even their defensive position left much to be desired."[32] Oil was only two dollars a barrel and the oil shaykhs did not want to give any more money, the Saudis were still suspicious of Nasir and his ties to the Soviets, and the Egyptian army was held in low repute. As if to underscore Fawzi's bleak assessment, Israeli forces landed on the Egyptian coast on December 23 and removed a complete Soviet radar complex by helicopter. The controlled Egyptian press did not mention the incident until a month later when Haykal published details and criticized the conspiracy of silence in his column.[33]

Nasir's standing in the Arab world was never lower, his resources never more sharply shown to be woefully inadequate, and his dependence on the Soviet Union never greater. His situation was so precarious that even a diplomatic rescue operation would carry severe risks; for example, in early January 1970 when the U.S. State Department informally inquired whether the Egyptians would be interested in a cease-fire, Riyad's answer was,

[31] *Al-Ahram*, December 13, 1969.

[32] ARR, No. 24 (December 16–31, 1969), p. 547. Haykal discussed the reasons for the failure of the Rabat conference on January 10, 1970. BBC/ME/3276/A/1-4 (January 12, 1970). See also, *NYT*, December 26, 1969, and December 27, 1969.

[33] BBC/ME/3288/A/3 (January 26, 1970).

"If we agreed to a cease-fire now, the Army would revolt." Once again, only the Russians stood between Nasir and disaster.

THE SOVIETS CROSS THE NILE

There had been hints of expanded Soviet military commitments-in-the-making even before Sadat's visit. After Zamiatin's allegation on October 31, 1969, that American combat pilots were flying for Israel, Soviet sources referred to this "as an act of aggression,"[34] not necessarily to encourage anti-U.S. feeling in the Arab world but to open the option of intervening in the area. A more portentous omen appeared at this time in *Kommunist*, the theoretical journal of the CPSU Central Committee, in the form of an article written by V. Rumiantsev, the chief of its International Department. The article discussed Soviet policy toward the Arab world, but particularly toward Egypt since 1955, and was the most detailed analysis on the subject to appear in *Kommunist* since the June War.[35]

Rumiantsev sketched in the background of Soviet-Egyptian relations prior to 1967. He described the 1955 arms deal as a "landmark" in modern Middle Eastern history, putting an end to the West's monopoly on arms sales to the Arabs, "a monopoly which made it possible for the imperialists to rule supreme in the area." Thanks to the support of the Soviet Union, Egypt was able to nationalize the Suez Canal Company and overcome the Anglo-French-Israeli aggression in October 1956. The deepening of Soviet-Egyptian ties was highlighted by cooperation in building the Aswan High Dam and resistance to imperialism. For a time the absence of "a revolutionary scientific ideology," which accounted for "negative survivals of the past and anti-communist prejudices," hindered the internal evolution of the Arab countries; but as a result of expanding contacts with the USSR they began to accept the principles of a truly revolutionary outlook, that of "scientific socialism." Over the years Egypt carried out major economic and social reforms, created a mass political organization "of working people," expanded the public sector, and tried to make a socialist revolution. It also encouraged the study of the classics of Marxism-Leninism and ended the persecution

---

[34] *Pravda*, November 14, 1969.

[35] V. Rumiantsev, "Arabskii vostok na novom puti" (The Arab East on a New Road), *Kommunist*, No. 16 (November 1969), 90-101.

"of Egyptian Marxists," who were given an opportunity to participate in the political life of the country. Having bestowed Moscow's imprimatur on Nasir's Egypt, Rumiantsev focused on the situation since June 1967.

In 1967, imperialism, spearheaded by the United States, launched a new assault against the progressive Arab regimes "in order not to allow a further weakening of the positions of the Western monopolies in the Middle East. The Middle East oil resources and the strategic position of the Arab countries are such that imperialism is not about to leave the Arabs in peace."[36] The aim of overthrowing "the progressive national regimes in the UAR and Syria" is motivated by a social and class basis and not a national one, as imperialist propagandists like to make out, said Rumiantsev. After Israel's aggression, the Soviet Union adopted "a principled and consistent position." It rendered Egypt and Syria "immediate and great assistance in strengthening their defensive capability, granted them economic aid, and sent these countries food and medicines free of charge," and also upheld their cause on the world scene.[37] But the struggle continues, abetted by "local reactionary forces, which regarded the situation as conducive to a struggle for the restoration of their influence and former privileges." Under Nasir's leadership, Egypt has taken measures "for the more effective study and utilization of the rich military experience of the Soviet Armed Forces."[38] In the economic and social sectors it has continued to implement progressive reforms. Quite promisingly, in September 1969, representatives of Egypt, Syria, Jordan, Iraq, and the Sudan agreed to coordinate their military efforts.[39] The Palestinian Arabs are widening their resistance in the struggle "for the restoration of their national rights." Rumiantsev drew attention to the struggle of "the revolutionary-democratic leaders of the Sudan and Libya," the evolution of the Iraqi Ba'thists in the direction "of opening a dialogue with the Iraqi Communist Party with the aim of creating a progressive national front in the country," and the improved conditions of Communists in Syria, Algeria, and Jordan.[40] These are symptomatic "of the growth of revolutionary processes in the Arab world" and of efforts to oppose the reactionary circles who seek "to squeeze the liberation struggle in the Procrustean

[36] *Ibid.*, p. 96.   [37] *Ibid.*, p. 97.
[38] *Ibid.*, p. 98.   [39] *Ibid.*, p. 99.
[40] *Ibid.*, p. 100.

bed of narrow nationalism and Islamism, to deprive it of its progressive social content and prevent the unification of all patriotic forces." With "the all-round selfless aid of the Soviet Union," the Arab peoples will prevail.[41]

The importance of Rumiantsev's analysis inhered in its timing, content, and the audience for which it was intended. The article was the probable result of a major policy debate in the Kremlin concerning the advantages and disadvantages of furnishing Egypt with significantly greater amounts of military assistance, of which an important component was the commitment of Soviet personnel to a combat role, and it was designed to alert party cadres to an imminent major development in Soviet foreign policy and to provide the justification for it. The Politburo knew from its subordinates in the field of Egypt's military vulnerability and realized that only direct Soviet involvement could prevent certain defeat should the situation continue to deteriorate. It weighed the risks and decided, by late October, to escalate Soviet aid and involvement, as necessary, though the actual decision to send combat troops in defense of this beleaguered, "progressive," non-Communist country was deferred pending developments. By the time of Nasir's secret trip three months later, the basic decision to send troops had already been taken.[42] All that was then needed was the final go-ahead.

In December and early January the line in the Soviet press hardened.[43] The Israeli bombing and the American supplying of Phantoms came in for scathing criticism: "Day by day the extremists in Tel-Aviv become more impudent, continually egged on by U.S. imperialist circles."[44] A major article by V. Kudriavtsev denounced Israel's proud claim that "all this is a prelude to 'the war of attrition'" and called the Rogers proposal of December 9 nothing more than a "peacemaking shell" disguising a pro-Israeli stand, which showed America's advocacy of the "Rhodes formula" to be a camouflage that "does not make for normaliza-

[41] *Ibid.*, p. 101.

[42] Up to then Soviet troops had not been sent into the Third World in significant numbers: handfuls of Soviet advisers had participated in counterinsurgency activities in Indonesia in the late 1950s and early 1960s at the request of Sukarno, and in South Yemen in the mid-1960s, when the Royalists claimed that they had shot down several Soviet pilots.

[43] For example, see *Pravda*, December 18, 1969, and *Izvestiia*, January 5, 1970.

[44] *Izvestiia*, January 8, 1970.

tion of the situation in the Middle East . . . but, on the contrary, for still greater aggravation of the situation."[45]

Buoyed by the audaciousness of their planes bombing Egyptian bases and hitting targets on the very outskirts of Cairo, Israeli commentators declared that, in the absence of a secure cease-fire, "Nasser will not be allowed to dictate the rules of the game along the canal . . . all Egyptian territory is fair game."[46] Confident of their military superiority over the Egyptians, some of the Israeli leaders may well have thought that the application of additional pressure might actually topple Nasir. However, by bringing the war into Nasir's living room, they threw down a challenge that neither he nor the Soviets could ignore.

Cairo newspapers warned the population to expect even more severe fighting.[47] Not until January 29 did they openly mention the deep penetration raids, whose existence, however, was no secret to the Egyptian public.[48] Sadat and 'Abd al-Muhsin Abu an-Nur, the ASU Secretary-General, on tour in the countryside, were quoted as saying: "We are passing through a delicate stage.

[45] *Izvestiia*, January 11, 1970.

[46] BBC/ME/3277/A/6-7 (January 13, 1970). The Israelis operated with growing impunity. Their extraordinary success against the MiG-21s in late 1969–early 1970 was due to superior pilots and to the timely deployment of a highly effective air-to-air missile, the Shafrir, developed in Israel after the June War. The existence of the 200-pound heat-seeking missile with a 25-pound explosive was not made public until early 1973. *The Jerusalem Post Weekly*, April 3, 1973.
The heavy losses of MiG-21s to Israeli-piloted French-built Mirage fighter aircraft—seven were down in one engagement over Syria in July 1969—helps explain the Soviet attempt (unsuccessful) to bribe a Lebanese air force officer to fly a Mirage to Baku; *NYT*, October 2, 1969. However, in December 1969, the French government gave the Soviets on a silver platter what they could not buy in stealth. As part of its policy to establish France as a major force in the Mediterranean and to assure itself adequate supplies of oil, it agreed to sell Mirages to Libya, thus making Tripoli the conduit to Moscow via Cairo. Although the agreement of sale stipulated that the Mirages were not to be deployed outside of Libya, the French government knew they were destined for Egypt and went along with the deception in order to promote its Arab policy. According to Haykal, in October 1969, Nasir had encouraged Qadhdhafi to purchase Mirages or Phantoms, FBIS/Egypt, February 4, 1972, p. G5.

[47] *Al-Ahram*, January 18, 1970.

[48] *Al-Ahram*, January 29, 1970. It reported that four enemy planes had attacked Mahdi (a suburb of Cairo): "No sirens were sounded because the attacks were outside of Cairo. The Minister of Interior and the Minister of War are meeting to discuss the possibility of improving the coordination regarding the use of sirens. Cairo's sirens should be used to alert people in the suburbs."

The aim of the enemy is to create fear in our home front."[49] To veteran Cairo-watchers such an obvious understatement suggested something was happening that could not yet be told.

On January 10, 1970, a delegation of members of the Supreme Soviet headed by D. A. Kunaev, a Politburo member and First Secretary of the CPSU Central Committee, arrived in Cairo for a ten-day visit. Before Kunaev's departure he was briefed by Nasir on the situation and given an urgent message for Brezhnev. Two days later, on January 22, Nasir flew secretly to Moscow for four days of talks with Kremlin leaders.

The trip has never been discussed in any Soviet source. Informed Egyptians knew of it within several weeks, though the Egyptian public was not officially told until Nasir's speech on July 23, 1970:

> I had requested that the visit be kept secret. We talked continuously for four days. During those days I sensed much interest on the part of the Soviet leaders—interest in the safety of the Egyptian people, in their cities and villages, in saving the Egyptian people from exposure to the enemy's raids and in ensuring Egypt's ability to defend its territory with all means. The Soviet leaders subsequently issued a decision saying that the Soviet Union would help us with all its power to defend our homeland against deep raids and threats to civilians and economic targets. They told me during my January visit that the support we required would reach us in no more than 30 days. The Soviet Union kept its promise.[50]

To understand the interdependent nature of the Soviet-Egyptian relationship, it is important to examine the probable reasons for Nasir's secret trip and for Moscow's response. Unlike his previous secret visit in 1958,[51] this one involved his own political

[49] *Al-Ahram*, January 19, 1970.

[50] BBC/ME/3439/A/9 (July 25, 1970). According to one Western diplomat, the first inkling of the visit was the remark of a barber in Heliopolis (a Cairo suburb with a heavy concentration of military barracks) that he had cut the hair of a number of officials in Nasir's entourage.

[51] Nasir had flown secretly to Moscow in July 1958, at the time of the overthrow of the Hashemite monarchy in Iraq, when there was reason to believe that the Turks, encouraged by the United States and Britain, might intervene to save Prime Minister Nuri Said and the remnants of his pro-Western regime. However, within a few days it became clear that the king and his family and also Nuri Said had been killed, thus eliminating any pretext for a Turkish intervention. See Dwight D. Eisenhower, *The White House Years:*

survival; never had he been in a more precarious position, not in 1956, not even in 1967.

First, Nasir's internal position was rapidly becoming untenable. Politically and militarily, the Israelis had him on the brink of disaster. Their deep penetration raids, which had the deposal of Nasir as their ultimate target, had struck repeatedly without difficulty and with few losses at targets in the Nile Delta and as near as five miles to downtown Cairo:

> Against those attacks, Egyptian manned MiG-21c/D interceptor aircraft and SA-2 *Guideline* surface-to-air missiles proved all but totally ineffective: from 1967 to mid-1970, the Israelis flew around or through the former and under the effective coverage of the latter. In the process some 150 of the UAR's small corps of trained pilots were shot down.[52]

With the growing demoralization of the Egyptian army, Nasir's main prop was corroding.

Second, in asking Moscow to commit its troops to combat, Nasir was making a momentous request. By going himself, he best conveyed the desperation of his situation (which the Soviets already knew from their own sources) and was in a position to respond immediately to any Soviet demands as when he gave Soviet forces exclusive jurisdiction over sections of six airfields (Cairo West airport, two in upper Egypt, one in the Delta, and two in the canal area) and a free hand to deploy Soviet missile and air defense personnel and pilots. Nasir agreed to this, despite an anticipated balkiness from some of his military men, because from his point of view it meant that the Soviet Union would not under any circumstances permit Egypt to be defeated, which after all was the key consideration.[53] The commitment of Soviet combat troops accorded with his strategy of enmeshing the Soviet Union militarily in the defense of Egypt, not only to strengthen Egypt's defense capability but, shrewdly, to exacerbate tension between the superpowers and force the internationalization of the Arab-Israeli conflict.

Waging Peace 1956–1961 (London: Heinemann, 1966), pp. 277-278; Oles M. Smolansky, *The Soviet Union and the Arab East Under Khrushchev* (Lewisburg, Penna.: Bucknell University Press, 1974), pp. 102-122.

[52] *Strategic Survey 1970* (London: International Institute for Strategic Studies, 1971), p. 46.

[53] See Haykal, as cited in CPR, No. 5599, September 18, 1970.

Nor is the affirmative Soviet response difficult to understand.[54] Moscow strengthened its military-strategic foothold: in addition to naval facilities at Alexandria and Port Said, it obtained freer use of airfields. With these it at last had the strategic plum it had coveted since the early 1960s, namely, an infrastructure in the eastern Mediterranean to compensate for the loss of the naval base at Vlone (Albania) in May 1961 and from which to neutralize the U.S. Sixth Fleet and to strengthen the USSR's ASW (antisubmarine warfare) capability against the Polaris submarines. The airfields also enabled the Soviets to reconnoiter the Red Sea area to the Horn of Africa. Moscow propped up Nasir because Soviet advances in the Middle East were in great measure linked to his fortunes. He was a known factor, and no successor was

[54] One scholar contends that the Soviet leadership was pleased by Nasir's plight and that it went so far as to suggest "that, if he came to Moscow, he might find the USSR surprisingly willing to make meaningful moves to rescue him." This, he argues, "is a far more likely explanation of his secret Moscow visit in January, 1970, than the version which claims that he decided, on his own initiative, to fly suddenly to the Soviet capital and ask for help. . . . The reason why the Soviet leaders may have preferred to bring the Egyptian President secretly to Moscow was to confront him, almost alone, with the full and united, awesome pressure of the Kremlin, at a time when he was in dire need of Soviet help." Uri Ra'anan, "Soviet Policy in the Middle East, 1969–1973," *Midstream*, 19, No. 10 (December 1973), 37. According to Ra'anan, Moscow maneuvered Cairo into requesting the assistance in order to intrude its combat forces into Egypt, a decision it made independently of Nasir.

This is a provocative and imaginative essay, though some of its assumptions and assertions are open to question. Ra'anan argues that the Soviets required more than two to three months to plan and implement the complex logistical aspects of the operation. This discounts the fact that the USSR had extensive stockpiles of SAM-2 and SAM-3 missiles in the Black Sea area preparatory to shipping them to North Vietnam. It was, then, no major problem, but the simplest of operations to send the ships loaded with radars and missiles across the Black Sea through the Bosphorus across the Mediterranean to Alexandria. Nor was Moscow, as he alleges, concerned that Israel or the United States would interdict Soviet shipping. The United States was fighting a war in Vietnam; the last thing it wanted was another with the Soviet Union. Nor is it likely that the Soviet Union "mentioned the plan" to its Warsaw Pact allies: when did Moscow ever consult with its East European satrapies on a decision of strategic importance? Finally, it is misleading to say that the Soviets decided to embark on a program of building aircraft carriers shortly before the war of attrition. The Soviet Union had begun to build its first generation of carriers in 1963–1964, under Khrushchev. The first Moskva-class helicopter carrier was designed for ASW (antisubmarine warfare) activities and became operational in mid-1967; a second was completed in 1969. Construction of a second generation of carriers, which may be what Ra'anan is referring to, began in Nikolaev sometime in 1969–1970, but the decision to do so must have been taken considerably earlier.

likely to be in a position to do more for the Soviet Union than he. By supporting him and like-minded Arab nationalists determined to cast off Western domination, the Soviet leadership nurtured Arab propensities toward nonalignment and closer ties with the Soviet bloc.

Nasir slowly, fitfully, but inexorably out of his own travail and ambition brought the USSR into the mainstream of Middle Eastern and Afro-Asian affairs. The Soviet leaders' decision to meet Nasir's request, a request they had expected from their knowledge of his straits, may have also been a function of internal politics. Those who had upheld the "forward policy" in Egypt and the Middle East could not shy away from securing that policy without leaving themselves vulnerable to attack from opponents in the leadership. Thus considerations of bureaucratic politics, as well as national strategic calculations, no doubt determined the Kremlin's response. The Soviet Union, for the first time in its history, undertook a commitment to participate directly in the defense of a non-Communist country.

Within a week of Nasir's return the curtain of doubt as to Soviet intentions began to lift. *Pravda* published a lengthy statement on the Middle East, preparatory to the Soviet government's note of January 31, 1970, to the United States, France, and Britain.[55] Warning that "the situation is becoming more inflamed," *Pravda* disabused those in the West who had expected that the Arabs would find "themselves all alone and thus become easy prey" for the Israelis, by reaffirming that the ties between the USSR and Egypt "have grown stronger and firmer" since June 1967 and stressing the even greater significance "at the present time" of the "many-faceted Arab-Soviet cooperation," which provides a guarantee of the sovereignty and independence of the Arab countries. The article noted (anticipated?) Egypt's growing "combat potential." While maintaining that the possibilities of a settlement still existed, its tone was firm: the Soviet Union was not going to let Egypt down. Furthermore, the United States must realize that there were to be no territorial concessions, no "reward" for Israel, and no participation by Israel in the determination of the fate of Gaza or Sharm el-Sheikh. The Soviet proposals contained none of the guarantees Israel deemed essential.

[55] *Pravda*, January 27, 1970.

Egyptian sources, reporting on the article, emphasized the danger of war.[56]

Premier Kosygin's note of January 31 warned of the danger in the Middle East, demanded an end to Israel's air attacks, and urged new Four Power talks, intimating that the USSR would take appropriate action unless the United States stopped supplying arms to Israel.[57] *Al-Ahram* interpreted the note more bluntly: Moscow was saying, "We would like to tell you very clearly that, as long as Israel persists in its adventures, the Soviet Union will place at the disposal of the Arab countries *everything* necessary for expelling the aggressors" (emphasis added).[58] On February 12 TASS reported that Kosygin had told the Western powers: "The Soviet Union is fully resolved to help to foil imperialist ventures and there should be no doubt about that."[59] Four days later, it issued a terse statement: "The Soviet Union will render the necessary support to the Arab states in strengthening their ability to uphold their security and their just interests."[60] Against this background of forceful warnings reports began to circulate of a growing number of Soviet ships putting into Egyptian ports.[61]

Officials in Washington discounted Kosygin's note as a "polemical gesture."[62] The White House, absorbed with Vietnam, SALT, and student unrest, did not take repeated Soviet admonitions to Israel seriously. It could not believe Moscow would take on a direct military responsibility or use troops to back up imperial ambitions in a Third World country not vital to its security. This would contravene establishmentarian assumptions, encrusted over a generation, about the determinants of Soviet behavior, to the effect that the combination of U.S. nuclear superiority and traditional Soviet caution would keep the bear con-

---

[56] *Egyptian Gazette*, January 28, 1970.

[57] *NYT*, February 5, 1970.

[58] BBC/ME/3299/A/4 (February 7, 1970).

[59] *Soviet News*, No. 5530 (February 7, 1970).

[60] *NYT*, February 17, 1970. Sadat later revealed that on the following day six Soviet soldiers died during an Israeli raid on a Soviet-manned missile site at Dahshur, 20 miles south of Cairo. *NYT*, January 5, 1971.

[61] The Black Sea Shipping Agency allocated an additional 20 ships to carry matériel to Egypt and other Arab countries. Moscow Radio in English for Africa, 1830 GMT, January 31, 1970, as cited in BBC/ME/W556/A/1 (February 1970).

[62] *NYT*, February 3, 1970.

fined to his own imperial den. Sustaining this comforting view of the constrained appetite of Soviet policymakers was the tendency of the White House to dismiss the possibility that the Soviets would jeopardize the superpower drift toward détente over some third rate real estate in an area of presumed secondary or tertiary importance to the Soviet Union. Actually, the same reasoning that could not admit of Soviet missile crews and combat pilots being sent to Egypt appears still to dominate much official U.S. thinking about Soviet policy in the Third World. That is to say, there exists a patronizing disdain for Brezhnev and company, who are seen as a bunch of third rate "faceless" bureaucrats concerned with preserving power, not expanding Soviet influence; a belief in Soviet "caution," extrapolated from post-World War II Soviet policy toward Western Europe—Moscow had never before committed troops outside the Soviet bloc, ergo, it will not do so (the 1970 incident being an exception); and a widely shared view that Moscow regards détente in the same broadly constructive, cooperative way that Washington does.

The hardening Soviet diplomatic position on the Middle East coincided with the intensification of a major anti-Zionist campaign in the Soviet Union. One aim of the hate campaign, which started in November 1969 and reached a peak in March 1970 when Soviet combat forces became operational in Egypt, was to prepare the Soviet people for the possibility of Soviet involvement in a war to defend Egypt.[63] Never before in Soviet history

---

[63] Jonathan Frankel, "The Anti-Zionist Press Campaigns in the USSR 1969–1971: An Internal Dialogue?" *Soviet Jewish Affairs*, No. 3 (May 1972), 5-6. In his excellent article, Professor Frankel examines four theories that might explain the anti-Zionist campaigns: 1) they are an integral element of a hard line attitude toward all Jews, both in the USSR and abroad, that is in keeping with traditional Russian anti-Semitism; 2) they are Machiavellian propaganda efforts "to divert the attention of the Arab world from the decision of the post-Khrushchev leadership to permit Jewish emigration to Israel"; 3) they are just another aspect of Soviet Middle Eastern policy, aimed at intimidating Israel, currying favor with the Arabs, and recruiting public support at home behind Moscow's "expensive and risky Middle East venture"; and 4) they are "a direct response to the mounting pressure from Jews in the Soviet Union—backed up by highly vocal support in the Western countries —for the right to emigrate to Israel." He concludes that in the 1969–1971 period it was "the internal Jewish problem which dominated the [Soviet] decision-making process."

Mr. Frankel correlated Soviet anti-Zionist diatribes with Soviet pilots flying combat missions *over the canal* in June and July 1970, instead of with the deployment of Soviet-manned missile sites in March and Soviet pilots

had the press given the Jewish question the saturation treatment it received in early 1970.

At an international meeting of parliamentarians in early February, Nasir publicly acknowledged Israeli deep penetration raids for the first time, saying "the attacks will not frighten us, instead they will strengthen us."[64] Denouncing the arming of Israel, he hinted the Soviet Union would more than match the American effort. In an interview with two American journalists on February 9 Nasir refused to comment on whether he had recently visited the Soviet Union but implied it was providing advanced SAM-3 missiles to check Israeli raids: "The Israelis today think they are masters of the area but this will not last long."[65] On February 14, twenty-four hours after Israeli planes had bombed a factory and taken a heavy toll of lives, he told James Reston of the *New York Times* that to accept direct air support from the USSR was "a delicate question," and he had "to think about it" (*sic!*).[66] Despite his seeming plight, Nasir was adamant, maintaining that unless there was a total Israeli evacuation from all Arab territories and a solution to "the problem of the refugees" there could be no peace. He did not "mind a Jewish homeland, but a Jewish state is intolerable." When Eric Rouleau of *Le Monde* asked if he would call for Soviet volunteers to beef up Egypt's air force, Nasir "visibly embarrassed by the question" smiled: "If the contingency arose, we would consider the possibility. But, you see, a one-sided decision on such a matter wouldn't be of much use."[67]

On March 10, in an interview on Cairo television, Haykal said "The Soviet government is on the point of taking an important decision on the Middle East crisis."[68] Five days later, Soviet-manned SAM-3 missiles were in place. The diplomatic cat-and-mouse game was over. The first Soviet troops had been openly committed to combat in the Middle East, a signal event.[69]

---

flying combat missions *over the Delta area* from early April on. The use of the former period as a measure of intensity is partially responsible for his underestimation of the Middle East as a policy determinant.

[64] *Al-Ahram*, February 3, 1970.

[65] BBC/ME/3302/A/5 (February 11, 1970).

[66] *NYT*, February 15, 1970.

[67] *Le Monde Weekly Selection*, No. 44, February 18, 1970.

[68] ARR, No. 5 (March 1–15, 1970), 158.

[69] The date of March 15, 1970, was pinpointed by Sadat in a speech on August 29, 1971. BBC/ME/3775/A/7 (September 1, 1971).

ISRAEL IN CHECK

Conscious of the political implications of the operation, the Soviets were careful to signal the defensive nature of their buildup to the United States, in order to preclude an American overreaction. Thus, though the Soviet government had insisted that the Egyptians maintain absolute secrecy about the buildup, the first Soviet missile units, arriving in late February, "which had been supposed to land in Alexandria at night, landed instead in broad daylight and took the main road" to their assigned camp, and Soviet pilots talked in Russian over their radios.[70]

Egypt's situation quickly improved. By April 18 the Israeli air force was effectively deterred from bombing inner Egypt. The Soviet intervention was already a success. Egyptian morale rose, at least among the civilians.[71] The battle now began for the canal area: as the Soviets pushed the air defense perimeter methodically toward the canal, the Israelis fought back to prevent the development of a new strategic situation that would expose all of the Israeli-held eastern bank of the canal to Egyptian attack and pave the way for an assault into Sinai. On April 14 Dayan defiantly told the Soviets that Israel would do everything it could to prevent the emplacement of missile sites along the canal: "We shall bomb you."[72] By late April there was no longer any doubt that Soviet pilots were flying combat missions over the heartland of Egypt (they did not make their appearance along the canal until June).[73] Israel faced a new situation. And so did the United States.

[70] CPR, No. 5668, July 28, 1972.

[71] General Chaim Herzog (ret.), a respected Israeli military analyst, suggested that there was a deterioration in the morale of the Egyptian army "following their acceptance of a situation whereby their defense is now in the hands of Russian operators of SAM-3 missiles, the operation of which is on no account to be entrusted to the Egyptian soldier. Obviously such an attitude must affect the morale of any army which has all along been advised that it was being prepared for the decisive struggle against Israel, and here now is being informed that not only is it incapable of defending the skies of Egypt but not even trustworthy enough to receive the new weapons for such defense." BBC/ME/3352/A/4 (April 14, 1970).

[72] BBC/ME/3354/A/3 (April 16, 1970). See also, BBC/ME/3376/A/6 (May 12, 1970).

[73] For the text of the Israeli government's statement of April 29, 1970, on the Soviet combat presence in Egypt, see NYT, April 30, 1970. See also, Edward H. Kolcum, "Soviets Accelerating Mideast Drive," Aviation Week and Space Technology, 92, No. 20 (May 18, 1970), 14-18.

On January 25 and again on January 30 President Nixon implied he accepted Soviet arms deliveries to Egypt as being defensive in character and intended for the preservation of a balance of power between Egypt and Israel. He accordingly refused to act on Israel's request for an additional commitment of aircraft, on the grounds that Israel enjoyed overwhelming air superiority:

> We will consider the Israeli arms requests based on the threats to them from states in the area. And we will honor those requests to the extent that we see—we determine—that they need additional arms in order to meet that threat. That decision will be made within the next 30 days.[74]

On March 23, after a seven-week delay, Rogers' announcement that the United States had decided not to sell Israel an additional 25 Phantoms and 100 Skyhawks signaled Nixon's desire to keep the fighting limited.

> In our judgment, Israel's air capacity is sufficient to meet its needs for the time being. Consequently, the President has decided to hold in abeyance for now a decision with respect to Israel's request for additional aircraft. In doing so, he has instructed that close watch be kept on the military balance in the area. The USA will be in a position to provide additional as well as replacement aircraft promptly if the situation requires it.[75]

As evidence accumulated that the Soviets intended to push the missile belt closer to the canal and to use their pilots there too, Nixon's dilemmas intensified: how to convince Moscow that he was prepared to accept a restoration of the balance of power between Egypt and Israel and yet not precipitate a new arms spiral? How to induce Moscow to cooperate in arranging a cease-fire without encouraging it to exploit the expanded Soviet military involvement to seek a decisive shift in relations between the local adversaries? The Egyptian-Israeli conflict was rapidly acquiring a global dimension that Washington wished to minimize. Haykal perceived that the Middle East was a magnet, that as the local conflict intensified it would suck the superpowers onto a collision course:

[74] *NYT*, January 31, 1970.
[75] ARR, No. 6 (March 16–31, 1970), 193.

There is a struggle in the Middle East mainly between Egypt and Israel. As the Middle East is in the heart of the Arab world, and its political, economic and strategic position is now important, the struggle in it will affect the world power struggle. Ultimately, the Middle East will become an important area in the struggle between today's two super powers—the USA and the Soviet Union, particularly in view of Israel's special relations with the USA and Egypt's strong friendship with the Soviet Union. . . .

The parties to the local struggle cannot impose peace and the parties to the international struggle cannot declare war. Therefore, the Middle East crisis has entered a strange state—a vacuum in which it is lost between war and peace.[76]

The Soviet-American talks, resumed on March 25, 1970, had not resulted in any change, especially on the matter of limiting arms deliveries. Washington was uneasy over Brezhnev's uncompromising remarks: "The sooner the leaders of the United States realize how pointless and dangerous is their connivance with the Israeli aggressor, the sooner this [a settlement] can be achieved."[77] Perplexed and piqued, on April 16, Rogers accused Moscow of not showing interest in a peaceful settlement: "We think there is a very strong likelihood that the Soviet Union would prefer what is referred to as 'controlled tension' in the area rather than a permanent peace."[78] On April 24 Sisco said the Soviet flow of weapons was complicating efforts to find a solution. U.S. alarm over Soviet intentions mounted, leading Nixon on April 29 to order an immediate evaluation of intelligence reports on Soviet involvement and its implications for the balance of power in the Middle East. Disbelief gave way to dismay: how far did the Soviets intend to go?

Washington was encouraged by Nasir's speech of May 1, appealing to Nixon to refrain from aiding Israel and to understand the Arab position and press Israel to fulfill the principles of Resolution 242: "I inform President Nixon that we have reached a decisive moment in Arab-American relations—either we will

[76] BBC/ME/3336/A/3 (March 23, 1970). While retaining his post as editor of *Al-Ahram*, Haykal was brought into the government on April 26 and made Minister of Information and National Guidance.
[77] *NYT*, April 15, 1970.
[78] ARR, No. 8 (April 16–30, 1970), 255.

be estranged forever or there will be a new, serious and definite start . . . the situation is delicate and . . . the consequences are extremely dangerous."[79] Riyad took pains to bring Nasir's speech to the attention of Washington by personally handing Donald Bergus, the head of the U.S. Interests Section, an English translation of the complete text.[80] Inexplicably, Washington was, as often in the past, slow to react. In what was interpreted as a deliberate prod to the White House, Nasir told an American journalist two weeks later that he intended to ask for more Soviet experts to operate the complex electronic equipment that is integral to air warfare: "we cannot dispense with the Russian experts *as long as we are at war with Israel and as long as there is no peace*. In fact we have asked the Russians for more equipment of this kind and more experts to operate them"[81] (emphasis added).

The fighting raged fiercely through May and June. Egyptian forces, though performing creditably, suffered heavy casualties from round-the-clock Israeli bombing. In the third week of June, the diplomatic situation took a sudden upturn, when Bergus broached the issue of a cease-fire and received a warm welcome. The Rogers' proposals were submitted to the foreign ministers of Egypt and Jordan on June 19, reached Nasir in Tripoli on June 21,[82] and were made public on June 25. They called for the "restoration of the ceasefire for at least a limited period," the resumption of talks under Jarring's aegis, and the willingness to carry out Resolution 242 "in all its parts."[83] As Nasir later remarked, they contained "nothing new," yet the overall situation was in need of a fresh assessment. To demonstrate its diplomatic activism and not be outdone by Washington, Moscow offered a plan of its own to the Four Powers at a meeting in New York on June 24, but it was the Rogers Plan that was on the bargaining table.[84] Broadcasts over Moscow domestic service allowed that the United States had made a number of suggestions for a solution, but one journal termed Rogers' proposal "rather vague" and commented that the plan had met "with a highly critical re-

79 BBC/ME/3369/A/14 (May 4, 1970).
80 CPR, No. 5453, May 3, 1970.
81 BBC/ME/3380/A/3 (May 16, 1970).
82 BBC/ME/3553/A/2 (December 7, 1970).
83 *NYT*, July 23, 1970.
84 *NYT*, July 2, 1970; October 16, 1970.

sponse in Arab capitals, where it was assessed as a camouflaged formula designed to enable Israel to achieve its objectives."[85]

DECISION IN MOSCOW

On June 29, on a few days' notice, Nasir flew to Moscow to discuss the Rogers Plan with Soviet leaders. Important decisions had to be made by both parties. In the five months since his previous trip, Egypt's political and military turnabout had been extraordinary. Israel's counterwar of attrition was blunted: the deep penetration raids were a thing of the past; the battering of Egyptian forces stationed along the canal continued, but Israel, too, was beginning to feel the sting, as Egyptian commando raids and Soviet SAMs took their toll; morale on the home front had improved despite shortages and difficulties. The Soviet intervention had made the difference. Now Moscow and Cairo had to plan for the future.

At first, Egyptian sources reported that Nasir did not expect to remain in the Soviet Union for more than a week: on July 2 Cairo Radio said the final meeting would be held on July 6;[86] but three days later, it reported, without comment, that Nasir would resume talks with Soviet leaders on July 9, after spending several days in a sanatorium undergoing a medical checkup; a third meeting was reported on July 12, and a fourth on July 16. Clearly the discussion—or the issues—were difficult.

The talks were conducted at the highest level: the key Soviet participants were Brezhnev, Podgornyi, Kosygin, Grechko, Ponomarev, Skachkov (chairman of the State Committee of the USSR Council of Ministers for External Economic Relations), Deputy Foreign Minister Vladimir Vinogradov, and Sergei Vinogradov, Ambassador to Egypt; on the Egyptian side, there were Nasir, Riyad, Fawzi, Haykal, Sabri, and Ghaleb, Ambassador to the Soviet Union. The joint communiqué of July 17,[87] though long, was revealing more for what was not said than for what was. It stated that the discussions were held in an atmosphere of "openness, friendship and complete mutual understanding," the use of the term "openness" suggesting that all options and their

---

[85] P. Demchenko, "Stiffening Rebuff," *New Times*, No. 27 (July 8, 1970), 9. See also, BBC/SU/3417/A4/1 (June 30, 1970).

[86] BBC/ME/3421/i (July 4, 1970).

[87] FBIS/USSR, July 20, 1970, pp. A1-A5.

implications had been candidly discussed and the differences were minor, "frankness" being the customary word for differences of more serious degree. The discussions focused on the Middle East and "questions of further development of all-round cooperation" between the USSR and Egypt, but there was no mention of the Rogers Plan, the fighting along the canal, the Soviet military involvement, or the gathering superpower crisis over it. More than half of the communiqué was diplomatic filler—material on extra-regional issues.

The two sides did stress the "similarity" (the version published in *Pravda* used the word "identicality") of their views on the Middle East: that Israel's "aggressive, expansionist policy" was possible only because of U.S. support; that there must be an end to Israel's armed attacks and a full withdrawal "from all the occupied Arab territories in accordance with the principle of non-acquisition of territories through war and by complete implementation" of Resolution 242; that every effort should be made to achieve a "political settlement"; and that United Nations decisions "on the questions of Palestinian refugees" should be implemented. However, the communiqué treated the Palestinian issue as a minor matter. In contrast to the December 1969 communiqué, which spoke of satisfaction of the just rights of the Palestinians as "resolutely essential" for any settlement, this one merely "expressed solidarity with the Arab people of Palestine." The relative downgrading of the Palestinian problem signified agreement on the need to give priority to the pressing diplomatic and military questions, whose outcome would determine the foreign policy course of Moscow and Cairo.

Another contrast to the December communiqué was Nasir's glowing tribute to Soviet assistance. He expressed "profound gratitude for the all-round assistance" of the Soviet Union and its "decisive support" during Egypt's "present complex and difficult struggle" against Israel. And well he might, and with full confidence about the future, because the Soviet leaders assured him of their "readiness to continue supporting the just struggle of the Arab peoples . . . and give them the necessary assistance in this." What these promises entailed became known very soon. In addition to cooperation in the military field, which predictably loomed large in the talks, the communiqué called for closer ties in other areas as well, party and governmental, with "culture, science and art" singled out for the first time. Finally, the two governments stressed their friendly and increasingly intimate relationship; and Brezhnev, Kosygin, and Podgornyi accepted invitations to visit Egypt.

The communiqué took on new meaning on July 23, when Nasir announced Egypt's acceptance of Rogers' proposals and agreed to a three-month cease-fire in place (foreign chancelleries had been informed two days earlier). On July 31, after bitter debate in the Knesset, the Israeli government also accepted, but on the understanding that the cease-fire would not be used to strengthen military positions in the canal area.[88] Its decision was influenced by Nixon's secret replacement of some aircraft losses in June and July and assurance of future deliveries to maintain the military balance. Dayan remarked that Israel "is not so strong that she can afford to lose allies."[89] Not even the combat successes of its air force could withstand the force of American arguments that the opportunity for Israel to stop fighting and start talking and for the United States to play a mediating role was too precious to waste.[90]

By accepting the American proposal, Nasir incurred the ire of the radical Arab regimes—Iraq, Algeria, and Libya, especially the former. He justified the recourse to political action on the basis of Egypt's growing strength:

> We are not acting from a weak position but from a strong one. There are many factors in favor of our strong position. . . . The first is the increasing ability of our armed forces to strike back. The second factor is increased Soviet political and military backing for us as a result of the sound Soviet appreciation of the fairness of our struggle and the importance of this struggle to the liberation movement in the world.[91]

He scoffed at Iraqi charges of betrayal of Arab unity and the Palestinians: "The Egyptian people are not used to the luxury

[88] One Israeli newspaper wrote prophetically that the opposition to a limited cease-fire was justified because it would "create the most convenient conditions for strengthening the Egyptian front and for continuing to slip Russian missiles into the ceasefire line." BBC/ME/3437/A/8 (July 23, 1970).

[89] NYT, July 29, 1970.

[90] On July 30, the day before the Israeli government accepted the cease-fire, Israeli Phantoms shot down five Soviet-piloted MiG-21s in less than one minute in a dogfight over the canal. According to one informed Cairene, there were "drunken parties" at Egyptian bases when the Soviet pilots were shot down.

[91] BBC/ME/3439/A/17 (July 25, 1970).

of fighting on speakers' platforms or in the corridors of political maneuvers."[92] The Soviets, on the other hand, praised his statesmanship and "great political courage" and denounced Arab "extremists."[93] An Iraqi Ba'thist delegation, which went to Moscow in early August, received a cool reception.

Much more embarrassing to Nasir were the Palestinians. Far from being uncritical admirers, many of them harbored resentment of Nasir's attitude toward them in the years prior to the Karamah battle of March 1968, and they were offended by the close surveillance of their activities in Cairo. On Tuesday evening, July 28, "The Voice of Assifa" (Storm), a daily one-hour broadcast of fiery commentary operated by Al-Fatah since May 11, 1968, was taken off the air and replaced by a program of Arabic songs, including one called, "Don't Forsake Me, Lover";[94] and the six-hour daily program, "Voice of Palestine," begun in 1964 under the aegis of the Palestine Liberation Organization, was also terminated. Both stations, which had been used to broadcast coded messages to operatives in Israel and Israeli-occupied territory, were discontinued by the Egyptian government because of their criticism of Cairo's acceptance of the cease-fire.

Nasir weathered these flurries. For the moment there was nothing to be done about the new cracks in the façade of Arab unity. Far more important for Egyptian foreign policy and the Egyptian-Soviet relationship were the implications of the cease-fire, which went into effect on August 7, 1970.

CEASE-FIRE OR RESPITE?

The aim of Nasir's visit had been to discuss the basic question of whether or not to go along with the Rogers Plan and the specifics of what could be expected from the USSR. His final decision was motivated by short-term diplomatic objectives and longer range military benefits, and presumably Soviet preferences.

[92] BBC/ME/3447/A/11 (August 4, 1970). Several weeks later Haykal commented caustically: "The Iraqi Baath Party stood where it always did and where it will always stand—a mere black market trader in a war which will decide the fate of his own nation, but unconcerned with anything but the pilfering of gain for himself even at the expense of the blood of fallen heroes." CPR, No. 5562, August 21, 1970.
[93] *Pravda*, July 30 and August 1, 1970. See also, I. Belyaev, "The Downed Phantoms and Peace Proposals," *New Times*, No. 32 (August 12, 1970), 4-5.
[94] *The Kuwait Times*, July 30, 1970.

First, Nasir agreed to the Rogers Plan in order to involve the United States directly in the process of forcing an Israeli withdrawal. Convinced of the impossibility of a military solution, because the United States would never permit Egypt, even if it had the capability, to defeat, occupy, and destroy Israel, he preferred to rely on political pressures. The weakening and ultimate defeat of Israel could be accomplished by diplomacy, with an occasional boost from military actions. To this end, it was essential that the Nixon Administration, which had often expressed a desire to follow an "evenhanded" policy in the Middle East, be encouraged to improve relations with the Arab world and detach itself from the partisan commitment to Israel. According to Haykal, Nasir confided to a visiting Sudanese delegation:

> The USA moved under pressure. We want to hold it in this position and do not want it to slip away. Israel will resist withdrawal from the occupied territory with all its means. Only the USA can put presssure on Israel to that end. In our opinion, Israel will be compelled to accept the U.S. proposals, but [and] her acceptance will split the ruling alliance there.[95]

Nasir expected America's diplomatic involvement to lead to a limitation of arms shipments to Israel, thereby enabling Egypt to close the military gap that much more quickly. The pause would also temper the surrogate U.S.-Soviet military confrontation, whose intensity threatened a complete polarization of superpower alignments in the Arab-Israeli conflict, thereby reducing his own independence and freedom of diplomatic action. Nasir's delicate task was to gain U.S. support without arousing the suspicions of the Kremlin that he was playing off the Soviets against the Americans and without seriously alienating his radical, anti-American constituencies in the Arab world.

Second, Nasir accepted the cease-fire in order to allay Soviet apprehension over the alarming extent to which the fighting was developing an impetus toward a direct U.S.-Soviet military confrontation. A canny, basically cautious man, with a grasp of tactical constraints and strategic realities, Nasir was not heedless of the risks of uncontrolled escalation or insensitive to new op-

[95] BBC/ME/3452/A/2 (August 10, 1970). For an informed Western assessment with this same general line of reasoning see, John C. Campbell, "Is America's Lone Hand Played Out?" *New Middle East*, No. 36 (September 1971), 11-15.

portunities and to the USSR's keen interest in SALT and détente in Europe. He knew there was a military limit beyond which Moscow might not wish to go. The Soviet Union had nothing further to gain from an expansion of Egypt's war. It had saved its client, and in the process acquired a substantial military foothold, and institutionalized Egypt's dependence on Soviet power and expertise, and demonstrated its credibility, which was no longer under a cloud in the Arab world. Its investment optimized, Moscow was ready to stop. Moreover, Egypt was not in a position to cross the canal and retake Sinai, hence the value of time to consolidate and to prepare for the future.

True, some of his entourage—Sadat for one—argued that acceptance "was a mistake." They reasoned that the tide was slowly but perceptibly turning against Israel, whose air force was beginning to meet its match in the SAMs: during the June 30–August 7 period, Israel lost five Phantoms along the canal, or about ten percent of its total, a loss ratio it could not sustain indefinitely, even allowing for some U.S. replacements. With the Soviet Union deeply committed to Egypt's defense and military success and the United States bogged down in Vietnam, Egypt should exploit this Soviet "dependency" and the favorable international situation to the hilt, persist, take the casualties, relentlessly drain Israel's strength, and in this way bring it to the conference table in a mood for a settlement on Arab terms. However, Nasir decided against this option and the questionable premises on which it rested.

Third, Nasir was promised continued military assistance, including the extension to the canal itself of the most concentrated and elaborate air defense system in the non-Communist world, in the event that he chose to accept a cease-fire. The Soviet missile belt was slowly being widened. Though the casualties from Israel's "flying artillery" were still extremely heavy, the rapid deployment of SAM-2 and SAM-3 batteries in the central and southern sectors of the canal area and the new tactics of launching SAMs in volleys were taking their toll of Israeli planes. A respite would permit the expeditious, painless emplacement of the SAM system. Should diplomacy fail, the Egyptian military position would have been enormously strengthened. It is this ratiocination that Nasir developed in a conversation with Boumedienne: "This is our only hope to build up a military force which will enable us one day to return to the battlefield";

a lull was essential because "it was our only hope of getting [Soviet] arms to resume fighting."[96]

Thus, though Moscow did not initiate the diplomatic process nor dictate to Nasir the decision culminating in the cease-fire of August 7, it did apparently use some leverage to encourage his acceptance of the Rogers Plan.[97]

The Soviet press welcomed the three-month cease-fire in-place that went into effect in the Middle East in the early hours of the morning of August 8 (officially, 2200 hours Greenwich Mean Time, August 7).[98] Hardly had the fighting stopped when, on August 13, Dayan accused Egypt of having egregiously violated the standstill provisions of the agreement, of moving missiles into the canal area the very night the cease-fire went into effect.[99] The controversy that followed raged for months and fore-shadowed the failure of the Rogers initiative: Israel demanded the removal of the missiles as a precondition for partici-pation in the Jarring talks; Egypt refused, asseverating that the missile sites had been under construction before the agreement came into effect; the United States wavered between annoyance with the Israelis for exposing the violations and with the Egyp-tians for committing them; and the USSR accused Israel of wrecking efforts at a settlement. However, after three weeks of indecision, prolonged by Rogers' reputed equivocation on the evidence gathered by his own agencies, the State Department con-

[96] BBC/ME/3475/A/2-3 (September 7, 1970).

[97] Haykal gave this view of Nasir's motives shortly after the Egyptian president's death: "In Moscow Brezhnev heard from Abd an-Nasir that Abd an-Nasir had decided to accept the U.S. initiative. Brezhnev asked him: Can you really do it, can you accept an initiative originated in Washington? Abd an-Nasir's answer was quite clear: Other than abandoning Arab territory —which I cannot do—and Palestine's right—because the Palestinian people have the right to self-determination—I am not going to restrict my free-dom." BBC/ME/3553/A/2 (December 7, 1970).

[98] *Pravda*, August 8, 1970.

[99] Dayan revealed that the cease-fire agreement had stipulated the follow-ing conditions: "Both sides will refrain from changing the military status quo in the areas extending 50 kilometers east and west of the ceasefire line. Neither side will introduce or set up any new military installations in these regions. Activities within these regions will be limited to the maintenance of existing installations in their present areas and positions and to the rota-tion and supply of the forces now present in these regions. In order to rein-force the observance of the ceasefire, each side will rely on its national means, including reconnaissance aircraft, which will be free to operate unhindered up to a distance of 10 kilometers from its side of the ceasefire line." BBC/ME/3457/A/3 (August 15, 1970).

firmed on September 3 that "there have been violations of the ceasefire standstill agreement."[100] A week later Moscow indirectly confirmed Israel's accusation. It said Israel was threatening the complete disruption of present diplomatic contacts by declaring it would not make an agreement based on "absolutely different conditions," i.e. violations of the cease-fire in the canal area:

> The UAR carried out in this zone some measures which are limited to maintaining former positions and personnel in proper condition. Israel and the USA are attempting to give out as true that these minimal measures, including individual transfers of missile installations from one place to another and the replacement of some installations there by others, which are necessary to ensure the security of the missiles positions and their personnel, constitute violations.[101]

The move of the missiles into the canal zone had been planned as part of Moscow's payoff to Nasir for agreeing to the cease-fire. Indeed, the Soviets even sent Marshal P. Kutakhov, Commander of the Air Force, to Cairo on August 1 to supervise the SAM deployments personally (and perhaps also to investigate the circumstances surrounding the downing of the five Soviet-piloted MiG-21s on July 30). It is entirely possible that they expected to have more time, that Israel's quick acceptance came as a surprise and confronted them with a dilemma: to refuse the cease-fire and take additional heavy casualties; or to accept the cease-fire, move up the missiles, and brazen out the diplomatic imbroglio. The latter won out because Moscow calculated that the United States, fearful of the collapse of its initiative, would pressure Israel to accept the violations and proceed from there under the new conditions.

By the time the first three-month period of the cease-fire drew to a close, no amount of diplomatic acrimony could obscure Egypt's vastly improved military situation:

> By the end of October, some 500-600 surface-to-air missile launchers covered the western approaches to the Canal, about

100 Appalled at the casuistic indifference of Rogers and Sisco to the implications of Soviet-Egyptian duplicity, the White House took firmer control of Middle East policy and signaled its displeasure to Moscow and Cairo by granting Israeli requests for more Phantoms.
101 *Izvestiia*, September 11, 1970.

200 of them being within 19 miles of that line. Moreover, the forward sites in the system, carefully spaced 7½ miles apart along the Canal itself in order to give overlapping coverage, also covered an area extending 12 miles into Israel-occupied territory.[102]

Sadat later confirmed that "The ceasefire was a wonderful opportunity for us to build and reinforce all our positions along the entire battle front. . . . Our forces did not lose a moment in the first ceasefire period."[103] The planned missile buildup immeasurably strengthened Egypt's military position, though the test of its lethal effectiveness was still three years off.

The furor over the missiles obscured something that took on added importance in the months ahead; namely, the tactical setback to Israel's diplomatic stance. Israel was forced to retreat from its demand for direct negotiations and agree to a temporary three-month cease-fire, whose renewal was conditional on progress being made by Jarring, instead of a return to the unlimited cease-fire established by the Security Council resolution of June 8, 1967. Egypt controlled the diplomatic play. As an uneasy calm set in along the canal, momentous events were unfolding elsewhere.

NASIR'S LEGACY

On September 1, 1970, an abortive attempt to assassinate King Husayn plunged Jordan into fierce fighting. After four weeks of fratricidal conflict between the Jordanian army and the Palestinian guerrillas based in the country, and a foiled Syrian armed intervention to help the Palestinians, the crisis was brought to an end by a combination of vigorous behind-the-scenes U.S.-Soviet-Israeli maneuvering and signaling of intentions,[104] Jor-

---

[102] *Strategic Survey 1970*, p. 48.

[103] He made this statement on January 2, 1971. *Speeches by President Anwar El Sadat, September 1970–March 1971* (Cairo: Ministry of Information, 1971), p. 91.

[104] For a discussion of Soviet behavior during the Jordanian crisis, see Abraham S. Becker, "The Superpowers in the Arab-Israeli Conflict, 1970–1973," in Abraham S. Becker, Bent Hansen, and Malcolm H. Kerr, *The Economics and Politics of the Middle East* (New York: American Elsevier Publishing Company, 1975), pp. 94-97.

danian arms, and Nasir's mediation. The main casualty of the Jordanian civil war proved to be Gamal 'Abd al-Nasir. He died on September 28, less than twenty-four hours after he arranged for an end to the war.

From his early days in power, when he moved tentatively from weakness and uncertainty, always surprised by the ease with which his opposition was cowed or vanquished, Nasir believed that the fates were with him, that he had a pact with the stars. His fatalism inured him to criticism and to advice whose implications he did not want to accept. It was a source of strength and a source of weakness.

Nasir ruled Egypt for almost two decades. The first Egyptian to rule in Egypt since the time of the Pharaohs, he captured the imagination of the Arab world, paradoxically, more in moments of defeat and distress than in victory, whose fruits in foreign policy he tasted only rarely. Under his leadership, Egypt cast off the remnants of British colonial rule, embarked sporadically on a program of extensive internal transformation, and became a leader in Arab and Afro-Asian affairs.

Nasir's career survived extraordinary vicissitudes. The Soviet Union saved him from the consequences of his own folly and Israeli power. It is Egypt's relationship with the USSR that constitutes Nasir's greatest legacy in foreign policy. It preserved Egypt from defeat and became the basis for Egypt's military renaissance. By inducing the Soviet Union to underwrite the defense of Egypt, Nasir bequeathed his heirs a priceless surety— a Soviet guarantee never to permit Egypt to be defeated by Israel, to restrict Israel to a "no-win" policy. This was the lesson of 1967 and 1970. Egypt was thus endowed with a new and enlarged margin of security and diplomatic flexibility. This de facto alliance is the quintessential feature of Egypt's foreign policy. It has given Egyptian leaders policy options they would otherwise not have and enabled them, notwithstanding the strains arising out of dependency, to pursue a more independent foreign policy.

Because of Soviet ambitions and irrespective of divergencies between Moscow and Cairo on specific issues, Nasir was able to maneuver the Soviet Union into a position on the Arab-Israeli conflict—the issue of paramount concern to him after 1967— wherein it would not accept any proposal that failed to meet with Cairo's approval. Thus, in any discussions with the United States,

Egypt retained a veto over Soviet freedom of action. Finally, Nasir enlisted the Soviet Union in Egypt's effort to overcome centuries of backwardness and move toward modernity—in the military sphere, of course, but, to a lesser yet important degree, in the economic one as well.

Chapter Five

SADAT'S UNEASY ALLIANCE WITH
THE SOVIET UNION

NASIR's death ushered in a period of uncertainty in Soviet-Egyptian relations. Though he had appointed Sadat as vice-president, Nasir had not designated an heir. His modus operandi had been to concentrate power in his own hands and operate through his personal secretariat. He left no political tradition and no obvious center of decisionmaking authority, but only power diffused among the oligarchs of the military, the ASU, the secret police, and the intelligence services. Moscow proceeded warily. The round-robins of visits and exchanges of missions were ill-suited to penetrating this idiosyncratic and changeable network of power. In Egypt, as elsewhere in the Third World, Moscow relied primarily on close ties with the official wielders of power. Such secret hopes as it may have harbored of encouraging a more ideologically and institutionally congenial leadership were not allowed to interfere with the pursuit of concrete state interests, which were military, diplomatic, and economic in character.

The Soviets quickly reaffirmed their friendship for the collective leadership in Cairo. A delegation of government and CPSU leaders led by Premier Kosygin and including First Deputy Defense Minister Marshal M. Zakharov and Col.-General V. Okunev (a specialist on missiles and air defense), attended the funeral and met several times with Egyptian leaders. The Soviets comported themselves "as masters of prudence" and conveyed Moscow's deep interest in a stable Egypt and its assurance of non-interference.[1] The joint communiqué issued on October 3 stated that both governments "have always regarded friendly relations between themselves as a permanent factor unaffected by changes

---

[1] Edward R. F. Sheehan, "Who Rules Egypt?" *NYT Magazine*, November 29, 1970. According to Haykal, Kosygin, shocked by the demonstration of public emotionality at Nasir's funeral, told him: "You must try to control things. The leadership must get a grip on things. If you allow yourselves to surrender to grief in this way anything may happen. The whole country could collapse," *The Sunday Times Weekly Review*, April 27, 1975.

in the international situation" and that they were resolved to continue strengthening their relationship.[2] Moscow agreed to provide new support and accelerate arms deliveries contracted for 1971, in order to show that it stood by Egypt.[3] The only curious feature of the communiqué was the absence of any reference to Resolution 242 or the need for a political settlement, a standard inclusion in previous and subsequent communiqués. The omission may have been accepted by Moscow in order to strengthen the position of those who controlled the state organs of power and professed strict adherence to Nasir's foreign policy line, and thereby to undercut a pro-Western oriented group, gathering around Zakariya Muhyi al-Din and supported by Haykal. In a bit of palace intrigue, Haykal had asked Muhyi al-Din, who had been politically shelved by Nasir in early 1968, to write the eulogy of Nasir for *Al-Ahram*, thus placing him again in the public eye. But Muhyi al-Din failed to catch the public's interest, and Haykal chose to resign as minister of information and national guidance on October 3 and return to full-time work as editor of *Al-Ahram*. Moscow's long-standing dislike of Haykal, its proposal of October 15 for a normalization of the Middle East situation, and its reaffirmation of the need for a peaceful settlement in the Soviet-Egyptian communiqué in December 1970, all lent credence to the view that the omission was an instance of Soviet compliance on a matter relating to internal political jockeying in Cairo and not a change in Soviet foreign policy.

The Soviet government's appointment on October 8 of Vladimir Vinogradov as ambassador to replace Sergei Vinogradov (no relation), who died in August 1970, showed its desire to maintain cordial relations with Egypt. Vladimir Vinogradov had dealt with the Egyptians since his promotion to the post of deputy foreign minister in 1967 and was one of the most respected men in the Soviet foreign service, a thorough professional.

THE EMERGENCE OF SADAT

On October 5 the Higher Executive Committee of the ASU Central Committee unanimously recommended the appointment of

[2] FBIS/United Arab Republic, October 5, 1970, pp. G1-G2.

[3] See Sadat's speech to the ASU National Congress on November 12, 1970. BBC/ME/3534/A/1 (November 13, 1970); and the one to a political rally in Tanta on January 4, 1971. *Speeches by President Anwar El Sadat, September 1970–March 1971* (Cairo: Ministry of Information, 1971), p. 118.

Anwar al-Sadat as president. Born in 1918, he joined the army in the 1930s, befriended Nasir, became a member of the "Free Officers," and held a number of high but largely honorific posts under Nasir. Never an intimate of Nasir, he was generally regarded as undistinguished and inoffensive, qualities that appealed to the oligarchs who aspired to wield power through their respective institutional strongholds. Sadat was an acceptable compromise because he had not made any enemies and had no power base of his own. Often referred to as an "Egyptian Harry Truman," he was a man of humble origins from whom little was expected. Originally intended as a slight, the accolade turned out to be remarkably prophetic. Sadat quickly superseded Nasir as the butt of the mordant political jokes that delight Egyptians. According to one joke, God was admitting deserving people into Heaven and asked each prospective applicant to prove his identity by referring to his outstanding characteristic. First, Nasir was recognized by his claim that he could talk for four hours at a time. Next Field Marshal 'Amir (who committed suicide after the defeat in 1967) said he smoked hashish, and he was admitted. When it was Sadat's turn, he started by saying, "There is nothing outstanding about me," "Ah, yes," interrupted God, "you must be Sadat," and admitted him.

Sadat was sworn in as president on October 17. 'Abd al-Muhsin Abu an-Nur was designated secretary-general of the ASU; Ali Sabri and Husayn Shafi'i (also a charter member of the original Revolutionary Command Council and long an intimate of Nasir) were appointed vice-presidents. In general, the design was continuity. The Cabinet was virtually the same one Nasir had appointed in 1968. Sadat acted to ameliorate some of Egypt's pressing problems and to broaden the base of his popular support. As his prime minister, he appointed Dr. Mahmud Fawzi, the 72-year-old veteran diplomat. A brilliant, thoughtful man with the bent of a philosopher and the tongue of a poet, the widely respected Fawzi had extensive diplomatic experience. He set about reorganizing the governmental administration with a view toward improving efficiency, stimulating production, and raising the standard of public services, especially in Cairo. The Sadat-Fawzi leadership wooed the lower classes: it lowered the prices of staples such as tea, sugar, and cooking oil, repaired roads, and made gestures toward alleviating the heavily burdened system of public transportation. It also started a cautious policy of reconciliation with the bourgeoisie by dropping the sequestration cases pending against private individuals and families, and by ordering the return of some of the land and property seized illegally and/or arbitrarily in the past. DeNasirization had begun, though in the name of Nasirism.

THE CEASE-FIRE IMBROGLIO

The foreign policy problem that required Sadat's immediate attention was the cease-fire. The United States, convinced of the validity of Israeli charges that the Soviet Union had violated the standstill provisions of the cease-fire, withdrew from the Four Power talks. Also, suspecting Moscow of complicity in the Syrian intervention in the Jordanian-Palestinian fighting the month before, it took a hard look at its previous assessments of Soviet intentions.

On October 8 the Soviet Ministry of Foreign Affairs accused the United States of "spreading various falsehoods" about the USSR and "alleging that the Soviet Union was 'violating its commitments' in connection with the cease-fire in the Suez Canal zone."[4] Declaring that the United States was trying "to mislead world public opinion and to shift the responsibility for the situation that has arisen in the Middle East on to the Soviet Union and the Arab countries," the ministry maintained that "the Soviet Union did not take part in drafting any of the cease-fire terms in the Suez Canal zone," that these had been advanced by the United States government. The implication was clear: the Soviet Union had not reneged on any obligation because it had not been a party to the cease-fire agreement. It also denied that Soviet personnel were manning missile sites in the canal area. The next day Rogers said that though the Soviet government had not actually signed any cease-fire document, its resort to legal hair-splitting to justify actions that undermined an agreement it had implicitly accepted could only destabilize an already tense situation.

Riyad told the United Nations that the United States had misled Nasir, agreeing not to send Israel any more planes, and was in fact conniving with Israel to build up Israeli positions in

[4] "Statement of Soviet Foreign Ministry," *Soviet News*, No. 5564 (October 13, 1970), 13; 19.

Sinai.[5] Egypt refused to concede any wrong-doing or withdraw a single missile, and Israel refused to participate in the Jarring talks until all the missiles were withdrawn. Despite the ensuing stalemate, neither side renewed the fighting. On November 4, Riyad announced that Egypt would extend the cease-fire for another three months, until February 5, 1971. Absorbed with the problems of an orderly succession and developing a political constituency of his own, Sadat used the time to strengthen Egypt's air defense system and train Egyptian personnel.

SABRI'S VISIT TO MOSCOW

Ali Sabri's visit to the Soviet Union on December 20 was front page news in Cairo.[6] The high level government and party delegation included Deputy Prime Minister and Minister of Industry 'Aziz Sidqi, Deputy Prime Minister and Foreign Minister Mahmud Riyad, and War Minister Muhammad Fawzi. *Pravda* reported that discussions had started on December 21 and published the text of the speeches of Kosygin and Sabri.[7] In his welcoming speech Kosygin noted that the Middle East had become "one of the most dangerous breeding grounds for the threat of war in the world" and cautioned "the Israeli extremists" not to believe they could strike a bargain that would enable them to retain any Arab lands.

Amidst reports that the Soviet Union had increased the number of Soviet personnel in Egypt to almost 20,000,[8] and that Boris N. Ponomarev, the CPSU's specialist on relations with foreign Communist and "progressive" parties, who had returned from Egypt on December 20, had promised full Soviet support "under all circumstances,"[9] the Kremlin talks assumed particular importance. Careful planning had gone into the Sabri visit. Ponomarev had concluded a ten-day party-to-party visit to Cairo in time to return to Moscow several hours before the Sabri delegation. While his visit purported to focus on party contacts, the Middle East no doubt figured prominently.

In view of the conjunction of the Ponomarev and Sabri visits

---

[5] *NYT*, October 17, 1970; BBC/ME/3519/A/7-13 (October 27, 1970).

[6] *Al-Ahram*, December 20, 1970.   [7] *Pravda*, December 22, 1970.

[8] *The Times* (London), December 17, 1970.

[9] *NYT*, December 13, 1970.

and their apparent interrelationship, the joint communiqués issued on December 20 and December 26, 1970, from Cairo and Moscow respectively, bear comparison.[10] Both contained the perennials: criticism of the United States, Israeli culpability for Middle East tensions, and Soviet support for the Arab cause. There were a number of important similarities: 1) a commitment to the "full implementation" of Resolution 242 as the way to a "fair and lasting peace in the Middle East," and reiteration of the need for "a peaceful settlement" (in marked contrast to their exclusion from the October 3 communiqué, issued shortly after Nasir's funeral); 2) an emphasis on better party-to-party relations; and 3) an expressed readiness of the Soviet Union "to continue to extend all kinds of support" to Egypt in its struggle against imperialism (the promise of greater military assistance). Egyptian newspapers attributed particular significance to Marshal Grechko's decision not to attend a Warsaw Pact ministerial meeting in order to participate in these Soviet-Egyptian talks.[11] On his return from Moscow, Sidqi reported that the Soviet Union had agreed to increase the exports of certain commodities, including 40,000 additional tons of steel ingots for the sheetrolling plant in Helwan, and assorted petroleum products; to join Egypt in carrying out a number of military production projects; and to sign a long-term trade and aid agreement during Sidqi's next visit to the USSR in March 1971.[12] These agreements were important in suggesting that the USSR and Egypt were making a smooth transition to the post-Nasir period and that Soviet aid was being liberally used to consolidate Moscow's standing with the new rulers in Cairo.

The differences in the communiqués, which admittedly may have stemmed from the different focus of each mission, still are worth noting. First, whereas the Cairo communiqué specified that the ASU's political line for bringing about "the social transformation of Egyptian society" was "on the course of socialism," the Moscow communiqué (drawn up by officials acting in a governmental capacity) made no mention of socialism, noting merely that Egypt was "fully resolved to advance firmly and consistently

[10] For the Cairo communiqué see, BBC/ME/3566/E/1-3 (December 22, 1970); for the Moscow one see, FBIS/USSR, December 28, 1970, pp. A1-A3.

[11] Al-Akhbar, December 23, 1970, as quoted in FBIS/United Arab Republic, December 23, 1970, p. G2.

[12] FBIS/United Arab Republic, December 28, 1970, p. G14.

along the road of socio-economic development with the aim of ensuring the people's welfare." The latter formulation fore-shadowed Sadat's policy of de facto deNasirization, a modest but noticeable retreat from nationalization and collectivization. Sadat was cautiously discarding Nasir's socially divisive policies and courting those technocratic and managerial groups who preferred a more relaxed and pragmatic governmental hand on the reins of power. Ponomarev was given reassurances in the interests of satisfying the Soviets ideologically about the commonality of out-look on the party-to-party level, but the Moscow communiqué put the Soviet leaders on notice that Sadat intended to slow down, and in certain instances even reverse, the trend toward "scientific socialism." Second, the December 26 communiqué de-voted somewhat less attention to the Palestinian question. It assuredly did not go as far in directly linking the Soviet bloc with the struggle of the Arab and Palestinian peoples as the December 20 communiqué, whose formulation on this point may have re-flected Ponomarev's insistence on a strong statement in order to answer Peking's charge that the USSR was selling out the Pales-tinian cause. In the Moscow meeting, diplomatic concerns pre-vailed. Whereas in party-to-party communiqués the Egyptians were prepared to cater to Soviet ideological necessities, they skill-fully avoided exposing their objectives to possible misunder-standing abroad or undermining the import of their private soundings in Washington (for example, in late December, at the time of Sabri's visit in Moscow, Sadat had passed the word to the State Department: "I want peace; move fast").[13]

Sabri's visit was acclaimed a success by Moscow.[14] It had cemented existing ties, reassured the Soviet leadership of con-tinuity in Egyptian policy, and paved the way for Podgornyi's visit.

The Soviet president arrived on January 13, 1971, with a strong economic delegation (there were no identifiable military men in the group) to inaugurate the official opening of the Aswan High Dam. In the communiqué of January 19 the Soviet govern-ment committed itself to two new major economic projects—the electrification of rural areas and the reclamation of 900,000 acres of new land with water drawn from Lake Nasir.[15] The importance

[13] Author's interview, December 1974.
[14] For example, *Izvestiia*, December 30, 1970.
[15] FBIS/USSR, January 20, 1971, pp. A1-A3.

of party contacts was stressed, and the two sides agreed to "an exchange of delegations of party functionaries on all levels," a development clearly advanced by Moscow. The USSR supported Egypt on the Middle East, and both sides called for a settlement in accordance with strict implementation of Resolution 242, noting "with satisfaction . . . the friendly ties and fruitful cooperation in the political, economic, *defense* and other fields" (emphasis added). For Egypt the occasion signified the inestimable utility of Soviet friendship. The Soviet Union also had reasons for satisfaction: it had helped to construct the greatest engineering achievement in the Middle East since the pyramids; its military had acquired a valuable network of bases; and it had established good relations with the new Egyptian leadership, all of whom were familiar faces, though not politically proven leaders. Soviet prestige had never been higher. Yet as is so often the case in the Middle East, nothing fails like success.

THE POLITICS OF REOPENING THE SUEZ CANAL

After early 1968 the possibility of reopening the canal was frequently discussed as part of an interim settlement that would lead eventually to a full settlement. The decision of the Israeli government on December 28, 1970, to resume indirect talks with Egypt through Jarring, revived hopes for progress on this matter. Israel had reluctantly recognized that Egypt would not pull back any missiles to the pre-August 7 line and had agreed to deal with Jarring. Departing from its stand of early 1968, Israel yielded to a combination of U.S. pressure (Washington no longer felt so strongly about keeping the canal closed, as the Vietnam war slowly wound down) and the conviction of leaders like Dayan who believed that diplomacy would prove more conducive than fighting to ending the state of war with the Egyptians, though the Israeli Cabinet was far from united on the precise concessions it was prepared to make.

On February 4 Sadat coupled an expected announcement of a thirty-day extension of the cease-fire until March 7 with a surprise proposal for reopening the canal.[16] After holding informal

16 *Speeches by President Anwar El Sadat*, p. 253. The idea of reopening the canal and establishing a demilitarized zone on the east bank had been raised in private talks that Dayan held with Kissinger, Rogers, and Sisco during a visit to Washington in November 1970. However, since the suggestion was not

talks in Cairo with Donald Bergus, Sadat expressed a readiness "to start at once in clearing" the Suez Canal to reopen it for international navigation, provided Israel withdrew its troops from the eastern bank and agreed to implement Resolution 242. What Sadat apparently had in mind was a preliminary Israeli withdrawal to El Arish.[17] In return he would reopen the canal within six months and prolong the cease-fire to enable Jarring to complete a settlement, after which Israeli shipping, too, would be permitted free passage. However, he ruled out the one condition that Israel had continually raised to test Egypt's good faith, that of a formal peace treaty.

The Israeli government responded cautiously, saying it had no intention of withdrawing to the lines of June 4, 1967, but asking for clarification on the questions of borders and refugees. It wanted to retain Sharm El-Sheikh, offering to lease it from Egypt, and to deal separately with the issues of withdrawal from Egyptian-held territory and withdrawal from the rest of the occupied Arab areas. Golan, part of the West Bank, and Jerusalem were regarded as nonnegotiable. But Israel was on the spot. Sadat's proposal led Rogers to suggest again, on March 16, 1971, as he first had in December 1969, that in the interest of a Middle East settlement Israel pull out of all lands occupied in 1967, except for some minor border adjustments. While Sadat's proposal of February 4 could be interpreted as a gambit to intensify American pressure on Israel, it could also have been a step toward a reconciliation with Washington, and a possible reassessment of relations with Moscow. These moves foreshadowed the spreading web of Sadat's diplomacy.

There were at least three prominent flies in Sadat's diplomatic ointment: his foreign minister, the Palestinians, and the Soviets. Riyad bitterly opposed any interim arrangement, arguing that it would become a permanent line of demarcation. But Sadat side-stepped Riyad, and dealt several times directly with Bergus and through Haykal on this delicate matter. These explorations, which continued throughout the spring, with Bergus arranging visits to Cairo for Sisco and Rogers, kindled a restrained opti-

---

an Israeli cabinet decision but only Dayan's personal view, and since Washington was then committed to the resumption of the Jarring talks, the matter had not been pursued.

[17] See Arnaud de Borchgrave's interview with Sadat. *International Herald Tribune*, February 15, 1971.

mism among top State Department officials, who believed a breakthrough was within reach. The White House was more skeptical, partly because it was less willing to pressure Israel as long as the Soviets were so heavily involved in Egypt.

The Palestinians were apprehensive about Sadat's diplomatic initiative. Though their political clout in Arab circles had diminished since their battering at the hands of King Husayn the previous September, they still could do mischief. On February 28 Sadat assured them that he would never conclude a separate peace with Israel or abandon the Palestinian people. He linked his strategy to Nasir's: to deepen the commitment of friends and isolate Israel internationally.[18] His reassurances, however, were not comforting to the Palestinians, who were still smarting over Nasir's acceptance of a cease-fire the previous August without consulting them. Sadat pleaded for understanding—and time. Citing the Arab proverb, "He who has his hand in the fire is unlike him who has his hand in the water," Sadat said that "we have our hands in the fire" and are speaking out and acting, while others "have their hands in the water" and are talking but not acting.[19] He faced a formidable challenge, trying to protect his fragile domestic base and his links to the Arab radical regimes, while groping also for ways to dispel past suspicions and improve relations with Saudi Arabia and the Persian Gulf shaykhdoms, his prospective bankers and rulers who were more congenial to his own political outlook and style.

The Soviets required different handling. In the absence of an Israeli withdrawal, Sadat was committed to resume fighting, if not immediately at the expiration of the cease-fire then in the not too distant future. He needed assurance that the Soviet Union would back him up. On March 1 Sadat flew secretly to Moscow for two days of intensive talks. He revealed the circumstances of the visit on March 7, during a nationwide address announcing the nonrenewal of the cease-fire. The meeting in Moscow, which had been agreed upon on February 27, had been held, he said, at the suggestion of the Soviet leaders.[20] "These leaders had sent to me saying that they considered circumstances necessitated consultations between us. I decided to travel to Moscow, myself, without announcement. I left Cairo on Monday,

18 *Speeches by President Anwar El Sadat*, pp. 280-281.
19 *Ibid.*, p. 276.
20 CPR, No. 5567, March 8, 1971, p. 14.

March 1st, at dawn, and returned in the evening of Tuesday, March 2nd."[21]

If we grant the accuracy of Sadat's account—no mention of the visit has ever appeared in the Soviet Union—the conclusion seems warranted that Soviet leaders were uneasy over Sadat's intentions and wanted to be clear that they and he understood the available options and their implications. The Kremlin was not keen on a new war in the Middle East: It was then completing final preparations for the CPSU's Twenty-fourth Congress, which was to set out formally a policy of promoting détente with the United States, and it wished to avoid a breakdown of the cease-fire. But it was also uneasy over how far Sadat was willing to go to improve relations with the United States. Soviet diplomats must have been following the internal debate, triggered on February 19 by a series of Haykal's articles, on whether any settlement was possible without the active support of the United States. This motive for a radical improvement in Egyptian-U.S. relations, coupled with Sadat's deNasirization decrees in December 1970 that signified a shift in Egypt's domestic orientation, required Moscow to scrutinize the situation in a new light.

It can as plausibly be argued that Sadat took the initiative in going to Moscow, risking remonstrance from opponents, because he had to obtain assurance of continued support and persuade a skeptical Soviet leadership of his need to end the cease-fire. Though unhappy over the latter, Soviet leaders accepted Sadat's assessment that his credibility at home depended on it. The reports of increased arms shipments in March and April[22] seem to indicate that Moscow granted Sadat's request for additional arms and planes, including a small number of improved MiG-21s, to demonstrate Soviet support and to allay Cairo's uneasiness that a U.S.-Soviet détente might be at Egypt's expense.

Coming so soon after Sadat's proposal of February 4 on reopen-

---

[21] *Speeches by Anwar El Sadat*, p. 292.

[22] ARR, No. 5 (March 1–15, 1971), p. 149; *Egyptian Gazette*, March 23, 1971; *NYT*, April 11, 1971, for example, reported that Soviet freighters had brought about 150 MiGs, 20 Sukhoi-7 fighter-bombers, and that the air defense system had been thickened in the interior of Egypt. A Soviet airlift in early April brought 30 transports in Cairo West airport: "The airlift represented the first flights to Egypt of the Antonov-22 transports, the largest of the Soviet air force" (the Antonov-22s were used extensively in the October 1973 war). See also, Edward H. Kolcum, "Soviets Spur Arms Flow to Egypt," *Aviation Week and Space Technology*, 94, No. 16 (April 19, 1971), 14-16.

ing the canal, Haykal's articles entitled "Reflections on the Great Conflict" attracted wide attention. Haykal ruminated about the unthinkable—the existence of the state of Israel—and its implications for Egyptian policy. Whereas he saw the liquidation of the consequences of 1967 as a sound, realizable objective, he maintained that the removal of "the consequences of the 1948 aggression by removing Israel altogether" was not.[23] His implication was clear: the existence of the state of Israel was a political fact that could not be realistically ignored or undone in the foreseeable future. For the moment, therefore, all efforts should concentrate on undoing the 1967 defeat. Even the Soviet Union, Haykal observed, for all its generous support, stood behind Egypt only in its quest for this objective, "but none other." Quoting Nasir, he expressed dismay that Egyptian troops were the only ones meaningfully engaging the enemy and they "could not go beyond the Egyptian border and Gaza in the most favorable circumstances" without precipitating a reaction from the United States that Egypt was in no position to handle.[24] As for the eastern front (Lebanon, Syria, Jordan), it was non-existent. The Palestinians, while commendably militant, were militarily incapable of affecting the strategic outcome. In another article Haykal pointed out that the United Nations cannot "achieve anything" because of the balance of power between the superpowers and their competing interests where the Middle East was concerned: "We must reconcile ourselves to this truth, whether we like it or not, because it is the prevailing law by reason of the fact that these two powers possess the greatest economic and political power and the greatest influencing power."[25] The key to success was "to neutralize the United States somehow." The United States should not, contrary to what so many argued, be viewed as the enemy in the same way that Israel was. If the American factor was to be handled, differentiation was essential:

> The method we apply in our conflict with the United States must not and cannot be a military one. If we allow this conflict to run this way, we will face the danger of exposing ourselves to what is beyond our capacity, bearing in mind that much more powerful countries would not go to war with the

[23] CPR, No. 5558, February 26, 1971, p. 3.
[24] Ibid., p. 4.
[25] CPR, No. 5564, March 5, 1971, p. 1.

United States, the Soviet Union and China being cases in point; and we would be allowing Israel to get exactly what she wants.

What we must do is to embarrass the United States by every possible means to push her away from the fighting front and we have the means by which to exert political pressure on the USA [i.e. the prospect of reopening the Canal and Arab oil]. The Egyptian people can defeat Israel if the United States of America is not with her on the front. If we allow Israel to bring the USA to the battlefield with her, we must then prepare ourselves for a long drawn battle which might continue for scores of years. I shall continue to believe that extremists in this regard are advocates of maximum capitulation.[26]

In early March, after Sadat ended the cease-fire, Haykal wrote "A Tribute to the Men," which praised the Egyptian army but said it faced a hopeless task. The net effect of his article was to discount the utility of the military option as long as only Egypt fought.[27] In such circumstances, the United States, not the Soviet Union, was the key to a Middle East settlement. Haykal also articulated a truth that was rarely mentioned in the Egyptian press, namely, that in 1956 it was the United States's opposition to the three-power attack on Egypt that had been instrumental in saving Egypt, and not the USSR's; not until nine (it was actually eight) days after the attack, when the tide had already turned, did the Soviet Union issue an ultimatum.[28] In 1967, though Nasir greatly appreciated the Soviet stand, he still did not cut off all contacts with the United States. In 1970 to help polarize American-Israeli differences, he had accepted Rogers' initiative, which had been overshadowed temporarily by the fracas over the emplacement of missiles in the canal area. With this hurdle now passed, the importance of the U.S. attitude was a crucial variable.

Haykal's opponents had a field day. They took him to task for "defeatism," arguing that he raised questions that did not have to be answered seriously, to wit, whether Egypt should go to war with the United States, and that furthermore he had

[26] *Ibid.*, p. 3.

[27] CPR, No. 5570, March 12, 1971, pp. 1-5.

[28] CPR, No. 5585, March 26, 1971, p. 3. For information on the precise timing and responses of the Soviet government during the Suez crisis, see Oles M. Smolansky, *The Soviet Union and the Arab East under Khrushchev* (Lewisburg: Bucknell University Press, 1974), pp. 51-53.

exaggerated the extent to which Washington could be neutralized or pressured into making Israel disgorge its conquests.[29] Ihsan 'Abd al-Quddus, for one, charged that the impossibility of war had apparently become an obsession with Haykal and "driven him to abandon completely the line he set for himself of writing only objectively . . ."; a recourse to war need not negate diplomatic and political efforts, indeed, it might even be salutary, and the objective of liberating all Arab lands was still valid and attainable. Ahmad Baha' al-Din said that Soviet national interests required support for the Arab countries so as to keep them from being used as Western military bases and that the USSR would continue to be an active friend in the ongoing international struggle against the United States, even if there were an improvement in U.S.-Soviet relations in other regions of the world.[30]

While Haykal's articles provoked controversy in Cairo and contumely from Moscow for the attempt by "certain Arab newspapers" to mislead Arab public opinion about the possible "new course" of the United States toward a Middle East settlement,[31] Sadat's proposal had caused a serious rift between Washington and Jerusalem. At a press conference on March 16, three days before a meeting with Israel's foreign minister, Rogers said that guarantees of Israel's security "do not necessarily require the acquisition of territory," that a combination of "insubstantial" border adjustments, demilitarization, and international guarantees, including "an international peacekeeping force—with a provision that it would be of a continuing nature, that it could not be removed by any unilateral decision, and that it would be located in areas that were critical—would provide . . . the greatest possible security for the parties."[32] The Israeli government bitterly rejected Rogers' scheme for a settlement founded on international guarantees.[33] (A month earlier it had refused to commit

[29] For example, Ibrahim Said in *Al-Musawwar*, as quoted in CPR Supplement, March 11, 1971; Ihsan 'Abd al-Quddus in *Akhbar al-Yawm*, as quoted in CPR, No. 5579, March 20, 1971; and Abd al-Hadi Nasif, a member of the ASU Secretariat in *Al-Gumhuriya* as quoted in FBIS/United Arab Republic, March 18, 1971, p. G2.

[30] Ahmad Baha' al-Din, as quoted in CPR Supplement, March 25, 1971, pp. 1-4.

[31] *Pravda*, March 20, 1971. [32] *NYT*, March 17, 1971.

[33] Prime Minister Golda Meir told the Knesset: "It is our experience in defending ourselves that has brought us to recognize that no guarantees of

itself to a Jarring memorandum, sent to Egypt and Israel, calling on the two parties to agree simultaneously to take on two commitments: the withdrawal of Israeli forces from Arab territories and the establishment of peace.)

Cairo took note of Washington's favorable attitude toward Egypt's terms for reopening the canal.[34] Sadat seemed within reach of a palpable breakthrough with the United States. His diplomacy, a skillful mixture of flexibility and obstinacy, of caution and threat,[35] of obeisance to Arab unity[36] and stimulus to Egyptian development, contrasted in subtlety and range with the narrow scope of Nasir's final years.

A Sisco visit to Cairo in late March had proved promising enough for Rogers to plan a meeting with Sadat in early May, and for Sadat to state in his May 1 speech at Helwan that he would welcome Rogers. Generally regarded as without standing in the White House in his capacity as Secretary of State, Rogers was overshadowed in foreign affairs by Dr. Henry A. Kissinger and the National Security Council staff he drove with Calvinistic discipline and intensity; and he was isolated from most of the significant international negotiations conducted by the Nixon administration. However, a highly respected lawyer, Rogers be-

---

any kind can be regarded as a substitute for defensible boundaries that we can defend by ourselves," *ibid.* The following day she struck an even stronger note: "We cannot trust Rogers' offer, even if it is proposed in good faith. . . . There are certain things beyond which our American friends have to realize we will not go," *NYT*, March 18, 1971.

From a military point of view Israel's reluctance to permit Egyptian troops to cross the canal related not so much to a possible breach by the Egyptians as to the problem that would arise if the Soviets crossed the canal. What would be the value of international guarantees then? Israel "is being asked to forego her trump card and her best possible line of defense. She is being pressed to give up a line that . . . gives her the best possible defense posture, given a state of war which continues. Withdrawal from the canal line without a peace agreement or a cessation of the state of belligerence means for Israel a move toward suicide, militarily speaking," *The Jerusalem Post*, April 20, 1971.

[34] *Egyptian Gazette*, April 3, 1971.

[35] A governmental decree invested all the governors of Egypt's 25 governorates with military powers for mobilizing and preparing for the war effort (a similar decree had been passed in February 1969, but applied only to the canal zone). *Egyptian Gazette*, March 26, 1971.

[36] On March 29, 1971, in a gesture to the Palestinians and to his critics in the Arab world, Sadat restored radio broadcasting rights to the "Voice of Assifa," the Al Fatah program, *NYT*, March 30, 1971.

lieved that the negotiating skill that had served him well in business would enable him to make his mark in diplomacy with a Middle East settlement.

Riyad went to Moscow (April 15–20) to inform Soviet leaders of the status of the U.S.-Egyptian dialogue and the upcoming Rogers visit. In an interview with the Moscow correspondent of MENA (Middle East News Agency), he declared that "the main issue now is liberation of all the occupied Arab territories . . . and not the reopening of the canal," thus closing ranks with the Soviets and also giving the most uncompromising twist to Sadat's plan.[37] The communiqué conveyed the message that Cairo and Moscow shared "a full identity of views on all questions discussed, above all, on Israel's aggression against Arab states" and that they "agreed on further joint steps to normalize the situation and strengthen peace and security in the Middle East."[38] Notwithstanding Riyad's reassurance, Moscow betrayed a certain nervousness as the date of Rogers' visit to Cairo approached. *Pravda* accused Rogers of being "hypocritical," of only pretending sympathy for Egypt while arming Israel;[39] and Soviet officials accused the United States of promoting its own interests by conducting secret bilateral negotiations with Egypt and Israel for a reopening of the canal.[40]

Rogers' visit to the Middle East—the first by an American Secretary of State since 1953—began on April 26. However, before he arrived in Cairo on May 4, an Egyptian contretemps had made a shambles of a once-promising overture.

THE SOVIET-EGYPTIAN TREATY OF MAY 27, 1971

The origins of the Soviet-Egyptian Treaty of Friendship and Cooperation are to be found in the nexus of the domestic upheaval that shook Egypt's power structure in early May and the politically corrosive eddies that accompanied the movement toward an interim Middle East settlement. The domestic components were especially crucial, and they shed light on the agents and parameters of the Soviet-Egyptian influence relationship.

On April 17 Sadat returned from Tripoli and announced that

37 FBIS/United Arab Republic, April 19, 1971, p. G1.
38 FBIS/USSR, April 21, 1971, pp. B1-B2.
39 Quoted in the *Jerusalem Post*, April 26, 1971.
40 Quoted in the *Jerusalem Post*, April 22, 1971.

Egypt, Libya, and Syria planned to establish a Federation of Arab Republics in accordance with a proposal made by Qadhdhafi in February. Though Sadat had originally requested five months to evaluate the proposal, he decided at Tripoli to proceed with it immediately. At a series of meetings of the ASU Central Committee on April 25–27 to discuss the statutes of the proposed federation, Sabri challenged Sadat, ostensibly objecting that Sadat had made too many concessions but really trying to unite the oligarchs against him, to settle the rulership of Egypt. Thus forewarned of a quickly coalescing opposition, Sadat moved with unexpected forcefulness. He determined to remove Sabri and told the Soviet ambassador so, impressing on him that it was a purely domestic affair and not intended as anti-Soviet. But Moscow was not convinced.[41] On May 2, two days before Rogers was due to arrive, Sadat dismissed Sabri from the vice-presidency, his first major step as president to secure his position. On May 4 *Pravda* reported Sabri's dismissal without comment, under the inconspicuous heading "Organizational Changes in the UAR Government." For the next two weeks the Soviet media said little about the deposed or the developments.

Sadat justified the dismissal and his discussions with Rogers to the ASU and Cabinet on May 10. Two days later, accompanied by General Fawzi, he visited the Suez Canal front area, where he consulted with field commanders and addressed the troops. Having convinced himself of the army's loyalty, the next day Sadat forced the resignation of Sha'rawi Gum'ah, Deputy Prime Minister and Minister of Interior, long regarded as one of the most powerful men in government. A mass resignation of others in the anti-Sadat cabal, who thought thereby to demonstrate Sadat's lack of support and force his resignation, only resulted in their incarceration.[42] In the next few days, Sadat jailed dozens of government and party officials. The list was a "Who's Who" of the Nasir era: Lt. General Muhammad Fawzi, War Minister;

[41] This was revealed by Sadat after the October War. FBIS/Egypt, March 30, 1976, p. D.8.

[42] For an intriguing account by the former chief of Egyptian intelligence, Ahmed Kamel, of the personalities and issues involved in the events of May 1971, see, P. J. Vatikiotis, "Egypt's Politics of Conspiracy," *Survey*, 18, No. 2 (Spring 1972), 83-96. See also, *Sadat's Speech of May 20, 1971* (Cairo: Ministry of Information, n.d.); and the statement of the Public Prosecutor on July 22: BBC/ME/3746/A/1-9 (July 28, 1971) and BBC/ME/3748/A/11-14 (July 30, 1971).

Sami Sharaf, Minister of State for Presidential Affairs and long responsible for Nasir's personal intelligence and security organization; Muhammad Fa'iq, Minister of Information; 'Abd al-Muhsin Abu an-Nur, head of the ASU; Ahmed Kamel, Chief of Intelligence; Labib Shuqayr, Speaker of the National Assembly. In all, 91 former dignitaries were held for trial for "high treason" on August 25, 1971. In a nationwide address on May 14, Sadat alleged that the conspirators had planned to create violent demonstrations on May 14–15 and seize power under the guise of defending public order. On May 20 he spoke in even greater detail about the plot, the endemic bugging of the secret police (no surprise to anyone in Cairo), the irregularities that had been perpetrated in ASU elections, and even the pilfering of damaging evidence from Nasir's personal safe shortly after his death.

What emerged from these extraordinary developments was the political ineptness of Sadat's opponents and the Pharaonic ease with which Sadat elicited loyalty and juggled officials. Nasir's old entourage had controlled every institution of political consequence, yet they had been unable to unseat Sadat. The purge impelled Sadat to concentrate on safeguarding his position and recruiting reliable political adherents. It also gave rise in Moscow to an unprecedented initiative.

After trying unsuccessfully for forty-eight hours to see Sadat, the Soviet ambassador saw Riyad on May 19. Two days later, when Vinogradov was finally able to see Sadat for the first time after the political upheaval, he raised the question of a visit to Cairo by a high-ranking Soviet delegation.[43] Late in the evening of May 23, Cairo Radio announced: "At the invitation of the UAR President and Chairman of the ASU, Anwar al-Sadat, the member of the Politburo of the Central Committee of the CPSU and Chairman of the USSR Supreme Soviet Presidium, Nikolai Viktorovich Podgornyi, will come to the UAR in the next few days on an unofficial and friendly visit." The visit may have been unofficial but it was high-powered and all business.

Up to this point, the Soviet-Egyptian relationship had operated on an ad hoc though continuing basis, but on May 27, 1971, its character was formalized with the signing of the Soviet-Egyptian Treaty of Friendship and Cooperation.[44] The treaty was gener-

[43] BBC/ME/3691/i (May 24, 1971). Also, ARR, No. 10 (May 16–31, 1971), 272.

[44] For provisions of the treaty, see *Pravda*, May 28, 1971; translated in

ally interpreted in the West as signifying both the increase and institutionalization of Soviet influence in Egypt.[45] The very fact that the Soviet Union was willing to commit itself explicitly to the defense of Egypt (something it had not done for any non-Communist country of the Third World) suggested that Moscow believed it would receive an important quid pro quo in terms of influence over Egyptian policy.[46] Articles 7 and 8 of the treaty confirmed this impression. Article 7 called for consultations reg-

---

CDSP, 23, No. 21 (June 22, 1971), 204; or FBIS/United Arab Republic, May 28, 1971, pp. G3-G5.

[45] For example, on October 19, 1971, Walter Z. Laqueur told a congressional committee that the treaty "undoubtedly constitutes a step forward from the Soviet point of view. President Sadat had to sign a document which stated that the UAR set itself the aim of reconstructing Egyptian society along socialist lines, despite the fact that 'socialism' now figures in Egyptian pronouncements less frequently (and Islam more often) than in Nasser's day . . . more sweeping and potentially more threatening is paragraph nine of the treaty which states that the high contracting parties will not take part in any grouping of states, *or in actions or measures* directed against the other high contracting party. This provision exposes Egypt, in theory, at any rate, to the application of the Brezhnev doctrine." Subcommittee on Europe and Subcommittee on the Near East, Committee on Foreign Affairs, House of Representatives, *Joint Hearings*, 92nd Congress, 1st Session (Washington, D.C.: Government Printing Office, 1971), p. 31. *NYT*, May 30, 1971, editorialized that "except for religion, it is difficult to think of a major area of Egyptian life which Mr. Sadat has not now promised to bring closely under Moscow's guidance."

In Oslo, Mrs. Meir's first reaction was that there is "nothing new" in the treaty, but in Jerusalem 12 days later she told the Knesset: "The Soviet-Egyptian pact may be regarded as a contractual framework that creates a new dimension in the process of Soviet entrenchment in the Middle East. The articles of the treaty recall the bilateral treaties between the Soviet Union and the nations of the Communist bloc. The articles of the treaty express both local and international commitments and are calculated to bind Egypt to the Soviet doctrine.

"The treaty covers every vital sphere of political and social life: the infrastructure of the economy, social, political and cultural life, relations between the Communist Party and the Arab Socialist Union, foreign and defense policy, and cooperation and military aid. . . . The Soviet-Egyptian treaty possesses a significance extending beyond the sphere of Israel-Egyptian relations. Egypt has undertaken to coordinate with the Soviet Union her moves and positions in the world political arena. The Soviet Union has gained control of Egypt's policy." The *Jerusalem Post Weekly*, June 15, 1971, p. 6.

[46] One must bear in mind that the Soviet Union by and large views treaties as serious obligations entered into for mutual benefit. Such an attitude has not necessarily been characteristic of Middle Eastern regimes in the past. As one Yugoslav suggested to the author in June 1973, the Soviet Union's failure to recognize this discrepancy may constitute an important drawback in its approach to the region. "We cautioned the Soviets," he recalled, "that Sadat was agreeing to the treaty too quickly for it to have any lasting value."

ularly "at various levels on all important matters affecting the interests of the two states." Article 8 spoke of

> . . . cooperation in the military field on the basis of the perti-
> nent agreements between them. This cooperation includes in
> particular aid in training the UAR armed forces and in en-
> abling them to absorb the equipment and weapons sent to the
> UAR to increase its ability to remove the effects of the aggres-
> sion as well as to strengthen its ability to oppose the aggression
> in general.

These provisions gave reason to anticipate a further expansion of the Soviet military presence in Egypt. In addition, the fifteen-year term of the treaty suggested a more permanent type of relationship in which the Soviet Union would be able to pursue its courtship of Egypt systematically and with long-term purposes in mind.

Moscow hoped extensive commitments would guarantee its status in Egypt and inhibit Egyptian leaders from flirting with the United States. Sadat assured Podgornyi that in his talks with Rogers he had not gone beyond the coordinated Cairo-Moscow political line on the Middle East and that he had not succumbed to "honeyed words."[47] In turn, Podgornyi expressed "a feeling of satisfaction" at Egypt's socialist course and promised the USSR's full support, without which he noted "the developing countries cannot achieve real political and economic independence and confront imperialist despotism."[48] The Soviets made much over the economic and political provisions of the treaty; the Egyptians stressed the military aspects. Soviet commentaries waxed ecstatic over the treaty.[49] They emphasized that it would frustrate American efforts "to drive a wedge" between the USSR and Egypt, that the Americans, who pose "as self-styled 'mediators' in the Arab-Israeli conflict in order to secure the kind of 'peaceful' settlement under which the United States, using Israel as a tool, could dictate its will to Arab countries," would find themselves stymied and their goals exposed for all to see.[50]

[47] FBIS/United Arab Republic, May 27, 1971, p. G7.
[48] *Ibid.*, p. G8.
[49] For example, E. Dmitriev, "Soviet-Arab Friendship: A New Stage," *International Affairs*, No. 8 (August 1971), 66-68.
[50] *Pravda* and *Izvestiia*, June 2, 1971. Evgenii Primakov dismissed the "Rogers Plan" as "nothing new," only a maneuver to sow dissension in Arab circles and between Egypt and the USSR. *Pravda*, June 5, 1971.

That the treaty indicated a major new Soviet commitment in its relationship with Egypt is beyond question. That it signaled a major increase in Soviet influence is problematic, as a close investigation of the circumstances surrounding the conclusion of the agreement tends to confirm.

In the first place, the treaty obviously resulted from a Soviet and not an Egyptian initiative.[51] The coming of the large Soviet delegation dispatched to Egypt for the negotiation and signing was announced on Cairo Radio a mere two days before its arrival on May 25. Moreover, the provisions of the treaty bore a remarkable resemblance to those of treaties between the Soviet Union and other Warsaw Pact nations, suggesting that the Soviet delegation had arrived with a prepared text in hand. Also, the delegation itself was an impressive one with significantly comprehensive representation of party, government, and military interests, including President Podgornyi as head of the delegation, Foreign Minister Gromyko, Deputy Defense Minister General Ivan Pavlovskii, and CPSU Secretary Boris Ponomarev. The last three were the principal Soviet representatives in the three working groups—one dealing with political affairs, one with military matters, and one with party-to-party relations—formed at Soviet suggestion on May 26 for working out the terms of the treaty. Finally, the treaty, which was ratified by Egypt on June 13 and by the USSR on June 28, was hailed with considerably more fanfare in Moscow than in Cairo.

Moscow's decision to up the ante so very dramatically in its

---

[51] On May 30, 1971, Agence France Presse reported that Nasir had proposed a similar treaty to Moscow shortly after the June War and that Sadat had raised the matter during his secret visit in March. ARR, No. 10 (May 16–31, 1971), 273. Semi-official confirmation of Nasir's alleged request came in August 1972 when Quddus revealed the incident, noting that Moscow refused "perhaps because then they did not deem their commitment required a treaty. Furthermore, their high esteem of Abdel Nasser's personality rendered the signing of a treaty unnecessary. Three years later, Sadat was surprised by a Soviet request to sign a treaty," *Akhbar al-Yawm*, August 19, 1972, as cited in Yaacov Ro'i and Ilana Dimant-Kass, "The Soviet Military Involvement in Egypt, January 1970–July 1972" (Jerusalem: The Soviet and East European Research Centre, Research Paper No. 6, February 1974), p. 36. Sadat contributed his confirmation of the incident in April 1974 (see Chapter I, n. 25). Musa Sabri of *Al Akhbar* said that the USSR had pressed for the 1971 treaty: "This treaty had been requested by President Gamal Abdel Nasser, more than once, during the three years following the Israeli aggression. But the Soviet leaders had hesitated, until the failure of the May plot, then it was desired and urgently demanded." CPR, No. 5705, September 3, 1972.

relationship with Egypt was due to a combination of factors in the Egyptian domestic scene and in the evolving foreign policy of Anwar Sadat. Sadat's purge, coming close on the heels of his own independent diplomatic soundings about the possibilities of an interim settlement, alarmed Moscow. Uncertain about the full implications of these developments, especially the decimation of the Nasirist network with which they had worked,[52] Soviet leaders sensed that their special position in Egypt was threatened. If the Rogers Plan were to materialize, Washington would deliver to Egypt by diplomacy what Moscow's considerable military inputs had not enabled Cairo to attain. Moreover, if Moscow were no longer able to speak for Cairo in discussions with the United States on the future of the Middle East, what function— other than that of quartermaster—would be left for it to play? The upshot was that within two weeks of Sadat's preemptive coup Moscow dispatched its delegation to Cairo with the proposal for a fifteen-year treaty. If Sadat signed, the Soviet Union was prepared to leave its fallen Egyptian sympathizers to their fate. As long as Cairo kept its relationship with the Soviet Union intact, Moscow was not particular about who governed in Egypt.[53]

Sadat's alacrity in signing the treaty was equally understandable. Eager to consolidate his domestic position, he saw the treaty as a recognition of the legitimacy of his rule and hence as a Soviet pledge not to interfere in Egyptian internal affairs, while the reaffirmation of Soviet promises of weapons and military advisers would sit well with the Egyptian military, upon whose loyalty he depended. In addition, the formalization and expansion of Soviet commitments could only strengthen Sadat's hand in future bargaining with the United States. In dealing with the Soviets Sadat was conciliatory but firm. After purging Sabri he made a gesture toward the Soviets by appointing Dr. Isma'il Sabri Abdullah, a former secretary of the Egyptian Communist Party

[52] FBIS/United Arab Republic, May 26, 1971, p. G11. What was perhaps most frustrating to the Soviets was the difficulty in restoring contacts between the Soviet and Egyptian intelligence and security services as a result of Sadat's sweeping purge, which removed many of the officials with whom the Soviets had previously dealt. Moscow acted quickly to repair the links, sending Minister of the Interior Nikolai Shchelokov for a four-day visit to Cairo (June 22–26, 1971).

[53] P. J. Vatikiotis, "Notes for an Assessment of the Soviet Impact on Egypt," in M. Confino and S. Shamir (eds.), *The U.S.S.R. and the Middle East* (New York: John Wiley and Sons, 1973), p. 282.

(which was dissolved in 1965, its members thereafter permitted to join the ASU), to his Cabinet as deputy minister of planning. But he chose the opening day of his talks with Podgornyi to disclose publicly that Ali Sabri had masterminded the plot against him.[54] In the weeks that followed, Sadat stressed the military provisions of the treaty.[55] He let Riyad have his way, and for the time being dropped the effort to encourage diplomatic movement through Washington.[56]

[54] ARR, No. 10 (May 16–31, 1971), 273.

[55] For example, see Sadat's speeches of June 2 to the ASU Election Committee and of June 22 to the Alexandria Naval College. BBC/ME/3700/A/4 (June 4, 1971) and BBC/ME/3717/A/6 (June 24, 1971), respectively.

[56] The Sadat-Riyad disagreement on how to proceed gave rise to a diplomatic brouhaha, known as the "Bergus affair," which sheds light on Sadat's predicament at the time. In mid-April 1971, the State Department succeeded in persuading the Israelis to come up with a new statement of their position, in response to Sadat's proposals of February 4, 1971. The essence of the Israeli position was informally conveyed to Cairo, and Sadat was asked to respond with a modified statement of Egypt's position. Several weeks later, Muhammad Riyad, an aide of Foreign Minister Mahmud Riyad, showed Bergus a draft of the Egyptian reply. Thinking he could be helpful, and aware of the negative tone of the Egyptian draft, Bergus drew up a memorandum that set out the probable specifics of an interim settlement. The "Bergus Memorandum" called, among other things, for an Israeli withdrawal halfway across Sinai, for an advance of Egyptian forces to a line approximately fifteen miles west of the new Israeli positions, and for a U.N. force in between.

On June 6, the same day that Sadat gave the State Department a formal statement of Egypt's position, remarkably similar to the Bergus Memorandum, Mahmud Riyad moved to scuttle the entire project: he declared that no partial agreement was possible unless Israel gave a public commitment to a full withdrawal from all Arab territories; on June 13 he said Rogers' proposals completely failed to answer any of Egypt's concerns. As the coup de grace, Riyad gave an interview to Roland Delcour of Le Monde, stating "As a matter of fact, there was never any negotiation [between him and Rogers on reopening the canal]. It is again American propaganda which makes believe there was." The interview published in Le Monde on June 18, 1971, did not attract the attention Riyad had hoped. Accordingly, he fed twisted details of the Bergus Memorandum to Joseph Kraft, a syndicated American journalist, whose story was published in the International Herald Tribune, June 29, 1971. This time Riyad was successful: the State Department disavowed knowledge of the "unauthorized" exploration by Bergus and did not reply to Sadat's statement; the Israeli government protested; and Sadat dropped the matter, angry at what he regarded as Washington's lack of good faith. Six months later in an interview with Arnaud de Borchgrave, Sadat said that he and Sisco had discussed in April all the points contained in the Bergus Memorandum. Newsweek, December 13, 1971, p. 44.

For an incomplete Egyptian account, but with additional details, see Mohamed Heikal, The Road to Ramadan (London: Collins, 1975), p. 146.

On the other hand, the Soviet leaders found themselves obliged to expand their commitments merely to preserve their existing position. The treaty did not positively improve that position in any significant area of Egyptian affairs; on the contrary, the Soviets were forced to sit back while Sadat suppressed "progressive" elements and took such "bourgeois" steps as increasing the permissible size of private landholdings. However, Moscow believed that the treaty thwarted Rogers' attempt to work out a settlement without Soviet participation and weakened the position of those like Haykal who favored increased contacts with the United States;[57] indeed, Podgornyi declared publicly that the USSR had foiled an American attempt "to use internal political complications [in Egypt] to cause a split among the patriotic forces of the Arab countries" and assume the guise of "peacemakers" in the Middle East: "The saying, the beard of an apostle and the teeth of a devil, fittingly describes such mediators."[58] Unlike the Egyptian media, the Soviet press seldom wrote on the military aspect of the treaty, but occasional pieces in military journals suggested that the Soviet military establishment approved this component of the relationship.[59] For all of this, in a little more than a year the Soviet position was shown to have been built on sand.

The communiqué issued on May 27, at the conclusion of Podgornyi's visit, repeated the amity and shared outlook and objectives of the treaty.[60] In it, the Soviet delegation declared its appreciation of the continuation of Nasir's "progressive and anti-imperialist line" and determination to bring about "the socialist transformation of society"; Sadat expressed his "profound gratitude to the Soviet Union for its aid and support"; and both parties called for close cooperation in all fields, saying agreement had been reached "on practical and specific measures for implementation of the 1971 party contacts program."

By early July, to Moscow's relief, the steam had gone out of Rogers' initiative. As was evident from the communiqué published at the end of Riyad's Moscow visit (June 29–July 4) to

[57] *Pravda*, June 5, 1971.   [58] *Pravda*, June 11, 1971.

[59] For example, Colonel A. Orlov, "Platsdarm mezhdunarodnogo imperializma i sionizma na Blizhnem Vostoke" (The Bridgehead of International Imperialism and Zionism in the Near East), *Voenno-istoricheskii zhurnal*, No. 6 (June 1972), 90-95.

[60] FBIS/United Arab Republic, May 28, 1971, pp. G1-G3.

exchange the instruments of ratification of the treaty, Sadat's flirtation with Washington was temporarily over. The communiqué emphasized two points of particular interest to Moscow and Riyad: that the treaty deals "a new blow at the plans of international imperialism," which is trying to sabotage Soviet-Egyptian friendship, and that "the problem of reopening the Suez Canal for international shipping cannot be solved in isolation from other problems of the settlement and should be in context with an agreement on the withdrawal of all Israeli troops to the lines held before June 5, 1967, with the establishment of fixed deadlines for this withdrawal."[61] To consolidate his domestic position, Sadat took a tougher line on foreign policy.

TACTICS IN SEARCH OF STRATEGY

During the summer Sadat displayed a versatility and feel for balance of power considerations that were to distinguish his diplomacy in the years ahead. Toward the Soviet Union he was propitiating: speeches larded with phrases about Egypt's commitment to a socialist transformation; expanded exchanges of party cadres, including even an invitation to Ponomarev to address the ASU National Congress during the July 23 celebrations; support for the Soviet position on international issues; and easy accessibility for the Soviet ambassador. But Sadat kept close watch on the Soviets, whose programmed pattern of behavior isolated them from Egyptian life. The more than 18,000 advisers, troops, and technicians did not mingle with their Egyptian counterparts, except officially. The Russians, whose reserve often masked contempt for Egyptian indolence, remained very much a Sphinx to the Egyptians, who referred to them as "the unsmiling ones"; to Sadat they were important only as provisioners and insurance agents.

In dealings with the United States Sadat vacillated between feeling encouraged and aggrieved. He reiterated his desire for better relations, asking that Washington follow an "even-handed" policy, which to him meant denying Israel weapons and pressuring it to return all Arab territories. He assured Nixon and Rogers that the treaty with the Soviet Union in no way changed Egypt's attitude or position. But if the mood in the State Department

[61] FBIS/USSR, July 6, 1971, pp. B3-B4.

was favorably disposed toward Egypt and critical of Israel, in the White House and much of the Pentagon it was anti-Soviet, hence suspicious of Egypt and pro-Israeli.

Unnoticed at the time but ultimately as portentous a development as the Soviet treaty was Sadat's rapprochement with King Faysal and his policy of improving relations with the conservative regimes in the Arab world and eschewing ideological pretensions for the attainment of non-ideological goals. Sadat thus reversed Nasir. He disavowed Egyptian expansionist ambitions in the Arab world and made no pretense of seeking any mantle of leadership outside of Egypt. Indeed, in personal relations with Arab leaders, he cultivated a modest, deferential manner and attempted to de-ideologize and depolarize Arab politics.[62]

Faysal's visit to Cairo in late June was important. Sadat apparently convinced the staunchly anti-Communist Faysal that Egypt had not, by signing the treaty, accepted Moscow's ideology, outlook, or ambitions, but only its weapons and shield; that he held Islamic precepts inviolable and considered them relevant to modernization; and that he had no political or imperial ambitions in the Persian Gulf area. Reconciliation with Faysal brought with it the promise of Saudi financial support and consolidated Sadat's position with the influential conservative Muslim religious leaders at home. In less than a month Sadat gave Faysal—and Moscow—a demonstration of Egypt's independence of the Soviet Union.

The Sudanese Communist Party seized power on July 19, but three days later the deposed government of Ga'far al-Numayri was restored, largely because of Egyptian and Libyan support. Moscow, which had welcomed the coup and pressed the Egyptian government to recognize the new regime, appealed fruitlessly to Sadat to intervene on behalf of condemned Communists. Sadat not only withheld recognition of the short-lived Communist government, but he helped to unseat it. His gratitude to the Soviet Union did not extend to sanctioning legitimacy for Communists

[62] Sensitive to criticisms of Nasir's ambitions and mishandling of the merger with Syria in 1958 and desirous of allaying suspicions among his prospective partners in the new Arab federation, Sadat, on May 1, called for a change in the name of the country: "In view of what I have sensed from large sectors of our masses and so that there will be no confusion of names, and after having honorably, faithfully, and with struggle, sweat and effort maintained the name of the UAR, I should like us to return to the name Egyptian Arab Republic." BBC/ME/3674/A/8 (May 2, 1971).

in the Arab world. Indeed, he told a closed session of the ASU on July 24 that Egypt would never recognize an Arab Communist government and that he had rejected a plea by Ponomarev to oppose the crackdown on the Communists.[63]

Relations deteriorated between the Sudan and the Soviet Union —which had provided military and economic assistance to Numayri from the time of his coming to power in May 1969, had overlooked Numayri's denunciation of the Sudanese Communist Party in February 1971, and had received a military delegation from Khartoum in late April.

But neither Moscow nor Cairo wanted the Sudanese affair to mar their relationship. Haykal commented that since the USSR was Egypt's "most important and closest friend" in the struggle against Israel and imperialism and its "greatest strategic guarantee" in the battle ahead, it was essential "to remove the summer cloud which had appeared in the atmosphere of Arab-Soviet relations as a result of the Sudanese events."[64] Earlier Haykal had observed that in the past similar differences had arisen with the Soviets over the actions of Arab Communists, notably the behavior of Iraqi Communists in 1958, that they had been contained within "natural limits," and that the current differences should be assessed in the light of the limited alternatives available to Egypt, in particular, the unavailability of any great power other than the Soviet Union to help in the battle against Israel.[65] This appeal to contain the public squabbling arising out of the Sudanese events was generally reciprocated by the Soviet press, though articles did appear expressing anger at the Sudan's anti-Communist campaign, at the "persecution and murder of Communists and other patriots and progressives in the Sudan," and at the "specious talks about the 'incompatibility of communism and Islam,' attempts to represent Marxism-Leninism as a 'foreign ideology' alien to the 'Arab national spirit'—all these devices of the organizers of the Sudan anti-Communist campaign" that are taken straight from "the imperialist ideological arsenal."[66] Ponomarev, who was in Cairo at the time of the coup, "got ugly," according to one diplomat, no doubt assuming that Moscow was

63 *NYT*, August 6, 1971.

64 BBC/ME/3768/A/3 (August 23, 1971).

65 BBC/ME/3756/A/4 (August 9, 1971).

66 "The Repression in Sudan," *New Times*, No. 32 (August 1971), 8. On August 2, 1971, the Soviet bloc countries condemned "the reign of terror" in the Sudan. ARR, No. 15 (August 1-15, 1971), 422.

entitled to some dividends from the treaty. Sadat quickly disabused him on this score. Yet Sadat had no desire to complicate or embitter his relations with Moscow at a time when he was proclaiming, as on July 23, "I shall not allow 1971 to pass without this battle [against Israel] being decided . . . 1971 will be a decisive year."[67]

He repeated this promise on a number of occasions in succeeding months, while pushing ahead with plans for the federation with Syria and Libya. The coming to power of General Hafiz al-Asad in November 1970 had paved the way for a reconciliation with Damascus. Asad's wing of the Ba'thist Party was more willing to coordinate policies with Cairo, and its agreement in April 1971 to federate with Egypt and Libya was an important turnabout, given Syria's lingering resentment at Egypt's overbearing behavior during the previous effort at unity in 1958–1961. On August 20 in Damascus, Sadat, Qadhdhafi, and Asad signed the Constitution of the Federation of Arab Republics, which was approved in referendums held in each of the three countries on September 1.[68]

Ten days later Egypt adopted its own new constitution, replacing the interim Charter of 1964, and shortly thereafter Sadat installed a new Cabinet, which was noteworthy for two reasons: it was enjoined by him to streamline economic ministries, especially those dealing with the public sector (in actuality, not much was done in the period prior to the October War); and it brought Murad Ghaleb, previously Egypt's ambassador to the Soviet Union for almost ten years and highly regarded by Moscow, to the post of minister of state for foreign affairs, with special responsibility for advising the president on relations with the Soviet Union. Coming soon after the trials of Ali Sabri and the other conspirators and the bitterness over the executed Sudanese Communists, Ghaleb's appointment on September 19 was an explicit gesture of goodwill toward the Soviet Union. Moscow approved of Sadat's efforts to revitalize the ASU, but it stressed the need to include Communists in the process.[69] Despite his absorption with

[67] BBC/ME/3744/A/17 (July 26, 1971).

[68] Egypt formally changed its name to the Arab Republic of Egypt on September 1, 1971.

[69] One Soviet commentator wrote: "At the same time there is no discounting the difficulties the Egyptians are confronted with in accomplishing what they set out to do. The role that belongs in this to the ASU would be hard to overrate. But the ASU is still very young as a political organization, and its new functionaries are younger still in organizational political experience.

internal reorganization and the reconstruction of a severely riven administrative superstructure, Sadat saw Vinogradov several times in an attempt to patch up the Soviet-Sudanese rift; and on September 17, the day after a fiery speech to the nation, they again met to discuss a working paper drawn up by Soviet and Egyptian specialists on Egypt's military position.[70]

Despite the political difficulties, the Soviet Union continued to supply weapons. In the year since the cease-fire, it particularly strengthened Egypt's air defense system and air force,[71] and provided sophisticated equipment, including quantities of SAM-6s not yet made available to its Warsaw Pact allies. The Israelis reported that the Egyptians had started building SAM sites two miles from the canal, extending their air umbrella ten miles over the Israeli-held east bank.[72] Yet Sadat was impatient with the Soviet military buildup. Intent on making 1971 "the decisive year," he determined to present his views personally to the Soviet leadership. On September 26 it was announced that he would pay an official state visit to the USSR in October. Less than five months after the signing of the milestone pact with the Soviet Union, Sadat felt compelled to press the Soviets on their promise to augment Egypt's military capability and "to increase its ability to remove the effects of the aggression," as Sadat saw it, to be able to go to war.

MISSION TO THE KREMLIN

Sadat arrived in Moscow on October 11 to an enthusiastic welcome, though *Pravda* had been critical two weeks earlier.[73] The

---

Survivals of a specious, purely formal approach are still strong. There also persists, as a legacy of the past, fear of participation by the broad working masses in conscious political activity. And local reactionaries do their best to cultivate the idea that people of the Marxist way of thinking must not be allowed to share in active political life, even under ASU slogans." V. Lykov, "New Stage in the Life of the UAR," *New Times*, No. 34 (August 1971), 8. Another analyst contended that the Arab federation would succeed "only if all the national progressive forces stand united. Any attempt to exclude the Communists and their parties from the common struggle can only weaken the united front and play into the hands of the imperialist forces and their agents." R. Petrov, "Step Towards Arab Unity," *New Times*, No. 35 (September 1971), 22.

[70] ARR, No. 18 (September 16–30, 1971), 514; and "Report From Cairo—Sadat's Joker," *New Middle East*, No. 37 (October 1971), 5.

[71] *NYT*, September 1, 1971. See also, "New Soviet Deliveries Bolster UAR Air Force," RFE Report, July 14, 1971.

[72] BBC/ME/3789/A/5 (September 16, 1971).

[73] *Pravda*, September 28, 1971.

newspapers printed his picture and biography with glowing tributes to Soviet-Egyptian friendship, and streamers and crowds lined the route to the Kremlin. The next day, however, the Soviets stripped away the gloss and laid bare festering resentments. At a Kremlin luncheon remarkable for its open display of discord Podgornyi welcomed Sadat and a "frank discussion of ripe questions" and a detailed exchange of views. Mincing no words, he condemned "the anti-Communist and anti-Soviet campaign, fanned by the imperialists and their agents," that sets "the Arab countries at loggerheads with their most loyal friends and allies"—the Soviet Union and the other Communist countries; he left no doubt as to the meaning of his comment that wise leaders "know full well who is their ally . . . and who is their enemy, and do not let themselves be fooled."[74] Sadat was being rebuked for his failure to requite their support. To his quest for additional military aid, Podgornyi countered with the need for a political settlement.

Sadat's reply did not ease the tensions that had suddenly flared into the open. He thanked the Soviet Union for "the great role" it had played "in supporting the movement for national liberation and social progress in Egypt," but said nothing to dispel any of the bitterness that was an outgrowth of the Sudanese Communist coup. Nor was he even faintly politic about a peaceful settlement; on the contrary, he asserted that the Egyptians had "made every effort possible to attain a peaceful settlement," but Israeli intransigence had convinced them "that force and only force is the method" to deal with Israel.[75] He said the newly established Federation of Arab Republics, which Podgornyi had not even mentioned, was "a national action" for consolidating Arab unity, and now the Arabs had come to take counsel with the Soviets on the matter of gravest concern, the battle that was to come.

Immediately after this strained luncheon, Sadat was informed that President Nixon would visit the Soviet Union the following May. Both the message and its timing were a calculated rebuff, a reminder that Soviet support was not to be resorted to in times of distress and forgotten in peaceful periods, and that the Soviet relationship with Egypt was only one facet of Soviet global interests. If Cairo Radio admitted being "surprised" by the an-

[74] FBIS/USSR, October 13, 1971, pp. B2-B3.
[75] Ibid., p. B6.

nouncement,[76] so must Sadat have been; this was antithetical to his expectations.

The joint communiqué of October 13, 1971, was long, detailed, and provides some additional particulars about the substantive disagreements, attested by the discussions having been held "in a spirit of frankness."[77] It was notable for Sadat's apparent accommodation to the Soviet position on all major political issues, his carefully hedged dissatisfaction with Soviet aid, and the attention devoted to military matters. Sadat went along with the call for a peaceful settlement of the Middle East crisis through Jarring's mediation and "a fair settlement on the basis of fulfillment of all the provisions" of Resolution 242; he affirmed Egypt's effort to undertake "a socialist reconstruction of society," which "will try to use the rich experience of the Soviet Union and other socialist countries and rely on their experience and support"; in an effort to mollify Soviet irritation over his role in the Sudanese affair and its aftermath, he agreed that "the attempts to spread anti-communism and anti-Sovietism are designed exclusively to split the ranks of Arab revolutionary fighters . . . and are also aimed at disrupting the solidarity and cooperation between the Arab peoples and their true friends, the countries of the socialist community" and condemned these divisive phenomena; he sided completely with the Soviet position on Berlin, disarmament, and European security: in a word, virtually everything Sadat agreed to was designed to please the Kremlin.

However, though Sadat "highly commented" on the "great assistance" given by the USSR, he did not, as in May, express "profound gratitude" for such support. Yet, other sections of the communiqué suggest that he may have thought satisfaction was only a matter of months away. In discussions the two sides examined, among other things, cooperation in "military-technical fields"; the Soviet Union reaffirmed its continued "all-round assistance and support" for Egypt; and the two sides "agreed specifically on measures aimed at further strengthening the military might of Egypt." It may be that this latter formulation and the discussions leading up to it were what led Sadat to believe that he had received a solid commitment for additional arms, and that they were the basis for his future disappointed accusation that the two sides had come "to a certain agreement in Octo-

[76] BBC/ME/3813/A/7 (October 15, 1971).
[77] FBIS/USSR, October 14, 1971, pp. B3-B7.

ber, after we had cleared everything up."[78] According to Sadat's understanding, certain kinds of Soviet weapons, and in stipulated quantities, were to have been delivered by the end of the year, but were not. An Egyptian military mission, headed by War Minister Muhammad Sadiq (who was appointed in May 1971), had arrived three days before Sadat and remained until October 16, conducting extensive talks with Grechko and the Soviet military. Murad Ghaleb remained until October 26, presumably to tidy up the details. Brezhnev again accepted an invitation to visit Egypt, and Sadat returned home still believing that 1971 would be "a decisive year," and certainly not a year in which "the Middle East does not have a military solution," as Soviet analysts later wrote.[79]

Cairo soon learned that it had not been given a clear "green light" for war, even though Moscow had not explicitly foreclosed this option. In light of Nixon's opening to Peking and coming visit to Moscow, of Moscow's quest for Western technology and credits, of the decision taken at the Twenty-fourth Congress of the CPSU in March 1971 to promote détente, of a seriousness of purpose in the SALT talks, and of the gathering storm over the subcontinent, the last thing the Soviet leadership desired was a new war in the Middle East, with highly unpredictable consequences for the improving superpower relationship and even for Moscow's relationship to its Arab clients. At a time when Moscow believed the "correlation of forces" in other parts of the world to be highly favorable to Soviet interests, the exercise of restraint over the explosive forces in the Middle East became an important though not easy assignment. "It would be difficult indeed," wrote one Soviet analyst, "to find a spot in the world where the situation is as contradictory as it is in the Near East."[80]

DEFERRING THE YEAR OF DECISION

On his return from Moscow, Sadat vowed that "the day is very near when the Egyptian people, and we with them, will take the

[78] Sadat in a speech on July 24, 1972, as quoted in *Journal of Palestine Studies*, 2, No. 1 (Autumn 1972), 180.

[79] For example, Evgenii M. Primakov, "Blizhnevostochnyi konflikt" (Middle Eastern Conflict), in V. V. Zhurkina and E. M. Primakov (eds.), *Mezhdunarodnye konflikty* (Moscow: "Mezhdunarodnye Otnosheniia" Publishing House, 1972), p. 135.

[80] Dmitri Volsky, "Middle East Prospects," *New Times*, No. 44 (October 29, 1971), 7.

conclusive decision that will affect our destiny and that of generations to come," and General Sadiq told the troops on the canal that zero hour was approaching.[81] Sadat assumed personal command of the armed forces on November 1, and soon afterward the press fed the expectancy of imminent war, publishing air raid instructions and assurances to the people of Soviet support. On November 11 Sadat told the inaugural session of the newly elected People's Assembly that the blame for the diplomatic impasse was the United States's because of its unwillingness to make Israel accept the reopening of the canal as a first step toward "a complete and comprehensive solution"; "1971 must be a decisive year because we cannot remain forever suspended in this state of no peace and no war"; the Soviet Union "has spared no effort and withheld no assistance to strengthen our military ability" (a surprising statement, obviously intended to prod Moscow into delivering the promised weaponry and to disarm anti-Soviet agitation).[82] On November 20 he told front-line troops: "The time for battle has come. There is no longer any hope whatsoever of peaceful or other solutions. . . . The road to the crossing [of the canal] is a one-way road. The next time we shall meet in Sinai."[83] The brinkmanship was meant for the USSR, the United States, and the United Nations; the battle plans remained his secret.

Rogers searched for a formula acceptable to Cairo and Jerusalem, meanwhile procrastinating on Israel's request for more planes, maintaining that the Soviet arms shipments in the three months following the Sudanese fracas were deemed moderate by U.S. intelligence.[84] He nourished the hope that the USSR would exercise restraint if the United States did, thus slowing down the arms race and giving diplomacy a chance without jeopardizing the security of either side or the incipient U.S.-Soviet détente.[85]

[81] ARR, No. 20 (October 16–31, 1971), 564.
[82] BBC/ME/3838/A/6-15 (November 13, 1971).
[83] BBC/ME/3845/A/6-7 (November 22, 1971).
[84] NYT, November 5, 1971.
[85] Rogers based his position on the assumption, shared by the leading Arabologists in the State Department, that Moscow would not frustrate the efforts to reach an interim settlement on reopening the canal, even though it was not a party to the process. Soviet sources had often expressed keen interest in seeing the canal reopened. For example, see Y. Primakov, "Why the Canal Must Be Reopened: A Soviet View," New Middle East, No. 46 (July 1972), 7-8; and Ia. Bronin, "Ekonomicheskie perspektivy Suetskogo Kanala" (Economic Perspectives on the Suez Canal), Mirovaia ekonomika i mezhdunarodnye otnosheniia, No. 10 (October 1972), pp. 81-84. However, Washington was not willing to multilateralize the diplomatic

The acceleration of Egyptian preparations for war coincided with the debate in the General Assembly on the Middle East. It was intended to rivet the attention of the great powers on the crisis and force them to act. The General Assembly, predictably, passed a resolution by an overwhelming 79 to 7 vote with 36 abstentions (the previous year the vote on a similar resolution had been 57 for, 16 against, with 39 abstentions), which reaffirmed "that the acquisition of territories by force is inadmissible," that Israel should withdraw from Arab territories occupied in the 1967 war, and that the Jarring mission should be reactivated.[86] But Egypt's success at the United Nations was ephemeral.

The storm clouds over the subcontinent had burst, drenching India and Pakistan in war and temporarily diverting the attention of the superpowers. The swell from South Asia upset Sadat's plans. It jumbled political alignments and tossed balance-of-power considerations into the proverbial cocked hat. Sadat bitterly deplored the fact that the U.S. position on the Middle East issue was not the same one it took on the Indo-Pakistani conflict, where it was calling for a cease-fire and a return to prewar boundaries;[87] but he conveniently ignored the political topsy-turvy of the USSR, which also took a position on South Asia contrary to the one it espoused on the Middle East, to wit, calling for a cease-fire without insisting on any return to prewar borders.

Moscow squelched whatever plans Sadat may have been considering for a limited crossing of the canal by the simple expedient of diverting to India the arms promised Egypt, and thereby communicating its disapproval in unambiguous terms. For a brief moment it had seemed otherwise. On December 16, Ambassador Vinogradov told a group of Egyptian journalists: "If there is to be war, we will support you so that it will be a war with

---

explorations. It showed little interest in the Soviet note to U Thant, sent on July 13, 1971, offering "to take part together with other powers—permanent members of the Security Council—in creating international guarantees for the political settlement in the Middle East." ARR, No. 14 (July 16–31, 1971), 392.

[86] General Assembly Resolution 2799 (XXVI) of December 13, 1971. It expressed "appreciation" of Egypt's positive response to Jarring's memorandum of February 8, 1971, and called for a similar response from Israel implying that in the event of refusal the Security Council would be asked to place an embargo on Israel.

[87] See the interview with C. L. Sulzberger, NYT, December 13, 1971.

minimum losses, and if it is to be peace, we will support you since it would be a solution with no losses. We will support you in peace and in war."[88] Moscow quickly issued a denial, in response to a worried inquiry from Washington, of any change in Soviet policy, insisting that Vinogradov had been misquoted, that the Soviet government did not favor war in the Middle East. Soviet newspapers criticized Israel, but implied that this was not the time for the Arabs to start any fighting and called on Jarring to work for a political settlement.[89] To underscore this view, the call for a settlement in the Middle East was juxtaposed to the piece in the "International Survey" section of *Pravda* that discussed the Indo-Pakistani war; and Iurii Glukhov, the Soviet correspondent in Cairo, commented in another article in the same issue on Egypt's "peaceful foreign policy" and the country's "consistent course for a political solution of the Middle East crisis."

But the Soviet leadership left nothing to chance and sent a clear message by removing missile crews, aircraft, and air defense equipment from the Aswan Dam area, purportedly as much to restrain Sadat as to aid India.[90] The USSR did airlift considerable weaponry to India via Egypt, though whether it was compelled by military exigency to weaken Egyptian defenses is open to question. It certainly wanted to make sure Sadat would not attempt anything on his own. Moscow used Soviet bases in Egypt to advance policy objectives on the Indian subcontinent—and the Egyptians tolerated this—although the official policy of the Egyptian government was to maintain a neutral position between India, its partner in nonalignment, and Pakistan, its brother in Islam.

For Sadat there was the painful realization that no battle would be fought in 1971. The Soviet Union was against a war, a crucial consideration. Without Soviet supplies Sadat's military option lost its viability. Moscow's stand gave added weight to those in the Egyptian high command who argued for more time to absorb Soviet equipment and training. Besides, the Arab world was still in disarray; if Egypt fought, it would have to fight

[88] *NYT*, December 17, 1971. Vinogradov's promise was blazoned on the front page of *Al-Gumhuriya*.

[89] *Pravda*, December 19, 1971.

[90] *Al-Nahar*, December 31, 1971, as quoted in ARR, No. 1 (January 1–15, 1972), 3. Also, BBC/ME/3909/A/2 (February 8, 1972).

alone. The assassination of the Jordanian prime minister in Cairo in late November had again chilled relations between Cairo and Amman; Syria's backing for the Palestinians kept Syrian-Jordanian relations at a low boil; Libya was at odds with Saudi Arabia, Jordan, and Morocco; and the Sudan and Iraq were preoccupied with rebellious minorities. Moreover, the United Nations could not be counted on to mobilize effective political pressure, as had been shown by India's peremptory rejection of the General Assembly's recommendation and the Security Council's helplessness in the face of a veto. Finally, Washington, furious at India, frustrated by its inability to prevent the humbling and disintegration of an ally whose defeat was at least to a small degree the consequence of Soviet intervention, and fearful of further erosion of its position in the Third World, might come unequivocally to Israel's support in the event of another war. Clearly, the time was not propitious for the battle.

Sadat gave the ASU Central Committee the embarrassing task of informing the country that the battle had to be postponed. The statement of December 28 was vague, disjointed, and uninformative, yet Egyptians understood the message: no war.[91] Sadat withheld any personal explanation for several weeks. At the end of December, the Egyptian army held maneuvers lasting more than a week, but they were for morale-building not canal-crossing.

Not until January 13, 1972, in what came to be known as his "fog" speech, did Sadat relate the circumstances that had necessitated postponement of "the battle."[92] He spoke of a decision that Nasir took on July 9, 1967, when an Israeli armored brigade was reported moving toward Qantarah East. Egyptian aircraft flew out to intercept the Israelis, but were stymied by fog. When the Egyptian command informed Nasir two hours later that the planes could not see their targets, Nasir canceled the strike, having concluded that the Israeli brigade was not moving to cross the canal but only to reinforce its existing positions. Sadat observed that in early December, with the troops in full readiness, "a fog similar to that of Sunday, July 9, 1967, developed. A battle broke out between two friendly countries, India and Pakistan." While the attention of the world turned to the subcontinent, the balance of power, "which we must never ignore when we enter

91 BBC/ME/3875/A/10-11 (December 30, 1971).
92 BBC/ME/3889/A/1-8 (January 15, 1972).

our battle or begin our battle, was confused and disturbed." Like Nasir, I, too, said Sadat, told the generals to wait. A reassessment is required as a result of the Indo-Pakistani war and the preoccupation of the Soviet Union with commitments elsewhere than the Middle East; but "continuous earnest negotiations are now taking place at the highest level" between the USSR and Egypt with a view toward coordinating political-military strategy.

The new year began unpromisingly. Nixon announced the sale to Israel of additional Phantoms and Skyhawks. The stated reason was the need to maintain the balance of power in the Middle East; the real reason was the reaction to the perceived Soviet gains from the Pakistani defeat and Nixon's desire to convey to Moscow his determination not to permit a similar setback in the Middle East. Reacting to the South Asian situation, Nixon flexed American power in the Middle East, indifferent for the moment to its effect on Cairo. Reflecting this indifference and the White House's belief that no interim settlement was likely was the removal of Donald Bergus, who had developed a close working relationship with Sadat and was identified in Cairo with those in the State Department who believed that Sadat was willing to reach a political settlement and reduce his dependence on the Soviet Union. He was replaced in early January by Joseph N. Greene, a non-Arabist, rather than, as expected, by Michael Sterner, an Arabologist like Bergus. The White House, not the State Department, was calling the diplomatic plays.

At home, Sadat reorganized his cabinet to bring in new blood and give his foreign policy a friendlier pro-Soviet face. On January 17 he made 'Aziz Sidqi, a known and welcome person in Moscow, prime minister (transferring Dr. Mahmud Fawzi to the post of special adviser to the president). Sidqi, an economist trained at Harvard University in urban affairs and economic development, was greatly enamored of Soviet gigantism and centralized control over the economy. Over the years he had developed close relations with Soviet officials assigned to advising Egypt on economic development and had acquired a reputation for being a tough, driving administrator, a trait he quickly displayed with a series of austerity measures aimed at curbing inefficiency and consumption of luxury goods. A technocrat, Sidqi was without a political base to challenge Sadat.

The surprise in the new cabinet was the replacement of Mahmud Riyad as foreign minister by Murad Ghaleb. Ostensibly,

Riyad was promoted to the post of adviser to the president with the rank of deputy prime minister; actually, Sadat was settling an old score, isolating his old opponent, and replacing him by a trusted aide, who was also on good terms with Moscow, having served as ambassador to the Soviet Union longer than any previous Egyptian.

Finally, there were the students. After more than three years of relative quiet, they were again troublesome. On January 19, at a meeting of supporters of the Palestine revolution in the Engineering Faculty of Cairo University, they demanded greater liberalization—a reaction to Sidqi's call for harsh domestic controls and Haykal's evasiveness on the issue of freedom of speech and press—and an end to the government's interminable procrastination toward Israel. The unrest spilled into the streets of Cairo. Some of it was fed by the bleak prospect of an indeterminate period of military service and an economy saddled with a surplus of college graduates but a paucity of jobs. Sadat was in a ticklish situation: faced with domestic restiveness, he was goaded and ridiculed for his indecisiveness, but was constrained from acting by military weakness and political uncertainty over Soviet support. One foreign journalist reported the following comment by an Egyptian official:

> Sadat talks of war, but knows that it is beyond his power. He wants peace, but dare not offer it. Like so many other Arab politicians he talks of unity and progress, while the Arab world is steadily sinking into a mire of hatred, debt, poverty, corruption and general regression.[93]

On January 25 Sadat spoke for several hours to representatives of political, trade union, and student organizations. He set forth and tried to clarify some of the contradictions of Egyptian politics. He said the decision for war had already been made, but gave no reason why there was no fighting, other than the "fog" created by the Indo-Pakistani war; the home front had been ready in December, but new calibrations for conflict had to be set; the students would be granted more democracy, but they had to operate within the limits dictated by the interests of the home front. Sadat likened himself to Churchill during Britain's darkest hours in 1941, when some elements asked that an investigation

[93] Karl Breyer, "Egypt's Fantasies," *To The Point* (February 26, 1972), p. 42.

into the causes of the setbacks be held but were refused on the ground that first the war must be won. Sadat asked for a vote of confidence, declaring that the time was not ripe for complete revelations and that the current phase through which Egypt was passing was very complicated. Extreme caution had to be exercised, "with maximum calculation and maximum accuracy." At several points in his speech, he revealed that consultations were proceeding with the Soviet Union, Egypt's "only friend," and that "the contacts are still going on and have not finished. They will be concluded with a visit on my part to the Soviet Union."

Sadat's mission to Moscow was to be the most important of his career.

Chapter Six

THE END OF ILLUSION

B REZHNEV greeted Sadat at Vnukovo Airport on February 2, 1972, and played host for three days, but his main interests lay elsewhere. In early 1972 the Middle East was overshadowed in Soviet eyes by the USSR's altering adversary relationship with the United States, the impending Nixon visit to China, détente in Europe, and the prospect of a SALT agreement. The decisions taken at the CPSU's Twenty-fourth Congress the year before connoted restraint in foreign policy, not the stoking of new conflicts. The postwar era of Cold War in Europe was passing, and key Soviet goals were within easy reach. The Soviet-West German Treaty of Friendship and Cooperation (ratified in May 1972) signified Western recognition of the two Germanies and the territorial status quo in Europe. Nixon's coming visit to Moscow in May was to be the final legitimizing cap on these achievements.

By 1972 Moscow's Mediterranean strategy had begun to prove itself. It had limited the political utility of the U.S. Sixth Fleet, whose interventionist capability on behalf of clients in the Third World had diminished since the 1950s and 1960s; it now had at its disposal a navy, vastly expanded since the mid-1960s, with credible strategic as well as tactical forces that exposed NATO's southern flank to the Soviet deterrent; it encouraged nonaligned proclivities in Italy, Greece, Turkey, and Iran, as much by a détentist policy as by growing military power. The military presence in Egypt, even if advantageous, was not absolutely essential for the effectuation of this strategy, although so expensively acquired and maintained a lease on real estate would not remain unused.

The only unpredictable danger was in the Middle East. Whereas China was a far more perplexing and intractable foreign policy problem for the Soviet Union, it was not in a position to frustrate Soviet policies in the above-mentioned areas the way Egypt could. With his potential for triggering a war, Sadat could endanger Soviet relations with the United States. Washington, smarting from defeats administered to its client-states in

South Vietnam and Pakistan at the hands of Soviet-armed North Vietnam and India, respectively, had drawn a line in the Middle East. An Arab-Israeli war was a tinderbox that could consume détente. In 1970, Nixon had interpreted the Soviet intervention in the war of attrition as an attempt to preserve, not upset, the military balance between Egypt and Israel. But his reaction to the Indo-Pakistani war had disconcerted the Soviets. Infuriated by India's crushing victory, by the open role of Soviet weaponry and diplomacy, and by what he considered the arrogance of Mrs. Indira Gandhi, for whom he had developed a strong dislike, Nixon sought to compensate for the change in the balance of power on the subcontinent by evincing a determination not to permit anything comparable to occur in the Middle East.

On January 1, 1972, the U.S. government announced the sale of additional aircraft to Israel—a decision Secretary of State Rogers had tenaciously resisted for almost a year in the hope of producing an interim agreement and inducing the Soviet Union to curb its arms shipments to Egypt. The hardening of the president's attitude was evident again on February 9, 1972, when his annual foreign policy report to the Congress was published. Nixon lashed out against the Soviet Union for using the Arab-Israeli conflict "to perpetuate and expand its own military position in Egypt":

> The USSR has taken advantage of Egypt's increasing dependence on Soviet military supply to gain the use of naval and air facilities in Egypt. This has serious implications for the stability of the balance of power locally, regionally in the Eastern Mediterranean, and globally. The Atlantic Alliance cannot ignore the possible implications of this move for the stability of the East-West relationship.[1]

He accused the USSR of refusing to cooperate in helping the local parties reach a settlement and of changing its mind in December 1969 "on a possible procedure for indirect Arab-Israeli talks."[2] Referring to the Soviet military involvement in

[1] *President Richard Nixon's Foreign Policy Report 1972* (Washington, D.C.: The White House, 1972), p. 154.

[2] *Ibid.*, p. 155. The contrast between the President's Report and the Secretary of State's was startling, as if two rival bureaucracies had drafted them with different purposes in mind. The latter was more restrained on the Middle East and less belligerent about Soviet behavior. See *United States*

the war of attrition and in the violations of the cease-fire agreement of August 7, 1970, he called on Moscow to refrain from further exploitation of the conflict. Nixon's anger was unmistakable, as was his message to Moscow; in the Middle East, the United States would not tolerate a setback attributable to Soviet arms. As far as the Kremlin was concerned the South Asian and Middle Eastern situations were quite different; however, it had no desire to argue the point at that time or fan new fires in the area.

Moscow had deferred Sadat's visit until the crisis on the subcontinent subsided. Irritated with his dwelling on the need for "battle" and repeated allusions to Moscow's diversion of arms to India as justification for his decision not to go to war in December 1971, Moscow had to convince Sadat that the international situation was not suitable for war and, moreover, that the Arabs were not ready for it: Egypt needed time to master its new weaponry; Syria was vulnerable to Israeli air power; Jordan stood aloof, more concerned with suppressing the Palestinians than fighting the Israelis. What more could Moscow be expected to do now?

THE KREMLIN VISITS

Haykal described Sadat's visit (February 2–4) "as among the most important and delicate in the history of Arab-Soviet relations"; it was the time to "concentrate on what is positive" and not to dwell on differences.[3] More pressing than military issues was the need for far-ranging candid discussions of their countries' basic political and strategic attitudes and aims, which were far from similar or convergent. Haykal called for a dispassionate approach to incidents such as the Sudanese affair and a curb on emotional outbursts—an allusion to criticisms in the Lebanese press of Soviet hesitation to help topple Israel[4]—in order that tensions over temporary disagreements did not vitiate the effectiveness of the Arabs' long-term relationship with the USSR. Arab emotionalism, he wrote, makes Moscow uneasy: it gives the Soviet leadership the impression that the Arabs are incapable of

Foreign Policy 1971: A Report of the Secretary of State (Washington, D.C.: Department of State Publication 8634, 1972), pp. 94-98.

[3] FBIS/Egypt, February 4, 1972, p. G4.

[4] *NYT*, January 30, 1972.

understanding the nuclear balance of power, and makes the Arabs "think they can enter into a maneuver that would lead to a confrontation between the two superpowers."[5] Too often, Arab-Soviet meetings were contrived gatherings, which "did not permit much frankness or a studied scientific discussion enabling each side to know the other side's limitations, views of the problems, and intentions":

> In most cases, the meetings began with courtesies, followed by insistence, and finally requests. This was not an ideal situation concerning relations between two sides bound by firm friendship and facing a complicated crisis. Instead of the courtesies, insistences, and requests, they should discuss policies, strategies, and plans.[6]

Sadat's purpose in this visit had been not so much to make a request for hardware as to get a commitment:

> What I want this time is a strategic decision, a decision that you will give us the opportunity to be equal to Israel. We do not want supremacy but equality. This is a strategic decision. After it has been made, any requests we make or any additions you give to our forces become a matter of detail.[7]

Sadat knew what the Soviets could do to help, if they had a mind: he had seen what a flood of arms had done in 1967 and 1970, and in 1971 in India.

But Egypt needed more. "It is becoming obvious," wrote a British journalist, "that Egypt's insatiable appetite for new and better weapons, though a perfectly natural response to Israel's ever-growing armoury, at the same time reflects a psychological need: it rationalizes their fear of using the ones they have."[8]

Though *Al-Ahram* called Sadat's visit "a huge success," a "turning point in the Middle East conflict,"[9] the joint communiqué of February 4 suggested the contrary: it showed the Soviets to be far less forthcoming than in the previous October.[10] The

[5] FBIS/Egypt, February 4, 1972, p. G8.
[6] *Ibid.*, p. G9.
[7] See Haykal's article in *Al-Ahram*, March 17, 1972, as quoted in BBC/ME/ 3944/A/2 (March 20, 1972).
[8] David Hirst, "Comrades in Arms—or at Odds?" *The Guardian*, February 4, 1972.
[9] ARR, No. 3 (February 1–14, 1972), 51.
[10] FBIS/USSR, February 7, 1972, pp. B1-B3.

February communiqué mentioned military aid only once: "the sides *again* considered measures to secure the lawful rights and interests of the Arab peoples, to render assistance to the Arab Republic of Egypt, in particular, in the field of further strengthening its defense capacity, and outlined a number of concrete steps in this direction" (emphasis added). By contrast, the October communiqué had referred to Soviet military aid in three different places. The use of the word "again" in the February communiqué was unusual. It seemed to indicate that the previous October there had not been quite the meeting of minds or the clarification of "misunderstandings" implied by Sadat in a statement at Aswan on January 30;[11] or, perhaps even more likely, that the Kremlin reconsidered its policy toward Egypt once the Indo-Pakistani crisis developed.

The communiqué simply mentioned an exchange of views. The parties did not, as they had in October, reaffirm or emphasize the "coincidence of their viewpoints," thus revealing that the differences were serious indeed. There were expressions of continued interest in a political solution in accordance with Resolution 242 and in the resumption of the Jarring mission, giving Sadat justification for a further postponement of any fighting. Finally, the absence of any mention of the U.S. effort to start proximity talks between Egypt and Israel in a New York hotel, with Sisco acting as the go-between, meant that neither Moscow nor Cairo wished to foreclose any new American initiative, though Sadat had declared the previous month that he had broken off all contacts and wanted nothing further to do with Washington. Other issues probably discussed, but not mentioned publicly, were manifestations of anti-Sovietism in Arab circles; Arab uneasiness over the growing emigration of Soviet Jews to Israel;[12] and domestic de-

---

[11] *NYT*, February 3, 1972; ARR, No. 3 (February 1–14, 1972), 52.

[12] An Arab analyst known for his outspoken views wrote that though the percentage of immigrants "is very small in comparison to the total number of Soviet Jewish citizens," and though the Soviets would surely not allow this exodus to grow into a problem with the Arabs, "the fact remains that any Soviet acceptance of Israel as a refuge for the Jews means that Soviet recognition of Israel would be an indication that it is a state for the world's Jews." This would "give a boost to the recognition of Zionism." Clovis Maqsud, "The Arabs and the Soviet Union," *al-Nahar*, February 6, 1972, as translated in Joint Publications Research Service, Translations on Near East (hereafter referred to as JPRS), No. 55563 (March 28, 1972), 2-3.

Soviet diplomats in defense of their policy regarding the emigration of Soviet Jews, are reputed to have retorted: "You Arabs have permitted one

velopments in Egypt. But these were peripheral to the main difficulties besetting the Soviet-Egyptian relationship.

Sadat stopped in Damascus and Benghazi on his way home, and in early March he traveled to Jiddah, as part of his practice of consulting regularly with Faysal. In Arab quarters the communiqué was interpreted as evidence of Soviet double-talk and double-dealing. *Al-Hawadith* observed:

> The picture depicted by Soviet propaganda was that friendship, principles and ideals were the only considerations which dictated to the Russians their attitudes vis-à-vis Arab causes. Now, however, the truth has become so obvious that it cannot be escaped. This is that the Soviet Union, exactly like the United States, is no more than an arms merchant and a seeker of spheres of influence—and that its policies are dictated by the same self-seeking interests which inspire the policies of any Great Power.[13]

On February 16 and 17, Sadat told the ASU National Congress of Egypt's need to establish a durable relationship with the Soviet Union, not only "for the battle but also for the post-battle period," a relationship based not merely on mutual interest, but on the principles of resistance to imperialism and capitalism.[14] He praised Soviet generosity, welcomed the presence of the Soviet fleet in the Mediterranean, and rebuked a questioner who asked what "conditions" Moscow had imposed in return for helping Egypt, saying that the sources of such invidious ideas were the United States and Israel, who sought to sow discord between the USSR and Egypt.[15] The speech was aimed at pleasing Moscow and gave no hint that unpleasantness between Egyptian officers and Soviet advisers was on the increase nor that rumors were circulating about the expulsion of a senior Soviet military adviser to War Minister Sadiq for allegedly telling a group of officers, "You are like a man with two wives and do not know which one to choose"—a gibe at Egypt's courting of both

---

million Jews to emigrate to Israel; do not criticize us for allowing 100,000 to go." For an example of this line of argument, see Boris Shumilin, the USSR Deputy Minister of Internal Affairs, "Zionist Fabrications and the Reality," *New Times*, No. 16 (April 1972), 12-13.

13 As quoted in *New Middle East*, No. 42-43 (March–April 1972), 63.

14 BBC/ME/3918/A/9 (February 18, 1972).

15 BBC/ME/3920/A/2-3 (February 21, 1972).

the USSR and the United States.[16] For the time being the lid was kept on such incidents.

As a follow-up to Sadat's visit, Soviet Defense Minister Grechko came to Cairo on February 18 at the head of a large military delegation. (Coincidentally, Jarring also arrived for the first time in almost three years to try to arrange for indirect Egyptian-Israeli talks.) Grechko met with Egyptian leaders, visited positions along the canal, observed maneuvers, and soothed ruffled feelings among the Egyptian military. The communiqué issued on February 21 reported that views had been "exchanged" (they were still far from identical) in an effort to build up "the fighting capacity" of Egypt.[17]

After Grechko's visit there were reports of increased arms deliveries to Egypt. Al-Ahram quoted Sadat as having said that Egyptian troops were "fast absorbing advanced sophisticated weaponry" from the USSR.[18] A Lebanese newspaper reported that the USSR had offered to build a MiG-21 plant in Egypt but that Sadiq had rejected the offer, supposedly because he was holding out for a more advanced MiG-23 plant.[19] A conference at Al-Ahram on Soviet-Egyptian relations, interesting because of the topic and the participation of Soviet analysts, went so far as to fix Soviet military aid to Egypt at $5 million a day.[20] Rumors of a major arms buildup wafted about the area, conflicting with the conjecture that Sadat was far from satisfied with Soviet arms deliveries.

If the actual flow of Soviet weaponry was shrouded in secrecy, the intensity of Soviet diplomatic activity was not. Israel was regularly denounced for trying "to torpedo and wreck" efforts to reach a settlement.[21] But the Soviet net was being cast over more than just the Egyptian-Israeli conflict. Moscow encouraged the efforts of Arab "progressive forces," which it claimed the con-

[16] NYT, February 18, 1972.
[17] BBC/ME/3922/E/1 (February 23, 1972).
[18] ARR, No. 5 (March 1–15, 1972), 107.
[19] ARR, No. 6 (March 16–31, 1972), 135.
[20] Al-Ahram, March 30, 1972. The conference was held at its Center of Political and Strategic Studies and included, on the Soviet side, E. M. Zhukov, V. Maevskii, and V. G. Solodovnikov.
[21] Izvestiia, March 5, 1972. On March 20, at the Fifteenth Congress of USSR Trade Unions, Brezhnev attributed the "dangerous hotbed of tension" in the Middle East to Israel's "stubborn refusal to withdraw from the Arab lands, [and to] the Israeli military's constant provocations . . . ," CDSP, 24, No. 12 (April 19, 1972), 7.

gress of the Lebanese Communist Party in January had brought together; it hosted Arab delegations, including a sizable one from Libya headed by the number two man Major 'Abd al-Salam Jallud; and it drew closer to Iraq, signing a Treaty of Friendship and Cooperation in April. Moscow was not putting all its Arab eggs in Egypt's basket.

The impression of a vast influx of Soviet weapons and an end to the misunderstanding with the Soviet Union over arms deliveries was rudely challenged by Haykal in the indirect fashion of questioning the feasibility of war as a realistic option. His articles, labeled "defeatist" by rival newspapers, argued that military solutions in the contemporary era were almost impossible to impose because of the superpowers' reluctance to risk nuclear war in pursuit of limited objectives—hence the United States did not overrun Cuba, which it could do in an hour, nor did the Soviet Union knock out China's atomic plants:

> In our conflict with Israel, I do not think that we shall in the near future possess the amount of military power necessary for a first step at Qantarah as an entrance to Sinai and up through the last step at Qunaytirah in the Syrian Heights. Neither is the amount of power so easily available nor are observable circumstances so suitable.[22]

Disappointed by the United Nations and lacking preponderant military power, Egypt should adopt a mixed approach, by which Haykal meant a combination of economic, military, and political moves and "enlightened propaganda which gains the maximum amount of support for this conflict and attitudes based on principles which guarantee the broadest front of friends and allies." The United States and the Jarring mission required still further cultivation, notwithstanding their dismal yield thus far. Egypt was not strong enough in its current condition to persuade the United States to diminish its support of Israel; therefore, it had to concentrate on putting its own house in order, build up its armed forces, and unify the fragmented Arab forces. Only then would the United States take a different view of the Middle East situation. This is not to say, Haykal hastened to add, that Egypt is "in a desperate position which might prompt it to embark on an adventure or to capitulate."[23] It is fully able to defer any de-

---

[22] BBC/ME/3932/A/2 (March 6, 1972).
[23] BBC/ME/3944/A/1 (March 20, 1972).

cision, reject any suggestion that did not meet its demands, and take any step that would in the process improve the negotiating position within which its aims might be achieved. He did not preclude the use of force in a local war, but did caution that success in such an instance depended on fully understanding the political limits of what could be applied and expected,[24] an elliptical reminder not to venture too far from the Soviet shield.

Haykal seemed to be counseling patience and temporary acceptance of the reality of uncertainty. He castigated Husayn for his plan, floated in late March, to establish a federation of the West Bank, Gaza, and Jordan, and to share Jerusalem with Israel as a dual capital. In this, and in upholding Sadat's break with Jordan and alignment with the Palestinians, he applied the tried and accepted formula of post-1967 Arab politics, namely, when in difficulty, denounce Husayn and defend the rights of the Palestinians. Haykal's articles alerted observers to Sadat's intensifying dilemmas and impatience with Soviet promises.

Internal oppositionists of the Right and the Left beset Sadat: the Rightists alleged undue Soviet influence over Egypt's policy and called for an assertion of national independence; the Leftists criticized the failure to fight, notwithstanding all the arms supplied by the USSR.[25] Sadat temporized between the two. To the former he replied that Egypt was its own master, that it would never establish a Marxist system, and that "the Soviet Union did not ask for military bases and at present it has no military bases," though it was being provided with "facilities"

[24] BBC/ME/3954/A/16 (April 4, 1972). In a previous article, he had suggested that Egypt seize "100 square kilometers of territory" and hold it. "This would change the whole picture of the crisis and would open the door to other direct developments in the course of the conflict," i.e. a superpower intervention to impose a solution. BBC/ME/3950/A/4 (March 27, 1972).

[25] BBC/ME/3967/A/1 (April 19, 1972). One outspoken Egyptian writer, who incurred official disfavor by publishing her views in an Israeli journal, maintained that the unrest in Egypt in the winter of 1972 was not motivated by a "desire to see the government launch a war. Personal observation and interviews with students during the riots convinced me that while the organizational core, which was leftist, favored some form of war of liberation, the majority of participants were merely nationalists expressing the diffuse sense of dissatisfaction with the regime that had been widespread since the defeat in 1967." Sana Hassan, "An Egyptian's Vision of Peace," *New Outlook*, 17, No. 3 (March–April 1974), 21. If her analysis is correct, the Leftists could have been exploiting Sadat's deferral of war as an issue to weaken his position internally.

because it was in Egypt's interest to do so.[26] To the latter group, he rejoined that Egypt would not be goaded into a premature attack, but would fight only when the moment was propitious.

Added to Sadat's worries at home was his anxiety over Nixon's forthcoming trip to Moscow. Fear of a Soviet-American deal on the Middle East at Egypt's expense impelled him to fly again to Moscow (April 27–29). His supersession of the visit that had been planned in late March for Murad Ghaleb[27] and his announcing as late as April 22 that he would go instead, indicate that the decision was a spur of the moment one. For the third time in less than eight months Sadat personally laid his case before the Kremlin.

Three days before his departure, at a meeting with ASU journalists and public media specialists, Sadat berated the "doubt-sowers" who foment suspicion of the Soviet Union. Referring to his upcoming negotiations with Moscow, he said: "I cannot carry a whip and threaten Russia with it. And [this] does not mean that the Soviet Union has taken a certain line or is laying down certain terms. The Soviet Union has not posed any conditions. There is friendship . . . and nothing more."[28] In the meantime, he indicated, Egypt was obtaining British and French military equipment through third parties (presumably Libya, thus substantiating the assumption that the Soviets were not furnishing all that Egypt wanted and that the issue of arms was the sore point between Cairo and Moscow).

Before he left, Sadat pushed an important opponent out of the mainstream of Egyptian decisionmaking, through the nomination of Mahmud Riyad for secretary-general of the League of Arab States to replace another Egyptian, 'Abd al-Khaliq Hassuna, who had served in that position since 1964. More than ever before, Sadat tightened his grip on the country's foreign policy.

The Moscow visit began and ended inauspiciously: neither Brezhnev nor Podgornyi was on hand to greet Sadat or see him off. Moscow's only comment on Brezhnev's absence from the welcoming ceremony was that he "was detained by a previous appointment"; it offered none for his failure to appear at departure time.[29] In light of the importance of the Egyptian connection to

26 ARR, No. 8 (April 16–30, 1972), 203.
27 FBIS/Egypt, March 27, 1972, p. G11; ARR, No. 7 (April 1–15, 1972), 175.
28 ARR, No. 8 (April 16–30, 1972), 203.
29 In his speech at Alexandria on May 1, 1972, Sadat, in the context of de-

the Soviet Union and the urgency of the visit for Sadat, the absence of Brezhnev and Podgornyi was a definite slight. Another unusual circumstance, given the centrality of military matters to the discussions, was the absence of War Minister Sadiq from Sadat's party. Furious over Soviet slights to Egyptian officers and Moscow's delay in supplying advanced weaponry, Sadiq had stayed in Cairo, but whether at his own insistence or Sadat's is not clear. The ranking Egyptian officer in the delegation was Air Vice-Marshal 'Abd al-Latif al-Baghdadi, who was appointed deputy minister of civil aviation, on April 24. According to one Arab source, Baghdadi, long an outspoken critic of the Soviets, was demoted to remove from the air force one leading exponent of its widespread anti-Soviet resentment, which was fed by rumors that Soviet advisers were deliberately going slowly in the training of Egyptian pilots, especially on advanced planes such as the MiG-23 and Su-11.[30]

A third indication of discord was the announcement that Sadat would leave twenty-four hours earlier than scheduled. In an attempt to answer the inevitable speculation this would engender, Kosygin devoted one-third of his unusually brief speech, given at the banquet for Sadat on the evening of April 28, to an explanation:

> The fact that the discussions were concluded quickly does not mean we have differed or that we have not reached agreement on certain matters. On the contrary, the real reason for the short talks was the common understanding and unity of aim. This has enabled us to reach the desired end in the shortest possible time.[31]

---

livering a rebuke to his right wing critics for "weeping" over Egypt's allegedly lost independence and its subservience to the USSR, offered an explanation of the Brezhnev incident: "Our enemies were very pleased. They said: Brezhnev did not receive Anwar as-Sadat at the airport. This means that the visit was a failure. . . . I take this opportunity to send, on your behalf, our greetings to him because we spent six hours together the first day and three hours the second day while he had a temperature of 39 degrees" (104 Fahrenheit). BBC/ME/3979/A/8 (May 3, 1972).

[30] *Al-Hawadith*, May 12, 1972 (a pro-Egyptian Beirut weekly), as quoted in Yaacov Ro'i and Ilana Dimant-Kass, "The Soviet Military Involvement in Egypt, January 1970–July 1972" (Jerusalem: The Hebrew University, The Soviet and East European Research Centre, Research Paper, No. 6, February 1974), p. 47.

[31] FBIS/Egypt, May 1, 1972, p. G1.

This explanation is highly implausible, especially when set in the context of the other irregularities attending the visit. In his equally brief comments, Sadat said several times that the discussions had been based on complete "frankness," the usual cue for basic disagreement. Also indicative of Cairo's disappointment was the inclusion of this term in Cairo's descriptions of the visit, but not in Moscow's, nor in the actual communiqué, which noted only that "the sides discussed a wide variety of questions connected with the situation now taking shape in the Middle East area."

The communiqué of April 29 attracted considerable attention abroad, for although it did not meet all of Egypt's demands for more arms, it did give Soviet sanction to Egypt's possible recourse to the use of arms. The Egyptians saw this as an important gain and later commented favorably on the April visit. In a formulation new to Soviet-Egyptian communiqués, the communiqué noted that, given the unregenerate hostility of Israel and the United States to a political settlement [satisfactory to the Arabs], "the Arab states . . . have every reason to use *other means* to regain the Arab lands captured by Israel" [in Arabic the words may be translated as 'various means' or 'all means,' and they have a stronger connotation than in English] (emphasis added).[32] For the first time, the Soviet government publicly acknowledged Egypt's right to use force to regain its territories if peaceful means failed. Thus, in principle, Moscow was not against a war, only a war for which it did not consider Egypt prepared. However, it was far from opening the arms tap all the way, as can be seen in the reference to the need "to study again" ways of increasing "the military potential" of Egypt. Moscow tried to reassure Egypt with the following: "The sides reached agreement on a further strengthening of military cooperation between them. The holding of appropriate important measures in this direction was arranged."

Why, so near to the Nixon visit, had the Soviet leadership agreed to the ominous phrasing of the communiqué? Two reasons may be suggested. First, the Kremlin was helping Sadat in his domestic need to bring back some sign that Moscow backed his assertions of inevitable war if Egypt's lands were not returned. Second, at the Moscow summit the phrase would strengthen the

32 FBIS/USSR, May 1, 1972, p. B2. The Russian meaning is similar to the English one.

Soviet argument that the Middle East situation was highly explosive and required the United States to intensify its pressure on Israel. It gave Moscow an added chip to use on Egypt's behalf.

The Egyptian and Soviet media both attributed great significance to the visit and stressed the indissoluble friendship of the two countries.[33] But it was the Egyptians, not the Soviets, who repeated the stipulation that the Arabs had the right to resort to war to regain their lands "because it has been confirmed that all political means have failed to achieve Israeli withdrawal peacefully and it is clear and certain now that war is inevitable to reach this goal";[34] and it was they who conveyed the impression that Moscow fully supported their determination to use force, if necessary. The Soviets were chary of commentary on this point.

Sadat returned to Egypt newly armed with a provocative phrase, but the military gap was far from being closed. The air vice-marshal stayed on for several more days, and two weeks later Grechko came to Cairo. Moscow gave no other sign that it favored escalation in the Middle East. With Nixon coming on May 22 and far-reaching military, economic, and political agreements with the United States in the offing, it adopted the mien of peace.

STASIS

The Egyptian military was seething with anti-Soviet sentiment. The economy was in deplorable condition. Low productivity, rising absenteeism, endemic shortages, and appalling waste mocked Sidqi's austerity and mobilization program. For the fellahin, the shortage of his staples—tomatoes, onions, and sugar —was of near-crisis proportions. The public mood was hardly total readiness for war, the objective set by the Sidqi Cabinet in January. Everywhere he turned, Sadat saw danger signals.

At a May Day rally in Alexandria, Sadat spoke out against those who disparaged the achievements of Egypt's socialist experiment and those who were in a panic about Egypt's independence and reliance on the Soviet Union: "When we befriend the USSR, we hear it said that a big power will occupy us? Why these complexes? . . . We are not in anyone's zone of influence.

[33] For example, *Pravda*, April 30 and May 5, 1972.
[34] See CPR, No. 5579, April 30, 1972; and BBC/ME/3981/A/2 (May 5, 1972).

We are the people who decide."[35] *Al-Gumhuriya*, the ASU's left-ist-oriented newspaper, parroted Sadat: can those who cast doubt on Egyptian-Soviet friendship "tell us in what way this friendship impairs our national independence, or can they tell us of an alternative to liberate the land and protect our national independence?"[36] But rhetoric did not still the doubts or answer the critics.

In a major speech on May 14, the first anniversary of "the corrective movement" (euphemism for the preemptive purge that had saved his position) Sadat told the People's Assembly that a group of former members of the 1952 Revolutionary Command Council (most prominent among whom were 'Abd al-Latif al-Baghdadi, Kamal al-Din Husayn, and Hasan Ibrahim) had petitioned him to establish a new national front that would supersede the ASU and be more avowedly Egyptian-centered (they had tried once before, shortly after Nasir's death).[37] He went on to say that it was permissible to disagree over government policy, but only within existing institutional structures—no extra-legal political groups would be tolerated; that his Soviet visit had been important, since Moscow upheld the right of the Arabs to use all means to regain their lands; and that Marshal Grechko was due to arrive that very day to implement the arrangements agreed on in Moscow.[38] His revelation that prominent individuals were urging him to change Egypt's policy toward the Soviet Union is interesting in that the petitioners were unlikely to have acted quixotically on their own, that is, without some institutional support, probably in the military, without some sense that they were expressing a politically formidable sentiment.

When Grechko arrived for the second time in three months (each visit following by several weeks a Sadat visit to Moscow),

[35] BBC/ME/3979/A/7-8 (May 3, 1972). Moscow's Cairo correspondent praised Sadat for dispelling rumors of growing strains in Soviet-Egyptian relations, for giving "a fitting rebuff to concocters of such fables." He also dismissed the hopes of "reactionaries" that the government's reexamination of cases relating to the sequestration of property on account of certain errors in any way presaged a restoration "of private capitalist companies that had been nationalized or placed under state control." V. Kudryavtsev, "Egypt's Ill-Wishers Rebuffed," *New Times*, No. 20 (May 1972), 11.

[36] CPR Supplement, May 4, 1972.

[37] ARR, No. 9 (May 1–15, 1972), p. 229. The proposal used the word *wataniyah*, which means "national" in the narrower sense, instead of *qawmiyah*, or "pan-Arab."

[38] BBC/ME/3990/A/1-14 (May 16, 1972).

he was greeted with great fanfare. Outwardly things went well. All the newspapers carried feature stories on Egyptian-Soviet friendship, as much to please the Soviets as to mobilize support behind Sadat's policy. *Al-Akhbar* wrote:

> The Soviet Union firmly believes in our right to employ all methods and means to restore our lands; and the Soviet Union is ready and willing to provide us with the means with which we can defeat the U.S.-Israeli imperialist alliance.[39]

A number of military displays were publicized: an overflight of Sinai by two MiG-25s, a Grechko-Sadiq visit to a Soviet naval squadron in Alexandria, and inspections of various military bases. On May 17, five days before the Moscow summit, the Cairo press used Grechko's visit as the occasion to report that a new Soviet-Egyptian arms agreement had been signed and that General Sadiq would visit the Soviet Union in the near future.[40] However, neither the joint communiqué issued the same day nor *Pravda's* report mentioned such an accord or hinted at any new arms deal.[41] As in February, the communiqué noted only that the two parties "exchanged views" to strengthen "the fighting capabilities of the Egyptian Armed Forces" in accordance with the statement of April 29, 1972. The "exchanged views" did not signify increased arms deliveries, and the communiqué did not break new ground, though Cairo newspapers gave the impression that it had.

Reservations about Moscow's fealty to the Arab cause continued to surface. On May 19 *Al-Ahram* published a lengthy account of a seminar on Soviet policies in the Middle East that had leveled a number of serious criticisms at Moscow.[42] First, the participants deplored the low priority of the Middle East in Soviet thinking and urged immediate steps to have the problem

[39] *Al-Akhbar*, May 17, 1972, as translated in CPR, No. 5596, May 17, 1972.
[40] FBIS/Egypt, May 18, 1972, p. G1.
[41] *Ibid.*, p. G2; *Pravda*, May 18, 1972.
[42] *Al-Ahram*, May 19, 1972, as quoted in CPR, Supplement, May 19, 1972. The participants included the following: Isma'il Fahmi, Under Secretary of Foreign Affairs; Tahsin Beshir, press spokesman for the Ministry of Foreign Affairs; Muhammad Awad al-Quni, former head of the Egyptian delegation to the UN; Osamah Al-Baz, Deputy Director of the Diplomatic Academy; Muhammad Hasanayn Haykal, Dr. 'Abd al-Malik Awdah, Muhammad Sayyid Ahmad, all editors on *Al-Ahram*; and Hatim Sadiq (the late President Nasir's son-in-law), Samih Sadiq, Jamil Matar, and Dr. Hazim al-Biblawi of *Al-Ahram*'s Center for Strategic and Political Studies.

placed on equal footing with Vietnam in upcoming Soviet discussions with Nixon. Second, they regretted that whereas the Soviet Union seemed satisfied with the existing situation of "no war, no peace" in the Arab-Israeli context, it was very actively extending its presence via a growing navy into the Mediterranean, the Persian Gulf, and the Indian Ocean, and establishing closer ties with Syria, Iraq, and Somalia, quite independently of considerations of Soviet-Egyptian relations. Third, observing that none of the communiqués issued at the end of high-level Soviet visits to these other countries contained any mention of Resolution 242, the Jarring talks, or the need for a political settlement, they deduced Soviet willingness to tailor its position to that of a courted client's attitude without regard for the Arab-Israeli issue or Egypt's position on the matter. This, they said, was something Egypt dare not overlook or accept in silence. Fourth, they argued that Soviet strategy, predicated on the assumption that the Arabs were incapable of an effective initiative that would require Moscow to adjust its approach, must be made to change. Fifth, they saw a convergence between the U.S. and Soviet strategies toward the Arab-Israeli problem, a de facto understanding to limit arms shipments to the protagonists, while allowing for Soviet professions of political support for the Arabs and assurances of eventual liberation. Unless Egypt marshaled sound reasons and firm actions to counter the insidious implications of such an approach, it would unwittingly be a party to the institutionalization of a Middle East stalemate. Sixth, lacking the wherewithal to challenge the economic dominance of the United States and Western Europe in the Middle East, the USSR depended on political and moral positions to enhance its presence in the Arab world. Should these prove to be antithetical to Arab interests, the Arabs would no longer look to Moscow as their "Qiblah" (i.e. the direction to which Muslims pray). Hence the Soviet Union should be made to realize what it stood to lose in acquiescing to the perpetuation of the present state of "no war, no peace." Finally, the participants warned that by freezing the status quo the Soviets were creating conditions for a Rightist turn toward the United States.

The published discussions created great excitement in Cairo and brought the participants under heavy fire. The Soviet ambassador demanded the removal of Haykal, Isma'il Fahmi, and the others involved in the seminar. Countervailing sentiments were widely disseminated: the very next day, Ihsan 'Abd al-Quddus lauded the Egyptian-Soviet relationship, upholding the need for faith in the Soviet Union;[43] a few days later, after the Moscow summit, other commentators professed to be encouraged by the dialogue that had occurred there on the Middle East; and the Egyptian (and Soviet) press devoted considerable space to celebrating the first anniversary of the Soviet-Egyptian treaty.[44]

Sadat assuaged his critics and importuned Moscow for more arms. He toured Egyptian air bases to soothe the military.[45] Isma'il Fahmi and Tahsin Beshir were placed on indefinite leaves of absence from the Ministry of Foreign Affairs for their part in the *Al-Ahram* seminar to appease the Soviets who had discreetly inquired whether the debate represented the official view of the government. Finally, Sadiq flew to Moscow (June 8–11).

The war minister's visit was a reversal of his behavior in late April when he had not accompanied Sadat. It was designed to ascertain once and for all what kind of shopping list Cairo could fill in Moscow and how quickly and to resolve the irritating grievances that were growing on the Egyptian side. Even the knowledgeable Lebanese journalist Fuad Matar was momentarily taken in by the visit, calling it a "turning point," because the Soviet military was so receptive, among other things putting on a demonstration of an amphibious assault in order to show its problems and possibilities.[46] But the display of amity in Moscow led nowhere; the Soviets kept up their criticisms of Israel but gave no sign of meeting Egypt's requests.[47] Sadiq returned empty-handed.

The Nixon-Brezhnev summit troubled Sadat; the low-key call for a political settlement; the lack of immediacy; the neglect of the Palestinians. As so often in the past it was Haykal who spoke to Cairo's innermost mood, this time its dismay over the situation of "no peace, no war."[48] Haykal likened the Middle East to a

[43] *Akhbar al-Yawm*, May 20, 1972.

[44] For example, FBIS/USSR International Affairs, May 30, 1972, p. B1; *Pravda*, May 27, 1972; *Al-Gumhuriya*, May 27, 1972. See D. Volsky, "Moscow and Cairo," *New Times*, No. 19 (May 1972), 9.

[45] An Israeli broadcast in Arabic on May 23 cited *Al-Hawadith*. BBC/ME/3998/i (May 25, 1972).

[46] *Al-Nahar*, June 15, 1972.   [47] *Pravda*, June 19, 1972.

[48] There was no direct response in the Soviet press to Haykal's series of articles. However, on July 6, Podgornyi welcomed Asad in the Kremlin and complained that "those saying that the Soviet Union benefits from the state

minefield that both the United States and the Soviet Union sought to traverse unscathed while proceeding to their détente. Taking pains to disavow any desire "to cast doubt" on the Soviet attitude out of a "profound belief in the importance of Arab-Soviet friendship" both in war and in peace, he said that the situation had to be seen as it was, irrespective of the embarrassing insights that were revealed and of the lack of enthusiasm for open discussion displayed by many "oversensitive" Soviet friends.[49]

The Soviet Union, he wrote, had given liberally to the Arab cause, but it, too, had benefited, gaining for itself a presence "in the warm seas" as a consequence. By cooperating (if only tacitly) to prevent war in the Middle East, the superpowers were pursuing their own ends. For its part, Egypt must terminate the state of "no peace, no war," which is "in our conditions, a crime" that could create a lack of credibility inside Egypt, weaken the ties between Egypt and the rest of the Arab world, and end the friendship between Egypt and the Soviet Union.[50] "By every means and in a calculated manner," Egypt had to break up the logjam lest Israel and the United States—the principal beneficiaries—retain their advantages permanently. He compared Moscow's role to that "of a lawyer who has come forward through conviction and interest to defend the Arab cause against an attempt to murder it. In his defense, this lawyer resorts to all methods he may find suitable, but he does not consider himself the victim of this murder attempt which is being continued on Arab soil."[51] That being the case there were several propositions that, though displeasing to the Soviets, needed to be stated: the Soviet Union is a superpower that is motivated by concrete national interests not just lofty principles as it is wont to claim, and as such it had to be considered in the same light as the United States; and Egyptian-Soviet friendship is not a one-way street:

. . . portraying Arab-Soviet friendship as an arrangement whereby the Arab side takes and the Soviet side gives is a distortion of the truth and is not in anyone's interest. The giving

of no peace, no war are repeating an imperialist propaganda against us." See Heikal, BBC/ME/4048/A/1 (July 24, 1972).

[49] BBC/ME/4012/A/2 (June 12, 1972).
[50] BBC/ME/4019/A/2-3 (June 20, 1972).
[51] BBC/ME/4030/A/7 (July 3, 1972).

and the taking is mutually serving the interests of both sides; otherwise, we would be transferring the relationship from the level of cooperation to the level of charity . . . this is not true of Egypt. Whatever Egypt gets from the Soviet Union is paid for.

Haykal identified the USSR's aims in the Arab world as follows: 1) to liquidate British and French domination and prevent the United States from supplanting the old imperialist powers; 2) to disseminate Marxism and substitute it for the feudalist capitalism that is collapsing in the region; 3) to strengthen its position through cooperation with the countries of the region; 4) to exploit its advantageous position in the Middle East to undermine American interests; and 5) to avail itself of the Arab region for passage to Africa and Asia.[52] He indicated that Moscow had been successful in realizing these goals and therefore had no grounds for questioning the benefits of its Arab investment or causing the Arabs to feel ungrateful for past and present assistance.

The articles were published at a time when Sadat was increasingly solicitous of his military, whose anger with Moscow had in no way been mitigated by Sadiq's visit. On June 11 the People's Assembly approved a draft law, prepared by Sadiq, reinstating with the same rank and seniority most of the officers who had been sacked for political reasons during the May 1971 purges.[53] In late June, almost a month earlier than originally planned, Sadat paid a two-day visit to the front line troops, in order, according to a Lebanese source, to deal with the disturbing climate of turmoil and recrimination.[54] Sadat spoke reassuringly, saying Egypt "would embark on the future with an advanced military industry, manufacturing her own aircraft and electronic equipment."[55] But the miasma of resentment was not easily dispelled.

In the meantime Sadat had sent two letters to Brezhnev requesting his assessment of the talks with Nixon, particularly as they related to the Middle East. After the second letter Ambassador Vinogradov brought a reply on July 8.[56] Haykal later related

[52] *Ibid.*, pp. A/3-4.   [53] CPR, No. 5621, June 11, 1972.
[54] ARR, No. 13 (July 1–15, 1972), 323.
[55] CPR, No. 5636, June 29, 1972.
[56] According to *Akhbar al-Yawm*, July 22, 1972, Sadat's decision to expel Soviet military personnel was communicated to the Soviet ambassador on July 8. CPR, No. 5662, July 22, 1972.

that Sadat listened until the translator had finished reading, then "twice asked if that was all and the Ambassador replied in the affirmative." Sadat then informed the ambassador that, effective July 17, the services of the Soviet military advisers would no longer be required.[57] He had decided that an "electric shock" was needed to straighten out the relationship. Two days later Sadat again saw Vinogradov, on the same day that he met with Syrian President Hafiz Asad, who had come directly from four days in Moscow hoping to smooth over the deteriorating relationship between Cairo and Moscow and to report on the eagerness with which Moscow gave him its pledge to strengthen "Syria's military potential" and continue bilateral military cooperation.[58] Ambassador Vinogradov saw Prime Minister Sidqi twice that day, and again on the following day. On July 12 Cairo announced that Sidqi would visit Moscow the next day for "a friendly business visit." Sadat was making a last-minute effort to forestall the implementation of his decision.

The Cairo press dutifully carried banner headlines and front page stories of Sidqi's talks and of Brezhnev's return to Moscow from an interrupted holiday in the Crimea to lead the Soviet side. Many Cairo journalists agreed with Quddus, who said the Soviet Union did not benefit from the situation of "no war, no peace"—a slap at Haykal, a long-standing rival.[59]

The delegation Sidqi took to Moscow was high level and broadly representative of Egypt's power structure; it included Foreign Minister Murad Ghaleb, a deputy war minister, the Minister of Interior Mamduh Salim, and top aides of Sidqi's who had worked closely on economic problems with Soviet ministries. The Soviet side included Brezhnev, Kosygin, Grechko,

[57] Haykal tells that his discussion with Sadat took place on July 11, making him the first Egyptian journalist to have been made privy to the decision. CPR, No. 5668, July 28, 1972.

[58] Cairo was also interested in the communiqué Asad had signed in Moscow because it formulated Soviet and Syrian support "for the Palestine resistance movement as a component part of the national liberation movement of the Arab people." Previous communiqués arising from Arab visits to Moscow had mentioned only the lawful and legitimate rights of the Arab people of Palestine. Moscow was now raising the Palestinian resistance movement to the status of a national liberation movement, which in its doctrinal pantheon is a necessary precursor of national independence. *Soviet News*, No. 5647 (July 18, 1972), 238-239; CPR, No. 5651 (July 11, 1972).

[59] CPR, No. 5655, July 15, 1972; see also *Ruz al-Yusif*, a weekly, and *Al-Masa'* of July 17, 1972, as quoted in FBIS/USSR, July 17, 1972, p. B2.

and Gromyko. All the discussions were held on July 14: one session, lasting about three hours, dealt with economic issues; the other, lasting for more than five hours, focused on military and political matters and was restricted to a few members on each side.[60] Scarcely twenty-eight hours after arriving, Sidqi left, returning to Cairo at 0300 on July 15 and reporting immediately to Sadat. The truncated visit belied the communiqué's reaffirmation of "the invariability and identity of their views both on the issues of further development and strengthening of friendly relations and all-round cooperation between the Soviet Union and the Arab Republic of Egypt and on topical international issues."[61] The lie was given to the usual implication of an "identity" of views by one glaring and highly portentous omission: for the first time since the Soviets had been dealing with Sadat, a political communiqué did not mention military aid or military cooperation directly. It used none of the pregnant phrases—strengthening defense capacity, or enhancing "the fighting capabilities," or "increasing the military potential," or satisfaction with "the development of cooperation between the armed forces" of the two countries. Only the unobtrusive and more ambiguous term "all-round cooperation" suggested any military collaboration at all. The agreement on economic matters was completely overshadowed by the disagreement on military issues. The visit was a total failure. What thoughts must have raced through Kosygin's mind as he endured Sidqi's after-dinner speech larded with fulsome praise of Soviet aid and Egyptian confidence and trust in the "Soviet brothers" who readily provide "all kinds and forms of support and backing in the various fields."[62]

On July 18 Sadat announced that as of July 17 the Soviet military mission in Egypt had been terminated.

EXODUS

After studying the situation in all its aspects and in full appreciation of the tremendous aid the Soviet Union has extended to us, and while fully anxious for the friendship of the Soviet Union, I found it appropriate, as we are on the threshold of a new stage of this friendship, to make the following decision:

[60] *Al-Ahram*, July 16, 1972, as quoted in FBIS/USSR, July 19, 1972, p. B3. See also BBC/ME/4040/i (July 14, 1972).
[61] FBIS/USSR, July 17, 1972, p. B3.　　[62] FBIS/Egypt, July 17, 1972, p. G2.

1. To terminate, as from 17 July, the mission of the Soviet military advisers and experts who came here in compliance with our request. Our men in the Armed Forces are to replace them in all the work they were doing.

2. All the military establishments and equipment which were set up on Egyptian soil in the period that followed the June 1967 aggression will become the exclusive property of the Arab Republic of Egypt and will fall under the administration of our Armed Forces.

3. To call for an Egypt-Soviet meeting on a level to be agreed to exchange views with regard to the coming stage. This should be done within the framework of the Cooperation and Friendship Treaty with the Soviet Union.

The first and second resolutions have been put into force as from yesterday.[63]

With these words Sadat electrified the ASU Central Committee, the country, and the world. Not since Nasir had nationalized the Suez Canal Company almost sixteen years earlier to the day had an Egyptian leader so captured the attention and imagination of the Arab world and the international community.

In his July 18 speech and in the ones that followed, Sadat reviewed the evolution of Egyptian-Soviet relations, especially since 1971, emphasizing that during his secret visit in March 1971 differences between Cairo and Moscow had emerged over the quality of armaments and the schedule of deliveries. After signing the Treaty of Friendship and Cooperation, he had naturally expected the Soviet Union to deliver the kinds of weapons necessary to ensure that 1971 would be a decisive year, but "those weapons failed to arrive on the dates agreed upon." Then the Soviet Union became involved in the Indo-Pakistani war, and there were further delays. Repeated visits failed to resolve the difficulties. The decision to terminate the presence in Egypt of Soviet military advisers was intended to encourage both parties to take a fresh look at their relationship. Ironically, the following day a Soviet delegation arrived to participate in a round of cultural events celebrating Egyptian-Soviet Friendship Week!

[63] *Egyptian Gazette*, July 19, 1972.

The expulsion of Soviet military personnel was a signal reaffirmation of the end of classic imperialism as we have known it in recent centuries. Like "gunboat diplomacy," a major military presence by a great power was no longer a guarantee of political hegemony. In an age of superpowers, the small powers had acquired a new lease on independent action and with it the practice of balance of power politics. The expulsion was a surprise not only to non-Arab analysts but to the well-informed Arab commentators, whose antennae are usually finely attuned to the slightest deviation in Arab policy. Fuad Matar said of the development: "The dimensions of Sadat's decision to oust Russia from Egypt will preoccupy the Arab world and shake it the way Nasir's decision in 1955 to let Russia enter Egypt" shook the Arab world.[64]

The departure went smoothly. For several days prior to July 17 Soviet military personnel had been literally taken off the streets of Cairo and Alexandria and driven under protective custody to various embarkation points for flights home. Sadat was not taking any chances on a counter-coup. But these precautions proved completely unnecessary. On July 17, twenty-four hours before Sadat's public announcement, Egyptian personnel replaced the Soviets operating the air defense system. Soviet dependents were gathered and either flown out of Cairo or sent home by ship from Alexandria. The entire operation was carried out with courtesy, discretion, and dispatch.

Within a month between 15,000 and 20,000 Soviet military personnel (there were approximately 600 advisers in the country before June 1967) had been removed, including all Soviet pilots. Fewer than one thousand instructors and technicians remained with Egyptian units. The removal of Soviet units included "120 MiG-21 Js, 20 Sukhoi-11s, about four MiG-23s, up to 260 SAM-3s at about 65 Soviet-controlled sites, some SAM-4s and SAM-6s, and a squadron of TU-16 maritime reconnaissance aircraft" disguised in Egyptian colors but flown by Soviet crews.[65] Thus, "Soviet interceptor aircraft engaged in defense against possible Israeli air raids" were removed, as were some of their radar and electronic equipment.[66] Egypt's air defense system was presumed

[64] *Al-Nahar*, July 19, 1972.

[65] *NYT*, July 19, 1972; also *Strategic Survey 1971* (London: Institute for Strategic Studies, 1971), p. 31.

[66] *NYT*, August 4, 1972. Much of this matériel was returned prior to the October War.

to have been weakened, but to what extent it was impossible to gauge.

The Soviet military relinquished the six air fields, or sections thereof, that had been their exclusive preserve since early 1970. No longer could Soviet planes reconnoiter the U.S. Sixth Fleet from Egyptian soil. This loss cut deeply into Moscow's strategic dividend, but the Soviets quickly absorbed it by keeping more ships on station and by satellite reconnaissance.

Sadat did not insist on the complete removal or uprooting of all vestiges of the Soviet presence in Egypt. Most particularly, he did not end the naval facilities enjoyed by the Soviet fleet at Alexandria, Port Said, and, to a much lesser degree, at Ras Banas (on the Red Sea). These were curtailed but not closed down. Soviet naval vessels retained docking, repair, refueling, and re-provisioning privileges, but no longer were sections of these ports fenced off, policed by Soviet personnel, and treated as extraterritorial Soviet enclaves. There was still strategic advantage left to Moscow in the new circumscribed conditions, when coupled with its alternative access to Syrian ports. After all, there was always the possibility of an improvement, of a return to the previous situation. Sadat's toleration of the residual presence showed he had no desire for a complete rupture.

The expulsion elated the Egyptian masses. This move of Sadat's evoked outbursts of pride, of exhilaration at Egypt's independence, of relief that the "new pashas" had been evicted so easily, and gained him a popularity greater than any he had heretofore enjoyed. He had rid himself of a constricting army of advisers without for the moment seriously weakening his military position vis-à-vis the Israelis: the SAM's could be operated by Egyptians. The anticipated decrease in efficiency of the air defense system was minimized as a result of soaring morale and motivation among the Egyptian officers.

Sadat had taken a major decision. He demonstrated that Egypt retained an independence that belied oversimplified explanations of how a great power exercises influence over a militarily dependent and economically heavily indebted Third World client state. Whatever merit there is to the argument that Moscow maneuvered Sadat into a situation where he acted the way he did, the crucial fact was that the actual decision had been Sadat's. Subsequent Soviet policy and premises had to proceed from the new reality that he created by his action.

EXEGESIS

Sadat gave three reasons for his decision: 1) Moscow's unwillingness to provide offensive weapons; 2) its failure to deliver weapons in the quantities and on the dates promised; 3) its "excessive caution" as an ally, its attempt to impose conditions on the use of the weapons that were given.[67] Let us examine these reasons and those Sadat did not mention.

Offensive weapons. The biggest canard in all Western reporting on the affair was the prevailing uncritical acceptance, certainly prior to October 6, 1973, of Sadat's claim that the Soviet Union had refused to supply him with the "offensive weapons" he needed to carry "the battle" to Israel.[68]

What offensive weapons did the Soviets withhold? Bombers? While useful as morale boosters and for hit-and-run attacks on Israeli urban centers, they would not have been strategically decisive. Moreover, the lack of a fighter plane to fly protective cover for bomber missions—the MiG-21 wanted the range—sharply reduced their military utility. Ground-to-ground missiles? The limited accuracy and small payloads of conventional explosives made ground-to-ground missiles "ridiculously ineffective as compared to their cost: a million dollars worth of these missiles delivers less of an effective punch than the payload of a single fighter-bomber sortie":

> In order to knock out Israeli rear installations and airfields in Sinai (the only feasible targets), it would take a sizeable chunk of the entire Russian inventory of battlefield and short-range missiles, weapons which have never been intended for use with non-nuclear warheads . . .[69]

Fighters? The Egyptians had ample numbers of MiG-21s to provide air cover and close support for any limited operation across the canal. The Soviets lacked a fighter-bomber comparable to the Phantoms, the MiG-23s not having the bomb capacity of the F-4s; and in any case they were not yet available in large enough

[67] *NYT*, July 25, 1972.
[68] For example, Edward R. F. Sheehan, "Why Sadat Packed Off the Russians," *NYT Magazine* (August 6, 1972). See also CPR, No. 5030, January 12, 1975.
[69] Edward Luttwak, "The Military Balance . . . Moscow Notwithstanding," *New Middle East*, No. 48 (September 1972), 16.

quantities to be a significant military factor. The Soviets were tired of being reminded, as the Egyptians well knew, that they did not possess an aircraft equal to the Phantoms. A month after Sadat's speech Haykal told this revealing anecdote:

> Certain persons in Egypt had been persistently demanding an aircraft equal to the Phantom. The persistence reached the extent of becoming a headache to the friends in Moscow until Brezhnev one day said verbatim: "Please, I do not want to hear any more about this aircraft for which you have been persistently asking. Do not bring up this subject again. When the time comes we shall broach this subject with you."[70]

Excluding nuclear weapons, of course, no other weapons in the Soviet arsenal were denied the Egyptians, who, in fact, had been supplied with an impressive array of offensive arms.

> This includes more than 1000 pieces of artillery (guns, howitzers and heavy mortars). Deployed as it is along the Canal, this static but powerful force could provide direct fire-support as well as effective interdiction from zero to fifteen miles east of the Canal. 200 attack (MiG-17) aircraft for close support, and for interdiction in the immediate rear of the battle zone (zero to one hundred miles from the Canal). 100 strike (Su-7) aircraft for deep interdiction in the entire Sinai and pre-1967 Israeli territory. In addition, the Egyptians also have 200 MiG-21 fighters . . .[71]

The Egyptians also had massive quantities of armor, artillery, and military equipment adequate for a canal-crossing operation.[72] Aside from the TU-22 bomber, the only other offensive "weapon" denied to the Egyptians was the use of Soviet combat pilots, and even this could have been reversed if necessary.

Unreliable deliveries. This is the most difficult of Sadat's allegations to evaluate. Though evidence is lacking for an informed judgment, it is entirely possible that the Egyptians were kept on short rations of ammunition and spare parts in order to optimize Soviet political leverage and forestall any adventurist Egyptian

[70] BBC/ME/4072/A/3 (August 21, 1972).
[71] Luttwak, "The Military Balance," p. 16.
[72] See, for example, *The Military Balance 1972–1973* (London: International Institute for Strategic Studies, 1972), p. 30.

military action. During the Indo-Pakistani war, the Soviet Union did divert weapons originally intended for Egypt to India and remove some air defense cover from around the Aswan Dam in order to dissuade Sadat from attempting anything rash while Moscow was preoccupied on the subcontinent. The USSR may well also have been dilatory about subsequent deliveries of promised arms shipments, as Sadat alleged, in the interest of exerting greater control while important negotiations were in progress with the United States.

Soviet restraint on the use of weapons. Was it Soviet, or Egyptian, caution that was operative? Two Lebanese journalists, 'Abd al-Karim Abu al-Nasr and Fuad Matar, say Sadat's attempt to blame the Soviets is suspect. They do not accept Sadat's image of an Egypt eager for "the battle" but frustrated by Soviet parsimony. Rather, they see the Egyptians as trying to deflect criticism from themselves by disseminating the idea that the USSR, because of its policy of détente with the United States, limited its arms deliveries to defensive weapons in order to prevent the Arabs from waging war. This is an old idea that began as a whisper and "metamorphosed into an accusation, especially after Nasir's death."[73] Abu al-Nasr seriously questioned Egypt's willingness to fight and quoted a "senior Soviet diplomat in an Arab capital" as saying, "We have given the Arabs weapons similar to those we gave to India and North Vietnam. The issue is not arms, but the ability to use these arms."[74] After all, the decision to fight lay in Egypt's hands, as Sadat himself had stated on a number of occasions. Fuad Matar, while critical of Sadat, did uphold his general thesis that the Soviet Union did not want either a war in the Middle East or a settlement, that it believed "the longer the conflict remains unresolved, the more its Arab allies or friends will need it."[75]

Two other reasons, given by Sadat after the October War, require comment. First, it was essential to his overall policy that the Arabs get credit for the decision to go to war. In March 1974, in an interview with Arnaud de Borchgrave, he stated:

[73] *Al-Nahar,* July 16, 1972.
[74] *Al-Nahar,* June 9, 1972; see also 'Abd al-Karim Abu al-Nasr, *Al-Nahar,* May 31, 1972.
[75] Fuad Matar, *Al-Nahar,* December 8, 1972.

No strategist in America or Israel guessed correctly why I asked Soviet military advisers to leave in July 1972. Everyone thought that I had abandoned war as a way of breaking the deadlock. They all said that without Soviet advisers I could not go to war. Well, with the Russian military out of the country, I was making sure that no one could claim that what we did in the future was inspired by the Soviets. If Arab victory there was to be, it had to be clearly Arab. A victory that the world would describe as a non-Arab victory would clearly have defeated my overall strategic objective. . . .[76]

Second, he expelled the Soviets in order to have a free hand to attack when he was ready, the implication being that if the Soviets were present they would prevent his doing so. His post facto rationale ignores a number of salient facts. In 1969, the Soviet military presence had not prevented Nasir from launching the war of attrition; indeed, it was an accepted assurance then, as in 1973, that Moscow would not stand aside if Egypt faced defeat. In 1972, there was no eastern front: the Syrians were not ready for war, and Sadat would have been most unlikely to take on the Israelis alone. Far from going to war without regard to Soviet wishes, Sadat prudently assured himself of Soviet backing several times before D-Day.

Skepticism of Sadat's explanations is reinforced when one looks at the reasons he chose not to mention but that must have been part of his calculations.

First, there was the role of the Egyptian military. According to an article on July 21 in *Al-Nida*, the organ of the Lebanese Communist Party, War Minister Sadiq had presented Sadat with an ultimatum on behalf of the senior officers: get rid of the Russians or "the army would impose the measure of direct interference in the country's political affairs."[77] Certainly rumors of the military's restiveness under Soviet tutelage were rife in Cairo. Egyptian officers did not get along well with their Soviet advisers, who were arrogant and disparaging. They also believed, rightly or not, that they were given obsolete equipment, kept low on spare parts and ammunition, and deliberately given unduly complicated instructions on the maintenance and operation of weap-

[76] CPR, No. 5736, March 18, 1974.
[77] ARR, No. 14 (July 16–31, 1972), 348.

ons. One story that made the rounds in Cairo was that early in 1972 the Egyptian planners realized that their Soviet advisers were not giving honest evaluations of their work, not pointing out the flaws in their estimates or contingency plans. A worrying belief spread that the Russians patronizingly approved any assessment, however faulty, that the Egyptians presented. To confirm this, a draft plan for the defense of a sector of the canal, deliberately omitting a number of elementary considerations, was shown to the Russians, who passed it with their usual, "That's fine." Though probably an apocryphal episode, there may have been enough truth in this and similar stories to account for the tense relationship between the Egyptian and Soviet military.

A second and related consideration that Sadat conveniently skirted in giving reasons for the strategic "pause" with the Soviets was the boost that their expulsion could provide his internal position. Domestic morale was low. In addition to the grumbling in the military, Sadat was faced with a dangerous combination of restiveness and anomie in the students because of their confused political motives and bleak personal prospects. It was they who had first brought the question of the Soviet-Egyptian relationship into the open with their taunts of "fight or settle." It was they who pressed the issue of the emigration of Soviet Jews to Israel: how can the Soviets be friends and still permit large numbers of Jews to leave for Israel?[78] This gesture might quiet them. As for the workers, they were essentially conservative: their ethos was rooted in Islam and was antithetical to Marxism. Perhaps an outpouring of patriotic and anti-Soviet fervor would temporarily drown out the clamor arising out of their economic grievances.

Third, to ensure success on the battlefield against Israel, Sadat needed Arab allies. Particularly important to him was his courtship of Saudi Arabia. Faysal was open to Sadat as he never had been to Nasir, but he was morbidly suspicious of Cairo's extensive Soviet connection. Sadat knew that expulsion of the Soviets would find favor with the deeply anti-communist Faysal. It would also be very popular with al-Qadhdhafi, who blamed the Soviet Union for the violent division of Muslim Pakistan. But above all Sadat's diplomacy in the Arab world was geared to reconciliation with the Saudis, to reversal of almost two decades of Saudi-Egyptian hostility that had its origins in Nasir's anti-monarchical pol-

---

[78] 'Abd-al-Karim Abu al-Nasr, *Al-Nahar*, July 19, 1972.

icy and ambitions in the Persian Gulf; and to ever-growing reliance on groups and policies grounded in Islamic conservatism.
Sadat kept Faysal well-briefed on his relationship with Moscow
and his overall diplomatic and military strategy against Israel.
Never far from his mind was the aim of attracting the fabulous
oil wealth of Saudi Arabia to the military support and economic
development of Egypt.

Fourth, somewhere in the process of weighing the pros and
cons of forcing a Soviet exodus, Sadat may also have reasoned
that his decision would bring a change in U.S. policy, something
the Saudis had told him would be forthcoming. Like Nasir before him, Sadat appreciated that Soviet power and assistance,
invaluable and impressive as they were, could not push back the
Israelis without Washington's help. The United States explained
its increased military aid to Israel as a response to the Soviet
buildup in Egypt; and Kissinger had stated several times that the
"expulsion" of Soviet military personnel from Egypt was a major
American objective. If the deed were done, the desired effects
might be forthcoming. Sadat had been raised on backgammon,
a game that requires skill but essentially depends on a lucky
throw of the dice that can change one's situation with dramatic
suddenness. His throw might find favor with Washington.

Finally, there was in Sadat's decision the unknown in the equa-
tion, the man himself—resistant to definition yet crucial to understanding. Lying beyond the calculations of costs and benefits,
of feasible and strategic options, beyond the disappointment with
Soviet arms and pressure from the Egyptian military, there was
the very personal anguish over the friend who is not a friend, the
"friend" who does not help when help is essential.[79] As far as
can be determined Sadat consulted no one; his decision was
his own.

Though no orator, in those speeches of July 18 and July 24,
Sadat held his audiences. What he lacked in suavity, verbal facility, or charisma, he made up for with a disarming and calculated

[79] In early October 1972, about two weeks after Israeli armor had struck in
Lebanon in retaliation for the murder of 11 Israeli athletes by Palestinian
terrorists at the Olympic games in Munich, Sadat said in an interview that
the Soviet Union had not given Egypt MiG-23 fighter-bombers capable of
"striking in depth" against Israel: "If I had a fighter-bomber, I would not
have allowed Israel to commit its aggression in southern Lebanon. *Russia is
a friend who is listed on my side but is not really so*" (emphasis added).
NYT, October 8, 1972.

candor. Throughout these speeches he harped on the themes of insincerity and fickleness: the United States had tried to mislead him, to gain time, and to induce him to despair of ever being able to bring Israel to withdrawal. But this was no shock to him because the United States is the friend of our enemy, Israel, committed to her. However, what pained him (and his tone and gestures were expressive of his emotions) was the USSR. The Soviets, he repeated several times, were friends, staunch friends since 1955, and Egypt went along with their excuses and understood their delays, for a friend should go along with a friend; but to his utter shock and disbelief, and here he many times exclaimed, "Allah!!", he discovered after long patience that this friend "makes accounts and demands accounts! My God!" (in Arabic: Yahsib wa yatahasab), and that he could say No! (i.e. refuse Egypt's requests for arms). This sense of personal affront and rejection, this denial of dignity, was one facet of the many-faceted truth that drove Sadat to take the decision he did.[80]

The immediate Soviet response was silence. Twenty-four hours later TASS issued a statement:

> Now the Soviet military personnel in the Arab Republic of Egypt has completed its functions. With the awareness of this, after the exchange of opinions, the sides deemed it expedient to bring back to the Soviet Union the military personnel that had been sent to Egypt for a limited period. This personnel will shortly return to the USSR.[81]

On July 23, in a lengthy article commemorating the twentieth anniversary of the Egyptian Revolution, *Pravda* reviewed the record of Soviet assistance in the transformation of Egypt's economy, in the development of a "powerful public sector, which includes nearly three-quarters of industry and all transport and communications," and in Egypt's military recovery since the 1967 defeat.[82] Soviet arms and advisers had restored Egypt's "com-

---

[80] For insight into the important cultural component implicit in Sadat's speeches I am indebted to Dr. Arieh Loya, an Israeli scholar, who has taught at several American universities. An interesting biographical essay on Sadat is: Jon Kimche, "The Riddle of Sadat," *Midstream*, 20, No. 4 (April 1974), 7-28.

[81] FBIS/USSR, July 20, 1972, p. B1.

[82] FBIS/USSR, July 24, 1972, p. B11.

bat might . . . in line with modern standards," but now that Soviet military personnel had completed their tasks and were returning home "the enemies of Soviet-Egyptian cooperation" were trying to exploit the completion of this aspect of their cooperation, alleging that the "foundations of Soviet-Egyptian friendship" had been weakened. Warning against "the attempts of rightist reactionary forces" in a number of Arab countries— "including Egypt"—to sabotage Soviet-Egyptian friendship and the progressive measures that had been taken in Egypt, *Pravda* reaffirmed the importance of the 1971 treaty. Increasingly, Soviet sources expressed concern over right wing efforts to reverse, "with assistance from outside," socialist measures and "undermine the moral condition of the armed forces."[83] Their criticism of Sadat's drift away from Nasir's socialist course grew, as Sadat showed signs of modifying foreign policy, too.[84]

On the surface Moscow accepted its strategic losses with equanimity. What it had long coveted, paid heavily for, and acquired in 1970—air and naval privileges in Egypt—it now lost almost completely. Only severely reduced naval facilities remained of the once extensive military presence. But aside from petty and self-defeating retaliation in the economic sphere, Moscow had no alternative to acquiescence. The absence of geographical contiguity, the high political costs of intervention, and the marginal importance of Egypt to Soviet national security, argued against any military response; the Brezhnev Doctrine did not encompass Egypt. Nor could Moscow, even if it had wanted to, precipitate a coup. Aid had not enabled it to build up a dependable political base whence to intervene in Egyptian domestic politics; the Soviet aid net had not caught the desirable Egyptian bureaucratic fish. The Soviets were also hampered by their social isola-

---

[83] Iu. Griadunov, "Arabskaia respublika Egipet," in *Mezhdunarodnyi ezhegodnik: politika i ekonomika, 1973* (Moscow: Politizdat, 1973), pp. 238-239. See also, D.V. [Volskii], "Stable Cooperation," *New Times*, No. 44 (October 1972), 7; D. Volsky, "Our Common Possession," *New Times*, No. 37 (September 1972), 5. Volskii criticized those harboring illusions, who do "not know that there are elements in the Arab countries who would like with the imperialists' help to block the process of socio-economic restructuring, consign the ideas of Nasserism to oblivion, and partake of the profits of the American and West European monopolies operating in the Middle East." See also, R. Petrov, "The Soviet Union and Arab Countries," *International Affairs*, No. 11 (November 1972), 28.

[84] For example, see E. Dimitreyev, "Twenty Years of the Egyptian Revolution," *International Affairs*, No. 8 (August 1972), 49-53.

tion; in a society where personal connections are crucial to institutional influence, they were outsiders.

Moscow could, however, have affected the timing and character of its leaving. During his visit to Moscow, which came five days after Sadat had told Vinogradov to have the Soviet troops removed but four days before the deadline for departure began, Sidqi had offered Soviet leaders a face-saving way out. A joint statement was to be issued:

> . . . saying something to the effect that the two sides had agreed on the withdrawal of Soviet experts and advisers . . . but for some reason the Soviet side did not agree to this. The Chairman of the Soviet Council of Ministers Alexei Kosygin said: We do not accept such a statement. The Soviet leader Leonid Brezhnev added: If you wish to make such decisions, then declare them unilaterally.[85]

The question whether Soviet leaders fumbled the chance or elected not to take it raises the bigger issue of Soviet aims. One line of thought says they blundered. Believing that Sadat was bluffing, that he would draw back from fear of the probable consequences, they risked a split with Egypt and a loss of prestige in the Arab world. If Moscow had thought Sadat was serious, it might have lessened the humiliation of leaving and even turned the incident to advantage with the United States, by "offering" to leave in the interests of détente, rather than by exiting under duress; yet this was not done. If this is true and the Soviets were guilty of poor judgment, happenstance amply made up for their error.

A second view, a variant of the first, was offered by Fuad Matar shortly after the event. He contended that the Soviets were prepared to negotiate on Sadat's request for more MiGs, SAMs, and other weapons, but that they were adamantly opposed to placing Soviet military compounds and bases, including Soviet troops, under Egyptian authority.[86] According to Matar, Brezhnev re-

---

[85] BBC/ME/4072/A/4 (August 21, 1972).

[86] Fuad Matar, *Russya al-nasiriyya wa Misr al-misriyya*, II (*Nasirite Russia and Egyptian Egypt*) (Beirut: Al-Nahar Publications, 1972), 21-22. Sadat subsequently confirmed Matar's contention. See FBIS/Egypt, September 9, 1975, p. D5: "My opinion regarding the withdrawal of the Russian experts was that there should be no Russian expert on Egyptian soil receiving orders from Russia. Whoever wants to work here must take his orders from the Egyptian command."

minded Sidqi that Moscow had on four different occasions offered to withdraw Soviet military advisers and troops, the implication being that Cairo had always backed off. Presumably, he
expected Sadat to do so again.

A more probable conjecture is that Moscow had shrewdly decided that incurring public embarrassment carried with it little
real risk. Détente, the paramount Soviet objective at the time,
would be easier to arrange if the United States thought there was
a serious deterioration in Soviet relations with Egypt, of which
one manifestation was the forced removal of Soviet troops. Washington would become satisfied that the Soviets represented no
threat in the Middle East. In the meantime, ties with Egypt,
though strained, would remain close, because in Moscow's view
Washington would not or could not pressure Israel into making
the concessions that might lead to a major reorientation of
Egyptian foreign policy and without which Egypt would not
have really new options. Nor would Israel be likely to use the
lull wisely to advance proposals attractive to Egypt. The net result would be the perpetuation of "no war, no peace," which
admirably suited Soviet policy in the area. Sadat, unable to gar-
ner support for a diplomatic settlement or to find other arms
suppliers, would discover that "sliding toward the West"[87] was
no substitute for Soviet weapons and good-will. Disappointed
when the turn to the West failed to produce a settlement, Egypt
would return with its shopping list unfilled, and Moscow could
set its own price, its key objectives in Europe by this time having
been realized. If Moscow had believed Sadat could succeed in
effecting a fundamental reversal of relations, it might, to forestall
a major improvement in U.S.-Arab relations, have shown more
interest in the American proposals for a limitation on arms deliveries to the contestants in the Arab-Israeli dispute. Its lack of
interest underscores the argument that the Soviet leadership was
not disturbed enough by Sadat's decision to undertake a policy
reevaluation. Also, withdrawal of its troops would demonstrate
to Third World countries that the Soviet Union honored sov-
ereign decisions of client states and did not, when censured or
dismissed, try to subvert or penalize them.

There is in addition the conjecture that Moscow actually
maneuvered Sadat to act as he did. The weakness of this line of

[87] *Al-Nahar*, August 22, 1972.

reasoning is its assumption of complete Soviet control over all policy variables and its postulation of prophetic qualities to Soviet decisionmaking that belie the unpredictability and capriciousness of international developments. What is beyond dispute was the short-lived duration of the derangement of the Soviet-Egyptian relationship.

When Washington welcomed the expulsion more than the decision that gave rise to it, Moscow had reason to be pleased. The Nixon administration used the development to gain congressional support for its policy toward the Soviet Union, but did nothing to exploit the possibilities that had suddenly appeared for a new Middle East initiative, which would have been more salubrious for Western interests than the cosmetic agreements it concluded with the USSR. Its fixation with the superpower relationship, to the virtual exclusion of the effect on alliance relationships, warped its perspective on what was needed to fashion a meaningful accommodation and minimized the political costs of Sadat's action to the Soviets.

RECONSIDERATION

Over the next fifteen months exodus affected the key actors in different ways. Whereas it lulled the United States into believing that the Middle East could be discreetly ignored, it led the USSR to revise previous assessments of Sadat and to accede, in time, to his requests for weapons; and whereas exodus swelled the Israeli Establishment's sense of military assuredness and thus made possible the "Pearl Harbor" of October 6, 1973, it facilitated Sadat's tasks of forging new alliances and intensifying the planning for war. While exodus engendered a sense of relief abroad, it actually brought the Arab-Israeli conflict to the threshold of an even more complex phase.

In the weeks immediately following the events of July, Sadat engaged in a spate of diplomatic activity aimed at exploring new options. He went to Libya, where on August 3 the two governments declared their intention to federate completely by September 3, 1973. Emissaries were sent to key Arab countries; others toured West European capitals in search of alternate arms suppliers and diplomatic support. The foreign minister met with U.N. Secretary General Kurt Waldheim and readied a strong presentation for the fall session of the General Assembly. And in the forums of the nonaligned countries, the Egyptians lobbied for the international isolation of Israel.

Egyptian-Soviet relations deteriorated precipitately in the weeks immediately after Sadat's speech of July 18. The Soviets ignored his call for high-level consultations. On August 7 *Al-Ahram* reported that Sadat had received an important message from Brezhnev that "is being carefully studied . . . and will pave the way" for a political summit.[88] For the next few days all of Cairo's newspapers carried items on the Soviet "request" for a summit conference.[89] It remained for *Al-Nahar* in Beirut to debunk these sanguine reports with the accurate speculation that Brezhnev's note was in reality a sharp criticism of the expulsion, a rejection of any summit meeting, and an enquiry about the effects of the proposed merger with Libya on the Soviet-Egyptian treaty, which prohibited alliances with nations hostile to either party.[90] Other sources said the note also accused Egypt of inciting Syria, the Arab Republic of Yemen, and the People's Democratic Republic of Yemen to follow its example and expel their Soviet advisers.[91] A report that the Arab Republic of Yemen had requested the USSR to withdraw its experts[92] was promptly denied by Sana.[93]

The occasional sugar-coated accounts of Soviet-Egyptian relations came to an abrupt end on August 11, when Haykal began a Cold War-of-the-presses. First he took pains to emphasize the importance of friendship with the Soviet Union:

> There is no substitute we can obtain in place of our friendship with the Soviet Union . . . our military investments with the Soviet Union are tremendous. The arms of our land armies and of our sea and air fleets are now all from the Soviet Union. If we allow an acute crisis to flare up between us and the Soviet Union, it would mean that we had decided to defer the liberation of our land for a long time. . . .

> Our investments in peace with the Soviet Union are enormous, particularly in industry and agriculture. We cannot stop in the middle of the road.[94]

[88] *Al-Ahram*, August 7, 1972.   [89] CPR, No. 5681, August 10, 1972.
[90] ARR, No. 15 (August 1–15, 1972), 371.
[91] Quoted in *USSR and Third World*, 2, No. 8 (1972), 447.
[92] CPR, No. 5676, August 5, 1972.
[93] ARR, No. 15 (August 1–15, 1972), 372.
[94] BBC/ME/4066/A/2 (August 14, 1972).

Then he proceeded to expose certain "secrets," which one Lebanese journalist chided him for presenting as if they were the
"secrets of an enemy, not a friendly, state."[95] Haykal said that
Soviet pilots were no better than Egyptian pilots in combat
against the Israelis, that they had been trounced in the summer
of 1970 when five Soviet aircraft were downed in less than one
minute; and he spoke of Soviet vexation at not having a plane
that was a match for the Phantom. The following day, Ihsan
'Abd al-Quddus, long an advocate of close ties with the Soviet
Union and one who was regarded in Cairo as being increasingly
in Sadat's confidence, joined the attack. "Until today," he said,
"none of the Soviet leaders has spoken about the causes underlying" their differences with Egypt:

> [Even] If the Soviet leaders are restricted by diplomatic meth-
> ods, [still] . . . none of the Soviet writers has attempted a de-
> tailed analysis of these causes, and none of the Soviet papers
> has published anything worth reading on the matter. In fact,
> the Soviet papers—after a long time—just said that the deci-
> sion was taken because the Soviet military advisers had actually
> terminated their military mission in Egypt! This is not true!
> The mission of the Soviet military experts had, perhaps, ended
> with regards to the weapons that the Soviet Union had pro-
> vided to us. But it would not have ended had the Soviet Union
> actually provided us with the weapons it had agreed upon![96]

Quddus questioned the USSR's sincerity about a settlement, be
it one wrought by war or diplomacy, and declared that its "imposed silence or secrecy on what took place between Brezhnev
and Nixon [at the Moscow summit] about the Middle East,
together with the pressure of historical complexes, was . . . the
straw that broke the camel's back, after the camel had borne the
weight of numerous differences." It was time to put the Soviet
Union on an equal footing with the United States, since the two
clearly have the same position:

> They do not support war; they talk about a peaceful solution
> without attempting to impose it; and if the U.S. is supplying
> Israel with arms, then the Soviet Union is supplying Israel
> with immigrants who carry these arms. . . .

95 *Al-Nahar*, August 19, 1972.   96 CPR, No. 5683, August 12, 1972.

Therefore, why should not the Arab world adopt a unified stand so as to maintain a balance between the U.S. and the Soviet Union and thus win over each of them? If the Soviet Union itself has proclaimed its friendship to the U.S., then, the friend's friend is also a friend! In other words, all the friends of the Soviet Union must be friends of the U.S. If the Soviet Union has benefited from the friendship with the U.S., and has given concessions to American and Japanese petroleum companies in Siberia, why should we not also benefit? If the Soviet Union has built the High Dam for Egypt, then perhaps the U.S. would implement the Qattara Depression project, etc. . . .[97]

Sadat intensfied the row. In a speech on August 17, he told the People's Assembly of his rejection of a personal letter from Brezhnev:

The language, contents and type of the letter are totally unacceptable. I could easily get angry with this type of letter and others I have received from the Soviet leaders. [But] I do not want to sever relations; I want to get them back on a healthy line.[98]

He caused a major stir with the accusation that the USSR had tried, by refusing to give offensive weapons, "to drive us to despair to the point where we will be forced to surrender."[99] The Soviet press did not mention this speech.

The next day Haykal thrust a bit further. At the Nixon-Brezhnev meeting the two superpowers agreed, he alleged, to exclude the Middle East dispute from their competitive rivalry so that it would not "even remotely lead to a confrontation between them":

This meant that the Soviet military presence no longer had any practical effect as far as the United States and Israel were concerned, as if this presence on Egyptian soil had become an artillery piece for which no serviceable ammunition existed, as if it had become a mere ornament which is decorative but not functional. Leaving aside the use of artillery or gold jew-

[97] *Ibid.*
[98] ARR, No. 16 (August 16–31, 1972), 394.
[99] *Ibid.*

elry as similes, the Soviet military presence in Egypt had become, or so it appeared, a matter connected more with the prestige of the Soviet Union and the spread of its international influence than with the liberation of the Arab territory occupied by Israel.[100]

Haykal criticized Moscow for indifference to Arab concern over the emigration of Soviet Jews to Israel: "No one thought the Soviet Union should imprison within its borders people who do not wish to live within these borders," but it should have been open in discussing the problem with Cairo.[101] He also discussed the split in the Syrian Communist Party caused by Moscow's opposition to its stress on a military solution of the Palestinian problem, to its tendency to view "all the Arab world questions through the Palestinian eye," and to the "unsound" theory and tactic of pressing for the elimination of Israel.[102] But despite these differences between the USSR and Arab positions, Haykal called for a dampening of the disputation and a period for allowing Arab leaders to hold discussions with the Soviets "with wisdom and care and without exploitation and excitement" because "regardless of anything and everything, to us Arab-Soviet relations are vital."

In an interview with *Le Figaro* published on August 21 Sadat said that the Soviets had not taken "the psychological factor" into consideration in their relations with Egypt, that for them the Middle East problem was "just one of many between them and the Americans."[103] He suggested, as he did several times in August in other interviews with Western and Arab journalists, that the time had come for Western Europe to respond positively to Egypt's expulsion of the Soviets and, among other things, to end the arms embargo that France and Britain had imposed after June 1967.

The initial Soviet response was restrained. A few articles on Soviet-Egyptian relations appeared, but said nothing of their difficulties. This relationship was overshadowed by the many

---

[100] BBC/ME/4072/A/3 (August 21, 1972).

[101] *Ibid.*, p. A/4.

[102] *Ibid.*, pp. A/5-6. For a detailed presentation by the Soviet delegation to the Syrian Communist Party meeting in May 1971 see, "The Soviet Attitude to the Palestine Problem," *Journal of Palestine Studies*, 2, No. 1 (Autumn 1972), 187-195.

[103] *NYT*, August 22, 1972.

commentaries on Soviet-American relations and their prospects. On August 19, *Pravda* warned that "imperialist and reactionary circles" were trying to drive a wedge between the Soviet Union and Egypt by continually harping on the supposed existence of incompatible interests, in particular on the USSR's alleged interest in the state of "no war, no peace."[104] V. Kudriavtsev deplored what he called a Peking-inspired campaign in the Arab world to equate the two superpowers and insinuate that the USSR aimed at establishing a sphere of influence in the Middle East.[105] On August 27 *Pravda* said the belief that U.S. policy would change the Middle East situation was an illusion and it cautioned against attempts to spread misinformation about Soviet-Arab relations.[106]

The sharpest rejoinder to the Sadat expulsion order came on August 29, when *Izvestiia* attacked Quddus in a lengthy, blistering article. Not since the open polemics between Khrushchev and Nasir in 1959 had a highly placed Egyptian been so spotted for criticizing the Soviet Union. *Izvestiia* denounced him for saying that, whereas the United States fought on the side of Israel, the Soviet Union limited its activity in Egypt to "expansion:"

He who speaks of Soviet "expansion" is simply adding grist to the mill of imperialist and Zionist falsifiers.

The construction of the Aswan dam and hydroelectric station, Soviet assistance for building up Egypt's developing national industry, Soviet credits and deliveries of equipment—to call all this "expansion" is to ignore elementary logic and truth, to confuse ideas and not be able to see beyond one's own nose.[107]

It rebuked Quddus for having the gall "to slander" the Soviet Union, for accusing Moscow of not fulfilling its obligations under the 1971 treaty in the military field, when, indeed, the Soviet side "completely fulfilled all these agreements, as was attested to by the Egyptian leaders at the time of the departure of the Soviet

---

[104] *Pravda*, August 19, 1972.

[105] *Izvestiia*, August 22, 1972.

[106] *Pravda*, August 27, 1972. See also, I. Gavrilov, "The Arab Press in the Near East," *New Times*, No. 36 (September 1972), 8-9.

[107] *Izvestiia*, August 29, 1972.

military specialists."[108] The fiery article was matched by the icy unreceptivity of the Soviet government to Egyptian efforts to arrange a high-level meeting.[109]

However, caustic and unchastened, Quddus returned to the fray, berating Soviet leaders for using their "holiday" in the Crimea as an excuse to avoid discussing the troubled Soviet-Egyptian relationship.[110] Egypt did not seek to involve the USSR in its fight against Israel, as Moscow implied, but the USSR was not providing the weapons it had promised and it had made a secret deal with the United States on the Middle East.

Pravda promptly denied the existence of any "deal" with the United States—"neither secret, nor open, there was none and there would not be any."[111] And it was scornful of the "clumsy attempts of the Western press and different newspapers of certain Arab countries wittingly to spread falsified reports about the policy of the Soviet Union toward Arab governments."

On September 3, Musa Sabri, editor of *Al-Akhbar* and a staunch supporter of Sadat, charged Soviet officials with filling their media with "packs of lies" about their relations with Egypt and hinted that they were implicated in Ali Sabri's abortive coup in May 1971.[112] Sadat dismissed Murad Ghaleb as foreign minister on September 8 and replaced him with Muhammad Hasan al-Zayyat, a veteran diplomat, then serving as minister of state for information. Ghaleb, who was originally appointed foreign minister to mollify Soviet uneasiness at the criticism of its policy raised at the *Al-Ahram* seminar in May, was now removed to convey Sadat's uneasiness at Soviet policy.

Despite the political frictions, both governments continued to exchange economic and cultural missions. Thus, for example, the Egyptian minister of power went to Moscow (August 30–September 15) where he signed several protocols providing for Soviet assistance in rural electrification and in the construction of an electric grid; Khalid (The "Red") Muhyi al-Din, the secretary-general of the Egyptian National Peace Council, an or-

---

108 *Ibid.* See also, V. Potomov, "Middle East: Alliance Against Progress," *New Times*, No. 34 (August 1972), 5; R. Petrov, "Soviet Union and Arab Countries," p. 28.

109 *Al-Gumhuriya* erroneously reported that a delegation from the CPSU Central Committee was coming to Cairo to discuss Soviet-Egyptian relations. CPR, No. 5704, September 2, 1972.

110 *Ibid.*   111 *Pravda*, September 3, 1972.

112 CPR, No. 5705, September 3, 1972.

ganization used to maintain contacts with Communist and Communist-front groups, led a four-man delegation (September 5–15) to the Soviet Union; and for its part, the Soviet government sent several economic and trade union delegations to Egypt during this same period. In these areas normalcy prevailed.

The acrimonious exchanges diminished somewhat in late September. On the anniversary of Nasir's death, Soviet eulogies recalled his policy of close cooperation with the USSR.[113] In his tribute Sadat included mention of a "frank and also friendly" letter he had written to Brezhnev (in late August) to which he was still awaiting a reply.[114] On September 26 *Al-Ahram* announced that Ambassador Vinogradov (absent from Cairo since early August) would return shortly (he arrived on October 4), and the next day Egypt's ambassador to the USSR (who had been in Cairo since August 12) returned to Moscow.[115] On September 30, MENA reported that Prime Minister Sidqi would visit the Soviet Union on October 16. The next day Asad arrived in Cairo from a two-day visit to Moscow, where he had helped to arrange for Sidqi's forthcoming meeting and concluded an agreement for Soviet arms, including SAM's and other air defense equipment.[116]

The Soviet press regarded the forthcoming talks as a positive development,[117] but the Egyptian commentators were less sanguine, even though Cairo was the one pursuing a reconciliation. Quddus referred to the admonishment delivered by Moscow in late August, to the effect that "friendship with the Soviet Union is not an ornament that could be worn or replaced at will." He said it went to the heart of the matter: "None wants to be an ornament worn by the other to be displayed at the international clubs or communities."[118] Admittedly, "the High Dam is no ornament," but the USSR, too, has benefited industrially and economically from it; however, the arms were "mere ornaments" because they were not sufficient to fight a war. The Soviet Union was "an ornament dealer," who had benefited militarily from

[113] *Izvestiia*, September 27, 1972. See Y. Potomov, "A Great Egyptian," *New Times*, No. 40 (October 1972), 12-13.

[114] BBC/ME/4106/A/9 (September 30, 1972).

[115] ARR, No. 18 (September 16–30, 1972), 447.

[116] BBC/ME/4105/A/6 (September 29, 1972); BBC/ME/4107/i (October 2, 1972).

[117] For example, *Pravda*, October 5 and October 9, 1972.

[118] CPR, No. 5738, October 7, 1972.

friendship with Egypt, becoming a power in the Mediterranean, obtaining Egyptian airfields that "did away with the need of building aircraft carriers which would have cost millions of dollars to the Soviet people," and furthering its global aims by having been able to use Egyptian airfields to supply India during the Indo-Pakistani war. Quddus likened the Soviet government to "a smart jeweler who manages to make a profit from his business without meeting his customers' requirements or losing their friendship." Musa Sabri called Sidqi's trip an attempt to clarify the Soviet position in regard to Egypt and not a prelude to any return of Soviet troops.[119] Haykal revealed that Nasir had informed Kosygin in 1970 that he had encouraged Libya to purchase Mirages from France in order to acquire fighter-bombers that were not available from the USSR:

> Nasser's strategy was to use the Soviet military presence in Egypt as a means of elevating the local conflict in the Middle East to a level where it would affect the higher world balance of power between the United States and the Soviet Union. The Soviets were reluctant to increase their presence in Egypt for fear of provoking sensitivities [of the United States] but Nasser assured them that this was his responsibility.[120]

Of the three quasi-official, Egyptian spokesmen, Haykal came out most strongly in favor of repairing the bridge to Moscow. But all of their comments substantiate Fuad Matar's assessment that Sadat's efforts to patch up the relationship were half-hearted and might best be called "the politics of lack of eagerness."[121] How else, for example, could one reconcile the drastic reversal of domestic economic policy, which could not be pleasing to the Soviets, with the dispatch of emissaries to Moscow? Matar's analysis pointed to the dilemmas Sadat faced.

Sadat had doubts about the wisdom of Nasir's strategy. As a result of its new relationship with the United States, the Soviet Union was apparently no longer to be inveigled into a direct involvement in Egypt's struggle. In a remarkable interview with *Al-Hawadith* (Beirut) on October 6, Sadat said Nasir made "serious mistakes, greater than many imagined" and he owned to serious disagreements with him: "the leadership of Abdul Nasser,

[119] CPR, No. 5739, October 8, 1972.
[120] CPR, No. 5744, October 13, 1972.
[121] *Al-Nahar*, October 6, 1972.

previously so firm [prior to 1967] was a broken reed—it spelled defeat."[122]

The belief in the centrality of the Soviet Union in Egyptian foreign policy had to be revised. Détente had thawed the tension between the superpowers in the Middle East. Though Moscow was lavishing aid on Syria and Iraq, as much to prevent Egypt's anti-Sovietism from spreading as to remind Egypt of its dependence on Moscow, the USSR knew that Syria would not go to war without Egypt; and without a war the superpowers were free to shelve the intractable Middle East problem and proceed apace with their global special arrangement. Whereas Nasir's general policy and political posture were Left-oriented, and as such attractive to Moscow, Sadat's domestic situation, foreign policy options, and personal predilections edged to the Right. They demanded:

> . . . a more cautious, moderate approach in inter-Arab affairs; a rapprochement with the oil-rich conservative regimes in the area; a greater distrust of the Soviet patron; a dissatisfaction with the revolutionary-socialist experiment associated with the Nasser power structure; and, of course, the desire of Egyptians for a less repressive regime at home and a more pragmatic, liberal national economic policy.[123]

Sadat was adrift internationally, beset by grave economic difficulties, as yet without a suitable substitute for Soviet arms, disappointed in the absence of any new initiative from the United States (then involved in a presidential campaign), unsure of supporters in the Arab world, and convinced of the need to use the military option to break the Israeli logjam. Now at a point beyond which few believed he could move, he cast about for a new strategy.

[122] As quoted in *Journal of Palestine Studies*, 2, No. 2 (Winter 1973), 182, 184.

[123] P. J. Vatikiotis, "Two Years After Nasser: The Chance of a New Beginning," *New Middle East*, No. 48 (September 1972), 8.

Chapter Seven

TOWARD CONFRONTATION

I<small>T</small> was during the period between Prime Minister Aziz Sidqi's visit to Moscow on October 16, 1972, and the triggering of the Fourth Arab-Israeli War on October 6, 1973, that Sadat showed his mettle as a national leader and not just as a clever politician. Whereas Nasir's strategy of drawing the USSR ever more directly into the defense of Egypt providentially coincided with a period of high tension between the USSR and the United States, Sadat had to bargain for Soviet support at a time when the incipient superpower détente was a Soviet priority and Soviet-Egyptian relations were deteriorating; whereas Nasir sought to monopolize and manipulate Pan-Arabism, Sadat espoused a confederational pluralism, which found far greater favor among ruling Arab elites; and whereas Nasir preempted the center stage, arousing enmity and suspicion, Sadat eschewed the limelight, posed no threat to other Arab leaders, and by so doing made his virtuoso performance possible.

On the day before Sidqi left for Moscow, Sadat told the People's Assembly of his hope that the mission would succeed. "It is not in us to deny good deeds, nor are we ungrateful for those who have performed them. We did not consider the matter as one of courtesies or favors; we understood Arab-Soviet friendship as representing a strategic friendship for us. We have not changed." Alluding to the expulsion of Soviet military advisers, Sadat said, "We were compelled to take an objective pause with our friend . . . We have made and will make every effort to surmount this transient condition in our relations with the Soviet Union." Good relations with Moscow were necessary, because it was proving more difficult than he had expected to tap Western Europe as an alternative source of weapons, and he had to keep the military-technological gap with Israel from widening.[1]

---

[1] BBC/ME/4120/A/12-13 (October 17, 1972). Sadat denounced American support for Israel, which "has turned into something like a pipeline through which pumping is never stopped day or night. The race between U.S. politicians to please Israel has become a farce or a tragedy unprecedented in international relations. The United States has foiled every attempt and

OVERTURE TO THE KREMLIN

Sidqi's visit (October 16–18) was front page news in Moscow and Cairo. On the military side the delegation was led by Ahmad Isma'il 'Ali, Chief of General Intelligence, and Major-General Husni Mubarak, Commander of the Air Force. Sadiq was not present. They were received at the airport by Kosygin, Gromyko, Ponomarev, and Iurii Andropov (the head of the KGB, who was to be given Politburo status the following April).

Kosygin set the mood for the deliberations at the Kremlin dinner that night: the tone was crisp, not quite brusque but less than friendly. He remarked there had been "many trials for Soviet-Egyptian friendship in the past year," with opponents of their friendship trying "to scare the Arabs with socialism" but failing, because "socialist ideas" were gaining ever wider acceptance among the Arab countries. Kosygin rapped "the invention that the Soviet Union had allegedly reached some 'collusion' with the imperialists concerning a Middle East settlement to the detriment of the Arab countries" and reminded Sidqi that the USSR had done everything it could to restore the defensive capability of the Arabs and that it would continue to support Egypt, in accordance with the 1971 treaty. In reply, Sidqi spoke of Egypt's gratitude for past assistance and stressed that what Egypt desired now was to discuss ways of implementing "the principles of struggle against imperialism" that they both shared.[2]

But the rift was there, as can be seen in the communiqué of October 18.[3] First, the talks had been held in "an atmosphere of frankness," the giveaway of mutual discord. Second, this was the first communiqué, since the one issued at the conclusion of Ponomarev's visit in July 1971, in which Egypt joined with the USSR in professing loyalty "to the principles of socialism." In view of Sadat's clear departure from Nasirism—from a policy of nationalization, statism, and hostility to the bourgeoisie—his agreement to this formulation can only have been intended as window-dressing to placate the Soviets. Third, though imperialism and colonialism were denounced ritualistically, there was no direct attack on the United States: Moscow, not Cairo, was eager

---

blocked every path in order to put us in a position of having to accept the fait accompli."

[2] FBIS/USSR, October 17, 1972, pp. B3-B4.

[3] FBIS/USSR, October 19, 1972, pp. B1-B2.

to signal to Washington its interest in a lessening of recrimina-
tions. In the afterglow of the Nixon visit Moscow justifiably
believed that most-favored-nation (MFN) treatment and extensive credits were within reach, hence its basic satisfaction with
the "objective pause" in Soviet-Egyptian relations. Fourth, although the communiqué affirmed the centrality of the 1971
Treaty of Friendship and Cooperation in providing a suitable
basis for "the further strengthening and deepening of friendly
contacts and cooperation between Egypt and the Soviet Union in
every field," there was no mention of new commitments, economic or military.[4] The Egyptian side did, however, express "its
gratitude to the Soviet Union for its great help . . . in developing
its economy [and] strengthening its military potential." The Soviets again confirmed the right of the Arab states "to liberate
their territories by diverse means," to use the military option,
if all else failed.

In the interests of accommodation, Cairo agreed to the Soviet-
sculpted communiqué: it accepted Moscow's priorities—socialism, détente, and anti-imperialism. For its part, Moscow reaffirmed the right of the Arab states to liberate their territories "by
diverse means," but there was nothing else in the communiqué
to gladden Cairo, and Sidqi's failure to be received by Brezhnev,
unlike the previous occasions, was ill-omened. Still the mission
did not return empty-handed: Moscow did ease up somewhat on
the quasi-embargo on spare parts and ammunition,[5] and it
promised to send some SAM-6s (advanced mobile missile launch-
ers), which had all been pulled out when the Soviets withdrew
in July.[6] Sadat was given enough to keep him amenable but not
enough to be confident that the July 1972 status quo ante arms
arrangement would be quickly restored.

Publicly Cairo praised the talks for achieving "their objectives
completely."[7] The press stressed Moscow's commitment to a full
Israeli withdrawal and its acceptance of invitations for Brezhnev,
Kosygin, and Podgornyi to visit Egypt. Informally, Sadat made
it clear that he expected the Soviet leaders to come to Cairo before he would again go to Moscow. The Soviets, however, were
in no hurry, though a dialogue of sorts between Moscow and
Cairo was resumed after the Sidqi mission.

[4] *Ibid.* See also, *Izvestiia*, October 21, 1972.
[5] *NYT*, October 20, 1972.   [6] *NYT*, November 2, 1972.
[7] *Al-Ahram*, October 18, 1972, as quoted in CPR, No. 5748, October 18, 1972.

Haykal expressed measured optimism over the prospect of the USSR's again becoming a reliable supplier. Given Egypt's complete reliance on Soviet arms, it was incontestable that "a correct and healthy relationship with the Soviet Union will be vital" in any recourse to fighting.[8] Arms could be obtained "in specific quantities from outside the Soviet Union under certain circumstances," but he professed considerable uneasiness over such an alternative because of the uncertainty pervading the international arms markets:

> I feel that such an adventure is like a meeting in the deep bottom of the sea with an octopus and its twisting tentacles and black poisons. I would prefer that the arms deals take place in daylight and on the surface. I prefer that the arms deals be transacted between one state and another. What is reassuring is my knowledge that President Sadat believes and insists on this view.[9]

On October 25 Sidqi told the ASU that his mission had been well received. Talking with the Soviets on developments since the previous July, he had rebutted the belief, "accepted by some in the Soviet Union," that since [May] 1971 Egypt had deviated from the socialist path. He had stressed the overriding importance of ending the Israeli occupation of Egyptian territory, and had explained that acceptance of the Rogers Plan did not signify a shift to the United States, but was in harmony with the policy, consistently espoused by the Soviet leaders themselves, of finding a peaceful solution if at all possible. At no time did they broach the subject of the termination of the Soviet military presence, reported Sidqi. They reaffirmed their support for Egypt and readiness to provide military assistance, and expected a military delegation to visit Moscow in mid-November to discuss specifics.[10] Sidqi's speech received wide coverage in the Soviet media and Soviet broadcasts to the Arab world.[11]

The following day War Minister Sadiq was forced to resign.

---

[8] BBC/ME/4125/A/5 (October 23, 1972).

[9] *Ibid.*

[10] BBC/ME/4129/A/3-5 (October 27, 1972). *Al-Ahram*, October 26, 1972, trying to comment positively on Sidqi's report could only observe that the Soviet Union "fully appreciates the situation and would perform its duty as far as it was able."

[11] For example, Moscow in Arabic to the Arab world, FBIS/USSR, October 30, 1972, p. B1.

Notwithstanding his strong support of Sadat in May 1971 and his acknowledged personal popularity with the army, he was expendable. During the next few weeks, in addition to Sadiq, the commander of the navy and dozens of the top aides of both men were removed. The shakeup mystified Cairo-watchers.

The prevailing Western interpretation was that they had been sacrificed to placate Moscow.[12] According to this view, Sadat was greatly disappointed by the results of Foreign Minister Zayyat's post-July canvas of West European capitals in quest of new arms suppliers and realized how desperately dependent on the Soviets he therefore was. To facilitate the process of normalization, he decided to purge the armed forces of past irritants to the USSR. Though within the realm of political possibility, this explanation fails to take into consideration that Sadat is unlikely to have acted so precipitately after Sidqi's return, if only to preserve appearances with the army and the conservative elements on whom he relied for his power.[13] A second interpretation was that Sadiq had been removed to forestall a military coup; a third, that Sadat, alarmed by the full consequences of his July decision, decided to purge the military of those who opposed improving relations with the USSR and who hoped to use Sadiq as their spearhead.

These suppositions are not without merit and may be contributing factors, but the most convincing explanation is that Sadiq was removed primarily because he was too defensive-minded a general. Unimpressive and unaggressive as a field commander, he believed the Israelis could not be dislodged by force, so he favored a defensive buildup along the western bank of the canal to deter an expected Israeli attack. His preoccupation with defense may also have been a function of his open disdain for Soviet weapons and tactics. What triggered his dismissal was alleged insubordination. According to Lt.-General Ahmad Isma'il 'Ali (Sadiq's successor) and Ihsan 'Abd al-Quddus, Sadiq was removed because of "failure to relay a certain decision communicated to him during the summer months and to carry out other decisions," and because he did not "perfectly carry out the President's directives."[14] The passivity with which the armed forces

12 For example, *NYT*, October 27 and October 29, 1972; *The Times*, October 27, 1972; *The Guardian*, October 28, 1972.

13 ARR, No. 20 (October 16–31, 1972), p. 499.

14 ARR, No. 20 (October 16–31, 1972), p. 499. See also, Mohamed Heikal, *The Road To Ramadan* (London: Collins, 1975), p. 181. After the October War, Sadat told Musa Sabri that Sadiq had been replaced for failing to convey

accepted the change suggests that the middle echelons, i.e. the colonels and majors, also appreciated the need for a more offensive-minded commanding officer. Whatever the reasons, there was no doubt that the Soviets were pleased. Soviet-Egyptian relations, frozen since July, began slowly to thaw.

Sadat next embarked on an ambitious policy of enormous complexity. The intricacy of the design was only dimly perceived at the time, and much of the operation is still secret. But for strategic planning and execution it has no counterpart in modern Arab history. From the resignation of Sadiq to the start of the fourth Arab-Israeli War, Sadat displayed an adeptness at balancing and reconciling political rivals, an understanding of the limits and uses of the international balance of power and the superpower détente, and a patience and sense of timing that far exceeded the diplomacy of his predecessor.

Sadat's strategy had four components: first, to prepare the home front and prime the military for war; second, to restore the flow of weapons and professional advice from the Soviet Union; third, to obtain financial support from the oil-rich Arab states, particularly from Saudi Arabia, Sadat's natural ally, to establish a military alliance with Syria, and to coordinate the military strategy of the confrontation states; and fourth, to lull the Israelis and the United States into a sense of security through purposeful but marginal diplomatic activity, and to cultivate the political and economic support of sympathetic non-Arab states. Sadat forged these components into a potent policy. For Egypt it was the most momentous period since Nasir had negotiated an end to the British presence in the Suez Canal zone in 1954 and brought the USSR directly into Middle Eastern politics with the arms deal of 1955.

THE HOME FRONT

Sadat had to cope with a number of troublesome internal problems simultaneously. Although some of them involved implicit challenges to his authority, they did not deflect him from his diplomatic course nor from ordering his war minister in December 1972 to prepare for war within six months.[15] Ironi-

---

his instructions to have the army placed in a state of military readiness. CPR, No. 5872, August 3, 1974; FBIS/Egypt, December 23, 1975, p. D 8.

[15] ARR, No. 24 (December 16–31, 1972), 595.

cally, and of interest as a historical footnote to this period, Sadat's adroit handling of these varied domestic difficulties reinforced rather than altered the prevailing view of him as an indecisive bumbler, lacking political vision, enmeshed in a web of bureaucratic intrigue that shortchanged Egypt's pressing socio-economic problems, and surviving only because of the even greater apathy and incompetence of his opponents. "After all, who," remarked one Egyptian, "would want to rule Egypt at such a time?" Not until October 1973 was Sadat's achievement appreciated.

Student Unrest. A new round of student disturbances started on December 5 at Alexandria University. Mounting in intensity, they spread to Cairo but were confined to campus, and the police did not intervene. On December 28, 1972, Sadat addressed the People's Assembly on student unrest and communal tensions between the Copts and Muslims.[16] Regarding the former, he expressed sympathy with the students' frustration at the seeming intractability of the country's problems and lack of progress, but cautioned against psychological manipulation from abroad, warning there would be no toleration of any internal polarization either "by those claiming to be the adventurous Left or the reactionary Right"[17] (this gave rise to the quip that no one was a member of either extreme but all belonged to the "artistic center"). Regarding the latter, he announced that a parliamentary committee had been formed to look into the roots of the religious tensions and to clear them up. In recognition of the sentiment for a showdown with Israel and to foster the nation's preparedness, Sadat established Higher Committees for War Affairs in every governorate with responsibility for drafting plans to ensure that the home front would be ready when the moment of decision arrived.

There were further disturbances in early January. These spilled over into Cairo proper, prompting police intervention.

[16] The Copts are Christians, constituting about 10 percent of the population. In October and November religious strife had erupted into violence in several towns in the delta. Sadat interfered quickly, but the tension remained. Two months later, in an interview with the head of the Lebanese Press Association, Sadat denied the existence of communal conflict in Egypt, stating he had "documents" proving "that the feud [between the Copts and Muslims] was planned in the United States and Canada." BBC/ME/4190/A/4 (January 10, 1973).

[17] BBC/ME/4181/A/6 (December 20, 1972).

Several hundred students were arrested, most of whom were released within a few weeks, and the universities were closed for
a month. Sadat reacted with moderation. Citing the findings of
a parliamentary report blaming the unrest on a small clique of
left-wing students, abetted by right-wingers, he attributed the
unrest to the unavoidable consequences of "liberalization," which
had not yet been able to resolve the many serious shortcomings
of society. He absolved the overwhelming body of students (250,-
000) of any culpability and concentrated on the leftist activists—
especially on Marxists with ties abroad—and on their rightist
collaborators, declaring "we shall no longer allow any group,
regardless of who it may be, to impose its trusteeship on the
people or tamper with their destiny."[18] At one point he made a
comment that could only have had Moscow in mind:

> It is a strange thing. Why does the Left, not just the adven-
> turous Left but the Left as a whole, regard 15th May [1971]
> as being directed against it? It is a problem, a problem which
> it is not up to us to solve. Why? Because we did not create it.[19]

Sadat feigned puzzlement at Moscow's suspicion of him ever since
his preemptive purge of May 1971. Insisting he had no desire to
change their relationship, he disarmingly ignored the fact that
he had already done so, both in foreign policy and in the country's economic and political orientation.

The student unrest passed. By early February, classes were
back to normal; the campuses were quiet, and the students were
permitted to carry on "a dialogue" with the authorities through
their newspapers. In May, those still in prison were permitted
to sit for their examinations; in late September, they were released in the general amnesty commemorating the third anniversary of Nasir's death.

Intellectuals. One result of the student disturbances was a
sweeping purge of critics and known leftists from the media. On
February 4, sixty-four were dismissed from the ASU and therefore from their positions on newspapers and in radio, television,
and the theatre. The Disciplinary Committee of the ASU accused
them of "seeking to provoke the masses by means of lies and
rumors," by casting doubt on the veracity of the government, and

[18] BBC/ME/4210/A/16 (February 2, 1973).
[19] *Ibid.*, p. A/11.

by "supplying foreign newspapers, radio and press agencies with false information, or signing misleading statements for distribution abroad with the intention of presenting the country as being in a state of chaos."[20]

Prominent among those purged was Loutfi al-Kholi, the pro-Soviet Marxist editor of *Al-Tali'a* (The Vanguard), a monthly published by the *Al Ahram* publishing house. A frequent visitor to the Soviet Union, he wrote often of Soviet generosity to Egypt and described anti-Soviet manifestations in the Arab world as the work of "infantile leftists or Arab reactionaries." Like Khalid Muhyi al-Din, he was used by the government to represent Egypt at the innumerable propaganda forums of international Communist organizations. The removal of Loutfi al-Kholi and the other leftists on *Al-Ahram* was important for its implicit criticism of Haykal, who, though still influential, no longer retained an intimacy with Sadat similar to that which he had had with Nasir. The brief coverage of the incident in the Soviet press indicates that Moscow, if annoyed, nevertheless realized the matter was a purely domestic affair. The crackdown came at a time when Sadat's relations with Moscow were on the mend and did not mar the success of Hafiz Isma'il's visit in early February. As with the students, most of the intellectuals were restored to their posts in the September amnesty.

Parliament. There was an unusual display of criticism in the People's Assembly in December 1972. Deputy Speaker Gamal el-Oteifi presented a report that took Sidqi to task for having on November 27 led the parliament to believe that a plan had already been prepared to retake the occupied territories from Israel.[21] The report was the first statement of the Assembly to come out forthrightly in favor of better relations with the USSR. Moreover, it criticized the government for failing to provide a satisfactory explanation for the expulsion of the Soviet military personnel, for the deterioration of relations in the first place,

[20] *NYT*, February 5, 1973.

[21] Mr. el-Oteifi, elected deputy speaker in October 1972, had achieved his prestige in the Assembly by the thorough and dispassionate way in which he chaired the fact-finding commission that investigated the Coptic-Muslim tensions. For Sidqi's speech of November 27, 1972, which included a cryptic allusion to increased appropriations for the armed forces, "including equipment, either from local production or through the provision of foreign exchange for purchases abroad," see BBC/ME/4157/A/5 (November 29, 1972).

and for the inadequate efforts being made to rectify the situation. Also for the first time, a parliamentary document questioned the wisdom of continuing to uphold, even formally, Resolution 242:

> If we had accepted the Security Council's Resolution 242, this was only because it constituted the string which tied our cause to the world and because it expressed the legality of our position, but it is our militant power which can force the Security Council's Resolution to move in the right direction. It can also condemn it to failure for when the noise of cannon fire reverberates, the resolution will then become irrelevant.[22]

The blockbuster, however, was the Assembly's willingness to go on record as being unconvinced that the government really had a plan "of preparing the state for war."[23] After three days of unprecedented public debate—Sidqi was in the Persian Gulf at the time—the Assembly accepted the government's general statement of policy and, on December 12, Sidqi's assurance that there was a separate war budget and that in the future replies to the Assembly's questions on foreign policy would be given by the foreign minister. In the months that followed, the Assembly did not reassert itself, but Sadat did make a point of meeting more frequently with it and its key members. The incident was an expression of Sadat's relative internal political relaxation, but conceivably derived also from his efforts to undermine opponents in the ASU. Too much importance should not be attached to it; in Egypt men still count more than institutions in the wielding of political power.

ASU. Seeking new faces, on March 26 Sadat replaced Sayyid Mar'i as first secretary of the ASU with Dr. Muhammad Hafiz Ghanim (there was no personal animus in the shift: Sadat's daughter married Mar'i's son on July 7, 1974, and Mar'i was made speaker of the People's Assembly after the October War). At the same time Sadat assumed the post of prime minister and proclaimed himself military governor-general, thus completing the centralization of power in his hands. His hold on the levers of power firmer than ever before, he eliminated or isolated remaining opponents and moved to a more right-of-center position

---

[22] Fuad Matar, "After the Deluge: Egypt's Parliament Finds Its Voice," as translated from *Al-Nahar* in *New Middle East*, No. 52/53 (January–February 1973), 47.

[23] *NYT*, December 11, 1972.

in domestic affairs—and toward entente with Saudi Arabia (nettling Qadhdhafi). The Nasirist legacy was being whittled away. David Hirst, a British journalist, saw in the elimination of the leftists from the ASU the growing influence "of the rural bourgeoisie."[24] Conservative, Muslim, suspicious of "socialism" and all that it connoted, this group represented the "traditionalists" within the hierarchy. They were not against change per se but wanted to regulate its pace and character. Quddus believed the differences between the government and the ASU had reached "the point at which there were two governments in Egypt; the official government and the government of the [Arab] Socialist Union, each ignoring the other in its actions."[25] Sadat's changes in the ASU leadership were made to curb this enervating infighting and to strengthen his position with the traditionalists as well as keep them in check.

Under Ghanim the ASU's role was more precisely and narrowly defined: it was to mobilize the masses and implement governmental decrees; it was not to be an independent source of decisionmaking power vying with the president. In his speech of March 26, Sadat said:

> The people see how people abroad are talking about the struggle between the Government and the ASU, between the ASU and the Government, between the People's Assembly and the ASU, and between the People's Assembly and Government. In a state of institutions, this is not possible, otherwise it would be a state of contradictions, not of institutions.[26]

He enunciated his concept of "the state of institutions," envisaging a delineation of responsibilities, in which the People's Assembly enacted the laws and the ASU implemented them. He castigated "certain elements" who sought to exploit the situation and, in particular, attacked "a great part of the Left Wing, which was linked to the centers of power."[27] Insisting that factionalism must be contained, Sadat molded the ASU into an effective instrument.

Economic Preparations. On February 11, to ready the economy for war,[28] the government decreed a series of austerity measures,

[24] *The Guardian*, February 7, 1973.
[25] ARR, No. 7 (April 1–15, 1973), 152.
[26] BBC/ME/4256/A/11 (March 28, 1973).
[27] *Ibid.*, p. A/13.   [28] *NYT*, February 12, 1973.

involving immediate curtailment of long-term projects. Salaries were frozen, new taxes levied, and restrictions on the importation of luxuries tightened. The Assembly granted Sadat sweeping powers to levy or increase taxes and duties without reference to the Assembly until "the end of the current year or the removal of the traces of aggression, whichever is earlier."[29] Extensive budget cuts were made in "services not directly related to production or public utilities."

Amidst reports of Egypt's dire economic conditions,[30] Sadat empowered Deputy Minister and Minister of Finance and Economy Dr. 'Abd al-Aziz Muhammad Higazi to introduce stringent measures and at the same time to press ahead with the introduction of free trade zones and the creation of an Egyptian International Bank for Foreign Trade and Development designed to attract Western and Arab capital.[31] The military budget, which consumed about one billion pounds (Egyptian) annually,[32] was given priority. The rest of the economy was squeezed to the utmost.

By mid-1973, secure in power politically, Sadat faced an uncertain future economically. Given his intention to launch a ten-year development plan (which had been shelved in early 1973, shortly after it had been adopted) and his realization that he could not expect to be bailed out by his oil-rich brethren unless he showed some decisiveness on the issue of Israeli occupation, Sadat may have made his decision to strike before the year was out as much because of the economic imperatives of his internal situation as for the political reasons. At the same time that he was putting his house in some kind of political order, Sadat was working on the problems of arms and money, and forging a military coalition.

SETTLING WITH THE SOVIETS

By the fall of 1972 Sadat appreciated that there was no substitute for access to the Soviet arsenal. The euphoria and expectations

[29] *Middle East Economic Digest* (hereafter referred to as MEED), 17, No. 8 (February 23, 1973), 213.

[30] *The Financial Times*, April 25, 1973.

[31] MEED, 16, No. 7 (February 18, 1972), 175. FBIS/Egypt, August 24, 1973, p. G3.

[32] This figure was cited by Sidqi on January 20, 1973. BBC/ME/4199/A/7 (January 20, 1973).

of July had given way by October to disappointment and dismay at the difficulties of buying weapons in Western Europe. War held risk of another defeat and with it probable political oblivion for Sadat, yet indefinite procrastination was almost as dangerous and far more exacting and humiliating. No solution was in prospect internationally. The superpowers, eager to develop their special relationship, were willing to relegate the Arab-Israeli conflict to a cul-de-sac whence it could not disturb their arrangements elsewhere. On November 25, 1972, Quddus wrote, "there is no doubt that nothing will change the situation we are living through, and also bring about a change in the position of the big powers around us, except war."[33] A new war of attrition was necessary.[34] The countries of Western Europe, while sympathetic, were not prepared to underwrite Egypt's military needs. And the nonaligned countries—though they voted with the Arabs on all issues relating to the Arab-Israeli dispute, upheld Egypt's position, and showed signs of readiness to reduce, even break off, diplomatic contacts with Israel—could not directly affect the military situation. War offered a way out, but it presupposed a steady supply of Soviet arms.

The initial efforts to restore the military relationship—the economic, technical assistance, and cultural programs had not been seriously disturbed by the expulsion—were not promising: Moscow kept Cairo at a distance. A mission led by General Mubarak (November 16–29), which was an outgrowth of Sidqi's visit, was not mentioned in the Soviet press, a sign that Moscow was not ready to resume its pre-July 1972 military role. It provided some spare parts, some replacements, and a limited number of SAM-6s, all of which had been agreed to during Sidqi's visit the previous month, but nothing more.[35] The Soviet media, quoting Sidqi and War Minister Ahmad Isma'il 'Ali, affirmed Moscow's support for the Arab cause, but Soviet behavior showed continued displeasure.[36] Moscow wanted Sadat to mull over the importance of retaining its goodwill.

[33] Quoted in Jebran Chamieh (ed.), *Record of the Arab World*, II (Beirut, 1972), 1185. A month later Fuad Matar wrote: "Sadat believes that the battle will improve relations with the USSR, and that Soviet leaders will do nothing unless Egypt starts a war; only a war will bring Egypt the sophisticated weapons it needs." *Al-Nahar*, December 21, 1972.

[34] *Al-Ahram*, December 5, 1972.

[35] *NYT*, November 12, 1972. The Egyptian press had no comment on the results of the Mubarak mission.

[36] For example, see, *Izvestiia*, October 28, 1972; *Pravda*, November 1, 1972.

Sadat made a conciliatory move. As he later related the incident, he decided unilaterally in December 1972 to extend the five-year agreement due to expire in March 1973, granting the Soviet Union naval facilities in Egypt:

> The agreement stipulates that, three months before it expires, the two sides will agree to either terminate or extend it. At that time, relations were severed, as I have exactly told you, and everything was at a standstill.

> I asked Field Marshal Ismail [Ali] to call the Russian general at the embassy here and tell him that we had decided, on our part, to extend the facilities for another period. This happened three months before the expiration of the agreement . . . The Field Marshal called the general and told him about this. The two of them concluded a deal [Sadat did not at this time tell whether the extension was for another five year term or for a shorter period]. After February 1973 our relations began to be, or to become, normal.[37]

On December 18 Vinogradov met with Sidqi and presidential adviser Hafiz Isma'il. The following day *Al-Ahram*'s Moscow correspondent reported that the CPSU Politburo had ordered a review of Soviet military, economic, and party relations with Egypt to be conducted under the chairmanship of Politburo member G. I. Voronov and to be reported to the full membership in January.[38] Nothing in the Soviet press suggested that any such committee had been established or that Voronov had been given any assignment to do with the Middle East. However, the Soviet leadership may have chosen this way to communicate its response to Sadat's renewal of port facilities, its willingness to reconsider Egypt's requests for arms.

In the next few weeks a major breakthrough occurred. On January 24 Vinogradov, who had just returned from consultations in Moscow, saw Sadat for the first time since resuming his duties on October 4, and arrangements were concluded for a Soviet military delegation to come to Cairo and for Hafiz Isma'il to visit Moscow. On February 2, Cairo briefly reported that a Soviet

---

[37] FBIS/Egypt, April 4, 1974, p. D7. In an interview with a Kuwaiti newspaper on October 22, 1975, Sadat for the first time mentioned that the naval facilities were renewed "for five more years after the expiration in 1973." FBIS/Egypt, October 23, 1975, p. D6.

[38] *NYT*, December 20, 1972; ARR, No. 24 (December 16–31, 1972), 596.

military mission, met at the airport by Vinogradov only, had arrived.[39] By contrast, Moscow gave Isma'il's visit of February 7–10 prime coverage, indicating a sharp upturn in Moscow's attitude.[40] Whatever its reservations over Sadat's shift away from a socialist economic orientation and crackdown on the Left,[41] it was eager to repair state-to-state relations with the prime target of its policy in the Third World. Isma'il was an able, experienced officer with extensive dealings with the Soviet military dating back to the arms negotiations of 1955 and a reputation for independent thinking that is reported to have included disagreement with Sadat's decision to expel the Soviet military advisers. While in Moscow, he, unlike Sidqi in October, had two meetings with Brezhnev, which were widely reported in the Soviet and Egyptian press.

The communiqué described the talks as having been held "in a friendly atmosphere" in which "an intense exchange of views took place on the Middle East situation."[42] The absence of the negative term "frankness" or its converse "an identity of views" meant that though there were still disagreements the serious ones had been reconciled or set aside, and that a convergence of positions on key issues had been achieved. Each side complied with the main wishes of the other. The Egyptians agreed to strive for a settlement based on the implementation of Resolution 242; rejected the "so-called partial settlement" to reopen the canal under U.S. auspices without an antecedent Israeli commitment to withdraw from all occupied Arab territories; implicitly reassured Moscow of a role in any settlement; and consulted with Soviet leaders on the position Isma'il would take during his scheduled trip to Washington. The Soviets, more open in their criticism of the United States than in the October communiqué, declared that no settlement was possible without due regard for "the legitimate rights of the Palestinian Arab people," and reaffirmed the right of the Arab states to use "any form of struggle in liberating their occupied territories." The two sides upheld the importance of the 1971 treaty. Most important of all for Cairo was Moscow's promise to strengthen Egypt's "military

[39] *Al-Ahram*, February 2, 1973.

[40] See *Pravda*, February 8, 9, 10, and 11, 1973.

[41] *Pravda*, February 2, 1973. *Pravda*, February 9, 1973, had only a very small item on the ouster of Loutfi al-Kholi.

[42] FBIS/USSR, February 12, 1973, pp. B4-B6.

capabilities." No details were given, but the praise accorded the visit in Cairo and Moscow meant that the USSR had agreed to meet most of Cairo's requests.[43]

The communiqué avoided mentioning socialism, party-to-party contacts, or anything remotely ideological. It stressed the need for firm, sound ties, "for a decisive checking of any attempt aimed at weakening the Soviet-Egyptian friendship and the close relations which bind Egypt and the other countries of the socialist community together." Finally, it emphasized the importance "of holding regular contacts between the leaders of the Soviet Union and Egypt to exchange viewpoints and coordinate the steps and actions" needed to cope with "the tense situation" in the Middle East.

The day after the communiqué was signed Sadat greeted the visiting Soviet military mission in a widely publicized audience.[44] Moscow blanketed the Arab world with word of its support for "the strengthening of Egypt's *military* power" and that of the other Arab countries locked in struggle with Israel (emphasis added).[45]

The atmosphere changed. General Ahmad Isma'il 'Ali, War Minister and Commander-in-Chief of Egypt's armed forces,[46] went to Moscow (February 26–March 2) for extensive talks with Grechko and other top Soviet marshals. He met with Brezhnev, who reportedly counseled moderation but denied that the USSR had ever favored an institutionalization of the state of "no war, no peace."[47] Isma'il 'Ali worked out the details of the Soviet military package, though the final communiqué noted only that "the two sides conducted a wide-ranging exchange of opinions on further development of cooperation between the armed forces of the two countries."[48] The Soviet arsenal was again open to Egypt.

[43] *Al-Ahram*, February 11, 1973.   [44] *Al-Ahram*, February 12, 1973.

[45] *FBIS/USSR*, February 13, 1973, p. B2; and FBIS/USSR, March 1, 1973, p. B3.

[46] The previous month, at the meeting of the Arab Defense Council, which was carefully reported by Moscow, General 'Ali had been given overall command of the combined Egyptian, Syrian, and Libyan forces.

[47] *Al-Ahram*, February 27, 1973. *Pravda*, February 28, 1973. *Al-Ahram*, February 28, 1973, reported that both the political and military aspects of the Middle East problem were discussed. ARR, No. 4 (February 15–28, 1973), 80.

[48] *Pravda*, March 3, 1973. In a speech at Alexandria University in April 1974, Sadat revealed that Soviet arms began to arrive again shortly after Isma'il 'Ali returned from the Soviet Union. FBIS/Egypt, April 4, 1973, p. D7.

An article in *Kommunist* alerted party cadres again, as in November 1969, to the importance of relations with Egypt.[49] Plainly intended to explain the felicitous turnabout in Soviet-Egyptian relations, it passed over the events of July 1972 and dwelt on the geo-strategic and economic significance of the Near East and the changes there favorable to the Soviet Union:

> Analysis of the situation in the Near East in the past year shows that the social-economic transformations in the majority of Arab governments are intensifying, the cooperation with the Soviet Union and the socialist community is expanding, and the socialist orientation of development in certain Arab countries is crystallizing.[50]

It added that the progressive, anti-imperialist policy of most Arab countries had been facilitated by Soviet aid and "today the Arab world is already not as it was several years ago. The progressive regimes have been strengthened, inter-Arab cooperation has increased, and their military-industrial potential has grown significantly. Sooner or later the long term effect of all these factors will start to count."[51] Saying there was nothing in the Brezhnev-Nixon communiqué of May 1972 that constituted a change in the Middle East course of the Soviet Union, the article set out the political rationale for aiding the Arabs and acknowledged the "'complexity" of finding a settlement. It did not doubt that Soviet influence in Arab countries was growing and that "all attempts of the enemies of the Arab countries to drive a wedge between the countries of the Arab East and the Soviet Union were doomed to fail."[52]

The Soviet resumption of full arms deliveries by March 1973 was confirmed by Egyptian and Soviet officials. On March 24 Quddus reported that Egypt was "importing arms from the Soviet Union . . . [and] is no longer concerned with the types of weapons," having solved the problem "of continuity of arms supply."[53] Two days later, Sadat said the recent contacts with Moscow had set "our cordial relations with the Soviet Union in their proper perspective and straightened them out complete-

---

[49] E. Dmitriev, "Problema likvidatsii ochaga voennoi opasnosti na Blizhnem Vostoke" (The Problem of the Liquidation of the Source of Military Danger in the Near East), *Kommunist*, No. 4 (March 1973), pp. 103-112.

[50] *Ibid.*, p. 104.   [51] *Ibid.*, p. 105.   [52] *Ibid.*, p. 109.

[53] FBIS/Middle East, March 26, 1973, p. G3.

ly."[54] Soon after, in an interview with *Newsweek*'s senior editor Arnaud de Borchgrave, he dismissed as irrelevant the idea of Soviet opposition to Egypt's use of force: "The decision is not theirs," and "Now they are supplying us with everything they can. I am completely satisfied."[55] In Cairo, the three main dailies interpreted this to mean that there was no alternative to war: "Egypt has exhausted all means for the sake of realizing an equitable peace in the Middle East . . . The Arabs will not be totally defeated in another battle."[56] During a press conference in Stockholm on April 6, Kosygin hinted, in reply to a question about renewed arms shipments, that the Soviet Union had resumed full-scale arms deliveries to Egypt:

> We have a treaty with Egypt. You know that very well. The treaty remains in force. We consider that Egypt is entitled to have a strong army at the present time, in order to defend itself from the aggressor and to liberate its lands.[57]

In a lecture delivered in Beirut on March 19, 1973, a leading Soviet specialist pointed out that while the Soviet Union favors a political settlement, "this does not mean that we are opposed to the use of other means to force Israel to desist from annexation as a means of ensuring its survival."[58] And on the occasion of the second anniversary of the treaty, another analyst dwelt on its military provisions:

> The treaty includes provisions on Soviet-Egyptian cooperation in the military field. Thanks to its military cooperation with the Soviet Union under Article 8, Egypt is in a position to strengthen its defence capacity, using the armaments and equipment it receives from the Soviet Union and availing itself of Soviet assistance in training military personnel.[59]

[54] BBC/ME/4256/A/5 (March 28, 1973).

[55] *Newsweek*, April 9, 1973; see Heikal, *The Road to Ramadan*, p. 181. However, in July 1973, Sadat complained that "we are not fully satisfied" with the supply of Soviet arms; and in September, that the USSR "does not give us up-to-date weapons." ARR, No. 17 (September 1–15, 1973), 387. However, as will be shown, this was part of a carefully prepared campaign of disinformation, intended to exaggerate Egyptian-Soviet difficulties and tranquilize the Israelis.

[56] CPR, No. 5395, April 2, 1973.

[57] *New Times*, No. 15 (April 1973), 8. *Pravda*, April 7, 1973.

[58] Igor Belyaev, "The Middle East in Contemporary World Affairs," *Journal of Palestine Studies*, 2, No. 4 (Summer 1973), 21.

[59] Y. Potomov, "In the Name of Progress," *New Times*, No. 21 (May 1973), 15.

The seriousness of Egypt's preparations was not lost on Jerusalem. Egyptian-Syrian military consultations increased. In late April, Sadat announced that the government had moved into a "war room," and on May 1 he acknowledged receiving aircraft from Iraq and Libya (for obvious political and commercial reasons, the French government officially denied any transfer of Libyan Mirages, though subsequently the reports were proved to have been correct).[60] There were a number of "false alarms" in early May, when heavy Egyptian and Syrian troop concentrations prompted the Israeli government to order a limited mobilization at considerable expense—a factor that helps account for the indecisiveness of Prime Minister Meir less than five months later. Despite Israeli reports of a major influx of air defense equipment into Egypt and Syria,[61] the overall military balance was considered stable by Israeli and Western analysts. Throughout the period from May to October, the Israeli and American intelligence communities tracked the movement of Soviet shipping into Egyptian (and Syrian) ports and generally concluded that the pattern of flow did not deviate significantly from the norm that might be expected to maintain Arab force levels. (The Israelis did take note of the introduction of SCUD missiles into Egypt and TU-22 bombers into Iraq.)

The regularization of the military relationship did not keep Sadat from caviling about aspects of the Soviet political position. While meant in one sense, in another deeper sense it was dissimulation, part of the diplomatic preparations for the coming battle, as Moscow probably understood quite well. The nits were picked periodically from May 1 on, when Sadat took exception to the Soviet commitment to continuation of the cease-fire, which he labeled "a U.S. policy":

Our friends in the Soviet Union must know that the peaceful solution, which the United States has been talking about, is

[60] On April 19, 1973, the Israeli chief of staff remarked prophetically: "I do not believe the Mirages or the Hunters or other planes of other Arab countries change dramatically the balance of power . . . but it may increase the Egyptian will to start the battle." ARR, No. 8 (April 16–30, 1973), 191.

The French intelligence services knew that Libya had lent the Mirages to Egypt, but "because of uncompleted aircraft deliveries to Libya chose to ignore the information." *The Financial Times*, June 10, 1975.

[61] BBC/ME/4328/A/3 (June 23, 1973).

fictitious. The peaceful solution which the United States has been talking about is a deception and a mirage.[62]

At the time when Moscow was preparing for Brezhnev's visit to the United States, Sadat threw back at the Soviets an accusation they had used when it was he who was trying to improve relations with Washington.

Moscow tried to calm Cairo's disquiet over the upcoming Washington summit. It said the Soviet Union was "carefully implementing the treaty" and "maintaining its support of the Egyptian people," and it regretted that "some people" seize every opportunity to invent "fabrications about the Soviet Union's policy and the Soviet-Egyptian treaty, thus, in fact [standing] in the same rank as the imperialist and Zionist propagandists."[63] One Soviet writer berated Quddus for representing the treaty "as a commercial 'deal' based on transient considerations" and equating "Soviet policy in the Middle East with the policy of the imperialist powers," in the process providing the first hint from a Soviet source that Moscow was receiving cash for its weapons.[64] During Foreign Minister Zayyat's visit (May 27–29), he was assured by Gromyko that no decisions prejudicial to Egyptian interests would be taken at the summit. The communiqué noted that the discussions had been held in "an atmosphere of friendship and understanding."[65] There was no mention of Resolution 242, and Zayyat left with the promise of full Soviet support for the Egyptian stand at the forthcoming Security Council debate on the Middle East. In an interview with a Yugoslav newspaper, however, Sadat complained that Moscow was still not giving sufficient weight in its political calculations to the Middle East problem: "In its assessment of the dangers in this

---

[62] BBC/ME/4285/A/6 (May 3, 1973). It was in this speech that Sadat mentioned that Iraq and Libya were providing Egypt with planes.

[63] FBIS/USSR, May 30, 1973, p. B2.

[64] Potomov, "In the Name of Progress," p. 15. During a visit to Cairo in late June 1973, Qadhdhafi shed some additional light on the Soviet merchandizing of arms for hard currency, revealing that Libya was purchasing Soviet weapons for cash: "Our relations with the Soviet Union are excellent today regarding trade, exchange of visits, development agreements, exchange of know-how, and *the purchase of arms*" (emphasis added). He continued that in international relations "everything has a price. Russia befriends us for a price: we also befriend it only in return for a price. . . . There is nothing free." BBC/ME/4336/A/3-4 (July 3, 1973).

[65] FBIS/Egypt, May 30, 1973, p. G17.

area, and its interest in lessening tension with the United States, the Soviet Union does not consider our own analysis as it ought to do."[66] Nonetheless, he did nothing to upset the process of normalization of Egyptian-Soviet relations: a CPSU delegation visited Cairo (June 12–20), making a liaison plan for 1973–1974 with the ASU; a high ranking Egyptian naval delegation visited Moscow (June 19–26); and a Soviet delegation from the Committee for the Defense of Peace came to Cairo at the invitation of the Egyptian Peace Council (June 19–30).

The meager attention paid the Middle East (only 89 words) in the Nixon-Brezhnev communiqué of June 24, 1973, provoked Cairo, which acted as if the absence of any mention of Resolution 242 purported a softening of the Soviet position, a yielding to the American preference for a partial settlement. No such thing was true (during his visit at San Clemente, Brezhnev told Nixon that war in the Middle East was likely). But so vociferous was Egyptian criticism that the Soviet government issued a disclaimer on June 27, assuring the Arabs that it still favored "a peaceful and political settlement" based on a complete Israeli withdrawal in keeping with the provisions set forth in the Security Council resolution.[67] The furor was stage-managed by Sadat; it contributed to the campaign of disinformation that deliberately exaggerated Egyptian disagreements with the Soviet Union, and brilliantly succeeded in adding to Israel's sense of confidence.

The gambit gained credibility with the recall of the Egyptian ambassador for consultations.[68] A week later Hafiz Isma'il was sent to Moscow (July 11–14) to obtain, according to Cairo, a firsthand account of the summit talks as they related to the Middle East. The Soviet press gave the visit extensive coverage, and a TASS statement on July 13 reported that the Isma'il-Brezhnev meeting had been "held in a friendly and frank atmosphere."[69] The belief that there were still serious disagreements was reinforced by the absence of a communiqué, the first time that one was not issued after an official visit by a top Egyptian since Sadat had come to power. In the weeks that followed, Sadat chided the Soviets mildly, once admonishing them "if the détente is going to mean for the Soviet Union the abandonment of the national liberation movements then it will be harmful to the Soviet

66 ARR, No. 10, (May 16–31, 1973), 223.
67 *NYT*, July 1, 1973. 68 *Al-Ahram*, July 4, 1973.
69 FBIS/USSR, July 16, 1973, p. B1.

Union, and even isolate it."[70] As other criticisms were widely reported by Beirut newspapers and Western journalists, the notion
took hold that the new edginess might presage another rupture
along the lines of July 1972,[71] though Sadat himself at no time
intimated that these differences might upset the post-February
1973 reconciliation.

Soviet leaders knew war to be an increasingly likely eventuality, at least from late spring on, that is to say, prior to the summit
meeting in Washington. By their arms shipments (which included SCUD missiles) and tacit cooperation with Sadat's diplomatic stratagems, they contributed to its inevitability. Soviet
objections to Egyptian criticism and lack of appreciation for assistance were misleading, as were Egyptian expressions of anti-
Soviet sentiment, which were journalistic opinions and not policy
statements. Considerations of prestige in the Arab world dictated
that the Soviets remonstrate against these manifestations of "the
tenacious character of old views and conceptions, the intensified
activity of reactionary circles, and the external pressure from
the forces of international imperialism";[72] against the resurgence
of the bourgeoisic in Egypt;[73] and against allegations that détente
was detrimental to Egyptian interests.[74] Soviet writers maintained
"that the development of Soviet-U.S. contacts has already had a
salutary effect on the Third World," that the "transition from
confrontation to stable peaceful coexistence makes it harder for
the aggressive neo-colonialist quarters to impose their diktat on
the newly-emerged national states."[75]

[70] BBC/ME/4355/A/9 (July 25, 1973).

[71] For example, see *An-Nahar Arab Report*, 4, No. 28 (July 9, 1973), 1, and
4, No. 37 (September 10, 1973), 1; Jean Riollot, "Soviet-Egyptian Relations
and the National Liberation Movement," *Radio Liberty Dispatch*, August 6,
1973; ARR, No. 18 (September 16–30, 1973), 419, which reported an increase
in Soviet-Syrian tensions, supposedly because the Soviets had refused to
assist the Syrians during the air battle with the Israelis of September 13.

[72] See E. Dmitriyev, "Middle East: Dangerous Tension Must Go," *International Affairs*, No. 7 (July 1973), 31.

[73] See P. Demchenko, "Egypt Today," *International Affairs*, No. 6 (June
1973), 75. Soviet writings intended for a predominately Soviet audience approached the problem of the progressive bourgeois elements in a more
sophisticated, less doctrinally rigid way. For example, G. Mirskii, "Natsionalizm
i nekapitalisticheskii put' razvitiia" ("Nationalism and the Non-capitalist
Path of Development"), *Mirovaia ekonomika i mezhdunarodnye otnosheniia*,
No. 10 (October 1972), 123.

[74] *Pravda*, July 21, 1973; August 28, 1973.

[75] D. Volsky, "Soviet-American Relations and the Third World," *New
Times*, No. 36 (September 1973), 4. See also V. Kudryavtsev, "The Peace

Soviet-Egyptian relations showed little signs of change. In the economic realm, efforts were made to increase Soviet-Egyptian trade, which had fallen by almost twenty percent in 1972.[76] More important, Sadat kept the military mission small. Whereas in Syria, Soviet advisers continued to fill operational roles at all levels of the army, in Egypt they were not reintroduced after the expulsion of July 1972, whether to permit Egypt maximum freedom of action, as Sadat later maintained, or because they were no longer vital and their absence contributed to the grand deception of Israel, may only be surmised.

In the summer of 1973 Soviet leaders, beset by dilemmas arising out of their interest in détente, their ambitions in the Arab world, and their rivalry with the United States, avoided making clearcut choices, possibly because of lack of consensus on their probable costs and benefits and because their aims in the Middle East were changing. Nevertheless, though the objectives were contradictory, the immediate activity was vigorous.

Brezhnev was committed to détente with the United States. He had presided over the attainment of all the major Soviet goals in Europe: Western recognition of the territorial status quo and Soviet hegemony over Eastern Europe; the permanent division of Germany and acceptance of the East German state; and a disunited, inadequately armed NATO, rent by jealousies, acrimony, and a lack of vision. The China problem was manageable. Though the Sino-American rapprochement was suspect, little of substance had crystallized, in large measure because of domestic uncertainties in each country and because Washington was absorbed with Moscow. The opening to the United States, agreed upon at the Party Congress in March 1971, was succeeding admirably. Only the Middle East troubled their relationship.

The Soviet investment in the Middle East had brought Moscow into the area in a major way. What had been denied it by Britain for more than 150 years, no Soviet leadership could now discard. There was no reason, as far as Moscow was concerned, why its inevitable rivalry with the United States should jeopardize negotiations on issues of mutual interest, why there should be a link tying Vietnam, SALT, or commercial transactions to the Arab-

---

Programme and the 'Third World,' " *International Affairs*, No. 9 (September 1973), 27-31.

[76] MEED, 17, No. 22 (June 1, 1973), 622.

Israeli conflict, the Soviet-Egyptian relationship, and political competition. This Soviet line of reasoning is logical, given the global dimensions of the superpower struggle; but it does not account for the full range of considerations that led Moscow to stay in the arms race in the Middle East and compete with the U.S. buildup of Israel that had expanded greatly from 1971 on, and, in so doing, raise the levels of tension and with them the risk of war. The reasons for such Soviet behavior lie not only at the heart of Soviet policy toward Egypt and the Middle East but also in its conception of political struggle.

First, the Soviets were persuaded by monetary considerations to reopen their arsenal: thanks to wealthy backers, Egypt could pay for arms in convertible currency. Being good businessmen and shrewd politicians, the Soviets saw a golden opportunity for earning the hard currency needed to help finance their imports of Western technology and food, for tapping the vast accumulated reserves of the oil-rich Arab states, and at the same time for complicating U.S. diplomacy in the area. Sadat's ability to pay dramatically enhanced his bargaining position and dissipated Moscow's reluctance to serve as Egypt's quartermaster. To deny him weapons now might appear vindictive to other Arab states and undermine both Moscow's reputation as a superpower patron, and the activities of Soviet arms merchants in the area. It might also encourage Egypt and other Arab states to persist in efforts to find alternate suppliers in Western Europe, where interest whetted by the prospect of a lucrative market for arms might override U.S. objections. This Moscow wanted to prevent, because its attraction for the Arabs was, as it had been from the very beginning of the Soviet diplomatic offensive in the mid-1950s, that it was a dependable alternative to the West in this coveted commodity. In line with this consideration is the possibility that Moscow originally resumed shipments not expecting Sadat to fight. Such an assessment paralleled those in Washington and Jerusalem. Sadat's shopping list was not unreasonable and was in accord with the 1971 treaty. Only in late spring or early summer did Moscow perceive Sadat's true intent.

A second reason for Soviet priming of Middle East tensions was its desire for the use of Egyptian ports for its fleet. When Sadat extended the Soviet privileges in December 1972, he strengthened the case of those in the Kremlin who favored supplying the arms in order to retain the strategic advantages inherent in the use of Egyptian ports. Superpowers do not readily relinquish real estate, and within the Soviet defense establishment the case for arms must have been strong, especially against the background of a possible return of other military advantages.

Third, notwithstanding Moscow's closer ties with Syria and Iraq, the linchpin of Soviet strategy in the Middle East was still Egypt. Its friendship was important for retaining good standing in the Arab world, for encouraging the nonaligned Arab line in world affairs, and for sustaining pressure on Turkey and Iran to opt for a policy of de facto nonalignment. The importance of this latter factor for Soviet strategic planners should not be underestimated.

Fourth, arms to Egypt helped to perpetuate NATO's disarray. It forced Washington to respond in kind in order to maintain the military balance between Israel and its neighbors, thereby angering the Arabs, discomforting the West Europeans whose dependence on Middle Eastern oil made them fearful of the economic consequences of another Arab-Israeli war, and encouraging independent foreign policy positions among the more restive or ambitious members of NATO.

Fifth, though raising the threshold of the arms race in the Middle East and intensifying the internal dynamics inherent in the situation of "no war, no peace" that it realized was unstable,[77] Moscow calculated that it could provide "defensive" weapons (SAMs, antitank weapons, tanks, and artillery) without upsetting the United States, which would accept this mini-Cold War as inevitable and escalate its countervailing shipments to Israel. Where this reasoning came a cropper was in Moscow's underestimation of the effect of escalation on Egypt; and in Washington's failure to view this development seriously enough. By accepting the Soviet and Egyptian description of the arms supplied as "defensive" ("offensive" weapons were identified as fighter-bombers and surface-to-surface missiles),[78] and by assessing the

[77] This point was made by Evgenii M. Primakov in "The International Political Conflict in the Middle East," a paper presented at a joint conference of the (USSR) Institute of World Economy and International Relations and the Stanford Research Institute in April 1973. According to Primakov, "The no war, no peace situation in the Middle East brings about not only violence . . . but could result in heavy losses [for the West] including those connected with the energy crisis in the United States."

[78] World Armaments and Disarmaments: SIPRI Yearbook 1973 (Stockholm: Stockholm International Peace Research Institute, 1973), pp. 299; 304.

military balance between Egypt and Syria, on the one hand, and Israel, on the other, as essentially unchanged,[79] Western and Israeli analysts underestimated the consequences of Soviet policy and the heightened danger of war.

Sixth, the arms deliveries were an answer to grating Chinese criticisms of Soviet "coziness" with Washington, to charges that Moscow did not want the Arabs to be in a position to liquidate the consequences of 1967, that it withheld weapons to promote its special relationship with the United States and exact better political and military concessions from the Arabs.

Finally, Soviet policy may have also been shaped by a mania to teach the Jews a lesson and vindicate Soviet arms and advice. Because we know virtually nothing about the motivations and drives of Soviet leaders, we tend to assume that their response to a foreign policy problem is the result of rational strategic calculations, that their decisionmaking process is unbiased by emotion. C. L. Sulzberger related that Kissinger felt that the Soviets "are not entirely rational on Israel. There is a hysterical edge. They are basically anti-Semitic and hate being licked by Jews. When Kissinger was in Moscow in 1968 he found he could talk to the Russians rationally on all subjects, even including Vietnam—except for Israel."[80]

[79] Overall, the figures compiled by the International Institute for Strategic Studies (IISS) showed only modest increases in Egypt's armed forces: for example, a 10-percent increase in tanks and a 30-percent increase in the number of SAM batteries during the period from July 1, 1972, to July 1, 1973. They showed a decline in combat aircraft from 768 to 620 and in the size of the Egyptian army from 285,000 to 260,000 during this same period; *The Military Balance 1972–1973* and *The Military Balance 1973–1974* (London: IISS, 1972 and 1973), pp. 30, 31, respectively. However, the modernization of Egyptian forces was notable, the number of T-34 tanks decreasing from 400 to 100, the more modern T54/55s increasing from 150 to 1,650, and the most advanced T-62s increasing from 10 to 100; see also *Arms Trade Registers: The Arms Trade With the Third World* (Cambridge, Mass.: The M.I.T. Press, 1975), pp. 44-46.

[80] C. L. Sulzberger, *An Age of Mediocrity: Memoirs and Diaries 1963–1972* (New York: Macmillan, 1973), p. 608. However, the implications of this observation should not be exaggerated. Stalin, whose anti-Semitic domestic policies after World War II were far more virulent than anything under Khrushchev or Brezhnev, permitted Czechoslovak arms to reach Israel in 1948–1949 because it was in his interest to see the British weakened in the Middle East.

And the lure of long-term credits and most-favored-nation treatment led Brezhnev to conclude an informal "understanding" with Kissinger in October 1974, whereby the USSR would allow up to 60,000 (mostly Jews) to emigrate annually in return for the economic concessions from the United States. Sev-

For some combination of reasons relating to their own policy objectives and quite independent of Sadat's purposes, and because of their unwillingness to risk the possible consequences of refusing to meet Egypt's request for arms, the Soviet leadership resumed and increased arms deliveries. Whatever the reasons, they served Sadat well. For his part, Sadat obtained the weapons at no cost other than cash: he made no concessions, no promises, and no changes of policy of benefit to Moscow.

SADAT COALIZES THE ARABS

In mobilizing the Arabs for war against Israel, Sadat succeeded where Nasir failed, and established himself as an astute leader and a masterful practitioner of power politics. Instead of polarizing the Arab world and having to fight alone, Sadat reconciled intra-Arab conflicts and worked out a coordinated plan of attack with Syria; instead of having to rely only on Soviet goodwill for his weapons, Sadat persuaded the oil-rich Arab leaderships to underwrite extensive military purchases from the USSR and, ultimately, to use oil as a political weapon. On the road to confrontation, he had to cope both with domestic problems and with four separate Arab entities—Syria, Libya, Saudi Arabia, and Jordan— among whom tensions were bitter and suspicions deeply rooted. He cosseted and coaxed, and forged a consensus, convincing highly skeptical autocrats, hardened by intrigue and duplicity, of his determination.

Syria was the least of the Arab hurdles. Coordination came quickly as Sadat developed a sound relationship with its President Hafiz Asad, who, like himself, had come to power in the fall of 1970, and who in his domestic politics also "represented liberalization, moderation, normalization, a search for consensus," without changing his country's "basic institutions and policies," and who assiduously mended "one fence after another with erstwhile opponents," both domestically and in the Arab world

---

eral months later, Moscow abrogated the "understanding," because of the Congress's unwillingness to grant the economic concessions that had been promised by the White House.

See also the comments of Professor Mircea Oprisan, an ex-Romanian Communist and, until June 1972, a counsellor to the Inner Cabinet of the Romanian government, now living in Israel, who says Soviet antisemitism reinforces the USSR's anti-Israel policy. *The Jerusalem Post Weekly,* July 29, 1975.

at large.[81] Both were nationalistic, pragmatic, leery of doctrinaire
formulations or solutions, and committed to a confederational
type of Pan-Arabism. They consulted often and agreed on the
need for thorough preparations before engaging Israel militarily.
Unlike Sadat, however, Asad steadily improved his relationship
with the Soviet Union and resisted Soviet blandishments to cap
their relationship with a treaty. In the fall of 1972, he strove
hard to mend the frayed ties between Cairo and Moscow, which
started lavishing military assistance on him. A joint Egyptian-
Syrian assault against Israel was threatened in May 1973. Whether
it was called off at the last minute because Syria's Soviet-built
air defense system (construction of which was started in late
1972) was not ready, or because the Israeli government ordered
a limited mobilization over the opposition of some Cabinet ministers who believed the exercise and the expenditures to be unnecessary, or because the feints were part of the grand deception is
open to debate, though the latter explanation seems the most
convincing.

Sadat's political artistry was put to the toughest test in dealing
with the erratic Qadhdhafi. In August 1972 the two leaders had
pledged to merge their respective countries on September 1, 1973.
Sadat coveted Libya's plentiful financial resources and realized
this puritanical, militant, tempestuous Libyan had great appeal
for many in the Arab world, though perhaps least for the comfort-
loving Western-oriented middle class in Egypt upon whom Sadat
based his plans for Egypt's future development. However,
Qadhdhafi's demands for a prompt merger were irksome, as were
his constant quarreling with King Faysal over the latter's friendly
relations with the United States and his insistence on immediate
war with Israel. He was also a bitter critic of the Soviet Union,
which thought Sadat was the instigator, thus complicating Cairo's
relations with Moscow.[82] Finally, Qadhdhafi was upset at the
dismissal of General Sadiq "not only because Sadek shared his
attitude concerning the futility of collaboration with the commu-

---

[81] Malcolm Kerr, "Hafiz Asad and the Changing Patterns of Syrian Politics,"
International Journal, 28, No. 4 (1973), 701. See also, C. L. Sulzberger, *NYT*,
May 1, 1974.

[82] Moscow approved of Qadhdhafi's elimination of Western bases and influence in Libya and his squeezing of the oil companies, despite his open
hostility to communism, his exposure of informal Soviet inquiries about the
possibility of acquiring port facilities, and his opposition to the Soviet-Egyptian treaty.

nists," but also because Sadiq had headed the armed forces of Syria and Libya as well as those of Egypt under the terms of the Federation of Arab Republics, and he felt "On this basis, the dismissal should have been preceded by consultation between the three heads of state."[83]

In April 1973 Qadhdhafi proclaimed a "cultural revolution" intended to turn the government over to the masses and institutionalize Islamic fundamentalism by replacing secular laws and standards with religious ones. Not limiting himself to Islamizing Libya, he wanted to put an end to Egyptian night clubs and hedonism. The more insistent he became (and he often showed up unexpectedly in Cairo, necessitating hasty trips by Sadat to the airport), the less interested was Sadat. The military, the middle class, and the bureaucracy, the key groups upon whom Sadat depended, were uncomfortable with Qadhdhafi's zeal and moral evangelism.

Sadat was offended at Qadhdhafi's carrying his high-pressure campaign into the center of Cairo in July, when 20,000 Libyans crossed the border in an effort to arouse popular support for immediate merger. He was not about to be stampeded into a premature political union, not with the more reliable Saudi Arabian financial alternative crystallizing. On July 23 Sadat upbraided Qadhdhafi: union could not be pushed impulsively, as the experience with Syria in 1958 showed; it required constitutional forms that gave due regard to economic, cultural, and regional differences; and it could not hope to be effective until the various social and political consequences of union and the administrative difficulties were first clarified.[84] Accordingly, at Sadat's insistence, a non-merger was decreed at the end of August: a Constituent Assembly composed of fifty members from each country was established and given the responsibility for working out the details and proposing a timetable for full union. Every-

83 *An-Nahar Arab Report*, 4, No. 3 (January 15, 1973), 3.

84 BBC/ME/4355/A/6 (July 25, 1973). Additional information on the July 1973 fracas came to light after the October War, when Sadat's relations with Qadhdhafi underwent serious strain. In one letter to the Libyan Revolutionary Command Council on May 7, 1974, Sadat complained of Qadhdhafi's irresponsible behavior: "Lack of seriousness is to imagine that unity can be accomplished extemporaneously and without study. . . . The sudden arrival of brother Mu'ammar [Qadhdhafi] in Egypt while I was absent from the country on a trip to Syria to offer that we sign a declaration announcing unity was also not a serious attitude, and, I may say, it was a theatrical gesture." BBC/ME/4610/A/9 (May 28, 1974).

thing was deliberately left vague and relations cooled.[85] The union of Egypt and Libya was lifeless, but Sadat managed to draw on Libyan resources until after the October War.

An absolutely essential component of Sadat's Arab strategy was his entente with King Faysal. This guaranteed that Saudi Arabian oil money would be available to finance the purchase of Soviet weapons, keep Egypt from economic insolvency, eliminate the need for union with Libya, and exert critical pressure on the United States. One of the most significant developments in Arab politics in a generation, it ended almost twenty years of intermittent animosity caused by Nasir's ambitions in the Arab world and marked the further dismantling of Nasirism.

Sadat was Faysal's kind of Arab leader: devout in religion, conservative in politics, eclectic in economics, a non-interventionist in the internal affairs of other Arab countries, a respecter of Saudi preeminence on the Arabian peninsula, and anti-Communist (though the 1971 treaty and the subsequent relationship with the USSR required continuing explanations).

Egyptian-Saudi Arabian interaction had intensified throughout 1972. Sadat kept Faysal closely informed of his deteriorating relationship with the Soviet Union; indeed, the Saudi defense minister was in Cairo at the time Sadat terminated the Soviet military presence (it is still not known whether there was any causal connection). Shortly thereafter a Saudi military mission came to consult on the implications of the decision and on possible ways to offset the deleterious impact on Egyptian military capability. Sadat's quest for Saudi financial backing to purchase weapons elsewhere took concrete shape at about this time.

Sadat also courted the Persian Gulf States, whose great wealth was a glittering contrast to their absorptive capacity and therefore a natural target of his attention. In early December 1972 he sent Sidqi to the United Arab Emirates and Kuwait in search of investment capital for development, and two weeks later sent a military mission to Kuwait to discuss arms purchases in Britain.

By late 1972 Egypt was hard-pressed: its worsening balance of payments problem resulted from rapidly growing import requirements in the face of slow growth in the volume of exports, heavy

[85] Another consequence of the non-merger was the alienation of Sadat from Haykal, a development already discernible in late 1972. Haykal's espousal of immediate union with Libya was generally interpreted in Cairo as implicit criticism of Sadat's foreign policy.

and increasing debt servicing obligations, and inadequate foreign exchange reserves. The preparations for war were responsible (along with higher import prices) for increased pressure on the balance of payments during the months prior to the October War.

Saudi and Gulf money was made available to Egypt (and Syria) in late December 1972–early 1973. At a special session of the Arab Defense Council in Cairo (January 27–30, 1973) Egypt was given the hard currency it needed to negotiate with Moscow for weapons.[86] Once Sadat had convinced Faysal and the Gulf shaykhs of his seriousness about war, their response enabled Hafiz Isma'il to clinch the arms deal during his visit in early February. The estimates of the sum given the Soviets usually range from $300 to $500 million.[87] In addition to financing the purchase of arms, Arab oil magnates provided between $400 to $500 million in 1973 in balance of payments support, exclusive of the $250 million annual subsidy agreed upon at Khartoum in 1967. This timely largesse allowed Egypt to sustain an enlarged trade deficit, settle various debt arrears, and temporarily increase its gross foreign exchange reserves.

The transfer of funds from the Arabs to the Soviets was arranged quietly. At the same time that the Soviets were agreeing to resume arms deliveries to Egypt in return for Saudi money, they were casting Saudi Arabia as "the bulwark of reaction throughout the Arab world generally"; and charging it with "urging an overt and covert war against all progressives in Arabia" and the Persian Gulf, with subverting Arab "cooperation with the socialist countries," and with thumping "the drums of 'holy war' against 'communism-zionism,' that fantastic invention of present-day obscurantists."[88] These criticisms of the Saudis, and especially

[86] See ARR, No. 2 (January 16–31, 1973), 48; BBC/ME/4208/A/3 (January 31, 1973); *Quarterly Economic Review: Egypt, Sudan* No. 1: 1973 (London: The Economist Intelligence Unit, 1973), p. 8 (hereafter referred to as QER).

[87] QER, No. 3: 1973, p. 5. Some estimates run as high as $700 million and upward. QER, No. 4: 1973, p. 5. For acknowledgement of Saudi Arabia's financing of the October War, see Quddus, as quoted in BBC/ME/4457/A/4 (November 22, 1973).

[88] D. Volsky, "King Faisal's 'Holy War,'" *New Times*, No. 5 (February 1973), 27. Denunciations of Faysal were commonplace. Another Soviet commentator wrote: Faysal "gives financial aid . . . in the name of an Arab 'holy war' against the Israelis, to pose as a patriot and even an anti-imperialist of a kind." R. Petrov, "The Middle East Needs a Just and Lasting Peace," *New Times*, No. 23 (June 1973), 5.

Faysal, did not deter Moscow from persistently trying to persuade Riyadh to enter into diplomatic relations with the Soviet Union. In international politics, hypocrisy is the twin of avarice.

By late March 1973 Sadat could confidentially allude to the de facto alliance with Saudi Arabia:

> There are bilateral contacts and there are indeed positive results from them. It is not the right time yet to disclose these positive results. It is better if we keep them going and if none of our enemies knows anything about them because what ultimately concerns us is the battle, the battle which is before and above everything else.[89]

A month later Egypt's war minister flew to Riyadh, between stopovers in Kuwait and Iraq; earlier he had been to Damascus. War was in the air.

Throughout the spring and summer Sadat and Faysal exchanged visits and emissaries. In what represented a potential policy change of great consequence, Saudi Arabia implied in mid-April that it was contemplating the use of oil as a political weapon against the United States and the West. The immediate expression of this was a statement by Shaykh Ahmad Zaki al-Yamani, Saudi Arabia's Minister of Oil, that his country was considering rejection of an increase in Saudi oil production until the United States adopted a "better" policy on the Middle East conflict, i.e. stopped its support of Israel. Quddus termed this development one of the significant changes at work in the Middle East that would eventually break the status quo that the United States and Israel tried tenaciously to maintain.[90]

---

[89] BBC/ME/4256/A/5 (March 28, 1973).

[90] CPR, No. 5421 April 28, 1973. See Haykal, CPR, No. 5503, July 13, 1973. Soviet analysts, too, pointed to the U.S. vulnerability to oil pressure: "A coordinated Arab policy in this sphere could be especially effective inasmuch as Israel's main backer, the United States, is displaying an increasing interest in the oil deposits of the Persian Gulf and in Libya," Victor Kudryavtsev, "On the Arab Diplomatic Front," *New Times*, No. 4 (January 1973), 12. "Skillful use of this lever [joint oil policy] could make Israel more tractable as regards a just political settlement. The annual income of only three oil-producing Arab countries—Libya, Saudi Arabia and Kuwait—is in excess of $6,000 million. Even if a small share of that sum were to be spent for resistance to the aggressor, this would greatly increase the effectiveness of the struggle. According to news agency reports, this view was given thorough consideration in Cairo." R. Petrov, "The Cairo Meeting," *New Times*, No. 6 (February 1973), 23.
The Soviets frequently urged Egyptian officials to use the oil weapon before resorting to war.

The pooling of Arab resources was producing results. In late August Sadat returned from a trip (unpublicized in Cairo) to Saudi Arabia and Qatar, with the promise of full financial support. This assured, the final step in Sadat's strategy was the reactivization of the "eastern front" through reconciliation with Husayn. At the conclusion of a three-day meeting in Cairo (September 10–12) Sadat, Asad, and Husayn agreed to resume diplomatic relations.[91] The Arab phalanx was in place.

COURTSHIP OF THE NON-ARAB CONSTITUENCY

In preparing for confrontation with Israel, Sadat could not gather the fruit of his diplomatic activism until the international tree had been shaken. Behind the breadth of his foreign policy moves was a determination not to have the adage "Out of sight, out of mind" apply to Egypt. His aim was to raise the threat level in the Middle East internationally, to sustain it, and eventually to compel the superpowers to intervene. Their détente must at all costs not be permitted to relegate the Arab-Israeli conflict to a regional side-show. In setting the stage, no prop was overlooked.

At the United Nations, Egyptian diplomats lobbied successfully and whittled away at the core of Israel's supporters. During the debates in the General Assembly in December 1972 and the Security Council in June–July 1973, only an American veto prevented a formal condemnation of Israel by the Security Council in July 1973.

In the courtship of Western Europe, top Egyptian officials were sent regularly to London, Paris, Rome, and Bonn; and West European officials were encouraged to visit Cairo. To the Germans and the Italians, Cairo held out the prospect of economic advantages; to the British, a return to better relations and large arms contracts; to the Spanish and French an opportunity to pursue an independent Mediterranean policy and consolidate their access to Arab markets. The argument was the same: Egypt wishes to improve relations with the countries of Western Europe, import massive amounts of goods and technology, and

[91] To seal the agreement and obtain the acceptance of the leadership of the Palestine Liberation Organization (PLO), Husayn released most of the Palestinians incarcerated in Jordan since the civil war of September 1970, in a general amnesty that included Abu Daud, the Al-Fatah leader.

expand trade; but it cannot do so until they help break the Middle East impasse.

Sadat sought African support, too; for example, in May 1973, he carried his plea for Afro-Arab solidarity to the Tenth Anniversary Conference of the Organization of African Unity in Addis Ababa. His lobbying paid off. In Black Africa Egypt seriously undermined the diplomatic achievements of twenty years of Israeli technical assistance and foreign aid. In the period prior to the October War more and more African states severed relations with Israel, most for Libyan money, a few out of conviction, a few out of domestic political concerns. Between February 1972 and October 1973, seven African states broke off diplomatic ties with Israel; after the October War the number doubled.

Egypt's links to the nonaligned countries were close. At the Fourth Conference of Nonaligned States in Algiers in early September 1973, Egypt overrode the reservations of Saudi Arabia and Libya about the value of the conference and led the Arab delegations to give their full support to the anti-colonialist and anti-apartheid resolutions of the Black African countries, at whose behest the conference had convened. In return, the Arabs were rewarded with strong resolutions condemning Israel and upholding the Arab cause. As a founding father of nonalignment, Egypt had impeccable credentials and could count on redeeming old IOU's. For Sadat, the conference's resolutions served two functions: first, they reinforced the Arabs' belief that the overwhelming number of countries in the world supported them in the struggle against Israel; and second, their moral injunctions could be translated into diplomatic action, and thus prove useful politically. The sum total of these diplomatic efforts was to deepen Israel's international isolation, but a sudden blow was needed to drive home their full impact.

THE MOMENT OF TRUTH

The writing of history always gives the impression that what happened was inevitable. Given the dearth of data on Egyptian (and Soviet) decisionmaking, we shall probably never know exactly when or why Sadat decided to cross the canal. In retrospect, we are left with imperfect clues, plus a few calculated cues.

For three years Sadat had talked like a lion but behaved like a hare. He had gained some grudging regard for the deftness with which he disposed of Nasir's old coterie and for his immensely popular peremptory dispatch of the Soviets. He had proved to be an accomplished intriguer, but his abilities in foreign affairs were unknown. He made no secret of his view that war was necessary, as in his interview with *Newsweek* in April 1973 when he expressed dismay that none of his overtures had evoked a promising response in Jerusalem or Washington and that the United States so completely underestimated the danger of a Middle East blow-up. He believed negotiations with Israel were possible, but only while fighting was in progress, as was the case between the United States and North Vietnam: "When we resume our fighting the whole picture will differ." Sadat felt threatened by détente. According to one Egyptian journalist, the Nixon-Brezhnev meeting in June reeked of collusion and confirmed Sadat's worst fears:

> Although we did not expect the talks between the two leaders to produce a specific position with regard to the crisis, we never thought that the problem would meet with this strangely negative attitude on their part.[92]

Sadat said the basic decision to go to war was made in April 1973, in consultation with Asad and Ahmad Isma'il 'Ali.[93] The final plans were made in Cairo in late August.[94]

With the acquisition of the wherewithal that opened the military option, the initiative shifted to Egypt. Notwithstanding public pronouncements favoring a political settlement, the Soviets would not have given their client-state the means to take the military plunge without recognizing the possibility that they might, in extremis, have to mount a rescue operation. Well aware of the region's insidious pulls and pressures, they could have kept a tighter control over the arms flow, except that this would have risked the political-military presence they had taken such pains and expense to acquire.

In July 1972 and again in October 1973 Sadat took far-reaching foreign policy initiatives without apparent regard for Soviet interests or preferences, these despite Egypt's complete dependence on Soviet arms and its heavy reliance on Soviet economic

[92] Ali Hamadi al-Gamal, Managing Editor of *Al-Ahram*, as quoted in *NYT*, June 26, 1973.
[93] BBC/ME/4565/A/2 (April 1, 1974).
[94] BBC/ME/4744/A/8 (November 1, 1974); Heikal, *The Road to Ramadan*, pp. 11–12.

assistance and foreign trade. His behavior revealed the ambiguous nature of dependency in the Egyptian-Soviet relationship and contradicted various social science theories of how he might have been expected to behave, given the severe limitations of his over-all situation.

In a speech commemorating the third anniversary of Nasir's death, Sadat referred sarcastically to the latest U.S. overtures for a "dialogue" and to "the Zionist glasses it puts on while talking to us":

> . . . I was surprised by the recent meeting of Mr. Kissinger, the new U.S. Secretary of State, because he says he wants to hear the Egyptian point of view. He says good and sweet things. I want to say to you and all our people that Mr. Kissinger knows our point of view very well and in detail.[95]

At that very moment Egyptian forces were being deployed into final position for the start of "the battle." Sadat was about to demonstrate that a small nation can affect its own destiny, defy the preference of its patron, and in the process force upon him far-reaching decisions of enormous complexity and high risk. Several months earlier he had told a Yugoslav journalist:

> The day all our mobilization for total confrontation is completed we shall not take into consideration the meetings or the discussions of the big powers.[96]

In this he did as he said.

[95] BBC/ME/4412/A/2 (October 1, 1973).
[96] An-Nahar Arab Report, 4, No. 23 (June 4, 1973), 1, see Chronology.

Chapter Eight

STRATEGIC IMPERATIVES AND
THE OCTOBER WAR

O N October 6, 1973, at 2 p.m., Egyptian and Syrian forces struck in Sinai and the Golan Heights.[1] The decision to start the Fourth Arab-Israeli War was made in Cairo: the tactics, the training, and the weapons were provided by Moscow. The preparations were orchestrated by Sadat.

The day was a special one for the Israelis and the Arabs, though this was as much coincidence as calculation: for the Jews, it was Yom Kippur—the Day of Atonement, the holiest day in the year; for the Muslims, it came in the holy month of Ramadan and marked the 1,350th anniversary of the Prophet Muhammad's victorious entry into Mecca after the Battle of Badr (the code name for the October War was Badr).

The October War has generated a voluminous literature,[2] and

[1] Initial Egyptian and Syrian communiqués accused Israel of starting the fighting. That Egypt and Syria started the war is clear from the reports of U.N. observers posted along the Suez Canal, from independent Western sources, and from the tactical advantages that go to the attacking parties in the beginning stages of any war. After the war, Egyptian officials no longer denied their responsibility. For example, see M. Abdel-Kader Hatem, *Information and the Arab Cause* (London: Longman Group Ltd., 1974), p. 270. Mr. Hatem was a deputy prime minister and the minister of culture and information at the time. See also Mohamed Heikal, *The Road to Ramadan* (London: Collins, 1975), p. 29. The Soviet media used only Arab-originated reports.

[2] Among the books and monographs, a few may be mentioned here. Additional sources are cited in the Selected Bibliography. Y. Ben-Porat, et al., *Kippur* (Tel-Aviv: Special Edition Publishers, 1974); Galia Golan, *Yom Kippur and After: The Soviet Union and the Middle East Crisis* (Cambridge: Cambridge University Press, 1976); Heikal, *The Road to Ramadan*; Chaim Herzog, *The War of Atonement* (London: Weidenfeld and Nicolson, 1975); Foy S. Kohler, Leon Goure, and Mose L. Harvey, *The Soviet Union and The October 1973 Middle East War: The Implications for Détente* (Coral Gables, Florida: Center for Advanced Studies, University of Miami, 1974); Marvin Kalb and Bernard Kalb, *Kissinger* (Boston: Little, Brown 1974); Walter Laqueur, *Confrontation: The Middle East and World Politics* (New York: Bantam Books, 1974); *Strategic Survey 1973* (London: IISS, 1974); and The Insight Team of the Sunday Times, *Insight on the Middle East War* (London: Andre-Deutsch, 1974).

need not be recapitulated here except insofar as it bears on assessment of the Soviet-Egyptian influence relationship. From almost any perspective the war wrought striking changes: in the international economic order; in NATO; in the political stature of the European Economic Community (EEC) and Japan; in Arab politics; in the prognosis for the Middle East combatants; in the fortunes of the Palestinians; and in the budding superpower détente. Paradoxically, the war had least impact on the relationship between Cairo and Moscow.

COUNTDOWN

The remarkable thing about the military preparations of Egypt and Syria was that they unfolded in full view of Israeli (and U.S.) intelligence, which egregiously failed to understand their meaning. In the words of one diplomat, "It was a classic case of intelligence correctly assessing the capabilities of an enemy, but not his intentions." It almost took the sound of the first shot to make the Israelis finally believe what their eyes had showed them earlier. The result, two and a half weeks later, was a stunning strategic setback for Israel, a major political triumph for Egypt, and a greatly magnified role in world affairs for the Arabs. Militarily, the war was a suspended contest, with Israel ahead on points.

Warning signs were accumulating throughout September and early October:[3] *Al-Nahar* reported that Sadat had told Arafat to alert Palestinian guerrillas that the cease-fire was about to be broken;[4] Syria altered its SAM defenses following the air battle of September 13; Egypt hardened the roads leading to the canal; in late September Syrian troops that had been stationed on the Jordanian border were shifted to the Golan cease-fire line,[5] a consequence of the reconciliation effected in Cairo on September

---

[3] In August there were reports that between 10 and 20 North Korean pilots had been seconded to the Egyptian (and Syrian) air forces. Egypt had an ample supply of MiGs but was short on experienced pilots. BBC/ME/4375/A/4 (August 17, 1973).

For a discussion of the growing concern in the Israeli intelligence community, see Herzog, *War of Atonement*, pp. 44-52, 60-62.

[4] *Kuwait Times*, September 22, 1973. Sadat was reported to have met with PLO leaders on September 19; the following day the PLO Executive Committee met to discuss a united front with other Palestinian groups. BBC/ME/4404/A/4 (September 21, 1973).

[5] *Middle East Journal*, 28, No. 1 (Winter 1974), 34.

12 and of the plan to consolidate the eastern front; on October
2 Cairo ordered "a full alert" in the northern and central zones
of the Suez Canal, alleging Israeli troop movements (which were
taking place about this time in Sinai, in response to Egyptian
troop concentrations) on the east bank;[6] on the same day Syria
put its army on "extreme alert" and recalled reservists and pen-
sioned officers;[7] on the night of October 5–6, Egyptian com-
mandos blocked up the pipes that Israel had laid to pump
napalm on the surface of the canal in the event of an attempted
crossing;[8] and on October 5 Israel's interception of Egyptian
communications traffic revealed that a new code had been put
into effect, and reports came in of the clearing of hospital beds
in southern Syria. The portents were everywhere.

The heavy concentrations along Israel's borders were known
to Chief of Staff Lt.-General David Elazar by October 3.[9] One
week earlier Dayan, on a tour of Golan, had told the troops that
they were facing hundreds of Syrian tanks and cannon, as well
as a SAM-system every bit as strong as the one along the canal,[10]
and had some reinforcements brought up. But neither the men-
ace of simultaneous concentrations of arms nor the reports
(patently false) over Damascus Radio on October 4 of "massive
hostile concentrations in the Golan Heights and in Sinai by
Israeli armed forces" led Israeli leaders to take appropriate defensive countermeasures or to question their assumptions concerning Arab strategy and intentions.[11] They delayed ordering
even a partial mobilization until the late morning of October 6,
so rigidly were they fixed on the doctrine, prevailing in the
Israeli intelligence community, that Egypt would not attack unless it were first assured of a measure of local air supremacy,
which could be achieved only by putting Israel's main airfields
out of commission; and that Syria would not attack unless Egypt
did so first.[12] After all, Egypt had held maneuvers along the canal

[6] *Kuwait Times*, October 3, 1973. [7] *Financial Times*, October 4, 1973.
[8] Riad Ashkar, "The Syrian and Egyptian Campaigns," *Journal of Palestine Studies*, 3, No. 2 (Winter 1974), 21; and Y. Ben-Porat, et al., *Kippur*, pp. 35–36.
[9] BBC/ME/4416/A/6 (October 5, 1973).
[10] BBC/ME/4410/A/4 (September 28, 1973).
[11] Jon Kimche, "Fall, 1973: The Soviet-Arab Scenario," *Midstream*, 19, No. 10 (December 1973), 16.
[12] Israeli journalists were pressed by the military and the government to minimize the seriousness of the Arab military moves and refrain from draw-ing attention to them. In all probability there was nothing behind this other

dozens of times since the June War, and the threat had never materialized. Moreover, the Israelis, relying on intelligence information, believed that if an attack came, it would come toward twilight.

THE SOVIET ROLE: COMPLICITY OR COLLUSION?

The Soviets primed the Egyptian gun, on this there can be no dispute. But did they have a finger on the trigger? If not, did they know when it was to be pulled? Did they try to dissuade Sadat? Or did they express readiness to back his move? As usual, the data are meager; they are also ambiguous and contradictory and suggest the possibility that Soviet leaders were of different minds about what to do. Let us examine what the Soviets did and said in the period immediately preceding the October War, and what are the probable explanations. Exegetics is, after all, inference writ large.

According to Western and Israeli officials, the Soviet military buildup of Egypt and Syria during the summer months was not alarming: the flow of weaponry was adequate to maintain rather than significantly expand existing force levels. What was unexpected, and of critical importance as it turned out, was the dramatic increase in the quantities of SAM-6s, SAM-7s, and *Sagger* antitank missiles (and their use in salvoes). The result of highly sophisticated military technology, these missiles were simple to operate and easy to maintain, hence their great utility for the Egyptians and Syrians. As far as can be determined, large numbers of these weapons were introduced into the normal supply process in late 1972 to Syria and in early 1973 to Egypt, after

---

than misapplied bureaucratism: in the midst of an election campaign the establishment did not want to inflate the importance of moves that it considered mere posturing, intended to impress the Arab masses and the superpowers, and by so doing lend credibility to the claims of the oppositionist Gahal Party, which had been predicting an Arab attack. Also having had several false alarms in 1973, the leadership wanted to avoid the expense of another costly mobilization.

One Israeli journalist, who had access to Israeli cabinet deliberations, has written that a chance of averting war was wasted "because of an overly optimistic intelligence evaluation, and because of the years of hostility of the prime minister toward her foreign minister." Matti Golan, *The Secret Conversations of Henry Kissinger: Step-by-Step Diplomacy in the Middle East* (New York: Quadrangle Books, 1976), pp. 42-43.

Hafiz Isma'il's visit in February. Thereafter they came regularly by ship.

Crucial to the argument that once Moscow was convinced of Sadat's resolve it decided to support his decision was the dispatch of Soviet-manned batteries of SCUD missiles—surface-to-surface missiles with a range of about 180 miles, normally intended for tactical nuclear warheads, but also capable of being fitted with a hefty conventional warhead. According to one American source, the SCUDs were shipped from a Black Sea port on or about September 12.[13] (Israeli intelligence officials told Washington in mid-June of the arrival in Egypt of the SCUDs). In either case, the deployment of SCUDs suggests that the Soviets knew sustained preparations for war were under way.

SCUDs were pawns positioned for possible use in an offensive situation. Their deployment outside of the Soviet Union did not connote a policy of restraint. Originally, SCUDs may have been introduced to deter Israeli air power from undertaking deep penetration raids, but deterrence is a partial explanation, since such raids had already been made prohibitively difficult during the latter days of the war of attrition and would have been even more so in 1973, when Egypt's air defense system was one of the best in the non-Communist world. SCUDs were also meant to meet the Egyptian need for a counter terror weapon. To compensate for the vulnerability of Soviet bombers and for Israeli air superiority that prescribed a stay-at-home policy for Egyptian and Syrian planes, Moscow sent the SCUDs so that Egypt might have a capability to inflict damage on the densely populated Israeli cities. Their dispatch—controlled by the Soviet military to prevent their being used "irresponsibly"—before October 1973, hardly seems fortuitous when one realizes their potential for restraining Israeli strikes against Egyptian industrial or urban targets. In early 1974 Moscow supplied SCUDs to Syria, thus bringing within range of these surface-to-surface missiles all of Israel's cities and not just Ashdod and Tel-Aviv. This Soviet policy added a qualitatively new military dimension to the Arab Israeli struggle, and it must raise serious doubts as to the peace-

---

[13] Cecil Brownlow, "Soviets Poise Three-Front Global Drive," *Aviation Week and Space Technology*, 99, No. 19 (November 5, 1973), 12.

SCUD (the NATO code name) was the most advanced surface-to-surface missile that the Soviets gave the Egyptians, far exceeding the FROG-3 and FROG-7 in throw weight and range. Israel's potential equivalent—the Jericho —has a shorter range, and it was still not deployed.

ful intent of Moscow's aims, whatever détentist jargon they were couched in. In October 1973 Moscow did not try to hold Sadat back as it had in December 1971.

Once the war was over, Soviet commentators verified that the Arabs had been well-provided with all types of offensive weapons, though the SCUDs were never mentioned. For example, without directly crediting the Soviet Union as the Arabs' supplier, one Soviet analyst claimed that various myths had been dispelled by the October War:

> The second myth to be blasted was that the Arab weaponry was inferior to that of Israel. Today this view, which regrettably was voiced at times in Arab countries as well, has been disproved by the facts of life. It has become clear that the Egyptian and Syrian troops have weapons of types Israel does not possess. The foreign press has noted that most of the aircraft lost by Israel were downed by new-type missiles against which the Phantoms and Skyhawks proved defenseless, and that in the Sinai desert and the Golan Heights hundreds of tanks were destroyed by new guided anti-tank rockets.[14]

In the weeks preceding the war, top level Soviet-Egyptian consultations took place. From mid-September on, Egyptian and Arab—but not Soviet—sources reported them: on September 17 *Al-Ahram* featured a report of an exchange of messages between Sadat and Brezhnev.[15] Three days later Agence France Press, citing a Beirut newspaper, told of a meeting between Sadat and Brezhnev that was in progress at an undisclosed site, presumably a followup to the exchange of correspondence of the previous week.[16] Their meeting (which has yet to be confirmed) allegedly was held in Bulgaria, where Brezhnev was on tour.[17] On Septem-

[14] Georgi Mirsky, "The Middle East: New Factors," *New Times*, No. 48 (November 1973), 18.

[15] BBC/ME/4401/A/2 (September 18, 1973). There was no mention of this in the Soviet press.

[16] FBIS/Egypt, September 20, 1973, p. G1. On September 18, MENA reported that Sadat was out of Cairo, *ibid.*; however, there was no implication that he was out of the country.

[17] Galia Golan, "Soviet Aims and the Middle East War," *Survival*, 16, No. 3 (May–June 1974), 106. Walter Laqueur, "Détente: What's Left of It?," *NYT Magazine* (December 16, 1973), p. 27. According to Laqueur, Sadat conferred with Brezhnev before going to war, as he was obligated to do under the 1971 treaty, in all likelihood "on or about September 22." Writing several months later, however, Laqueur dropped the assertion about a meeting and limited

ber 24 Sadat received Vinogradov in Alexandria (he was to see him again on October 1, 3, and 4).[18] These Sadat-Vinogradov meetings brought assurances of Soviet support. Also on September 24, in Tashkent, Brezhnev delivered his second major speech in a week and avoided, as he had earlier in Sofia on September 18, any mention of the Middle East, though touching on all other important foreign policy issues. By this time Brezhnev's own sources may have provided information of the concentrations of Egyptian and Syrian troops. At a later date Gromyko stated that political consultations between the Soviet Union and Egypt, which were held in accordance with the provisions of the 1971 treaty, "played an important part in the coordination of our actions in the period before October 1973 and during the events of last October."[19] By late September–early October the Soviets were fully aware of the imminence of war. They did not need to receive this information from their own intelligence operatives, for they had been told in so many words by Sadat himself (and by Asad on October 4).[20]

---

himself to saying that there was an exchange of letters at that time; see *Confrontation*, p. 83.

[18] In *The Road to Ramadan*, Haykal mentions two meetings between Sadat and Vinogradov: on October 1 and 4. Sadat says there were three meetings during this crucial period. FBIS/Egypt, September 16, 1975, pp. D4-D5.

[19] Gromyko made the remark in a luncheon speech, given in honor of Isma'il Fahmi, the Egyptian foreign minister, then in Moscow. FBIS/USSR, March 5, 1974, pp. F2-F3.

[20] In a speech on September 15, 1975, Sadat revealed that he and Asad had agreed in August 1973 to tell the Soviets on Thursday, October 4, the time that military operations were to begin:

"The agreement between us was, and this is being said publicly for the first time, that I would summon the Soviet ambassador on Wednesday 3 October and that he would summon the Soviet ambassador in Damascus on Thursday 4 October. The message I was to convey to the Soviet Union on Wednesday was supposed to be: Egypt and Syria have decided to embark on a military operation to put an end to the no peace, no war situation. The question I was to pose in the message was: What is the opinion of the Soviet Government regarding this offensive?

"I did in fact summon the Soviet ambassador. I summoned him on Wednesday 3 October and informed him of the situation. He asked me: When is the offensive to be? I told him that President al-Asad and I had not yet decided on the zero hour. Why? Because President al-Asad and I had agreed in August in Bludan that we would tell the Russians the time of the operation on Thursday 4 October. I would just ask the Soviet Government what its attitude to the action would be. So when the Soviet ambassador asked when the offensive was to be, I told him we had not yet agreed on the zero hour, but that I wanted a reply to my question, that is, what attitude would the Soviet Union adopt.

In the weeks prior to the time Israel actually reinforced both fronts, the Soviet media disseminated false reports of an Israeli buildup, reminiscent of May 1967.[21] These may have been intended to prepare the Soviet public for war. There had been similar intermittent reports in August, "which leads one to the conclusion that the Soviet Union was indeed preparing the public for some outbreak, although the fact that the reports began in August suggests that Moscow was not informed of the date of the impending operation."[22] On September 23 *Krasnaia zvezda* berated Israel for inflaming the situation. The next day Pavel Demchenko editorialized that "new tendencies" (i.e. the Sadat-Asad rapprochement with Husayn), favoring joint action "by Arab states with different political regimes against Tel-Aviv's continuing aggression," are gaining the upper hand.[23] Another denunciation of Israel followed in *Pravda* on September 26. As the countdown began, these reports of "provocations" became key pieces of the puzzle. Then came a week of relative quiet and relative neglect. The Soviet press had taken its cue from Brezhnev's Tashkent speech of September 24; and the Middle East was suddenly but temporarily "ignored." If we assume the propaganda had been intended to prepare the Soviet public for war, the lull is perplexing. There is no supportive evidence, but one wonders whether the Soviet leadership was debating the merits of the position it was to adopt in the coming conflict.

On October 2 the Bulgarian press agency issued a release in English of Syrian and Egyptian preparations for an imminent attack, but since the report was not repeated or carried in Bulgarian, the assumption was that it had been released by mistake.[24] The next day the USSR launched a recoverable photo-reconnaissance satellite, and five more during the next two weeks.[25] On

---

"As agreed, Al-Asad summoned the Soviet ambassador in Damascus on Thursday and told him of the time of the offensive. This was all as we had agreed." FBIS/Egypt, September 16, 1975, pp. D4-D5.

21 Kohler, et al., *The Soviet Union*, pp. 47-48.

22 Golan, "*Soviet Aims*," p. 106. 23 *Pravda*, September 24, 1973.

24 Golan, "*Soviet Aims*," p. 107. Haykal said that MENA released an item by mistake that day "to the effect that the Second and Third Armies—the two which were to launch the attack across the canal—had been put on a state of alert." *The Road to Ramadan*, p. 28. The Bulgarians might have picked it up.

25 *Aviation Week and Space Technology*, 99, No. 17. (October 22, 1973), 16. Normally, such satellites are launched "at about two week intervals and remain aloft 12–14 days." Those orbited on October 3 and during the war were kept up for only six days.

October 4, 5, and 6, Moscow mounted a sudden airlift to evacuate the families and dependents of Soviet advisers in Syria and Egypt. On October 4 *Pravda* wrote of Israel's increasing diplomatic isolation, especially as it related to the new reaction of the Black African countries to the "expansionist essence of Israeli policy."[26] TASS reported Israeli troop concentrations along the Lebanese border and the cease-fire line with Syria, repeating this allegation the following day.[27] On October 4, Soviet naval ships left Alexandria and Port Said,[28] and *Izvestiia*'s Beirut correspondent said that Israeli leaders were building up their forces on the Golan Heights "as an 'alibi' and as justification for their future actions."[29] At 0630 hours on October 6 Radio Sofia announced: "An adventure in the Middle East is [quite] possible at this particular moment."[30] *Pravda*'s morning edition carried a story from its Cairo correspondent, datelined October 5, alerting the Soviet public to speculations in the Egyptian press that "Tel-Aviv is preparing a massive attack:"

> Israeli tanks and heavy artillery have been concentrated on the Syrian cease-fire line. Israeli planes are patrolling along the entire line and the Lebanese frontier . . .

> Damascus Radio comments on the introduction of the emergency situation in the Israeli settlements on the occupied Golan Heights.

> The Syrian newspaper "Al-Thawra" concludes that Israel is preparing itself for a military adventure. A comparison of the declarations of Israeli leaders, made now and before the June 1967 war, writes the newspaper, clearly and vividly shows the similarity of Israel's tactics in preparing for aggression.

> Attention is paid in Cairo to yesterday's threat made by the head of Israel's Chief of Staff Elazar, who declared that Israel's military forces have a "long hand," which is capable of delivering a blow deep inside Arab territories. In light of the last provocation, writes the newspaper "Al-Ahram," this declaration is a signal for the preparation of a new aggression.[31]

26 *Pravda*, October 4, 1973.
27 *FBIS/USSR*, October 5, 1973, p. F2; October 9, 1973, p. F3.
28 Herzog, *War of Atonement*, p. 48.
29 *FBIS/USSR*, October 12, 1973, p. F4.
30 Radio Free Europe, Bulgarian Situation Report/36 (October 12, 1973), p. 7.
31 *Pravda*, October 6, 1973.

Shortly after noon on October 6 TASS reported "that within the next few days Israel intends to strike a blow at the neighboring Arab countries in order to impose on them by force its variant of solving the Middle East crisis."[32] Thirty minutes later, it announced that "Israeli troops attacked the advance position of the Syrian Army throughout the entire cease-fire line."

While the events are reasonably incontrovertible, the interpretations are admittedly not. Thus one can contend that the Soviet arms buildup was only an equivalent response to Israel's growing strength, an effort to keep Egypt from falling behind militarily; and the supplying of SCUDs was merely part of Moscow's all-round effort to strengthen Egypt. However, it is difficult to believe that the significance of the SCUD deployment was lost on the Kremlin: first, by providing Egypt with this deterrent weapon, the USSR was enhancing the offensive potential of Egypt's existing force structure; second, it recognized Sadat's resolve for war in his personally difficult but militarily compelling decision to permit Soviet personnel once again to control weapons on Egyptian soil; and third, coming on top of the large quantities of weapons shipped since early 1973, the SCUDs could not help but encourage Sadat to believe he had Soviet backing, certainly for limited military objectives.

Some elements in the Kremlin, possibly even Brezhnev, may still have doubted Sadat's ability to carry off a war in a creditable manner and feared there would be a stiff price to pay in relations with the United States. Nevertheless, Moscow did not interfere. Indeed, on several occasions, it gave assurances of "full support."

In the four days before the war, Moscow generated a variety of "signals" that were not understood perhaps because they contravened accepted premises and because the nature of analysis in intelligence work is such that discordant information, especially when new to the operator or weakly transmitted, is simply not "heard" or is set into some familiar pattern where it is assumed more or less to fit. What we witnessed in the early days of October was a flagrant error in Israeli and American judgment and a skillful combination of Egyptian and Syrian coordination, crowned by extraordinarily good luck. Secretary of State Henry A. Kissinger (who replaced Rogers in September) admitted the United States was caught unaware:

32 *FBIS/USSR*, October 9, 1973, p. F4.

The crisis for us started at 6 a.m. on October 6, when I was awakened with the information that another Arab-Israeli war was probable.

I mention this personal detail because it answers the question that the United States intervention prevented Israel from taking pre-emptive action [as implied by Prime Minister Golda Meir on October 6 and 13]. The United States made no demarche to either side before October 6, because all the intelligence at our disposal and all the intelligence given to us by foreign countries suggested that there was no possibility of the outbreak of a war.[33]

The Soviet "signals" were far from clear, but they were stronger than one would expect if the Soviets had been cooperating in a grand deception. The argument, put forth by a few, that Brezhnev orchestrated the entire scenario, managing Sadat's every move, is theoretically conceivable, but politically improbable, presupposing, as it does, Soviet foresight concerning the reactions of the Israelis and the Americans and a control over the behavior of each of the actors that is rare in international relations.[34] More plausible is the assumption that Moscow decided to keep its options open, to go along for the moment to see what would happen.

[33] Press conference, October 25, 1973 in *NYT*, October 26, 1973. On October 6, in her speech to the nation, Premier Golda Meir said: "For several days now the Israel intelligence service has known that the armies of Egypt and Syria were massing for a combined attack. . . . Our forces made the *necessary* preparations to meet the danger. . . . We *appealed* to influential political elements to work for the prevention of the heinous initiative on the part of the rulers of Egypt and Syria. We acquainted *friendly political elements in good time* with the information on the plans to launch an attack on Israel . . ." (emphasis added). *NYT*, October 7, 1973. On October 10, Israel's ambassador to the United States echoed the same line: "We would have destroyed them when the Egyptians and Syrians were sitting like ducks . . . [but Israel chose not to attack] because we wanted everyone to be sure this time that Israel had done everything to prevent war." *NYT*, October 11, 1973.

While Mrs. Meir had rejected on political grounds General Elazar's proposal for a preemptive strike, she was not accurate in saying that the "necessary preparations" had been taken—witness the unpreparedness of the frontline troops along the canal, nor had she apprised Kissinger of the facts "in good time." She later admitted that she was in possession of all the facts, but had misinterpreted them: "There was a fatal mistake of evaluation." *NYT*, December 7 and 10, 1973.

[34] See Uri Ra'anan, "The USSR and the Middle East: Some Reflections on the Soviet Decisionmaking Process," *ORBIS*, 17, No. 3 (Fall 1973), 946-977.

Retrospective examination indicates that the signals should have evoked a far greater response than they did. They were perplexingly inconsistent with Moscow's military support of Egypt since 1967 and suggested uncertainty more than disinformation. That they were weak is true; but that they were sent at all was significant.

Let us look at the signals. First, there was Brezhnev's conspicuous, and we must assume deliberate, omission of the Middle East in two speeches in which he touched on all other areas of the world. Any alarm in the West over this irregularity, however, was possibly forestalled by Gromyko's bitter attack on Israel in the General Assembly on September 25, when he warned that the situation in the Middle East "is dangerous" and even though "there are no actual flames, but only embers, in that center of war, there is the risk of another military confrontation at any time, and there is no telling to what consequences it might lead."[35]

Second, there were the "leaks" from Bulgarian and Czechoslovak news agencies. Neither of these conduits of carefully filtered information would initiate such portentous news without prior approval from Moscow, unless, as is entirely possible, they were only repeating information obtained from Arab news sources. Minor manifestations in themselves, in context they were suggestive. Yet because of the omniverous nature of intelligence-gathering and collating bureaucracies, they may have been ignored in the rush or been unassimilated.

Third, and perhaps most important, there were the reports on October 4, 5, and 6 of the evacuation of Soviet dependents from Egypt and Syria.[36] These were vented in the Western, not Soviet, press. The information was known in Jerusalem and Washington. The diversion of Soviet airliners to remove the dependents began on October 3. The explanation at the time by Western and Israeli sources was that Soviet refusal to help the Syrians in their air battle with Israeli planes on September 13 had aggravated Soviet-Syrian tensions, which presaged a possible expulsion of Soviet advisers, a repeat of Sadat's move fourteen months

[35] *Soviet News*, No. 5708 (October 9, 1973), p. 425.

[36] This point is not treated in depth in any of the works that I have seen on the October War. The Israelis viewed the evacuation as evidence that the Soviets had failed to persuade Egypt and Syria to give up their plans for war. BBC/ME/4418/A/8 (October 8, 1973).

earlier.[37] But unlike the Soviet departure from Egypt in 1972, this one took place without any formal or officially announced Syrian request. Of course, such a request could have been made informally to spare the Soviets humiliation, but there is no evidence that such was the case. Nor in this situation, unlike in 1972, was there any slowdown of Soviet arms to Syria, any discord over repayment, or any diminution of the Soviet strengthening of the Syrian air defense system.

Sadat said the initiative for the evacuation came from Moscow.[38] When on October 4 Brezhnev "asked for permission to withdraw Russian civilian advisers and their families from Egypt,"[39] Sadat "reluctantly agreed to it and took the opportunity to press for the speedy delivery of some equipment which had been ordered but not delivered." But he was puzzled by the request, fearing it mirrored Soviet foreboding about the outcome of the war or hesitation about providing the help Egypt expected.[40]

Some Western and Israeli officials believe that Moscow, sensing the imminence of war, removed its people out of humanitarian concern for their safety.[41] If so, it was the first time the Soviet leadership ever removed its citizens from danger *before* the actual outbreak of fighting in a Third World setting. Neither prior to nor during the June War did the Soviet government evacuate any personnel from Cairo and Damascus. It did remove embassy women and children from Amman during the Jordanian-Syrian-Fedayeen conflict in September 1970, and it did evacuate dependents from both East and West Pakistan during the Indo-Pakistani war in December 1971. But in both cases the evacua-

---

[37] For example, on September 27 a Beirut newspaper reported that the movements of Soviet military assistance personnel in Syria were being restricted. If true, the restriction would have hindered intelligence reporting to Moscow but possibly alerted Moscow to Syria's military intentions. BBC/ME/ 4411/i (September 29, 1973).

The speculation concerning a serious Soviet-Syrian rift seemed sound because no prominent Soviet leader had attended the ceremony inaugurating the Euphrates Dam, Moscow's show-piece effort in Syria and symbol of the friendship between the two countries in much the same way that the Aswan Dam is of Soviet-Egyptian friendship. *Sketch*, November 9, 1973, p. 15.

A more likely interpretation is that these and other such incidents were part of Syria's disinformation campaign.

[38] *FBIS/Egypt*, January 14, 1975, p. D6.

[39] Heikal, *The Road to Ramadan*, p. 34.

[40] *Ibid.*, p. 35.

[41] Author's interviews in June and December 1974.

tions took place during the course of actual hostilities and not in the period of mounting tensions.[42] Had Moscow participated in the decision to attack on October 6 it would hardly have made such a revealing move lest it heighten the vigilance of the foe it was working to catch unawares—unless, as seems most unlikely, the Soviets adopted this stratagem in the belief it would be incorrectly interpreted as a sign of Egyptian-Soviet discord, thus confirming the assessment of Israeli and Western intelligence that nothing was afoot. If so, it was a very risky dodge that almost backfired and raised an alert. Even if this first such Soviet evacuation were pure happenstance, it should have sounded alarm bells because evacuation is a *political* act, whatever may be its intent, and Moscow, realizing this, still went ahead.

Very likely, Moscow, which now knew the war was coming on October 6, wanted to maintain a certain diplomatic distance from the attack: it wanted to be sufficiently aloof so that when war broke out it would not be accused by the United States of complicity, thereby endangering the advantages it gained from détente. Also, Moscow went out of its way to indicate that the decision to go to war was an Arab not a Soviet one, because it did not want to get dragged into the fighting.

The weakest of the signals were the gleanings from the Soviet press. Their attempts to prepare the Soviet public for the possibility of war were sporadic and low key for the most part. Short items discussing simmering tensions were TASS staples, and only the most careful observer might have discerned suggestive differences between the presentations in the August and September issues and the April and May ones, for example. Not until the morning of October 6 was the message clear.[43]

By no means did any of these signals that could have been intended to alert Washington to the oncoming war convey an unequivocal warning. With the exception of the evacuation of the dependents, they were extremely weak and ambiguous, probably

[42] Two other minor instances of the evacuation of dependents may be noted. One was from Peking at the height of the cultural revolution (1967–1969) when the Soviet embassy was under siege. Another was the evacuation from Phnom Penh at different times over the past few years when that city appeared to be more than usually threatened. This, of course, had political as well as humanitarian motives in that it was intended to demonstrate lack of confidence in the Lon Nol government.

[43] The dispatch by Iurii Glukhov from Cairo on October 5 came close to predicting the outbreak of the war. See *Pravda*, October 6, 1973.

reflecting the Kremlin's ambivalence. Moscow did not really want a war, and up to the very end it questioned the determination of the Egyptians and Syrians and expected that an Israeli mobilization would suffice to deter them. Had the Kremlin desired, the signals could have been loud and clear, especially after October 1, when Sadat informed Vinogradov that war was likely to occur at any moment. But the fact is that the Soviet leadership, though not wanting to be directly involved, was not quite sure but that it might benefit by allowing events to unfold. After all, its invasion of Czechoslovakia had not prevented détente. The obscure signaling suggests uncertainty in Moscow and the possibility that the leadership basically believed it could keep the Middle East imbroglio under control and still have détente, though it was hedging its bets.

Had the Israelis been less complacent and more efficient in alerting and reinforcing their front line units, Arab losses would have been considerably heavier, their attack blunted at an earlier stage, and their political gains less sizable; in which event, some onus would have fallen on the Soviets, who in the future might have been more hesitant about feverishly feeding the Middle East arms race.

Foreign policy is the art of adapting to opportunity, and the Soviets have proved themselves masters of it. They had armed Egypt for a war they did not want just then. They could have tried to dissuade Sadat, for example, by withdrawing the SCUD missiles or the Soviet military personnel attached to the Syrian units; but this might have embittered their relations with Cairo and Damascus, and seriously exacerbated possible disagreements in the Kremlin between the supposed "détente-firsters" and "Arab-firsters." A policy of ambivalence, on the other hand, may have been acceptable to all factions. Once war came, however, after forty-eight hours of hesitation, Moscow grew protective of its clients, solicitous over its investment, and intrigued by the flowering prospects of a weakened Western alliance. Its ad hoc diplomacy evolved in response to the events on the battlefield: the text was improvisation, not ideology.

CONFLICT

At the start of the war, TASS broadcast the reports originating in Arab countries to the effect that Israel had launched attacks against Egypt and Syria, which were "answering enemy fire."[44] In Cairo, Moscow tried for a quick cease-fire. According to Sadat, six hours after the fighting had begun, Vinogradov asked for an audience, claiming that he was acting as a go-between for Asad to seek an immediate cease-fire.[45] The Soviet version of the incident is quite different: Vinogradov supposedly told Sadat that Asad had told Moscow that he wanted "the USSR to take rapid action to obtain a United Nations resolution on a cease-fire within forty-eight hours of the start of the fighting, as the situation would then be favorable to the Arabs. I said to President Sadat that Moscow wanted to know his view on Syria's request. President Sadat asked me to inform the Soviet leaders that it was too early to think of such a thing and that he would get in touch with President Asad to convince him of this."[46] When queried by Sadat, Asad denied that he had made such a request. What is clear from both versions is the Soviet interest in a prompt cease-fire at a moment when Syrian gains could be preserved. Moscow did not want to underwrite a major war. It did want to preserve the early gains of its Syrian client.

(Sadat later charged the Soviet Union and Syria with collusion, saying Asad had asked the Russians "even before the start of the

[44] FBIS/USSR, October 9, 1973, p. F5.

[45] See, for example, Sadat's interview of March 29, 1974, in Al-Anwar, as quoted in NYT, March 30, 1974; and his interview with Der Stern, as quoted in FBIS/Egypt, April 15, 1974, pp. D1-D2; see also his speech to the People's Assembly on April 18, 1974, in BBC/ME/4579/A/6 (April 20, 1974). A few days after Sadat's accusation against Vinogradov, Moscow announced the appointment of a new ambassador, V. P. Poliakov, who arrived in Cairo on May 14, 1974. See Heikal, The Road to Ramadan, pp. 208-209, 212-214.

[46] The Beirut daily Al-Safir (April 16, 1974), published the account which it attributed to Vinogradov. See Journal of Palestine Studies, 3, No. 4 (Summer 1974), 161-163. According to Vinogradov, on October 7, "I received another message from Moscow to the effect that Syria had repeated her request, that she believed that the military situation and the liberation of the Bar-Lev line were favorable to the Arabs' objectives. She wanted a ceasefire, and I was asked by the Soviet command about President Sadat's views on the new request." Sadat, contended Vinogradov, still demurred, arguing that "the goal was the accomplishment of a specific action to change the balance of military and political power in the Arabs' favor, to destroy the theory of Israeli security, and to unblock the crisis. I informed the President of the Soviet command's view that this goal had already been achieved, and that it was logical to ask for a ceasefire at this stage, before Israel recovered from the shock of the surprise defeat—unless other and wider objectives were intended. The President replied that he wanted to exploit the immense military success achieved on the Egyptian front to develop the attack and to advance to recover the passes."

battle" to demand a cease-fire shortly after the fighting had begun.[47] In his view, this was motivated, first, by the Soviet-Syrian expectation of a Syrian recapture of the Golan Heights within forty-eight hours, after which the U.N. Security Council would intervene to bring an end to the fighting, leaving the Syrians with a clearcut victory; and second, by their belief that the Egyptians would probably be defeated by the Israelis or, at best, might just surmount stiff Israeli resistance in their attempt to cross the canal: neither Moscow nor Damascus thought highly of Egypt's ability. Under such circumstances an early cease-fire would provide Syria, Moscow's prized client, with a dramatic military-political triumph and leave Sadat in dire straits, possibly weakened internally as a consequence. The Soviet-Syrian intrigue failed as a result of Egypt's impressive performance on October 6 and 7, Asad's inability (for reasons of domestic and Arab politics) to admit his preference for a quick cease-fire, and Sadat's concern for what King Faysal would think. According to Sadat, Faysal had told him: "If you are unable to enter a protracted battle and you ask for a cease-fire after a day or two, then we will be unable to support you in the Arab field."[48] The implication was clear: if Egypt was not going to make a serious fight of it, Saudi Arabia would not take the momentous step of using the oil weapon in support of Egypt.)

In public, the Soviet assessment was dogmatic and cast in ideological terms. On October 7, Evgenii Primakov, Deputy Director of the Institute of World Economy and International Relations, said that Israel launched the attack because it wanted "to change the nature of certain Arab regimes and to wipe out in general the progressive national liberation trends in the Arab world," and to alter by arms the political setbacks it had recently suffered:

> The nonaligned countries in Algiers [The Fourth Conference of Nonaligned Countries had been held in September] condemned Israel. There was the serious diplomatic defeat: eight non-Arab African countries have broken off relations with Israel lately. Finally, the Israeli leadership could not fail to be disturbed by the stand taken by the Austrian chancellor, Dr.

[47] FBIS/Egypt, October 29, 1975, p. D19; see also FBIS/Egypt, September 14, 1975, pp. D4–D5.
[48] FBIS/Egypt, August 19, 1975, p. D13; FBIS/Egypt, October 23, 1975, p. D8.

Kreisky, who, despite the pressures put on him, has categorically confirmed the decision to close the camp on Austrian territory for immigrants going to Israel.[49]

A few hours later, the Soviet government issued a carefully
worded statement, its first since the war began, in which it said
that Israel was responsible for the war.[50] Beyond this, however,
it was noncommittal. The statement intoned that "the Soviet
Union consistently comes out as a reliable friend of the Arab
states . . . [and] resolutely supports the legitimate demands of
the Arab states for [the] relinquishing [of] all Arab territories
occupied by Israel in 1967," but it did not specifically reaffirm
the USSR's "full support" for Arab military efforts, an omission
that was consistent with its effort to arrange an early cease-fire.
That Moscow was moving cautiously, appraising Arab prospects
and the risks and stakes involved, may also be inferred from "the
fact that the wave of protest against Israeli aggression failed to
spread in the Soviet Union in the wake of a Radio Moscow report on the holding of a protest meeting in a Soviet factory on
October 8."[51] Initially opposed to convening a meeting of the
Security Council, the Kremlin acceded to Washington's persis-
tence in the exchange of messages between Nixon and Brezhnev
during the evening of October 7–8,[52] an exchange that continued
actively throughout the crisis.

The U.S. government policy of keeping in close touch with
Moscow and withholding any help for Israel, verbal or material,
seemed to be working: American and Soviet officials refrained
from making any inflammatory remarks; neither side supplied
weapons or ammunition to the combatants; and in the eastern
Mediterranean, the Soviet naval force steadily reinforced, held
its position off Crete, as did the U.S. Sixth Fleet. The Security
Council, however, at the behest of the Arabs, the non-aligned
countries, and the USSR, dismissed an informally circulated
American proposal for a cease-fire status quo ante.

Late on October 8, Moscow shifted suddenly into partisan
gear. Pleased (surprised?) by the performance of its clients—

[49] FBIS/USSR, October 9, 1973, p. F12.

[50] Ibid., pp. F1–F2.

[51] Jean Riollot, "Soviet Reaction to the Middle East War," Parts I and II,
Radio Liberty Dispatch, October 12, and October 13, 1973, p. 3 and pp. 2-3,
respectively.

[52] NYT, October 9, 1973.

Syria and Egypt had seized important chunks of territory and were still on the offensive—but no doubt under some pressure from Arab governments, it decided to come off the sidelines. The catalyst was a letter sent on October 7 to the heads of government of the United States, France, and Great Britain and to the Soviet president, premier, and Communist Party secretary-general by Algerian President Houari Boumedienne in his capacity as chairman of the Fourth Conference of Nonaligned Countries, which had been held in Algiers the previous month.[53] On October 8, a small item in *Pravda* reported that Boumedienne in a letter "directed to the nonaligned and socialist countries" indicated that the "nonaligned countries . . . will not fail to render precisely in this moment appropriate political, moral, and material support for the Arab countries."[54] What is noteworthy is that the *Pravda* account was faulty on two counts: Boumedienne's letter was sent to the four great powers and not to all nonaligned and socialist countries, and it did not contain the strong expression of active and direct support described by *Pravda* in what purported to be a direct quote from Boumedienne's letter.

Brezhnev's reply was made public by the Algerian government on October 9 (it has never been published, or even mentioned, by the Soviet media); and according to an unidentified "Soviet source," similar messages were also delivered to all Arab governments with which the USSR had diplomatic relations.[55] Brezhnev urged the Arabs not to stand aloof from the struggle being waged by Syria and Egypt "against a treacherous enemy" and stressed the "urgent need for the widest aid and support." By way of justifying the Soviet desire to avoid any direct involvement, he referred to the complexity of the international scene and expressed confidence that the Algerian leaders would "understand full well all the peculiarities of the present situation and that, guided by the ideals of fraternal solidarity, will use every means and take every step required to give their support to Syria and Egypt in the tough struggle imposed by the Israeli aggressor."[56] Brezhnev wanted the Arabs to assume the primary burden of

---

[53] FBIS/Northern Africa, October 9, 1973, p. T2.
[54] *Pravda*, October 8, 1973. [55] *NYT*, October 10, 1973.
[56] BBC/ME/4421/A/5 (October 11, 1973). For the text of the Brezhnev response, see also Riad N. El-Rayyes and Dunia Nahas (eds.), *The October War* (Beirut: An-Nahar Report Books, 1974), p. 24.

aiding Syria and Egypt by contributing their Soviet arms and their troops to the struggle. (In Moscow Podgornyi expressed surprise to an Iraqi envoy that the Arab states were not hurrying more aid to the front.[57]) The promptness of Brezhnev's reply and the strong spurs to greater Arab involvement suggest that it was Brezhnev's intention to egg the Arabs on, not to restrain them, but to do so in a way that would leave Moscow with maximum diplomatic flexibility.

By the evening of October 8, however, Moscow felt impelled toward direct involvement. The Soviet ambassador in Cairo told Sadat that an airlift of arms would start shortly.[58] In less than forty-eight hours a major airlift was begun, soon to be overshadowed by a major resupply by sea. The Soviet escalation had begun. We may never know why, whether out of elation at the prospect, seemingly within reach, of a defeat of Israel, whether out of concern that the tide was going to shift against the Arabs unless Moscow took a direct hand in the conflict, whether as a consequence of urgent requests for assistance from the Arabs themselves, or whether as a result of American inaction.

The critical step was the decision to resupply the Arabs. Early on October 10, the Soviets began to airlift military supplies to Syria,[59] and on October 11, to Egypt. The quality of weapons was high but generally no higher than that already possessed. Critical items such as surface-to-air missiles and equipment and anti-tank ammunition had priority during this stage. The replenishment operation, characterized as "moderate" by Kissinger in his press conference on October 12, soon acquired a massive dimension. Meanwhile, Israeli losses in planes and tanks were heavy. Israeli forces had repulsed and reversed the Syrian advance on the Golan Heights and were consolidating their positions in Sinai, ten to twelve miles east of the canal, but they were growing short of equipment and ammunition and finding the Arabs formidable opponents. Israeli nervousness mounted with the ac-

---

[57] Heikal, *The Road to Ramadan*, p. 218.

[58] *Ibid.*, p. 214. In Syria, Soviet advisers were already in the front line with Syrian troops. *Strategic Survey 1973* (London: IISS, 1974), p. 25. According to an American official, some Soviet troops had manned SAM sites in Egypt during the fighting, but they had "not actively engaged themselves in hostilities." *NYT*, November 6, 1973.

[59] The next day the Arab ambassadors in Moscow thanked Gromyko for the "all-round assistance and support" rendered by Moscow. *NYT*, October 12, 1973.

celerating Soviet airlift and the dwindling of their own ordnance.[60]

October 10 to 13 was the testing time of détente, which was found wanting. In a real sense it was much more revealing of the limits of détente in competitive conflictual situations than was the crisis of October 24–25. Growing Soviet involvement occasioned great concern (and dismay among the détentists) in Washington, which increased its efforts, seeking now to gain Soviet acceptance for a cease-fire in place and no longer one that would require the belligerents to withdraw behind the lines of October 6. Moscow agreed, telling Kissinger it felt certain Sadat would go along. However, it insisted that neither superpower introduce the proposal. Moscow did not want to antagonize the radicals of the Arab spectrum or expose itself to the inevitable Chinese charges of collusion with the United States. It expected Kissinger to produce Israel's acquiescence (which he did), but was not willing to assume the responsibility for doing the same with its client. The Kremlin was unwilling to upset its connections with Cairo and Damascus in the interest of détente with the United States and cleverly tried to assure itself of political dividends at no risk.

Kissinger turned to the British for assistance, asking them to take the initiative and expecting that they would immediately make such a proposal in the Security Council. The British, however, thought the move would be opposed by Cairo and be seen as anti-Egyptian. Having recently improved relations with Egypt and imposed an embargo on arms to the area at the outbreak of the war to ingratiate themselves further with the Arabs, they were not about to risk this on Kissinger's say-so of what the Soviets had told him. They asked their ambassador in Cairo to sound out Sadat privately. Sadat, under little pressure from the Soviets, mindful of Faysal's admonition against a premature cease-fire, and now somewhat disturbed by the deepening plight of the Syrian forces, angrily rejected the proposal, unless Israel agreed to withdraw from all the territories. Kissinger was furious and interpreted the British handling of the matter as excessive kowtowing to Egyptian sensibilities. In his view the British

[60] To test Soviet determination to reprovision the Syrians, the Israelis bombed Aleppo airfield with Soviet transports on it, losing a couple of planes in the process. However, the Antonovs kept coming, landing on the cratered air strips and in Damascus, thus making Moscow's intention unmistakeable.

should not have inquired, but merely introduced the proposal on his assurance. Twelve hours later, at 4 p.m. on Saturday, October 13, the British ambassador again saw Sadat and received the same answer. From this the British concluded that Kissinger's plan was unworkable and they refused to go along with it, thereby provoking a minor crisis in Anglo-American relations.[61] The failure of this American initiative persuaded Nixon to sanction a relief airlift to Israel. All stops were pulled. On October 9, Nixon had permitted El Al to take on several loads of spare parts and electronic countermeasures (ECM) equipment; on October 12, he responded to Israel's call for assistance by countering the Soviet airlift with a modest American one; and on October 13, he authorized an all-out effort. Kissinger's attempt to obtain Soviet participation in what is frequently termed rather euphemistically "crisis management" had failed. Diplomacy had to wait upon developments from the battlefield.

At his first press conference since becoming secretary of state, held on October 12 when he still had hopes for the Soviets' assurance that Sadat would accept a cease-fire in place, Kissinger admitted that some Soviet actions, such as the airlift, Brezhnev's message of October 8 to Boumedienne, and Moscow's lack of interest in a mutual arms freeze to the combatants, had not been "helpful" in confining the crisis. Nonetheless, he said, "We also do not consider that Soviet actions as of now constitute the irresponsibility . . . that would threaten détente."[62] If the Soviet Union had foreknowledge of the war, he ruminated, it would have been an encouraging sign for détente to have shared this knowledge:

In an ideal world, one would expect closer consultation but, given the particular volatility of the Middle East, it would have been a heavy responsibility to make known certain advance information. Nevertheless, we would like to stress that if either side in this relationship has certain knowledge of imminent military operations in any explosive part of the world, we would consider it consistent and, indeed, required—by the principles that have been signed between the United States

[61] The Insight Team of *The Sunday Times*, pp. 135-136. According to the British, Kissinger later told their ambassador in Washington privately that the Soviets had admitted they misjudged Sadat's mood.

[62] Press conference, October 12, 1973 (News release, Bureau of Public Affairs, Department of State), p. 7.

and the Soviet Union—that an opportunity be given to both sides to calm the situation.[63]

While agreeing that the Middle East was an area where local rivalries that have their own momentum could draw the superpowers into a confrontation they did not seek, Kissinger pointed out that "if you compare their conduct in this crisis to their conduct in 1967, one has to say that Soviet behavior has been less provocative, less incendiary and less geared to military threats than in the previous crisis"; and he claimed to see hope in "the relative restraint that has been shown in public media in the Soviet Union and in the conduct of their representatives at the Security Council."[64]

Kissinger's plea for cooperation and his velvet warning evoked no calming response from Moscow. On the contrary, Soviet commentaries paid glowing tribute to Arab successes, the improved military performance of Arab armies, and the effectiveness of the SAMs and air defense system,[65] while the Soviet replenishment increased.

Jordan's entry into the war on October 13 threatened to expand its scope, but the Jordanians contented themselves with the commitment of a brigade (about 5,000 men) to the Syrian front; the Jordan River area and the West Bank remained quiet. By October 15 the USSR airlift had exceeded 200 planeloads, in addition to the tanks, artillery, and other heavy equipment that began arriving in Syria by sea on October 10.[66] Moscow wanted a win, not a draw.

Moscow assured Boumedienne, during his visit on October 14–15, that it would "contribute in every way to the liberation of all Arab territories occupied by Israel"—the communiqué standing as a marked contrast to the visit in June 1967 that had ended in bitterness.[67] But Moscow was far from generous, de-

[63] *Ibid.*, p. 9.

[64] *Ibid.*, p. 12. It is disquieting that for clues to the USSR's intentions, Kissinger referred to its press and behavior in the Security Council rather than to the resupply effort and disposition of its military forces. Presumably, he knew better, but preferred not to draw attention to the Soviet military effort, because the U.S. government was not yet fully involved in its own and he wanted to minimize the pressures being brought to bear on him.

[65] For example, *Krasnaia zvezda*, October 13, 1973; *Pravda*, October 13, 1973.

[66] BBC/ME/4427/A/3 (October 18, 1973). By mid-October, Soviet ships docked in increasing numbers in Syrian ports, and Soviet crews drove the tanks directly to Damascus.

[67] BBC/ME/4426/A/1 (October 17, 1973).

manding some payment, whereupon Boumedienne immediately gave the Soviets 200 million dollars; nor did it play up the visit, if we judge by the conspicuously greater coverage given to the visit of the Danish prime minister who arrived in Moscow on October 15.

Soviet behavior blatantly contravened the principles agreed to by Brezhnev and Nixon at their summit meetings and indicated Soviet determination to back its clients to the utmost, short of nuclear war and in the expectation of continuing détente.[68] On October 18 TASS acknowledged for the first time that the USSR was rendering military aid to Syria, Egypt, and Iraq.[69]

On October 16 Sadat made his first public appearance since the fighting began. Exuding confidence, he sketchily reviewed the course of the previous ten days and asserted that the Arabs were better able to bear a protracted war than Israel. He hinted at severe reprisals if Israel threatened "the Arab hinterland," by which he meant Egyptian cities, since Damascus, Homs, Tartus, and Latakia had already been hit hard, with heavy damage to prime economic installations:

> We are aware of the responsibility of using certain types of arms, and we of ourselves restrain ourselves from using them. The Israelis should remember what I once said and still say: an eye for an eye, a tooth for a tooth and depth for depth.[70]

This may have been an allusion to the Soviet-manned SCUDs in Egypt, because the Egyptian-developed Zafir rockets that he did mention by name were not highly regarded. (Soviet coverage of the speech omitted any reference to the missiles.) Sadat also mentioned his rejection of a U.S. "maneuver," i.e. Kissinger's effort on October 12–13 to gain acceptance for a cease-fire in place. Surprisingly, he made no mention of Soviet assistance, but addressed a proposal to Nixon for a cease-fire based on a withdrawal of Israeli forces from all Arab territories, to the June 4, 1967 lines.[71] The rebuff to the Soviets was calculated, a glimmer of Sadat's fury with Moscow for what he regarded as a less than openhanded policy of supplying weapons and avaricious in-

---

[68] Kosygin made the latter point in Moscow on October 15, at a dinner for the Danish prime minister. *Soviet News*, No. 5709, (October 16, 1973), p. 440.

[69] *NYT*, October 19, 1973.

[70] BBC/ME/4426/A/19 (October 17, 1973).

[71] BBC/ME/4427/A/8 (October 18, 1973). This citation refers to the second part of Sadat's speech of October 16.

sistence on payment while the war was still going on.[72] This grievance surfaced after the war.[73] It helps explain Sadat's eager embracing of Kissinger's efforts to find a settlement, leaving the USSR odd man out-in-the-cold, and his subsequent search for alternate arms suppliers in the West.

By October 16 the combatants had all suffered heavy casualties in men and material, but supplied by their superpower patrons they fought on in costly, exhausting combat. The tide had turned in Israel's favor. Israeli forces had driven the Syrians off the Golan Heights and advanced to the plain near Sassa, twenty miles from Damascus. In Sinai, they contained the Egyptian advance along a strip about ten to twelve miles from the canal after a major Egyptian defeat on October 14. And, on October 15–16, an Israeli column in "an audacious but risky tactical stroke designed to loosen Egypt's grip on the Sinai bridgehead" had crossed over to the Egyptian side of the canal just across the northern part of the Great Bitter Lake between Ismailia and Suez.[74]

The superpowers' naval buildup grew ominous, as did the seaborne resupply effort. The Soviet flotilla contained a small amphibious group in a holding pattern off Cyprus and two *Moskva*-class helicopter-carriers within quick steaming distance of Egypt and Syria.[75] For the first time Moscow deployed its navy in strength to protect and advance overseas interests.

On October 16 Kosygin flew secretly to Cairo; his presence was not officially announced until October 18. He came to press Egypt to accept an immediate cease-fire. To Moscow, the reasons were compelling: a) the Arabs had initially scored military suc-

[72] There were persistent reports of oil-producing Arab governments seeking quick loans in Western Europe to satisfy Soviet demands. *NYT*, October 19, 1973. For example, Abu Dhabi, one of the Persian Gulf shaykhdoms requested a 250 million dollar loan from Western banks. *NYT*, October 22, 1973.

[73] In an interview with *Der Stern* in April 1974, Sadat said that Boumedienne had to pay the Soviets 100 million dollars during his visit on October 14–15, 1973, and that Moscow had not provided all the heavy weaponry Egypt desired. FBIS/Egypt, April 15, 1974, p. D1. Also, *NYT*, April 22, 1974.

[74] *NYT*, October 19, 1973.

[75] Western naval experts were disturbed by departures from the pattern of Soviet behavior in the crisis of September 1970: first, the Soviet Union continued to augment its force levels; second, whereas in previous local conflicts the Soviet navy had pulled back when the U.S. Sixth Fleet projected its power, this time it did not; third, the Soviet navy in the area included a large number of landing craft; finally, there were more nuclear submarines operating in the Mediterranean than on any other occasion—fifteen had been the previous maximum.

cesses (but on the Syrian front they were being rapidly wiped out) and the time had come to translate them into effective diplomatic action; b) soon after his arrival, Kosygin learned that Israeli General Ariel Sharon's forces had crossed the canal and consolidated their bridgehead on the western bank and were expanding it, thereby posing a growing threat to the Egyptian army. He used this to exert pressure on Sadat to agree to a cease-fire.[76] The ante was being raised by the influx of arms from the two superpowers, but it was the Israelis and not the Arabs who were driving inexorably toward another crushing victory that could be prevented only by an immediate cease-fire or by a direct Soviet military intervention; and c) the fabric of détente had been stretched thin and Moscow had no wish to test the breaking point; hence its responsiveness now to Kissinger's call for a cease-fire.

Actually, neither superpower wanted an Israeli victory. It would lock the Soviets into an untenable position regarding their clients and make a cease-fire more difficult to negotiate, and possibly even provoke Moscow to intervene directly to prevent a 1967-type defeat. Kissinger tried to procrastinate on resupplying the Israelis—shifting the onus to the Pentagon and eliciting sharp disclaimers from Secretary of Defense James A. Schlesinger—in order to induce the Soviets to moderate their arms deliveries and to make Jerusalem more responsive to American wishes.[77] According to one story that later made the rounds in Washington, when Kissinger congratulated Deputy Secretary of Defense William P. Clements, Jr., who was generally regarded as pro-Arab in Pentagon circles, for his performance in organizing the airlift, he playfully chided him for doing it so impressively.

Nixon's green light on October 13 had complicated matters for Kissinger. The administration's concern over Arab cuts in oil production announced on October 17 had little effect on the strategic-political decisions at the time, though Washington did assume that a prolonged war and further assistance to Israel could only polarize the situation, driving Arab oil producers to use the oil weapon to the maximum. On October 17, in a decision that presaged cold and costly days ahead, the Organization of Arab Petroleum Exporting Countries (OAPEC), meeting in

[76] FBIS/Egypt, September 16, 1975, p. D6.

[77] See James Reston, "The Hidden Compromise," *NYT*, October 19, 1973; also *NYT*, April 21, 1974, and June 23, 1974.

Kuwait, had agreed to a five percent a month cutback in oil production until Israel withdrew from Arab territories.[78] The Saudis were the prime movers behind the OAPEC decision. When the U.S. airlift to Israel started, they had been kept informed by the White House and seemingly accepted the explanation that the move was a response to Soviet shipments and the United States was seeking only to maintain the balance of power in the area. However, what apparently embittered Faysal and impelled him to act was the White House's request, made for its effect on domestic politics ("Why should we let Senator Jackson get the credit?" one White House aide is reported to have said), for a $2.2 billion appropriation from Congress to finance Israel's purchases of weapons.

The Arabs had unveiled a new weapon, nonlethal, yet more far-reaching in its effects and implications than any of those being used on the battlefield or supplied by the superpowers.

On October 19 at 2 a.m. Sadat decided to accept a cease-fire and informed Kosygin of this prior to his departure for Moscow. On October 20, in response to an urgent message from Brezhnev, Kissinger flew to Moscow, arriving some twenty-four hours after Kosygin's return from Cairo. The Kremlin wanted a quick cease-fire, and a proposal was drafted the next day and jointly sponsored in the Security Council on October 22. Israeli Prime Minister Meir temporized in order to give General Sharon time to complete the encirclement of the Egyptian Third Army in the Suez area, but Brezhnev insisted on an immediate cease-fire, and in this he was supported by Nixon.

Security Council Resolution 338 of October 22, 1973, called for a cease-fire within twelve hours and for the start immediately thereafter of negotiations "between the parties concerned under appropriate auspices" for the implementation of it and of Resolution 242.[79] But the fighting in Sinai did not stop notwithstanding formal Israeli and Egyptian acceptance of the resolution (fighting continued on the Syrian front because Damascus did not agree to the cease-fire until October 24). In a last-minute drive to secure the fruits of its bold thrust across the canal, Israel triggered a series of developments that precipitated a Soviet-American confrontation.

[78] ARR, No. 20 (October 16–31, 1973), 470.
[79] NYT, October 23, 1973.

THE SKIP TO THE BRINK

The failure of the cease-fire to take hold gave rise to a second Soviet-American effort, Resolution 339 of October 23, which called for "immediate cessation of all kinds of firing and of all military action, and urges that the forces be returned to the positions they occupied at the moment the ceasefire became effective." The purpose of the resolution was to keep Israeli forces from closing the ring around the Egyptian Third Army, deployed on the eastern side of the canal, and from sealing off the city of Suez, situated at the southern terminal of the canal. In a strong statement, the Soviet government warned Israel of grave consequences. Sadat appealed to Brezhnev and Nixon to send troops to supervise the cease-fire, causing a White House spokesman to declare that the United States "has no intention of sending troops to the Middle East . . . [and] we hope that other outside powers will not send troops to the Middle East."[80] Washington strenuously opposed any direct intervention by the great powers.

Late on the evening of October 24 Brezhnev sent Nixon a "very urgent" message. It arrived soon after U.S. intelligence had reported that "four more divisions of Soviet airborne troops had been placed on alert, bringing the total to seven divisions, or roughly fifty thousand troops," that an airborne command post had been established in the southern part of the country, and that an unprecedented number of Soviet naval and amphibious craft had concentrated in the eastern Mediterranean.[81] Brezhnev warned Nixon: "I will say it straight that if you find it impossible to act together with us in this matter [i.e. stopping the Israeli encirclement], we should be faced with the necessity urgently to consider the question of taking appropriate steps unilaterally."[82] On the basis of this note and the menacing movements of Soviet forces, Kissinger recommended, and Nixon approved, a worldwide alert of U.S. military forces.[83] The time was 11:30 p.m. on

[80] ARR, No. 20 (October 16–31, 1973), 476.
[81] Kalb, *Kissinger*, p. 488.   [82] *Ibid.*, p. 490.
[83] The question of whether the U.S. alert was an appropriate and necessary response to a threatened Soviet intervention can be answered only in the light of how one assesses Soviet policy in the Middle East and Moscow's perceptions at the time. At a press conference on October 25 Kissinger gave his explanation of the move to the American public: "We became aware of the alerting of

October 24. The next morning the CIA reported that a Soviet ship carrying "nuclear material" had passed through the Bosphorus; presumably, the ship carried tactical nuclear weapons that could be tipped to SCUD missiles. Moscow was signaling its unwillingness to tolerate an Egyptian defeat.

The crisis broke as suddenly as it had developed. The Soviet government responded to the alert, agreeing on October 25 to an amended version of the non-permanent members' proposal for a U.N. peacekeeping force that excluded troops from the five permanent members—at the insistence of the United States—but did allow for observers from the United States and the Soviet Union;[84] the Israelis agreed to permit the Egyptians to resupply the surrounded Third Army with food and water and desisted from a crushing military triumph; and the alert was raised within seventy-two hours. On October 26, speaking in Moscow at the World Peace Council Congress of Peace Forces, Brezhnev sounded a conciliatory tone: "In the matter of normalizing the Middle East situation, the Soviet Union is prepared to cooperate with all interested countries."[85] He expressed his undiminished interest in proceeding with Soviet-American cooperation, praised the Arabs' "courageous struggle," and emphasized the USSR's

---

certain Soviet units and we were puzzled by the behavior of some representatives in the discussions that took place. We do not consider ourselves in a confrontation with the Soviet Union; we do not believe it is necessary at this moment to have a confrontation. . . . But cooperative action precludes unilateral action, and the President decided that it was essential that we make clear our attitude towards unilateral steps. . . . When we took the precautionary steps of which you are all aware, we did so because we thought there might be a possibility that matters might go beyond the limits which I have described." *NYT*, October 26, 1973.

Washington's fears of a Soviet intervention were intensified by a garbled intercepted Egyptian message reporting that the first contingent had arrived in Cairo. It turned out to be 36 Soviet cease-fire observers and an equal number of interpreters, and not, as was first feared, the advance guard of Soviet combat troops.

While critics contend the alert was a shrill signal intended to deflect public attention away from the seamy Watergate affair and give President Nixon's prestige a much-needed boost, any appraisal must also take into consideration the relative weakness of the conventional forces available to the United States to counter, if need be, a Soviet intervention; the worldwide deficiencies in U.S. stockpiles of arms and ammunition exposed by the airlift to Israel; and the strong domestic opposition—a reaction to Vietnam—to the use of American troops in any foreign war.

[84] UN Security Council Resolution 340 (October 25, 1973).

[85] *New Times*, No. 44 (November 1973), 6.

readiness to make a "constructive contribution" to negotiations aimed at establishing peace in the Middle East. He dismissed the U.S. nuclear alert "as the artificial whipping up of sentiment with all kinds of fantastic rumors about the intentions of the Soviet Union in the Middle East," averring that it had not served the interest of cooperation.

On October 29 Sadat sent Isma'il Fahmi, the acting Foreign Minister, to Washington to pave the way for Kissinger's visit to Cairo, the implementation of the cease-fire, and the resumption of diplomatic relations with the United States.[86] On November 11 Israel and Egypt signed a cease-fire agreement that quickly led to a disengagement of forces. The Middle East conflict shifted from the battlefield to the conference table, and Soviet-Egyptian relations entered a new period of friction.

The October crisis was over. Whatever else happened, Brezhnev had kept his commitment to Sadat.

THE UNENIGMATIC KREMLIN

Soviet policy in the crisis of October 1973 augured the advent of "The New Cold War"—an evolving and competitive superpower relationship that seeks stability at the nuclear level, limited cooperation in areas of mutual concern, but continued rivalry at varying levels of intensity in pivotal regions of the Third World. The Soviet leadership views détente practically. It is not motivated by internationalist or humanitarian aspirations toward ever-widening cooperation for congruent strategic, political, economic, and military goals or by anguish over the plight of the ill-fed, ill-housed, ill-clothed half of humanity; and one should

[86] Isma'il Fahmi replaced Hasan al-Zayyat as foreign minister on October 31, 1973. Zayyat's days as foreign minister were numbered after he replied, "frankly no," to the question posed on a TV discussion program in New York on October 7 as to whether he was certain Egypt would win. That the rest of his answer was, "But you don't struggle because you're assured of success. You struggle because you are right," was irrelevant. The damage had been done. *NYT*, October 8, 1973.

There was another factor. Fahmi is a Foreign Office technician and a tough negotiator. U.S. officials trying to obtain information about Egypt's intentions and actions turned increasingly to Fahmi in Cairo, rather than to al-Zayyat in New York. Sadat knew Washington would find it easier to talk to Fahmi, an experienced, professional diplomat, than to Zayyat, who was more philosophical and intellectual in discussions. He also knew that Washington would consider the appointment of Fahmi, who is disliked by Moscow, a sign of his desire to improve relations between Egypt and the United States.

not read into Soviet pronouncements sentiments that are not borne out by deeds.

The term "détente" has entered the Soviet lexicon only since 1972. Till then, whenever Soviet leaders wanted to convey the adoption of a relatively conciliatory line, they would use the term "peaceful coexistence," which signifies a temporary and tactical acceptance of struggle and competition, short of war, between different social and economic systems, at a state-to-state level. It does not brook compromise on ideological hostility or rejection of the class struggle, though both are to some extent unavoidable at the level of formal governmental interaction. G. A. Arbatov, Director of the USSR Academy of Sciences Institute for the United States and a top foreign policy adviser, cogently expressed the thinking underlying the Soviet view of détente:

> It is important to emphasize . . . that relations with the United States, as with other capitalist countries, will remain, in the historical sense, relations of struggle, no matter how successful the process of normalization and détente . . .

> Thus, it is not a question of whether or not the struggle between the two systems will continue. It is historically inevitable. The question is what sort of forms this struggle will take . . .[87]

The era of détente between the Soviet Union and the United States, ushered in by the Moscow summit meeting of May 1972, was supposed to rest on a number of mutually accepted assumptions set forth in the Statement of Basic Principles of Mutual Relations of May 29. This document pledged the two countries to cooperate to avoid nuclear war, to consult with each other to prevent local conflicts from escalating, and to refrain from trying to upset the power relationship between their respective clients in different regions of the world.

These principles were enunciated in more detail in the Nixon-Brezhnev statement on "Prevention of Nuclear War" of June 22, 1973. The two leaders agreed:

> a) that they will act in such a manner as to prevent the development of situations capable of causing a dangerous exacerba-

[87] G. A. Arbatov, in *Kommunist* (March 1973), as translated in "On Soviet-American Relations," *Survival*, 25, No. 3 (May–June, 1973), p. 128.

tion of their relations, as to avoid military confrontations, and
as to exclude the outbreak of nuclear war between them. . . ;

b) that each Party will refrain from the threat or use of force
against the other Party, against the allies of the other Party and
against other countries, in circumstances which may endanger
international peace and security;

c) [that] if at any time relations between the Parties or between either Party and other countries appear to involve the
risk of a nuclear conflict, or if relations between countries not
parties to this Agreement appear to involve the risk of nuclear
war between the United States of America and the Union of
Soviet Socialist Republics or between either Party and other
countries, the United States and the Soviet Union, acting in
accordance with the provisions of this Agreement, shall immediately enter into urgent consultations with each other and
make every effort to avert this risk.

Like any poor cosmetic, it cracked at the first sign of heat.

The behavior of the Soviet Union reveals that imperial ambitions overshadowed its quest for cooperation with the United
States. While striving through the crisis to pursue a dual policy
—effective support for the Arabs, tempered by some restraining
efforts, and continued contacts with the United States to insure
against confrontation—when forced to choose, Moscow sided
with its clients.

First, Soviet leaders did not forewarn Washington of the war
once they knew it to be imminent. Soviet diplomats say that
Moscow did warn Washington of just such a danger on a number
of occasions in the months prior to October 6; for example, one
relates that Brezhnev had told Nixon in June 1973 that "the
political situation was so bad in the Arab countries as to be militarily explosive" and that "there was going to be war."[88] These
were general warnings, however; they were not impellingly conveyed. And they beg the question of why Moscow failed to alert
Washington in the days and hours immediately preceding the
outbreak of hostilities when it possessed solid information, and
as it was obliged to do by the summit accords. Kissinger's rueful
comment that "in an ideal world" one might have hoped for a

[88] *NYT*, December 21, 1973.

more forthright show of concern was really beside the point: what is one entitled to expect in this not ideal world?

Second, once the fighting started, Moscow did not show a pressing concern to bring the war to a quick halt or to ensure that the superpowers not become involved. True, it did explore the possibility of a cease-fire in collusion with the Syrians, but it did so within the context of advancing Arab interests and strengthening its position with Syria, and not with a view toward cooperating with the United States and pushing its oft-implied quest for full membership in a condominium—"an agreed sharing of effective power *only* with America in a kind of permanent and somewhat institutionalized version of the power-balance as at the end of the Second World War."[89] Moscow wanted to be the benefactor of the Arabs, not the partner of the United States. This needs to be kept in mind in assessing Soviet policy after the October War.

Third, from October 8 on, Moscow moved from partisan observer to active incendiary. Rejected in its tentative feeler for an early cease-fire, but seeing the Arabs in trouble, it responded with substantial arms shipments, thereby openly committing itself and raising the threshold of risk. This policy rudely dashed the hopes of those in the West who believed that while Moscow would, of course, try to expand its presence and position in the Arab world, it would nonetheless be willing to "set increasingly agreed limits to the provisions of arms," to show restraint before escalating the Middle East arms race to avoid great power confrontations.[90] Moscow did more than resupply its clients: as the crisis deepened,

[89] Coral Bell, "The October Middle East War: A Case Study in Crisis Management During Detente," *International Affairs*, 50, No. 4 (October 1974), 535. The case for condominium is not convincing. If this had been Moscow's main aim, then it could have been more easily attained before, not after, the crisis had escalated to confrontation; it could have been an unavoidable reality for Washington if Moscow had cooperated openly and at an early stage in trying to end the fighting and had not waited until its clients were on the verge of defeat.

The October crisis may be likened to a big power game, with new chips continually being thrown into the pot and heightening the tension, more than to an instance of crisis management with its assumption of calmly conceived, dispassionate moves. In October 1973, the local actors had too much potential leverage over the great powers for comfort.

[90] For example, F. Duchene, "The Arms Trade and the Middle East," *Political Quarterly*, 44, No. 4 (October–December 1973), 458; 459–460.

it positioned its naval forces to provide maximum political support and, if need be, military assistance: for example, during the October 24–25 crisis, Soviet ships were interposed between the U.S. Sixth Fleet and the Egyptian coast to be better positioned to defend possible Soviet reinforcements; its missile crews manned sites in Egypt, though they were apparently not called upon to participate in action; and some of its senior officers served in a close advisory capacity on the Syrian front.[91]

Fourth, in contrast to its position of 1967, in the United Nations Moscow showed no interest publicly in a cease-fire. On the contrary, initial Egyptian and Syrian successes spurred Moscow on to greater risks. When the tide changed and the Arabs faced disaster, the Soviet leadership relied on its military power, not on the United Nations, to bring Israel into line.

Fifth, Moscow used its military capability, greatly increased since 1967, in pursuit of political objectives in the Middle East. It concentrated a formidable naval force (about ninety ships) in the eastern Mediterranean, inaugurated the newly acquired jumbo air transport fleet to supply Egypt and Syria,[92] and readied seven elite divisions for a possible intervention. Moscow flexed its military power, and the risk of a superpower clash took on added reality.

Finally, Soviet leaders showed a keen grasp of Middle East realities. They played a cautious, measured, but ambitious hand. Alert to opportunities, they also sensed pitfalls and reacted quickly to use their power most advantageously, as in shifting the impact of their diplomatic efforts from Damascus to Cairo by the second week of the war; they adapted policy in response to changes on the battlefield, but political objectives were kept central, notwithstanding a deepening military involvement. The Soviets were sensitive to the needs of their clients, but took care that these did not adversely affect Soviet interests. Throughout, they kept in close contact with the U.S. government and worked in private, if not always in public, to keep the war limited. Perhaps most significantly, they took decisions quickly, implemented them competently, and made necessary adjustments skillfully, in line with their basic political aims.

[91] BBC/ME/4642/A/1 (July 4, 1974).
[92] Drew Middleton, "Big Soviet Airlift and Airborne Capacity Altering Power Balance," *NYT*, October 26, 1973.

THE STRATEGIC HARVEST

Underlying the diplomatic and strategic initiatives that Sadat had painstakingly fashioned and impelling him to war was a current of political desperation dangerously swollen by economic tribulations. Egyptian birth statistics were alarming: the population had doubled since 1952 and increased by more than five million between 1967 and 1973, an annual growth rate of almost three percent, one of the highest in the world. An even greater exigency was the country's bankruptcy. Sadat related that in October 1973 Egypt's economy had reached "a critical point:"

> Securing a loaf of bread in 1974 was not on the horizon. We had debts due for payment in December according to international regulations, and there was no way we could repay them. We did not have 1 mil's worth of hard currency. This was one of the factors which contributed to my decision to go to war, because if 1974 were to come with us in that state, Israel would not have needed to fire a single shot.[93]

Egypt received $500 million in aid from Arab countries, but only after going to war: "You must realize that it was not possible for us to get one dollar of this Arab aid before we wrote the heroic story of the crossing with our blood. During the first week after the October battle, the Arab brothers sent us this aid." The situation may have been more severe than Sadat admitted. Given the enormous allocations to the military—defense expenditures from 1967 to 1973 were five times those allotted for development—the decision to go to war could scarcely have had worse consequences than continued despairing acceptance of the status quo.[94] At the end of August, during Sadat's visit to Damascus, he and Asad set the date for the attack.[95]

[93] FBIS/Egypt, September 3, 1974, p. D2.

[94] Egypt's parlous economic condition was mentioned for the first time by a Soviet analyst after the October War. Yevgeni Primakov, "The Fourth Arab-Israeli War," *World Marxist Review*, 16, No. 12 (December 1973), 17. Primakov wrote: "At the threshold of the 1973 war, the Arab countries' economic and political difficulties born of the aggression were increasing visibly. Egypt was compelled to keep a mass army and spend about 1,000 million Egyptian pounds per year on defense. Syria's defense spending claimed 60 per cent of its budget appropriations. Many observers noted that the delay in settlement might generate an acute political crisis in both countries."

[95] BBC/ME/4744/A/8 (November 1, 1974). Sadat related that Arafat was the only other Arab who knew beforehand; but he added, "I did not tell him the exact date."

Sadat's achievements were considerable, and none was to Moscow's liking. First, by his decision, Sadat demonstrated his independence and acquired diplomatic options that lessened Egypt's dependence on the Soviet Union. "The decision," he never tired of repeating, "was 100 per cent Egyptian." Second, he forced the Arab-Israeli conflict back to the center of the international stage, frustrating superpower attempts to shelve it until such time as they were prepared to tackle it:

> We simply could not allow the situation to continue as it was before October—no peace, no war. The two superpowers froze the Middle East dispute and put it in a refrigerator. The Americans have viewed us as a motionless corpse since the six-day war in 1967. This was worse than war.[96]

Third, he precipitated and exploited a crisis in Soviet-American relations. Though Moscow expected it would be short lived on the assumption that Washington would race to forget October 1973 as quickly as it had August 1968,[97] the Soviet intervention on behalf of Egypt and Syria did damage détente and give Sadat the opportunity to play one superpower off against the other. He gambled, successfully, that dread of an Arab defeat would keep Moscow committed. Fourth, to the consternation of the Soviets, Sadat brought Washington to the forefront of Middle East negotiations and encouraged it to try on its own for a settlement of the Arab-Israeli conflict. Moscow was again on the outside, its bid for entry into the diplomatic inner circle stymied for the moment. The fighting had barely stopped when, with not so much as a nod to Moscow's role, Sadat resumed full diplomatic relations with the United States for the first time since Egypt had

[96] FBIS/Egypt, April 15, 1974. p. D1.

[97] In discussion with a group of Soviet analysts in Moscow in December 1970, I asked why the USSR did not return to Japan several tiny islands having no strategic value and little economic importance other than fishing, and suggested that such a gesture would enhance Soviet prestige and induce the Japanese government to press more vigorously in support of the massive investment in Siberia that the USSR wanted. They gave two reasons: first, there were other considerations involved, i.e. Chinese claims, in any relinquishment of Soviet territory; and second, the capitalist economic order was incapable of resolving its "contradictions," Japanese-American economic relations would not always be cordial, and Japan would turn gladly to the USSR and its markets once the economic troubles become serious. "We can afford to wait," they agreed. The Soviets are confident that they need not make major concessions to the United States, that if they are patient they will get what they want at little cost.

severed them on June 6, 1967. His preference for an American-engineered settlement galled Moscow. Sadat has no illusions about Brezhnev (nor he about Sadat). One can find dutiful public expressions, but there is no real gratitude in Cairo for Soviet assistance. The contrast with the United States rankled: Washington had quickly authorized $2.2 billion in arms for Israel on a combination of grants and generous long-term loans. Finally, Sadat consolidated his position in Egypt and in the Arab world. For the foreseeable future, he is the leader with whom Moscow has to negotiate.

The Soviet Union, too, has accomplishments, though they do not include enhanced influence in Egypt, where ironically, the effect of Soviet policy was to intensify Sadat's quest for better relations with the United States. The case of those in the leadership who place a premium on the Arab countries has been buttressed. The point has been made that for years to come Soviet arms are indispensable and the Soviet Union is Egypt's ultimate shield from defeat. This transcendent fact of Middle East international politics is one Sadat dare not forget, and it alone is sufficient to ensure the Soviet Union of a foothold in the area. As long as the Arab-Israeli conflict is considered unfinished and pressing business in Cairo and in the Arab world, any Egyptian leadership must preserve the lifelines to Moscow.

Beyond the immediate context of Soviet-Egyptian relations, which, if anything, deteriorated after the war, the Soviet Union realized munificent dividends that reinforced its most optimistic assessments of the shift in the balance of world power.[98] Its main accomplishments are evident in the advantages that have come as a windfall in its strategic rivalry with the United States.

[98] On the eve of the October War two coming luminaries among the younger generation of Soviet scholar-diplomats argued this thesis. They contended that the United States had found it necessary to adapt its policies to the new international realities, to show greater readiness to conclude businesslike arrangements with the USSR, and to accept the Soviet Union as a major force in the world. There were a number of reasons for this: 1) the growing strength of the socialist camp; 2) the change in the strategic relationship between the United States and the Soviet Union; 3) the irreconcilable economic rivalries among the capitalist countries that preclude political unity among them; and 4) the realization by the United States that it could not carry on a policy of global rivalry with the Soviet Union, without undermining its own socio-economic and political position and stability. Anatoli Gromyko and A. Kokoshin, "U.S. Foreign Policy Strategy for the 1970s," *International Affairs*, No. 10 (October 1973), 67-69.

First, the war widened the rifts in NATO, leading Kissinger to remark in pique, "I don't care what happens to NATO. I'm so disgusted."[99] The Western European countries were annoyed at Washington for failing to keep them abreast of the developing crisis or to consult on the use of NATO facilities for military operations in an area not covered by the alliance and toward which individual members followed very different policies. When Kissinger informed the NATO members of the alert, the British ambassador in Washington is said to have commented: "Why tell us, Henry? Tell your friends—the Russians."[100] The West Europeans, dependent on Middle East oil, adopted a position of neutrality with a pronounced pro-Arab tilt, hoping to be spared the economic consequences of America's support for Israel and its rivalry with the USSR in the Middle East. But under Faysal's leadership the Arab oil producers ignored EEC's accommodating overtures and globalized the Arab-Israeli conflict. The West European countries behaved like ostriches, hiding their heads, hoping the Arabs would leave them alone, while the United States, the keeper of the Western preserve, was indifferent to the needs and weaknesses of its wards. No doubt the United States had treated its allies in a clumsy, offhand manner. The result was a disarray greater than any in NATO's history. Moscow could not have been more delighted.

Second, Arab oil policy has been an economic boon to the Soviet Union. It has brought in substantially higher revenues from Soviet oil exports to the West, thus enabling the USSR to meet its debt payments in the West and reducing its pressing need for credits.[101] The skyrocketing price of oil goes a long way toward defraying the costs of provisioning Arab clients at bargain prices: what the Soviets "lose" in arms sold on easy terms, they recoup from the increased earnings from oil, which quadrupled in price during the 1973–1974 period alone. It has also made the countries of Eastern Europe (except Romania) more dependent on the USSR economically.[102] In general, the energy crisis revealed the extreme vulnerability of Western Europe and Japan to oil pressure and increased their readiness to consider long-term

---

[99] *NYT*, October 31, 1973.   [100] Kalb, *Kissinger*, p. 62.

[101] *International Herald Tribune*, October 15, 1974. See Marshall I. Goldman, "The Soviet Union," in "The Oil Crisis: In Perspective," *Daedalus*, 104, No. 4 (Fall 1975), 137-138.

[102] *The Sunday Telegraph*, October 27, 1974.

commercial agreements with the USSR on terms favoring the latter. To offset soaring oil prices and world inflation, NATO members have curtailed their military expenditures, notwithstanding the glaring disparity between NATO and Warsaw Pact force levels in Central Europe.

Soviet commentators seized on the international ramifications of Arab oil policy and the nationalization of Western holdings, exulting in the Arabs' newfound power to use "oil as a political weapon in their efforts to eliminate the consequences of the Israeli aggression, making imperialism pay a high price for the support it has given for years to the Tel Aviv rulers' expansionist policy":

> Were the Arab countries to withdraw if only half of their holdings [from West European and American banks] this would seriously shake the finances of many West European countries.[103]

They have emphasized that the "Arab oil producing states are legally exercising their right to dispose of their own natural resources" and to pursue a carefully considered policy.[104]

Moscow is engaged in an internal "debate" over the implications of the centrifugal internal and external tensions that face the Western world.[105] Never in its wildest fantasy forecasting the doom of the Western system did Moscow expect the upheaval that has beset the Western world since the Arabs turned oil into a political and economic weapon.[106]

[103] Ruben Andreasyan, "Middle East: The Oil Factor," *New Times*, No. 45–46 (November 1973), 18.

[104] CDSP, 25, No. 47 (1973), pp. 11-12.

[105] The literature on the West's distress in serious Soviet publications has been extensive since the fall of 1973. For example, see the following: "Tendentsii razvitiia kapitalisticheskoi ekonomiki v 1974g." (The Tendencies of Development in Capitalist Economies in 1974) *Mirovaia ekonomika i mezhdunarodnye otnosheniia* (hereafter referred to as MEMO), No. 9 (September 1974), 38-49; E. Primakov, "Energeticheskii krizis v kapitalisticheskikh stranakh," (The Energy Crisis in Capitalist Countries), MEMO, No. 2 (February 1974), 65-88; and V. Cherniavina, "Energeticheskie problemy stran E. E. S." (The Energy Problems of the EEC Countries), MEMO, No. 4 (April 1974), 56-65. For an authoritative assessment see Nikolai Inozemtsev, *Pravda*, August 20, 1974.

[106] Jean Riollot, "Moscow and the Oil Crisis," Radio Liberty Dispatch (January 10, 1974). The author writes: "There is . . . evidence that Soviet analysts were giving serious thought to the relation between the looming energy crisis and Arab oil as early as the first months of 1973. . . . Today,

Finally, militarily, the USSR receives the lion's share of benefits from the reopening of the Suez Canal on June 5, 1975.[107] Economically, all nations, especially Egypt and the countries of Western Europe and South Asia, expect to be beneficiaries.[108] But for the Soviets the development opens new possibilities for political maneuvering in the Persian Gulf–Indian Ocean area.

Only through underwriting Egypt and Syria and through bear-like doggedness on behalf of a policy of confrontation were these accomplishments brought to pass. Their impact will be far-reaching and long-lasting, more than ample compensation for the difficulties arising out of the mercurial political shifts of the Egyptian leadership. The subsidizing of Arab surrogates has been a small price for the havoc they have wreaked on the Western world and the American alliance systems. In the jargon of Marxism-Leninism, the October War, subjectively speaking, was unanticipated, but, objectively speaking, it produced Moscow's greatest triumph since 1945.

---

most of what Soviet policy planners foresaw in the past years has come true: the oil boycott, further nationalizations of foreign oil companies, the threat of a withdrawal of Arab money from Western banks and the aggravation of the energy crisis with the prospect of serious economic and social consequences for the Western economies. And this has happened thanks to a demonstration of 'solidarity' on the part of the Arab oil-producing countries which they apparently hesitated to include in their calculations until the last moment," pp. 4-5, see also, *NYT*, July 10, 1973.

[107] See Arnold Hottinger, "The Re-opening of the Suez Canal: The Race for Power in the Indian Ocean," *Round Table*, No. 256 (October 1974), 393-402. A. Shakai, "Suetskii kanal i ego rol' v mezhdunarodnoi torgovle" (The Suez Canal and Its Role in International Trade), MEMO, No. 4 (April 1974), 132-134.

[108] S. Karpov, "The Closure of the Suez Canal: Economic Consequences," *International Affairs*, No. 4 (April 1974), 83-85. See UNCTAD Report, *The Economic Effects of the Closure of the Suez Canal* (New York: United Nations, 1973). Document TD/B/C.4/104/Rev.1.

Chapter Nine

THE DIPLOMACY OF DISCORD

THE strains that emerged between Cairo and Moscow after the October War and that have dominated their relationship ever since are baffling only if one looks for antithetical policy objectives as the cause. Their genesis is to be found also in passion, duplicity, and mutual suspicion: in the personal quirks of President Anwar Sadat and the indirection of Soviet leaders. The strains persist for reasons endemic to the politics of the Middle East.

Hardly had the cease-fire taken effect when Sadat jolted Moscow by restoring diplomatic relations with the United States and appointing Isma'il Fahmi, whom the Soviets considered pro-Western, as his foreign minister. With stunning alacrity Sadat proceeded to plump all his eggs ostentatiously in Kissinger's basket, leaving the Soviets empty-handed and furious. They had provisioned Egypt, shielded it from certain defeat, and imperiled their détente with the United States, only to find their relations with Sadat worse than ever and the Soviet government relegated to the sidelines in the negotiations that were under way for a Middle East settlement. The U.N.-sponsored conference, convened in Geneva on December 21 under the joint chairmanship of the United States and the Soviet Union, was adjourned two days later, when Egypt, Israel, and the United States (the Soviet Union had no real say in the matter) privately agreed that bilateral talks would be more appropriate for the foreseeable future. Given the Syrian boycott of the Geneva talks and the Israeli refusal to come to the same conference table with the Palestinians, the bilateral venue was considered easier to manage and more likely to generate some movement toward serious diplomatic negotiations between the protagonists. And on January 20, 1974, it did succeed, in that the Egyptian and Israeli chiefs of staff concluded a first-stage separation of forces agreement and accepted a concomitant interposition of U.N. troops between their forces. Sadat's diplomatic move was vindicated; however, the praise and green light for Kissinger increased the distance between Moscow and Cairo.

POST-OCTOBER DIVERGENCES

Sadat's mercurial turn to Washington and open alienation of Moscow was motivated by a number of factors. First, he was enraged by what he considered the mercenary demand for payment and limited resupply effort during the October War—which he contrasted with America's generosity toward Israel.

Second, and very important, Sadat felt personal animus against the Soviets. An Egyptian official in a position to know what the USSR had done for Egypt in the war, when asked how he explained Sadat's response, exploded, "Because he hates the Russians. It's as simple as that." In Sadat's mind the USSR's meanness was symptomatic not only of Moscow's ulterior purposes but also of an antipathy toward him. This bitter feeling may be traced back to late April 1961 when Sadat, then speaker of the National Assembly, was head of a visiting delegation to whom Khrushchev administered a public dressing down on the Egyptian leadership's ignorance of the ABC's of socialist development.[1] It was later sharply intensified by the realization that the Soviet Union and Syria had surreptitiously arranged to pressure him into an early cease-fire without regard for Egypt's situation. The duplicity of the two heightened his suspicion of Asad in the period after the war.

Third, Sadat was persuaded by Kissinger in their very first meetings that the key to a disengagement agreement and ultimately to further withdrawals was to be found in Washington: American mediation and a step-by-step approach could produce what Soviet arms could not.[2] Kissinger made this point in an interview during a visit to Cairo shortly after the war: "The USSR can give you arms, but the United States can give you back

[1] Oles M. Smolansky, *The Soviet Union and the Arab East under Khrushchev* (Lewisburg, Pa.: Bucknell University Press, 1974), pp. 145-146; and Yaacov Ro'i (ed.), *From Encroachment to Involvement: A Documentary Study of Soviet Policy in the Middle East, 1945–1973* (New York: John Wiley and Sons, 1974), pp. 337-344.

[2] For insights into Kissinger's approach, see William B. Quandt, "Kissinger and the Arab-Israeli Disengagement Negotiations," *Journal of International Affairs*, 29, No. 1 (Spring 1975), 33-48.

your territories, especially as you have been able to really change the situation in the Middle East."[3] Perceiving that the situation would occasion an American initiative, which in itself would represent a desired change in U.S. policy, Sadat gave Kissinger a free hand, allowing him to move from the highly structured multilateral framework at Geneva to an open-ended bilateral one.

Fourth, Sadat needed rapid progress that would make it politically possible for him to reopen the Suez Canal, attract desperately needed foreign capital, and begin the reconstruction and development of the canal cities: never far behind the need to prepare for a possible new war were the demands of Egypt's steadily worsening economic plight. The Kissinger approach, with its focus on Egypt and Israel, promised quick returns and facilitated the U.S.-Egyptian reconciliation. It also kept the Soviets at a distance and increased Sadat's diplomatic options and maneuverability.

Fifth, Sadat took for granted the continuation of a sizable Soviet commitment: Moscow had poured too much into Egypt to sever its connections out of irritation. He had no illusions about the nature of Soviet interests in Egypt, but he also knew the USSR needed to maintain a residual relationship with Egypt in order to pursue its aims elsewhere in the Arab world. In this, he relied on the immanence of the Soviet-American strategic rivalry.

Finally, as Haykal later observed, Sadat felt impelled to exhaust the American approach in order to satisfy "a certain conservative audience in the Arab world."[4] King Faysal, in particular, wanted the Soviets kept on the periphery of the diplomatic process; his suspicion of the Soviet Union was no less rabid than his hostility toward Israel.[5]

The decision to risk a rupture with the Soviets precipitated a break between Sadat and some of his ablest supporters.[6] They

---

[3] As quoted in *Journal of Palestine Studies*, 3, No. 2 (Winter 1974), 214.

[4] *International Herald Tribune*, January 20, 1975.

[5] King Faysal identified communism and Zionism as the twin, mutually supportive threats to the Arabs: "Collusion between world Zionism and international communism has become a firm and indisputable fact." BBC/ME/4729/A/6 (October 15, 1974).

[6] The rift led to Haykal's dismissal in February 1974; he had served as editor-in-chief on *Al-Ahram* since 1957. Haykal had disagreed with Sadat on previous occasions: in October 1972 regarding Sadiq's dismissal; in March 1973, when he refused to fire the journalists purged by Sadat and continued to pay their salaries; and in the summer of 1973, when he approved of

argued that the Soviet Union had played, and still played, a vital role in support of Egypt, that it should not be isolated from the process of bargaining with the United States and Israel, and that Soviet arms remained indispensable.[7] Haykal, for one, felt that the USSR could have given Egypt more arms:

> But not wishing to take risks vis-à-vis the other superpower, it gave us what we managed to use in performing the October miracle . . . we must also bear in mind that the major strategic ambition of the United States in the Middle East has always been to see the Soviet Union out of the Arab world . . . Previously, the United States had tried to keep the USSR away from the area. Now the U.S. strategy is to keep the area away from the USSR.[8]

A high-ranking Egyptian official was even more emphatic, telling this writer that "the United States gave Israel more than the USSR gave Egypt, but the USSR nonetheless gave Egypt enough weapons to do what had to be done. President Sadat's criticisms of the Soviet Union are unjustified."

Whether Sadat would have behaved as he did had the Soviets been more forthcoming during the war is a moot question. The USSR had acted in its own interests in promoting Egypt's objectives, but had not wished to get involved in a war with the United States. As it was, Moscow had gambled away some of the dividends from détente. But what Sadat saw intensified his suspicion of the Soviets: they doled out arms with an eye to their relationship with the United States; yet they balked at his policy with the United States and halted arms shipments in late November as petty retaliation. Moscow behaved out of self-interest; so, too, must Egypt.

Qadhdhafi's efforts to pressure Sadat into a union with Libya. See also Desmond Stewart, "The Rise and Fall of Muhammad Heikal," *Encounter*, 42, No. 6 (June 1974), 87-93. The irony, of course, is that Haykal, whom the Soviets long disliked for his criticisms of USSR policy, was dismissed for being too pro-Soviet in the post-October political ambience. Hafiz Isma'il, Sadat's Adviser on National Security Affairs, was reassigned to serve as ambassador to the Soviet Union; and Chief of Staff General Sa'ad al-Din al-Shazli was sent to Great Britain as ambassador and then, in the summer of 1975, reassigned to Portugal.

[7] For example, Haykal, as quoted in CPR, No. 5622, November 11, 1973; and Muhammad Sayed Ahmed in CPR, Supplement, December 3, 1973.

[8] CPR, No. 5641, November 30, 1973.

For its part, Moscow saw no reason why it should resupply Sadat gratis; or encourage the Egyptian military to consider another round of fighting against Israel, especially since the Arabs now had the oil weapon to force a favorable political solution; or not resent being frozen out of the negotiating process after the Geneva conference adjourned; or assist Sadat's resumption of diplomatic relations with the United States (though Syria followed suit during Nixon's visit on June 16, 1974); nor was it, in any event, under any obligation to treat Egypt and Syria alike.

Sadat did try to mollify Moscow. On January 21, 1974, three days after the separation of forces agreement had been signed at kilometer 101, Fahmi flew to Moscow to brief the Soviet leadership and explain Egypt's approach to the next stage.[9] The composition of the Egyptian delegation and the failure of the joint communiqué to mention military or economic matters indicate that the crux of the problem was political in nature. There was certainly no evidence for the contention of Hamdi Fu'ad, *Al-Ahram's* diplomatic correspondent who accompanied Fahmi, that the USSR had agreed, among other things, to "strengthen Egypt's army."[10]

The communiqué of January 24 said that "a unified conclusion" had been reached concerning the importance of Soviet-Egyptian cooperation, which "is not based on transient interests but on the long-term principled bases which guide the two sides in developing relations between them," and it reaffirmed the need "to develop and consolidate relations" on the basis of the provisions of the 1971 treaty.[11] But the omissions betrayed the troubled relationship: there was no allusion to weapons and no word of Soviet aid. The two sides spoke of the importance of convening the Geneva conference and promised to "do their utmost to ensure its success, but each understood the ulterior purposes of the other: the Soviet Union, as co-chairman, would then automatically be part of the settlement process; and Egypt acceded in public to what it opposed in private in order to satisfy the Arab militants, who saw the Geneva conference as the key to providing final legitimacy for the Palestinian movement.

[9] *Al-Ahram*, January 22, 1974. On the same day, Sadat flew to visit Syria, Saudi Arabia, Kuwait, Bahrain, Qatar, the United Arab Emirates, Abu Dhabi, and Algeria to give personal briefings on the Aswan talks with Kissinger and the military disengagement in Sinai.

[10] *Al-Ahram*, January 25, 1974.

[11] FBIS/Egypt, January 25, 1974, pp. G4-G6.

Finally, the Soviets conceded that the separation of forces agreement was "positive and important," but only a first step toward an overall settlement, in accordance with Security Council Resolutions 242 and 338 (October 22, 1973); and it said that "the Palestinian question cannot be discussed and solved without the representatives of the Arab people of Palestine," who must be part of the Geneva conference.

The Soviets had argued for an immediate role in the negotiations and a commitment by the Americans and Israelis to a precise time-table for the return to the June 1967 boundaries, on the grounds that it would obviate recurrence of the state of no war, no peace; but for the moment they kept their reservations about Sadat's policy private. Brezhnev even received Fahmi at the end of the visit, thus putting a friendly public face on the new rift. However, TASS's reporting of the Egyptian-Israeli disengagement of forces agreement without comment, the criticisms of it bruited about by the organs of the pro-Moscow Lebanese Communist Party, the alleged refusal of Sadat to receive a prominent Soviet leader before the agreement was signed, and Sadat's warm words for U.S. diplomacy—with not so much as a "thank you" for the USSR—all indicated the existence of serious, not easily reconciled differences.[12] Soviet commentaries, reacting to Sadat's snub, pointed out that the disengagement agreement would have been impossible without Moscow, who was ready to participate in bringing about a settlement.[13]

The "American factor" in the deteriorating Soviet-Egyptian relationship was evident on March 1, when Kissinger's presence at the flag-raising ceremony of the American embassy in Cairo, formalizing the resumption of full diplomatic relations, coincided with Gromyko's arrival from Damascus. Given Sadat's talent for staging politically symbolic events, the overlap seems intentional. At the time, Gromyko was emulating Kissinger, shuttling between Damascus and Cairo, intent on claiming a role for the USSR as an interested party and preventing Kissinger, who was trying to work out a disengagement agreement between Syria and Israel, from preempting the diplomatic stage. Sadat further heightened the public spectacle of superpowers in rivalry, by studiedly giving Gromyko "equal time," meeting with him for

[12] *Le Matin–An-Nahar Arab Report*, 5, No. 4 (January 28, 1974), 2-3.
[13] *Pravda*, January 30, 1974, and March 9, 1974. P. Demchenko, "The Middle East: From War to Peace," *International Affairs*, No. 5 (May 1974), 68.

four hours also, and arranging, as he had for Kissinger, an "impromptu" press conference, which he duly attended.[14]

Gromyko had been expected to arrive with a large economic contingent,[15] but he came with neither economists nor military men, a clear signal to Cairo that the resolution of political differences must precede consideration of Egypt's requests in those critical areas. Gromyko did not mince words. Soviet-Egyptian cooperation had been important before and during the October War, and it was "of no less significance now, when the situation has qualitatively changed, and the period of political settlement of the Near East conflict, marked by the opening of the Geneva conference, has begun"; he warned against "a drifting apart," saying "every available good opportunity for moving forward must be taken . . . The Soviet Union can firmly and definitely state that it will work specifically in that direction. If Egypt does so too, our friendship will be no less strong than the famous Egyptian pyramids." He questioned whether U.S. policy had really changed and reproved Egypt for not seeing the aims that motivated it:

> The opponents of a just peace in the Near East would like to substitute various half-measures and so-called "partial solutions" for a real settlement of the Near East conflict. For these ends they would like to split the Arabs and their allies and start them squabbling with each other. Our answer to this must be a further strengthening of unity, a still effective use of the mechanism of political consultations.[16]

At his press conference he told reporters, "It is no longer possible to solve any world problem away from the Soviet Union or against its will."[17] No more succinct statement of Soviet imperial ambitions had ever been made by a Soviet foreign minister.

The joint communiqué was equally revealing.[18] It stated the

14 *NYT*, March 4, 1974.

15 CPR, No. 5715, February 25, 1974. *Pravda*, March 6, 1974: Gromyko was accompanied by M. D. Sytenko, Iu. N. Cherniakov, V. G. Makarov, and P. S. Akopov, all from the Ministry of Foreign Affairs.

16 FBIS/USSR, March 5, 1974, p. F3.

17 CPR, No. 5721, March 3, 1974.

18 FBIS/Egypt, March 6, 1974, pp. G1-G3. While not immediately related to Soviet-Egyptian affairs, Arafat's meeting with Gromyko was mentioned in the communiqué. This was the first time the Soviet government officially acknowledged talks with a Palestinian leader; previously, contacts were conducted through Soviet nongovernmental front organizations. The meeting

talks were held "in a cordial and constructive atmosphere," but that the two sides held "detailed debates"—a sobriquet for discord—on the approach to unresolved issues. In keeping with the communiqué issued during Fahmi's visit in January, the two parties agreed that the disengagement in Sinai "must be considered as a first step toward reaching . . . a comprehensive settlement in the Middle East" and that the Geneva conference "must help" in this process. Moreover, in an evident concession to the Soviet position, Egypt agreed it was "important and necessary for the Soviet Union to participate in all stages of the settlement in the Middle East, including the working committees which the Geneva conference forms." But, as in January, Egypt said one thing and proceeded to do another: it opposed a reconvening of the Geneva conference, to the anger of the Soviets.

Cairo even dragged its feet on the routine matter of gratifying the Soviet desire to take part in the Suez Canal clearing operation. It "received with appreciation the Soviet Union's preparedness in principle to participate" in the enterprise. This was a teasing tactic; Moscow had made the offer weeks before, but had to watch American and British teams arrive in Egypt and begin dredging operations. In late March the Egyptians finally gave official permission, but not until late May did they assign the Soviets an actual role.[19]

Sadat renewed his invitation to Brezhnev to visit Egypt, and Gromyko invited Fahmi to come to Moscow. Cairo's dissatisfaction with the Soviet stand on military and economic issues was obvious in the absence of any expression of gratitude for past Soviet assistance. This omission acquired added significance when contrasted with the tribute contained in the Syrian-Soviet communiqué issued two days later in Damascus. To Gromyko's hope for closer cooperation, Sadat countered with the hope for a resumption of arms shipments and an agreement on debt deferral. Finally, there was no mention of socialism and no call for closer party-to-party ties.

The disagreement implicit in the communiqué was expressed openly in each capital. No sooner had Gromyko left Egypt than the Soviet news agency Novosti denounced U.S. efforts to promote

marked another step toward Moscow's recognition of the PLO as the representative of a nascent Palestinian state.

[19] *Pravda*, March 22, 1974; and FBIS/Egypt, June 3, 1974, p. D10.

peace as insincere and called for continuation of the oil embargo:

> The ban on oil exports to countries backing Israeli aggressors proved an effective weapon in the Arabs' hands . . . [it] had enabled the Arabs to overcome obstacles in the Arab-Israeli negotiations and had drawn the attention of the entire world to their demands. More important, it put an end to the military and political humiliation they had suffered for a quarter of a century.[20]

Since Egypt was pressing for lifting the embargo, the target of Novosti's proposal was clear. *Pravda* discounted the "apparent 'reorientation'" in U.S. policy, pointing out that Washington still supported Israel, both militarily and economically, and "when you get down to the actual facts, it turns out that the 'mountain has produced a mouse.'"[21] It castigated "some observers" (i.e. Sadat) who have already concluded that "the gestures" made by the United States toward the Arab countries are sufficient grounds for the Arabs to lift the embargo. At a state banquet for Asad, Brezhnev warned that "ersatz plans" for disengagement would mean "replacing an overall settlement with partial agreements of a different kind."[22] To invest Asad's visit (April 11–16) with special significance and contrast the closeness between the USSR and Syria with the growing cleavage between the USSR and Egypt, Brezhnev personally greeted him on his arrival, military and economic aid were lavished on Syria, and a protocol regularizing contacts between the Syrian Ba'th Party and the CPSU was signed.[23] The dispute between Moscow and Cairo was no longer to be encapsulated in diplomatic phraseology.

[20] *Le Matin–An-Nahar Arab Report*, 5, No. 10 (March 11, 1974), 2-3. See also, FBIS/USSR, March 12, 1974, p. F2. Moscow repeatedly opposed the lifting of the oil embargo: *Izvestiia*, February 24, 1974; FBIS/USSR, February 22, 1974, pp. F3-F4; FBIS/USSR, March 1, 1974, p. F4. This opposition intensified after Gromyko's visit.

[21] CDSP, 26, No. 11 (1974), 21. *New Times*, No. 10 (March 1974), p. 1, editorialized that friendship with Arab countries was "a matter of principle with the USSR, a policy not influenced by transient considerations," in contrast, it implied, with U.S. policy.

[22] *NYT*, April 12, 1974; Dmitry Volsky, "Support the Arab Peoples Can Count On," *New Times*, No. 18-19 (May 1974), 19.

[23] *Middle-East Intelligence Survey* (hereafter referred to as M.I.S.), 2, No. 3 (May 1, 1974), 18.

THE ADO ABOUT ARMS

The acrimony over arms that predated the October War increased after the fighting. In late November, Sadat told one Western ambassador, "We pay for everything we get." Moscow had kept the Arabs supplied during the war; however, given Sadat's changed foreign policy orientation after the fighting stopped, it did not feel obligated to give the Egyptians any bonuses. The arms delivered up to the end of November 1973 were essentially those contracted for earlier in the year: its airlift and stepped-up shipments by sea accelerated previously arranged delivery schedules. By the end of the year, it halted new supplies of weapons and sophisticated electronic equipment, though its depots remained open to Syria, which was promptly and amply re-equipped, with no haggling over repayment. By rewarding Asad and by ending the supply of arms to Egypt, Moscow put Cairo on notice that the Soviet Union was not an eleemosynary institution.

Sadat—dissatisfied with the results of Gromyko's March 1974 visit, pressed by his military for new weapons, and optimistic over prospects for attracting Arab and Western capital—vented his grievances. On March 29, he told of Vinogradov's attempt on October 6 to persuade him that Asad was requesting an immediate cease-fire.[24] The following day, visiting with Tito to stress Egypt's commitment to nonalignment and policy of equidistance between the superpowers, Sadat revealed that after the October cease-fire Yugoslavia had sent 150 tanks and Algeria 100, in contrast to the nonsupport of the USSR since then.[25] On April 3, he dwelt on past difficulties with Soviet arms deliveries, adding details about the 1971–1972 period and the Soviet opposition to a war.[26] In a speech at a joint session of the People's Assembly and the ASU Central Committee on April 18, at which time he presented his "October Paper" on economic development and institutional reform, Sadat announced his intention to diversify Egypt's sources of arms.[27] This intention had been manifest in his overtures to the British after the expulsion of the Soviets

[24] CPR, No. 5747, March 29, 1974.   [25] CPR, No. 5748, March 30, 1974.

[26] FBIS/Egypt, April 4, 1974, pp. D5-D8. After this speech to the Egyptian Students Federation at Alexandria University, the Soviet delegates to the conference received a cable ordering them back to Moscow. FBIS/Egypt, April 8, 1974, p. D9.

[27] CPR, No. 5766, April 19, 1974.

in 1972, but the public expression of it was new. Three days later he accused Moscow of using arms as an "instrument of policy leverage" and said he would "be very happy" if the United States would sell him arms; true, diversification meant retraining and retooling, but vital long-term considerations were involved. His four official requests to Brezhnev for arms since the October War had brought only the reply that the matter was "under study":

> They cannot possibly be under study for six months when I know that these demands do not include anything extraordinary or impossible; never, they were very ordinary.[28]

No single factor contributed more to the exacerbation of post-October War strains than Sadat's decision to go public in criticizing Moscow. By impugning Soviet good faith and support for the Arab cause, he pointed a questioning finger at its presence in the Arab world. His motives inhere both in the reasons he gave and in some he left unsaid. First, having unsuccessfully tried to settle the matter privately during Fahmi's visit to Moscow in January and Gromyko's visit to Cairo in March, he felt the quarrel was so profound that he could not possibly damage the situation by airing it. Given his longstanding animosity toward the Soviets and his belief he had nothing to lose, he decided to embarrass the Soviet leadership by not suffering their squeeze in silence. If Moscow chose to place him at a disadvantage, he would repay it in kind. Second, Sadat felt he could gain an edge in future bargaining, on the assumption that the injuring party would make concessions to the aggrieved, once normalization of ties was desired. Third, Sadat was concerned about the continuing fighting on the Syrian front, supported by lavish Soviet supplies. The absence of a Syrian-Israeli disengagement agreement heightened the possibility of Arab pressure on him to desist from further exploration of another disengagement in Sinai and to resume fighting. By pleading serious shortages of weapons and blaming the Soviets, Sadat sought to neutralize his Arab and domestic opponents, who criticized his reliance on Kissinger to the detriment of good relations with the Soviet Union.[29]

A fourth reason for Sadat's public criticism was amplified by Quddus, who indicated that the discord involved far more than

---

[28] FBIS/Egypt, April 19, 1974, p. D7.
[29] For example, Fuad Matar, "The Alexandria Speech," *Al-Nahar*, April 5, 1974, as cited in FBIS/Lebanon, April 9, 1974, pp. G1-G2.

arms. He accused the Soviets of helping Sadat's opponents, who were coalescing and hiding behind the slogan of "Nasirism" because of their opposition to Sadat's internal reforms and his desire to maintain good relations with both superpowers. Quddus denounced the Soviet Union's assumption that Egypt should consult it "before addressing a single word to the United States":

> It seems that Soviet statesmen believe that détente should be restricted to the two superpowers alone. They alone can agree and disagree, while small states such as Egypt have no right to agree or disagree except under the guidance of one of the two superpowers.[30]

If they are unhappy over being upstaged by Kissinger, they should not ignore the alternative, which is "to match his activity." Quddus castigated the Soviet government for an article in *Pravda,* based on Lebanese sources, attacking Sadat for deviating from Nasir's socialist line and calling on him to consult regularly with the USSR: "*Pravda* does not represent itself only; it is the official paper of the CPSU and whatever it publishes represents the state's views, even if it is quoting foreign newspapers." He cited evidence that Moscow said one thing in its Arabic-language commentaries and another in its Russian ones; that it applauded "the progressive forces in the Arab world" supporting continuation of the oil boycott and conveniently said nothing in its Arabic programs about Libyan, and for that matter Soviet, oil reaching the United States, "because it was anxious to deal with the Libyan government, with which it had recently concluded an arms deal requiring that a number of Libyan army officers depart for Russia for training." "The Soviet diplomatic mentality" that refuses to rid itself of "the inferiority complex" that America would receive sole credit for a solution in the Middle East "is exhausting the Soviet Union and exhausting us."[31]

Finally, Sadat may have calculated that being critical of Moscow was music to American ears and would facilitate his overall rapprochement with Washington. Not only might the United States government sell arms to Egypt, but the energy crisis and Egypt's improved political-military position might help sway those in Congress and in other key institutions who did not hold partisan positions on the Arab-Israeli dispute toward a more

[30] FBIS/Egypt, April 17, 1974, p. D15.
[31] *Ibid.*, p. D17.

favorable view of the Egyptian side. Moreover, his attitude pleased Faysal, thus assuring ample funds for arms purchases in the West.

In the months following, Sadat reproached the Soviets frequently for their failure to furnish arms. Thus, for example, on August 14, 1974: "I have not had any for nine months and there are no signs that they will send me anything";[32] on August 26, a statement that Egypt has not yet received a single plane from the USSR to replace the 120 lost in the war;[33] on August 29: "As to arms contracts, which were to be carried out to the end of 1973, we received nothing at all. . . . In addition, the Soviet Union has not up till now replaced the planes which we lost in battle although the Soviet Union and the whole world know that the United States had replaced all Israel's losses and sent her planes with their pilots before the ceasefire";[34] on September 24, "I shall tell you a secret which no one knew up to now. We entered the battle with half our helicopters out of operation due to a spare parts shortage. The required spare parts could have been sent in only two boxes aboard an ordinary airliner. But the Soviet friends did not supply the spares . . .";[35] on January 8, 1975, "Egypt wanted every Arab to know that Egypt has not till the present moment made up for her losses in war, although the Soviet Union made up Syria's losses fourteen months ago";[36] and on January 22, "They refused to replace the material that we lost during the October War or to deliver us the sophisticated, late model arms that they have furnished without difficulty to Syria."[37]

No doubt the arms imbroglio upset relations between Cairo and Moscow. But how serious for Egypt was the problem really? That the USSR did not satisfy Egypt's desires as it did Syria's is true, but this does not mean Sadat was as disadvantaged militarily as he was wont to complain. On the contrary, and aside from the merits of his other grievances against the Soviets, by the end of 1974 his force levels exceeded those of October 1973, except in frontline aircraft.[38]

32 FBIS/Egypt, August 15, 1974, p. D6.
33 *Le Matin–An-Nahar Arab Report*, 5, No. 35 (September 2, 1974), 2.
34 CPR, No. 5898, August 29, 1974.
35 CPR Supplement, September 24, 1974.
36 CPR, No. 5027, January 9, 1975.   37 *Le Monde*, January 22, 1975.
38 The figures given in *The Military Balance 1973–1974* (London: IISS, 1973), pp. 31-32, and *The Military Balance 1974–1975* (London: IISS, 1974),

For this we have the testimony of Sadat himself. On April 18, 1974, he told the People's Assembly: "I assure you that regardless of the demands to which the Soviet Union has not responded, your armed forces are now stronger than they were in October 1973";[39] on June 27 in an interview with *Al-Anwar*: ". . . since the October War we have been supplying our army with the most modern weapons, although the Soviet Union has given us nothing since the ceasefire";[40] on August 26 to the Preparatory Committee of the All-Arab People's Conference: "We are now in the right position and possess weapons which enable us to strike Israel in depth";[41] on the same day, to another group: "I reassure you that some of our Arab brothers have brought planes which are on their way to us to compensate for our planes [lost] in the October War";[42] in an interview with a Kuwaiti journalist on April 12, 1975: "What is important now is that we are strong. When Kissinger failed [in March 1975, to bring about another Egyptian-Israeli disengagement], we had the upper hand. If we succeed or fail in Geneva, we will be in a position of strength."[43] Sadat did not claim that Egypt was stronger vis-à-vis Israel, only that it was stronger than in October. It is true that in certain areas, ECM capabilities for one, Egypt's position was weaker. But Sadat's statements require a reconsideration of the extent to which the Soviets had actually damaged Egypt's military capability.

Sadat has obtained considerable quantities of weapons from a

pp. 32-33, are not very detailed, restricting comparisons to general categories: some show increases; others (e.g. heavy artillery) show no change; and aircraft are down from 620 to 568. In August 1974, Israeli estimates placed Egypt's force levels at the October 1973 level, except in aircraft. *NYT*, August 8, 1974.

On the second anniversary of the October War, War Minister General Gamasi declared that the arms we have "greatly exceeds what we had before 6 October [1973]." FBIS/Egypt, October 7, 1975, p. D11.

[39] BBC/ME/4579/A/9 (April 20, 1974). Later in this speech he did qualify his statement: "You have heard me say now that apart from some demands we have made to the USSR and which have not yet been fulfilled, our forces are again complete. But these demands include basic and essential matters. . . ."

[40] CPR, No. 5835, June 27, 1974.

[41] CPR, No. 5895, August 26, 1974. In late November 1975, a high-ranking Egyptian said in a closed seminar that the SCUD missiles were still in Egypt, and that they were manned and controlled by Egyptian personnel.

[42] FBIS/Egypt, August 30, 1974, p. D4.

[43] FBIS/Egypt, April 14, 1975, p. D5.

variety of sources—Syria, Algeria, France, and Yugoslavia,[44] the cash for which comes from Saudi Arabia, the Persian Gulf states,[45] and Algeria. During a visit to France in late January 1975, Sadat concluded an agreement to purchase Mirages, to be delivered over a period of years. Though the replacement of aircraft has proceeded slowly, in the event of another Arab-Israeli war Egypt has every reason to expect that Arab oil money will be made available to buy—from the Soviet Union if need be—all the material needed. Also, given the mounting sales of American weapons to the oil-rich Arab states in the Persian Gulf area since the October War, Sadat has access to the most sophisticated American weaponry as well: it is inconceivable that these arms are not shared with Egypt, as they certainly would be in the event of war. Furthermore, from at least early 1975 on, Sadat admitted to receiving regular arms shipments once again directly from the Soviet Union.[46] During his visit to France, he told a group of French journalists that Egypt "cannot give up Russian armaments, for no other power is in a position to replace the USSR in this sphere"; and he said, "Certainly, I receive Soviet armaments, thanks to the purchases made by my friend President Boumedienne, as well as equipment from West Europe paid for by King Faisal."[47]

[44] Fuad Matar, *Al-Nahar*, May 23, 1974; also FBIS/Egypt, March 1, 1974, p. G13 (Sadat told of receiving "hundreds of millions of dollars for the purchase of new arms and planes" from Boumedienne); and FBIS/Egypt, September 4, 1974, p. D1.

[45] For example, CPR, No. 5907, September 7, 1974: "My brother Faisal and the Kingdom of Saudi Arabia have made my task easy and have contributed to the compensation [necessary to buy new weapons]"; CPR, No. 5939, October 9, 1974; *Kuwait Times*, October 10, 1974; *The Daily Star* (Beirut), December 13, 1974. In January 1976, Kuwait concluded its first arms deal with the Soviet Union. FBIS/Arabian Peninsula, January 16, 1976, p. C2. The weapons are presumed to be intended for Egypt.

[46] FBIS/Egypt, January 13, 1975, p. D9; FBIS/Egypt, March 20, 1975, p. D1; and on May 1, 1975, Sadat said that from October 22, 1973 (the day of the cease-fire) until January 1975 "we did not receive anything from the Soviet Union except a tank deal which had been agreed upon earlier and part of the price of which had been paid by Boumedienne during the battle." In December 1974 the Soviet Union "agreed to deliver weapons provided for in contracts concluded between us which should have been fulfilled in 1973 and 1974. From January 1975 these weapons began to reach us." BBC/ME/4894/A/4 (May 3, 1975). See *NYT*, February 8, 1975; and Roger F. Pajak, "Soviet Arms and Egypt," *Survival*, 17, No. 4 (July–August 1975), 172. In January 1976, Sadat said that the Soviet Union had begun to resupply arms in February and March, 1975, according to previous agreements, but that it had stopped soon thereafter. FBIS/Egypt, January 9, 1976, p. D8.

[47] FBIS/Egypt, January 23, 1975, p. D4. Mirage-3 fighter planes purchased

In extremis, Sadat could draw on the vast stores of Soviet arms that Libya has purchased since mid-1974.[48] One should not be misled by the malicious charges and counter-charges that have filled the air between Cairo and Tripoli, especially in the spring and summer of 1975: Qadhdhafi called Sadat a thief who sold out to the United States and a traitor, because he reopened the Suez Canal, and even accused his wife of corruption; Sadat described Qadhdhafi as "mad" and "obsessed by the devil,"[49] and one who is "sick in heart and motivated by deep-rooted rancor, the rancor of failure and incompetence."[50] In the event of war, no Arab leader possessing Qadhdhafi's cache of arms could refuse to share them against Israel. The weapons are stockpiled near the Egyptian border and could be quickly dispatched to the "confrontation" states. Far exceeding Libya's absorptive capacity and needs, the arms have no other feasible military function, since Libya is in no position to attack Egypt. Politically, however, they have become a highly publicized and indeterminate part of the twists in the Soviet-Egyptian, Egyptian-Libyan, and Libyan-Soviet relationships.

Relations between Libya and the Soviet Union took a sudden upswing in the spring of 1974, in the wake of a sharp deterioration between the Soviet Union and Egypt and between Egypt and Libya. In May, Libyan Prime Minister Major 'Abd al-Salam Jallud concluded an arms agreement in Moscow, reputedly in the vicinity of $1 to $2 billion; a similar agreement was signed a year later. Formerly bitterly antagonistic toward the USSR for ideological, religious, and political reasons, Qadhdhafi found that his antagonism toward Sadat for accepting a cease-fire and improving relations with Washington superseded his dislike for communism and Moscow's atheism. He regarded the reemergence

---

from France with Saudi Arabian funds began to arrive in Egypt. *NYT*, October 7, 1975.

[48] *NYT*, September 9, 1974: "In a military parade last week, the Libyans displayed for the first time advanced Soviet-supplied SAM-6 ground-to-air missiles and about 300 Soviet-built tanks, including heavy T-62's. There also were SAM-3's and SAM-4's, which had been paraded before. Delivery of 110 French Mirage fighter-bombers, which began in 1970, has been completed according to informed sources." CPR, No. 5928, September 28, 1974: "Libya has received a huge quantity of Soviet weapons including surface-to-air missiles, modern fighter aircraft, and light arms. . . . Libya paid in cash for the consignment." Additional Libyan purchases, exceeding one billion dollars, were arranged in May 1975, during Kosygin's visit to Libya.

[49] M.I.S., 3, No. 7 (July 1, 1975), 50.

[50] FBIS/Egypt, July 23, 1975, p. D12.

of the United States as a key actor in the Arab world as the main threat to Arab revolutionary movements. Therefore, for the moment, Moscow's shared commitment to anti-imperialism and hostility to Sadat served his own purposes and called for an expedient rapprochement.

What Libya considered a masterstroke turned out, paradoxically, to be of great value both to Egypt and the Soviet Union. In the event of war, the Egyptians could turn to Libya for arms, and Qadhdhafi would find it politically impossible to deny them. Thus, while Cairo professes surprise at the Soviet-Libyan arms deal, interpreting it as a form of Soviet pressure against Egypt, it knows the arms may some day find their way to Egypt. For their part, if fighting should break out, the Soviets are now in a position to be spared the need to send any arms for at least a month. This would, in the absence of a direct Soviet intercession, increase the pressure on the United States to refrain from resupplying Israel lest it provoke an Arab oil embargo and incur a new wave of Arab hostility that could kill Washington's efforts to improve relations with the Arabs for years to come. Short of war, Qadhdhafi's stockpiles serve as a lever for use against Sadat in their touchy on-again-off-again relationship and for stoking revolutions in Eritrea and Oman, aims congenial to the Soviet Union. In the process, Moscow has also cornered an extremely lucrative market, alleviating its shortage of hard currency and opening the way for the possible acquisition of naval and air facilities on the North African littoral.

The preceding considerations suggest that Sadat's complaints about arms will not lead to an open split in Soviet-Egyptian relationship. Sadat calculates that the Soviets for their own political reasons will not break off ties, but will choose instead to absorb the rebukes. One Yugoslav official pointed out an irony in the situation. Brezhnev was in a position comparable to Tito's during World War II; in 1942–1943, Stalin had spoken of the heroic struggle of the Chetniks (the pro-monarchy, anti-Communist Yugoslav guerrillas) out of his desire to maintain good relations with the United States and Britain, who were then still committed to them, even though he knew as well as Tito that the Chetniks were collaborating with the Germans. However, bigger issues than Tito's sensitivities were at stake; Soviet state interests took precedence. As Stalin then banked on Tito's overlooking his criticisms, Sadat now counts on the Soviets' realizing that his criticisms on the issue of arms are intended for their impact elsewhere and not only on Soviet-Egyptian relations.

MOSCOW SEEKS LEGITIMIZATION OF ITS MIDDLE EAST ROLE

The USSR's admission to the inner circle of the Middle East club is an eventuality the United States has labored to forestall throughout the post-1945 period. The offhand adjournment of the Geneva conference in December 1973 was a bitter disappointment for Moscow, which had this long-coveted goal within its grasp, only to see it snatched away. To be shunted aside in an unused by-station because of Sadat's preference for the Kissinger track grated Soviet leaders, who remained unconvinced by Fahmi's explanations in Moscow a month later.

When Gromyko visited Cairo in March 1974, he established the USSR's interest in Geneva: "We attach a special importance to the Geneva conference."[51] When at the end of May a disengagement agreement was reached between Syria and Israel, Brezhnev claimed some of the credit, saying it had come to fruition because the Soviet Union and Syria had acted together "from a united position"; and he urged that "following the completion of the disengagement . . . the Geneva peace conference should lose no time in passing onto the examination and solution of all the questions concerning a settlement."[52] Several months later, Lev Tolkunov, the editor of *Izvestiia*, in one of three major articles on Soviet policy in the Middle East, wrote that "The Soviet Union believes in the Geneva conference as a basic tool for bringing about a settlement in the Middle East. The conference must therefore resume the full range of its efforts."[53] In a speech in Kishinev (Soviet Moldavia) on October 11, 1974, Brezhnev said the disengagement agreements were useful as initial measures, but they were not a substitute "for an effective and early resumption of the Geneva peace conference, with all the parties concerned, including the Palestinians, taking part,"[54] points he

[51] FBIS/Egypt, March 4, 1974, p. G3.
[52] *Soviet News*, No. 5740 (June 4, 1974), 197.
[53] BBC/SU/4667/A4/1 (August 2, 1974).
[54] *The Times* (London), October 12, 1974; see also, Dmitry Volsky, "Middle East: Time Presses," *New Times*, No. 42 (October 1974), 9.

made forcefully and often, for example, during the visit of British Prime Minister Harold Wilson in February 1975.[55]

Moscow was accustomed to roseate reassurances from American officials:

> As we go into the next phase of negotiations in the Middle East, which will certainly involve the Geneva forum in some manner, the Soviet Union participates in those as the co-chairman, and in any event, whatever the Soviet role in a particular negotiation, there is no American intention of expelling the Soviet Union from the Middle East.[56]

It paid such words no heed, well aware that despite Kissinger's protestations about détente the United States wanted to keep the USSR from participating in the actual Arab-Israeli negotiations and to arrange agreements that Moscow would have no alternative but to ratify. Behind the façade of a supposed common interest in peace, the superpowers jockeyed for strategic and economic advantage. Their adversarial relationship was also clear to the local protagonists, whose diplomacy aimed at exploiting it for their own purposes.

Throughout 1974 and early 1975 all Soviet-Egyptian communiqués affirmed the need for the Geneva conference, as at the end of Gromyko's visit to Cairo in February 1975:

> The USSR and the Arab Republic of Egypt reiterated their conviction that the Geneva conference on peace in the Middle East was the most suitable forum for discussing all aspects of the settlement. The two sides call for the resumption of the Geneva conference immediately with the participation of all the parties concerned, including representatives of the PLO.[57]

However, Sadat refused to be pinned down to a specific date, for reasons Moscow knew. He stood to be the main beneficiary of another piecemeal disengagement. The return of additional territory would strengthen his military position in Sinai and his domestic position. By holding out the promise of a diminished likelihood of a new war, the disengagement would be an added enticement to foreign capital to cooperate in rebuilding the canal

[55] *The Times*, February 15, 1975.
[56] This remark was made by Secretary of State Henry A. Kissinger at a press conference on June 6, 1974. *NYT*, June 7, 1974.
[57] BBC/ME/4824/E/1-2 (February 7, 1975).

cities and developing Egypt's economy, without waiting for a full settlement that might be years away. Furthermore, it would demonstrate the validity of his diplomatic strategy in the eyes of his supporters in the Arab world, whose desire was to minimize the Soviet presence in the area. Perhaps for these very reasons, in addition to wanting wider recognition of its role in bringing about the new situation in the Middle East, the Soviet leadership pressed for the Geneva conference: to embarrass Sadat, to align itself with his critics and Arab militants, and to sustain the pressure on the United States to force additional Israeli withdrawals. Tactics consumed strategy, as Soviet dissatisfaction during this period was shown in the postponement of two visits that were eagerly desired by the Egyptians: the one planned for Fahmi in July 1974, the other a projected visit from Brezhnev in January 1975.

Fahmi's trip had been billed by the Egyptians as a prelude to a summit meeting. An exchange of letters between Sadat and Brezhnev in April 1974—after a six-month hiatus—resulted in a lowering of the decibels of public discord, so that by late May, on the occasion of the third anniversary of the Treaty of Friendship and Cooperation, both sides spoke glowingly of the treaty's importance. On June 11 Cairo announced that Fahmi would go to Moscow the following month to prepare for a meeting between Sadat and Brezhnev.[58] The timing of the announcement, on the eve of Nixon's visit to Egypt, was seen by the Soviets as a subtle attempt to pressure Brezhnev to follow suit and thus enhance Sadat's prestige at home and abroad. On June 20 the Cairo newspapers carried the headlines: "Arrangements for Summit Meeting Between El Sadat and Brezhnev—Foreign Minister to Fly to Moscow in Mid-July Accompanied by Some Ministers to Prepare for the Meeting."[59] Three days later, in an interview with an American television network, Sadat stated that he had already been to the Soviet Union four times and that Brezhnev had yet to come to Egypt. One well-informed Arab analyst noted Sadat believed himself to be in a strong position "to settle accounts with the USSR, which had been unfriendly to him more than once,"[60] and, besides, for internal reasons he deemed it undesirable to go to Moscow. During visits to Romania and Bulgaria at the end of June, Sadat sought to allay Soviet concern

[58] *Al-Ahram*, June 12, 1974. [59] CPR, No. 5828, June 20, 1974.
[60] Fuad Matar, *Al-Nahar*, June 26, 1974.

over the results of Nixon's visit to Egypt and "to use the two Eastern European capitals as channels to press" Brezhnev to accept his invitation.[61]

On July 10, without warning, Moscow requested a postponement of the visit. The moderate leftist and normally pro-Soviet newspaper, *Al-Gumhuriya*, said the cancellation "caused astonishment and some queries" and was "unfortunate."[62] It was unmistakably a snub, and was so interpreted in Cairo; but the postponement then was due to dissatisfaction with Fahmi rather than to the frozen disagreement on issues.

Several days before, while Fahmi was in Bonn, *Al-Ahram* reported that he would delay his trip from July 15 to July 17, in order to be in Cairo for the visit of U.S. Secretary of the Treasury William Simon.[63] On the morning of July 10 Cairo newspapers reported that Sadat had instructed Fahmi to go to Moscow as scheduled, but it was too late to undo the damage. The Soviet request for a postponement until October came later in the day, alleging that more time was needed to prepare for the meeting. Undoubtedly, Moscow was giving Cairo pointers on how to deal with the Kremlin: a summit conference was not to be considered a foregone conclusion before the arrival of a mission, nor was any meeting with Soviet leaders to be taken for granted.

Cairo minimized the incident and played up the importance of economic negotiations then in progress in Moscow between the Egyptian minister of industry and Soviet officials. Sadat explained: "In my opinion, the causes of tension are latent in the style of their dealing with us."[64] As long as "doubt, guesswork and anxiety remained," it was futile to talk of sound relations. "The deplorable thing in our relations with the Soviets is that I have found that the improvement of our relations with America is unacceptable to them. They make many interpretations of these relations. This is their own business." Later, he expressed the hope that "the misunderstanding between us" would be eliminated and the day would come when the Soviets "will realize that some of their misinterpretations of our policy are incorrect" as has been the case more than once in the past.[65] The relationship, which he described in late August as "frozen,"[66] thawed

[61] *NYT*, June 28, 1974.   [62] CPR, No. 5850, July 12, 1974.
[63] A fine account of this incident is Henry Tanner's. *NYT*, July 11, 1974.
[64] CPR, No. 5858, July 20, 1974.
[65] BBC/ME/4660/A/1 (July 25, 1974).
[66] BBC/ME/4690/A/1 (August 30, 1974).

somewhat in September with an invitation from Moscow for Fahmi and reports of a resumption of Soviet arms shipments to Egypt.[67]

Fahmi arrived (October 14–18) with a large contingent and high hopes. The Egyptian delegation was the most comprehensive ever sent; its expertise covered military affairs, planning, economic development, foreign trade, civil aviation, and finance.[68] At the initial meeting, Brezhnev, according to an Egyptian source, had some blunt words for Fahmi:

> You still think the Americans will help you get your territory back? I bet you that, unless the Soviet Union enters the talks, the Israelis will not withdraw another ten kilometers in your lifetime or mine. Now let's go and talk.[69]

After three hours of talks a joint statement was issued announcing that Brezhnev would visit Cairo on January 15, 1975. The news was acclaimed in the Egyptian media.

The topics raised by Fahmi ranged from military cooperation to debt rescheduling, from new industrial projects to the Geneva conference, from the Palestinians to new loans. Joint specialized committees were established to work out all problems prior to the summit meeting. Fahmi said the discussions "proved that there were no insoluble problems . . . that both sides are concerned about mutual relations";[70] Gromyko, that the Soviet government would immediately start preparations for the visit because "Brezhnev's visit to Egypt must be successful."[71] These remarks veneered the troubles in the conference room.

The Fahmi visit was unusual in several ways. The announcement of Brezhnev's upcoming visit was made early during Fahmi's stay rather than at the end; and in place of the customary joint communiqué, there were a statement dealing only with the Palestinian issue and a routine departure announcement.[72] The care-

---

[67] BBC/ME/4702/A/2 (September 13, 1974). In Bulgaria in early September, Higazi (who was elevated to the post of prime minister on September 27, indicating Sadat's concern over economic problems) met Podgornyi, who gave him a message for Sadat. FBIS/Egypt, September 12, 1974, p. D2. A few days later Fahmi's visit was officially announced.

[68] FBIS/Egypt, October 15, 1974, p. D8.

[69] Quoted by Henry Tanner, *International Herald Tribune*, November 23-24, 1974.

[70] FBIS/USSR, October 17, 1974, pp. F1-F2.

[71] FBIS/USSR, October 18, 1974, p. F3.

[72] *Pravda*, October 19, 1974.

ful wording on the Palestinian problem reflected the importance officially attributed by the Soviet government to the Geneva conference and called for the creation of a "national home" for the Palestinians and support for the "independent participation of representatives of the Palestine Liberation Organization on equal terms with other participants at the Geneva peace conference on the Middle East."

Nothing was said of the work of the specialized committees, suggesting no progress on the substantive issues for which the large Egyptian delegation had been brought along. Fahmi later reasoned "that neither the Egyptian nor Soviet side assumed that the aim of the three day meetings of the working groups was to conclude new agreements . . . The aim and the purpose was, above all, to open hearts and minds and bring the spotlight to bear on present and future cooperation between the two countries in these fields in a new climate of mutual confidence and understanding."[73] Apart from Brezhnev's planned visit, which Fahmi called "a political turning point in Egyptian-Soviet relations," the Egyptians had nothing to take home but a Soviet agreement to build twenty-eight small-size tankers for Egypt on a long term basis.[74] Cairo gave the Fahmi visit a positive assessment, but it boded ill for the future.

On December 28, Isma'il Fahmi and War Minister Muhammad 'Abd al-Ghani al-Gamasi[75] were summoned to Moscow without explanation. Cairo Radio guessed they intended "to settle old differences" and to assure the success of Brezhnev's visit.[76] After a round of talks, held in what TASS described as a "friendly atmosphere," came the bombshell that Brezhnev had "postponed" his visit and that "a new date for the visit will be set." Sadat refused to comment other than to say that he was "convinced by the reasons" offered by Moscow. Against the background of his relations with the Soviets, the incident was merely another trying disappointment. There was no brooding over any affront; and the relationship, discord and all, went on, as was

[73] FBIS/Egypt, October 23, 1974, p. D1. After speaking with Fahmi, Musa Sabri of Akhbar al-Yawm wrote that one reason for Soviet dissatisfaction was the absence of the coordination between Egypt and the Soviet Union that was stipulated in Article 6 of the 1971 treaty.
[74] FBIS/USSR, October 18, 1974, p. F6.
[75] General Gamasi was appointed war minister to succeed Field Marshal Ahmad Isma'il 'Ali, who died on December 25, 1974.
[76] BBC/ME/4791/A/2 (December 30, 1974).

later reflected in the communiqué issued at the end of Gromyko's visit in February 1975.[77]

The Soviet rebuff gave rise to the inevitable speculations: that Brezhnev was ill with leukemia or cancer;[78] that he wanted to give Kissinger more time to produce some progress, in this way deflecting Sadat's demand for new weapons and limiting his military option (this view was advanced by Soviet journalists in Cairo);[79] that the Kremlin was evincing displeasure at Sadat's unwillingness to return to Geneva and involve Moscow in the diplomatic negotiations; that Sadat had failed to meet Moscow's expectations—political or military—out of concern that Faysal would be extremely discomforted by any Soviet-Egyptian rapprochement; that a faction in the Kremlin was challenging Brezhnev, ostensibly for going to Cairo without substantial concessions from Sadat but in actuality for his détente policy; and that Brezhnev decided against squandering his prestige on a showy but inconclusive visit that would have benefited mainly Sadat: he did not want to arouse the kind of reaction from the Politburo that Khrushchev had by his visit to Egypt in May 1964, with possibly similar consequences. And as one diplomat observed, "The Soviets want the final communiqué written before Brezhnev gets there. They don't want surprises."[80]

Certainly, Brezhnev saw no reason to make new inputs and inflate Egyptian expectations,[81] which his visit would surely have done, without a commensurate return; and there is some evidence that he really was ill. His wait-and-see decision was predicated on skepticism of Kissinger's policy, on the belief that it would ultimately prove wanting and that sooner or later the parties would have to go to Geneva; on annoyance with Sadat's public bickering and innuendo about Soviet reliability; on satisfaction with the existing level of Soviet involvement in Egypt; and on anticipation of a better price being had for a visit to Egypt by the secretary-general of the CPSU.[82]

---

[77] BBC/ME/4824/E/1-2 (February 7, 1975).

[78] On February 14, 1975, during British Prime Minister Wilson's visit, Brezhnev made his first public appearance since December 24, 1974, and appeared in good health. *International Herald Tribune*, February 15-16, 1975.

[79] Author's interview in Cairo in January 1975.

[80] *International Herald Tribune*, December 30, 1974.

[81] For example, Ali Amin of *Akhbar al-Yawm* had already predicted that during his visit to Egypt Brezhnev would make an offer that "will cause a world uproar." CPR, No. 5997, December 7, 1974.

[82] In an interview with *Al-Nahar* several weeks later, Sadat gave Israel three

Both the collapse on March 23, 1975, of an intensive Kissinger effort to arrange a second-stage Egyptian-Israeli disengagement and Egypt's formal request on March 31 to the United States and the Soviet Union to reconvene the Geneva conference seemed to open the way for its assembling and for an end to Soviet-Egyptian tension over this issue. But Sadat, on March 29, in an unexpected diplomatic hedge, announced, to harsh criticisms from the Palestinians and Arab critics, that Egypt would reopen the Suez Canal on June 5—on the eighth anniversary of its closure. In this way he gave a boost to Egypt's sagging economy and to U.S. arguments with Israel for a further pullback. Geneva was for him a resort of final desperation: given Palestinian disunity, Arab inability to fashion a collective position that Israel might accept, U.S. opposition, and Israel's refusal to recognize the PLO as a separate political entity, he feared Geneva would produce a petrifying stalemate and not a settlement.

The Soviets, believing that a reconvocation of the Geneva conference was now possible, quickly took diplomatic soundings. They sent envoys on a secret mission to persuade Israeli leaders to seek a settlement at Geneva, reportedly in return for a promise of renewed diplomatic relations and a Soviet guarantee of Israel's security within its 1967 boundaries.[83] On April 23, at a banquet in Moscow held for Syria's foreign minister, Gromyko said:

> Israel may receive, if it wishes, the strictest guarantees with the participation—in an appropriate agreement—of the Soviet Union, too, [guarantees] which would ensure peaceful conditions for the existence and development of all governments in the Middle East.[84]

By making the statement in the presence of the foreign minister of Syria, one of the militant Arab states, Gromyko implicitly called for Arab acceptance of Israel, but he avoided specifying the 1967 borders as the ones the USSR would be prepared to

---

months to withdraw "on all three fronts," warning that "if nothing is accomplished very soon, we will go to Geneva, all of us Arabs including the Palestinians, and explode everything there." CPR, No. 5035, January 17, 1975. There may have been a connection between Brezhnev's "postponement" and the pressure that Sadat felt to set a time limit for Kissinger to show some results.

[83] *The Times*, April 12, 1975.   [84] *Pravda*, April 24, 1975.

uphold. His reticence was due in part to a desire not to alienate Arafat, who was due to arrive on April 28. After discussions with him, and subsequent talks with all the parties concerned, Moscow, too, decided not to press for an early return to Geneva. What had been assumed to be a key Brezhnev demand, surprisingly lost its critical urgency for Moscow.

The USSR's sudden caution is significant. First, like Washington, Moscow is not keen on sponsoring a conference that has little prospect of success. It stands to lose ground with the Arabs from a meeting that degenerates into political name-calling and that shows the USSR incapable of delivering what they want, either at the conference table or on the battlefield. Second, in the late spring and early summer of 1975, Helsinki had priority over Geneva. Brezhnev wanted the 35-nation summit meeting to take place and to ratify the work of the Conference on Security and Cooperation in Europe (CSCE), before facing up to the knottier Middle East problems. Thus, for tactical reasons Moscow decided to proceed slowly toward Geneva. Third, a Geneva conference would confront Soviet decisionmakers with dilemmas. It would reveal the inconsistency of their position—support for the Palestinians and acceptance of the existence of Israel. Finally, the Soviet government had sought a conference for eighteen months on the assumption that Geneva would be an undisputed gain for the USSR. When this became doubtful, Moscow's eagerness waned. The USSR does want equal status with the United States in diplomatic forums dealing with the Middle East, but not at the expense of its standing with key Arab clients. And once the issue of hurrying a return to Geneva could no longer hurt Sadat, the Soviet leadership was prepared to wait until the situation promised it substantive advantages.

THE PALESTINIAN FACTOR

Palestinian opposition to Sadat's reliance on Kissinger's diplomatic efforts gave Moscow the opportunity to add to Sadat's difficulties through its encouragement of their demands. Though minor participants in the October War, the Palestinians were major beneficiaries, whose fortunes rose with Arab oil. Heretofore too weak militarily to challenge Israel's control of the West Bank and Gaza and too factionalized by personal feuds and conflicting ideologies to warrant serious diplomatic attention abroad or compel a unified Arab position on their fate,[85] they emerged from the war with increased popular appeal among the masses, such that no Arab government could afford to risk domestic unrest by appearing less than wholehearted in its commitment to their cause.

After 1967 the USSR maintained contacts with most of the Palestinian organizations, but favored the PLO because it enjoyed the widest support. Soviet policy adapted to the progressive elevation of the PLO's position in the Arab world. On November 15, 1973, Brezhnev joined Tito in calling for recognition of "the lawful national rights of the Arab people of Palestine," the first time he had used the term "national rights" (a higher status than "national liberation movement") in referring to them.[86] After December 1973, the Soviets insisted on the participation of the Palestinians in the Geneva conference, arguing that "no durable peace" was possible "until the legitimate national rights of the Palestinian Arabs are duly safeguarded,"[87] a stand they knew would complicate Sadat's efforts to achieve another Israeli withdrawal through Kissinger's good offices. In August 1974, the Soviet government permitted the PLO to open an office in Moscow, in effect recognizing it as the sole representative of the Palestinian Arabs and empowered to sit in its own right at the Geneva conference.[88] In October and November Brezhnev emphasized the Palestinians' "right to a national home."[89] Moscow had come to the threshold of recognizing the existence of a Palestinian Arab state but refrained from specifying its precise boundaries, leaving that for the future peace conference. Likewise, the Soviet government has never openly stated what borders it favors for Israel.[90] Indeed, since it states that Israel was solely responsible

[85] In September 1972 Sadat had suggested that the PLO establish a provisional government-in-exile, but this was rejected by the Palestinian groups because of their inability to agree on a leadership or a policy.

[86] BBC/SU/4453/C/2 (November 17, 1973).

[87] *Izvestiia*, July 24, 1974, as quoted in BBC/SU/4662/A4/3 (July 27, 1974).

[88] In addition, Moscow was reported to have agreed to provide the PLO with modern weapons and to assist in the formation of an "anti-imperialist Arab front" to strengthen the resistance to U.S. penetration in the area. *Le Matin–An-Nahar Arab Report*, 5, No. 32 (August 12, 1974), 1; *NYT*, August 5, 1974 (On this occasion, Arafat was hosted by B. N. Ponomarev, the head of the International Section of the CPSU Central Committee); see also, FBIS/Inter-Arab Affairs, February 5, 1975, p. A3.

[89] For example, *NYT*, November 7, 1974; FBIS/Egypt, November 27, 1974, p. D1.

[90] Some Soviet commentators have called for a return to the lines of June

for the first Arab-Israeli war in 1948–1949, and since it places no blame on the Arab governments for the failure to create a separate Palestinian state on the West Bank and Gaza when the opportunity was available prior to June 1967, it may be strongly presumed that Moscow prefers to keep the issue uncertain out of consideration for its relations with the PLO and as leverage in negotiations with Israel.[91]

Soviet policy has evolved in response to the requirements of Arab politics.[92] It is a step-by-step accommodation to the emerging new force in Middle Eastern politics. The Arab summit conference at Rabat in October 1974 averred that the Palestinians were entitled to a state of their own and that they would not, under any circumstances, be forced again under Jordan's control.[93] Arafat's unprecedented appearance before the U.N. General Assembly the following month resulted in greater readiness among non-Arab states to recognize the PLO as the incipient provisional government of a nascent Palestinian state.

1967 and the establishment of a Palestinian state on the West Bank and Gaza; they have not, however, made any proposal about the future of Jerusalem. For example, V. Vladimirov, "A Peaceful Settlement for the Middle East," *International Affairs*, No. 11 (November 1974), 112.

[91] L. Tolkunov, "Blizhnii Vostok: istoki krizisa i puti ego uregulirovaniia" (The Middle East: The Sources of the Crisis and the Ways for Its Resolution), *Kommunist*, No. 13 (September 1974), 99-100, 104-105. By virtue of his position as editor of *Izvestiia*, Tolkunov's idea of blaming the Israelis for the 1948–1949 war and avoiding any criticism of Arab behavior at the time must be seen as the official Soviet view; it keeps the possibility open for supporting PLO claims for a return to the original partition plan.

[92] With the move toward recognition of the Palestinians as a national movement, Moscow shifted from an emphasis on Resolution 242, which makes no mention of Palestinians and calls only "for achieving a just settlement of the refugee problem," to Resolution 338, which calls for "the implementation of Resolution 242 in all its parts" and specifies also that there should be a "settlement of the Palestinian question." Soviet coolness to Resolution 242 was evident before the October War, a function of its courtship of the PLO; for example, the June 1973 communiqué at the Washington summit meeting between the Soviet Union and the United States failed to mention it because of the difficulty of formulating mutually acceptable references. However, at the 1974 Moscow summit and at the Vladivostok summit between Leonid Brezhnev and Gerald Ford, the references are to Resolution 338, which the Soviets know is more congenial to the Palestinians.

[93] Israel missed whatever chance it may have had to help shape an alternative to the PLO's idea of a Palestinian state, by neglecting to explore seriously an arrangement whereby the Palestinians would have been returned to Jordanian jurisdiction prior to the October War, when such a possibility might have attracted a measure of support among West Bank notables and Jordan's leadership.

The USSR's espousal of the Palestinians' position made the Soviet-Libyan reconciliation of 1974 that much easier for Qadhdhafi and improved Moscow's relations with the militant Arab regimes. At the same time, it spotlights Sadat's gravitation toward the United States, thereby further complicating his relations with these Arab regimes. But Moscow can go only so far in using this as an issue with which to embarrass Sadat, for it, too, has not yet come out in support of the PLO covenant calling for the establishment of a "secular democratic state"—a euphemism for dismantling Israel and subsuming it into the whole of pre-1947 Palestine.[94] From a long-term perspective, a separate Palestinian state would complicate U.S. relations with those Arab governments who have no need to reconcile themselves to the existence of the state of Israel. As such it would provide Moscow with room for diplomatic maneuver and establish an Arab need for a permanent Soviet presence in the area. Moscow assumes that any Palestinian government will, at best, adopt a policy of cold coexistence with Israel, whose umbilical ties to the United States will inevitably create countervailing pro-Soviet propensities on the part of the Palestinian state and its active supporters. For the moment, though, Moscow, like Cairo, operates within a political setting that must include the United States and acceptance of the state of Israel.

DENASIRIZATION

The Soviets distrust deNasirization, believing it diminishes economic and political ties to the USSR. The term encompasses a variety of policies, all of them anathema to Moscow: reliance on private foreign capital for economic development; reversal of Nasir's collectivist economic course; restoration of the bourgeois technocracy to political and social prominence; and a diminished political role for the ASU. They see the United States as the guiding force, exerting pressure through Saudi Arabia. Uneasy over the process even before the October War, they are disturbed by the momentum it has gained since then.

While probably coincidental, on March 6, 1974, the day after Gromyko left, Sadat ordered an extensive shakeup of entrenched bureaucracies in an effort to increase their responsiveness to

[94] M.I.S., 2, No. 10 (August 15, 1974), 76.

foreign businessmen and facilitate private investment in Egypt. In April Sadat issued a 20,000-word document, called "The October Paper" (to symbolize his contention that the October War opened the way to a new era for Egypt). It called for extensive reforms and held out the promise of a better life for the Egyptian people.

DeNasirization took many forms. Attacks on Nasir became freer. One editor charged that during the Nasir period "the Egyptian was looked upon as the ugly man throughout the Arab world. . . . For twenty years every Egyptian seemed to have turned into a spy and a saboteur. The abominable picture has changed as Egypt now has a ruler and not a leader."[95] Another wrote that after 1961 "the centers of power launched a violent campaign of injustice, coercion, oppression and humiliation which turned peaceful Egypt into a gloomy scene of torture and punishment, the likes of which was not witnessed even in the darkest days of the medieval ages and is unprecedented in history."[96] Sadat claimed to have restored the independence of the judiciary, canceled all the extra-legal measures "the revolution had adopted throughout its 18 years" (i.e. from 1952 to 1970), and opened the doors "to expatriate Egyptians who had been abroad since the fifties for their safe return home without exception."[97] Indicative of the extent of the process is the frequent contrasting of Nasir's failure in 1967 with Sadat's success in 1973. For example, on the occasion of the second anniversary of the October War, at a conference in Cairo nominally sponsored by Cairo University but actually organized and run by the Egyptian military, the official spokesmen talked about their "glorious triumph in 1973" and stressed that in 1967 "the political leadership," and not the army, had been responsible for the defeat. With the denigration of Nasir came the cult of Sadat.

Sadat granted many amnesties, hoping to enlist on his side former opponents of Nasir and the generally conservative, religiously orthodox social subgroups they attracted, and to form a new consensus behind his domestic policies. In late 1971 he released after seventeen years under house arrest ex-General Muhammad Nagib, who was the figurehead behind whom Nasir

[95] Quoted in *BRIEF*, No. 78 (March 16–31, 1974), p. 3.
[96] *Al-Ahram*, February 27, 1974, as quoted in FBIS/Egypt, March 7, 1974, p. G6; see also, *Le Matin–An-Nahar Arab Report*, 5, No. 11 (March 18, 1974), 1.
[97] FBIS/Egypt, October 20, 1975, p. D7; also FBIS/Egypt, July 7, 1975, p. D6.

operated during his early years in power. After the October War, Sadat permitted interviews in which Nagib sullied Nasir and the revolution to be published in Egyptian journals.[98] He also pardoned a number of senior officers such as former War Minister Shams Badran and the Chief of Intelligence Salah Nasr.[99] And he made minor but symbolic gestures (appreciated by Faysal) such as the grant of Egyptian nationality to ex-Libyan King Muhammad Idriss al-Senussi and his family, who had lived in Cairo since the Libyan revolution of September 1969; and the return of property confiscated from members of the former royal regime.[100]

Western investors were courted, as Sadat did not disguise his preference for Western technology and technical assistance. Along with the removal of some of the fetters on the private sector came the restoration of former privileges to the bourgeoisie in the fields of foreign trade, banking, and tourism. The government's Western orientation was evident in cabinet appointments; for example, in late September 1974, Sadat relinquished the post of prime minister to Deputy Prime Minister 'Abd al-'Aziz Higazi, with a mandate to attract foreign capital and to free prospective investors from stifling bureaucratic controls. Higazi's ineffectiveness led to his replacement in April 1975 by the former Governor of Alexandria and the Minister of Interior since May 1971, Mamduh Salim, who, though no economist, is expected to keep a firm grip on the country in the economically trying period ahead.[101]

Soviet commentators deplored Sadat's deNasirization, defending Nasir and his policies.[102] *Pravda* cited an appeal by Lebanese political figures calling for a halt to the attacks. It criticized those who belittled Nasir's leadership,[103] as did Soviet broadcasts to the

---

[98] *BRIEF*, No. 108 (June 16–30, 1975), p. 4.

[99] *The Times*, October 24, 1974. See Najib E. Saliba, "The Decline of Nasirism in Sadat's Egypt," *World Affairs*, 138, No. 1 (Summer 1975), 52-53.

[100] FBIS/Egypt, May 20, 1975, p. D6.

[101] At the same time, Lt.-General Husni Mubarak was appointed vice-president and thus became President Sadat's immediate successor in case of any emergency; Fahmi and Gamasi assumed added responsibilities as deputy prime ministers. *The Times*, April 17, 1975.

[102] An important Soviet study emphasizing the progressive and socialist policies of Nasir was published in early 1974 and, by implication, contrasted Nasir's orientation with Sadat's. See, I. P. Beliaev and E. M. Primakov, *Egipet: vremia prezidenta Nasera* (Moscow: Mysl, 1974). The study stresses Nasir's domestic policies and has little on Soviet-Egyptian relations or foreign policy.

[103] *Pravda*, March 25, 1974.

Arab world with far greater asperity.[104] Moscow was disturbed by Egypt's drift away from "scientific socialism" and its reconsideration of the general trend toward establishing a strong public economic sector "that plays a decisive role in the economic life of the country" in favor of developing the private sector.[105] It testily defended the "vitality and soundness of the noncapitalist path of development in Egypt" against the "vast number of fabrications about the slow rate of development and the ever-lasting budget deficit," which it attributed to enormous defense expenditures and to difficulties that were temporary and could be overcome.[106] There were commentaries on the dangers of relying on foreign private capital.[107] In the spring of 1974, Soviet analysts remarked on the deluge of visits by Western capitalists who "spare no promises" in quest of "profitable deals."[108] By autumn, they reported that the clamor raised in the Egyptian press for foreign and private capital had given rise to "an obviously exaggerated appraisal" of the available possibilities: "The first sobering-up period . . . had already begun."[109] They warned that Egypt could not in the long run rely on support from non-socialist countries.[110]

The Soviets closely followed the debates on the reorganization of the ASU. They approved the official Egyptian line that "liberalization" did not entail dismantling the public sector or the alliance of "People's Working Forces" (i.e. the workers' and peasants' associations) and aligned themselves with those who opposed attempts to form several political parties and abolish "the provision for a 50 percent representation of the workers and peasants in the ASU under the invalid pretext that this provision, as they claim, is overtly communist."[111] They criticized "the venomous lies against communists and the whole communist movement" and blamed "the Arab reaction" for using the hoary cry of anticommunism to undermine the essentials of the Nasirite

---

[104] For example, FBIS/USSR, March 22, 1974, pp. F1-F2.

[105] FBIS/USSR, March 8, 1974, p. F8. At a later date, Haykal added his disapproval of Sadat's economic policies, alleging that "a parasite class" is emerging. NYT, October 24, 1975.

[106] FBIS/USSR, March 5, 1974, p. F8; USSR and the Third World, 4, No. 2 (1974), 76.

[107] Pavel Naumov, "In Egypt Today," New Times, No. 12 (March 1974), 24.

[108] FBIS/USSR, March 7, 1974, p. F4.

[109] FBIS/USSR, October 11, 1974, p. F12.

[110] FBIS/USSR, October 21, 1974, p. F2.

[111] FBIS/USSR, September 26, 1974, p. F5.

achievement.[112] Moscow took umbrage at Sadat's accusation that Communists and "Marxists" fomented domestic unrest and sabotage during the workers' riots on January 1, 1975,[113] and at the periodic slurs against the Aswan Dam,[114] which generally centered on the failure of the Soviets to anticipate its full ecological impact: "Those in Egypt and those outside it who are trying to prove that the dam is unnecessary, are in fact, morally speaking, joining forces with the Israeli militarists,"[115] It was further provoked by the openly anti-Soviet propaganda that had government sanction.[116] The individual components of deNasirization were irritation enough; but the totality of the assault on Nasir's policies, if sustained for any length of time and buttressed by assistance from the West, was dismaying, signifying Sadat's search for alternative domestic and foreign policy options. For Soviet policymakers the phenomenon required stocktaking.

SKIRTING THE BRINK

Sadat's efforts to optimize the diplomatic opportunities that had presented themselves fulfilled his desire to disengage politically from the USSR. They conformed nicely to the changing situation in the Middle East, where differentiation supplanted polarization; where both inter-Arab and superpower relationships were confronted with new uncertainties and dilemmas; and where the United States, which in 1967 had refrained from involvement only to incur the hostility of most of the Arab world, in 1973 intervened militarily and, paradoxically, wound up being wooed by it.

[112] FBIS/USSR, October 3, 1974, p. F3.

[113] FBIS/Egypt, January 9, 1975, p. D6.

[114] For example, Sayyid Mar'i, the Speaker of the People's Assembly (and Sadat's brother-in-law), raised questions in a journal article: "Have we benefited fully from the dam? I say no. . . . Have we benefited fully from the land reclaimed as we should have? I say partly, but not fully." *International Herald Tribune*, December 19, 1974. However, soon after Mar'i's article, Sadat lauded the High Dam, pointing out that in 1972 it had saved the country from the consequences of a low flood: "one-half or one-third of the land would not have been cultivated" had it not been for the Dam. CPR, No. 5021, January 3, 1975. See also, *NYT*, February 23, 1975, and May 4, 1975.

[115] *Soviet News*, No. 5772 (February 4, 1975).

[116] For example, in May 1975, the government, over the objection of the Soviet embassy, approved the showing of a play that derides the people and country represented by an imaginary foreign delegation that is friendly to Egypt. FBIS/Egypt, May 6, 1975, p. D12. See also, *NYT*, July 16, 1975.

Moscow had confidently expected to retain its preeminent and privileged relationship with Egypt but instead found itself hoisted on the petard of détente. It denied charges that its détente with the United States constituted a deviation from its policy of promoting the Arab cause, that it sought to keep Egypt isolated in an anti-imperialist box, or that its own quest for economic concessions in the West were no different from Egypt's opening its economy to Western capital.[117]

But Sadat was not swallowing any of this. In his May Day speech at Helwan in 1974, he rebuked the Soviets for denying the Arabs the diplomatic flexibility they claimed for themselves:

> The political adolescents and those whose voices are as loud as their hearts are weak and who are still afraid to believe in the newly acquired elements of Arab strength—those are the ones who fail to see the Arab and international changes and who do not believe it to be the right of their own nation to practice today with self-confidence what the other nations practice. For Kissinger to visit Moscow and Peking is acceptable, but for him to visit Cairo, Damascus or Algiers is treason. Kissinger's mediation in the Vietnam war and his discussions with North Vietnam are considered a victory for Vietnam and not directed against the USSR, but his mediation in the Middle East and his talks with us are considered defeatism and an act directed against the USSR. For the American Chase Manhattan Bank to open a branch in Moscow is acceptable, but for the same bank to open a branch in Egypt is considered a threat to us. American, German, and Japanese capital investment to build factories in Russia and exploit the gas fields in Siberia is acceptable, but the use of such funds to reconstruct the Canal towns and to reclaim the Western Desert is unacceptable. This is political adolescence. The least one can say is that it conceals a sickness and lack of self-confidence.[118]

Sadat premised his diplomacy on several assumptions: one, that Egypt would benefit from better relations with the United States and that Saudi Arabia preferred this orientation; two, that Western and Arab capital would flow into Egyptian coffers if conditions were made attractive enough; three, that Moscow

---

[117] See, FBIS/USSR, May 31, 1974, p. F7; BBC/SU/4647/A4/1 (July 10, 1974); and FBIS/USSR, January 24, 1975, p. F1.

[118] Quoted in USSR and the Third World, 4, No. 4 (1974), 223.

would continue its economic assistance for the sake of maintaining a presence. Confident in his assets, Sadat made the Soviets the scapegoat for the tensions in their bilateral relationship. While recognizing that his military dependency required a continuing relationship with the Soviet Union because even under the best of circumstances diversification and the creation of an Egyptian arms industry would be a slow process and only Soviet weapons could satisfy the battle needs of the Egyptian army in the foreseeable future, Sadat raised the level of recrimination, inviting invidious comparisons between the United States and the Soviet Union.[119] Furthermore, perhaps because his economic prospects depended primarily on the goodwill of Arab oil producers and Western investors who were generally wary of any notable Soviet-Egyptian rapprochement, he was not averse to extending his criticisms to the economic realm when Moscow rejected his repeated requests for a ten-year moratorium on debt repayments (about 200 to 300 million dollars a year), similar to the one granted Syria in the spring of 1974.[120] Sadat acknowledged the debts, but asked for a period of grace to help tide Egypt over difficult years, calling on the USSR to "appreciate our circumstances."[121] Moscow's insistence that Egypt meet the debt payments due on arms purchased from 1967 moved Sadat to recall that "under conditions similar to ours . . . the Soviet Union paid only one installment on the price of the arms it obtained during World War II under the Lend-Lease Act. It paid a token installment after 30 years."[122] In late June 1975, with the deadlock seemingly frozen, Sadat declared that if the Soviet Union continues "to ignore our demands and take no notice of our economic situation

[119] One Egyptian journalist minced no words: "Is Egypt supposed to seek the friendship of the Soviet Union and accept its conditions so they will supply us with arms? . . . Moscow refuses today to give us arms because we do not agree to its request, mainly to go immediately to Geneva and [accept] the return of the [Soviet] experts. . . . I ask every Arab to quietly compare the vast difference between the Soviet Union's friendship with Egypt and the U.S. friendship with Israel. Egypt groans under debts. Has the Soviet Union attempted to reduce these debts? The United States has written off Israel's debts. Egypt needs arms for which it will pay, but Russia refuses. Israel receives free arms supplied by the United States from the U.S. Army. Egypt wants to purchase arms from Russia, but meets only refusal." FBIS/Egypt, January 30, 1975, p. D4.

[120] See, CPR, No. 5035, January 17, 1975; Le Figaro, January 25–26, 1975; and BBC/SU/4836/A4/1 (February 21, 1975).

[121] FBIS/Egypt, May 2, 1975, p. D11.

[122] FBIS/Egypt, May 15, 1975, p. D8.

in regard to the moratorium I have asked for, by God, we will have something to talk about but quietly since there is no justification for anger or reaction."[123] On July 22, amidst reports that Cairo had started to curtail Soviet naval and air facilities in Egypt,[124] the Egyptian finance minister took a delegation to Moscow to discuss the matter of debt rescheduling. Sadat decided to try to exercise some leverage of his own, showing once again that the debtor is not without assets in dealing with the creditor.[125]

In September 1975, Kissinger succeeded in arranging another limited disengagement between Israel and Egypt. Under the Sinai Agreement, Egypt regained possession of the oil fields at Ras Sudar and Abu Rudeis, located along the upper eastern half of the Sinai peninsula; Israel pulled back its forces to the eastern ends of the Mitla and Gidi Passes, the key strategic routes dominating most of the Sinai peninsula, thus returning to Egypt an additional 1,900 square miles of territory; and the United States agreed to help Egypt build an early warning system at the eastern terminuses of the passes in order to guard against any surprise Israeli attack, and to station 200 to 250 American civilian technicians there to assist in the inspection system. For their part, the Egyptians have privately given assurances that nonmilitary cargoes destined for Israel and carried in non-Israeli ships shall be permitted to transit the Suez Canal; that Egypt will not blockade the Bab el Mandeb Strait, which leads to the Red Sea; and that the accord, and the cease-fire that is an integral part of it, shall remain in effect for at least three years and be operative until superseded by a new agreement.

The Syrians and Palestinians, among others, denounced the Sinai Agreement, especially Article I, which stipulates that the conflict between Egypt and Israel "and in the Middle East shall not be resolved by military force but by peaceful means." The Soviets, also critical, generally exercised more restraint than Sadat's Arab critics. There were a few exceptions, such as the

[123] FBIS/Egypt, June 24, 1975, p. D8.
[124] FBIS/Egypt, July 21, 1975, p. D11; and *NYT*, July 27, 1975.
[125] The finance minister returned from Moscow on August 2, seemingly without any progress having been made. On August 21, in an interview with the Lebanese magazine *Al-Hawadith*, Sadat said that a Soviet delegation would come to Cairo to continue the discussions: "I had no intention of abrogating the treaty and the idea was not basically raised for discussion" [in Moscow]. FBIS/Egypt, August 22, 1975, p. D4.

eve of Sadat's visit to the United States, when *Pravda* lashed out at the increasingly frequent commentaries in the Egyptian press that "aimed at casting a shadow on the Soviet Union and on its policy in the Middle East, in particular, vis-à-vis Egypt."[126] It deplored the insinuations of scant Soviet economic and military assistance, noted Egypt's growing isolation in the Arab world, and insisted that the Soviet Union was not opposed to the possibility of implementing partial measures, provided these partial measures were part of an overall settlement and were adopted within the framework of the Geneva conference: "Moreover, this [Sinai] agreement envisaging entry of American personnel into the Egyptian-Israeli disengagement zone, introduces a new element in the Middle East situation which is fraught with far-reaching dangerous consequences."[127] Notwithstanding these criticisms, Moscow sent a delegation to Cairo in late November 1975 to pursue the possible renegotiation of Egypt's debts to the USSR.[128] Three weeks of negotiations failed to break the deadlock;[129] but new talks were scheduled for early 1976.

In public at least, the Soviet side proffered an olive twig. On February 24, 1976, addressing the Twenty-fifth Congress of the CPSU, Brezhnev warned of the "persistent attempts" of "certain forces . . . to undermine Soviet-Egyptian relations," but he declared:

> As far as the USSR is concerned, we remain faithful to the fundamental line of strengthening them. This is reflected in the Treaty of Friendship and Cooperation between the USSR and Egypt, which we regard as a long-term basis for relations conforming with the interests not only of our two countries, but of the entire Arab world.[130]

These words, however, and the unsatisfactory gist of Soviet diplomatic notes, only fed Sadat's annoyance. On March 14, 1976, he administered another shock treatment to Moscow, calling for the termination of the 1971 treaty. Less than twenty-four hours later, Egypt's People's Assembly approved his request by a vote of 358 to 2, and Soviet-Egyptian relations plummeted to a new

126 *Pravda*, October 25, 1975.
127 See also, *Pravda*, November 16, 1975.
128 FBIS/Egypt, November 19, 1975, p. D1.
129 *NYT*, December 14, 1975.
130 *Socialism: Theory and Practice* (Moscow), No. 3 (March 1976), 18-19.

low. The move caught the Kremlin by surprise. In July 1972, when Sadat had sent the Soviet contingents packing, the Soviet government had been forewarned; but not in March 1976.

The reasons for Sadat's abrogation of the treaty are many and complex. In his speech to the People's Assembly on March 14, he gave most of them:[131] first, in pursuit of Soviet interests, Brezhnev opposed "the trend toward peace which had taken shape" since the October War; and he also opposed, as he had since 1971, Egypt's "open-door policy," the economic, social, and political changes that Egypt had been carrying out.[132] More serious, the Soviets refused to reschedule Egypt's debt repayments and meet Egypt's military needs. "What is worse," Sadat said, "they demand interest on the military loans":

> I do not forget 23 December 1973 [the day after the Geneva Conference was adjourned and Sadat had signified his intention of encouraging Kissinger's step-by-step diplomacy, which deprived the Soviets of a role in the negotiating process], when they told me that the Arab Republic of Egypt had been late in repaying the 22.1 million [rubles] Egypt had to pay in April and hence it should pay the interest on loans made for arms deals. Not only do they want the cost of arms but also the interest on the arms loans.

Finally, Moscow not only would not overhaul Egypt's aircraft or provide spare parts, but it also forbade India, which manufactures MiG-21 engines on license from the USSR, from doing so. This Soviet pressure on India was the last straw: "I can tell you this, the question with India . . . was really the main cause for ending the treaty."[133] By failing to build up and strengthen

---

131 FBIS/Egypt, March 16, 1976, pp. D24-D29.

132 On the next day, in a memorandum to Prime Minister Mamduh Salim on Egyptian-Soviet relations, Foreign Minister Fahmi took Sadat's criticisms a step further, charging Soviet officials with having violated Article 1 of the treaty by intervening, directly or indirectly, in Egyptian internal affairs. By way of example, he cited Brezhnev's comment at the Twenty-fifth Congress of the CPSU on the "strong pressures being exercised by domestic and foreign reaction . . . to undermine the social and political achievements of the Egyptian revolution." Such unwarranted intrusions, said Fahmi, "had regrettably been reflected in several pieces of correspondence recently addressed by the Soviet leaders to the Egyptian leadership." FBIS/Egypt, March 17, 1976, p. D3.

133 FBIS/Egypt, March 30, 1976, p. D7; FBIS/Egypt, March 31, 1976, p. D1.

Egypt's military potential, the Soviet Union, Sadat later noted, had violated Article 8 of the 1971 treaty, which called for the USSR's "strengthening the defense capacity of the United Arab Republic." For a brief period he held off closing Egyptian ports to the Soviet fleet, possibly to see whether Soviet leaders would relent somewhat. On April 4, however, while in Paris, Sadat announced that naval facilities for the Soviet Union had been canceled.[134]

From Sadat's subsequent elaborations on the circumstances prompting him to terminate the treaty, two other considerations appear to have motivated him, one personal, the other political. On a personal level the decision was symbolic; it signified the final act of disgorging a bone that had stuck in his craw since May 1971. Unsuccessful then in convincing Soviet leaders that the purge of Ali Sabri and the leading Nasirist figures was not directed against them, he had acceded to Podgornyi's entreaties and signed the pact in May rather than in July as he preferred, knowing that the Soviets still distrusted him nonetheless. In March 1976, with the termination of the treaty, he effaced the mortification he had felt in May 1971. On a political level, Sadat's revelation that the People's Republic of China had, in late 1975, made Egypt a gift of thirty MiG engines and a large quantity of spare parts was followed by an official visit to Peking by Vice President Husni Mubarak,[135] indicating that Egypt would look also to China for arms and aid.[136]

Soviet commentators accused Sadat of "gross distortions of the history of Soviet-Egyptian relations," kowtowing to reactionary forces by resorting to the "open doors policy" in order to obtain a U.S. pledge of economic assistance, and "a new manipulation of the unfriendly policy in regard to the Soviet Union that he has been actually pursuing already for a long time now."[137] They also viewed the cancelation of the Soviet-Egyptian treaty as a

134 *NYT*, April 5, 1976. The last Soviet naval units left Alexandria one hour before midnight on April 14. FBIS/Egypt, April 19, 1976, p. D3.

135 FBIS/Egypt, March 26, 1976, p. D8.

136 Some Egyptian officials privately questioned Sadat's wisdom in having gone so far in provoking the Soviets. (Author's interviews.)

Ambassador Hafiz Isma'il had requested reassignment prior to the March decision, no doubt because he felt his usefulness in Moscow had ended. FBIS/Egypt, February 11, 1976, p. D5. His replacement was former Minister of Aviation Hamdi Abu Zayd. FBIS/Egypt, April 5, 1976, p. D1.

137 FBIS/USSR, March 16, 1976, pp. F1-F3.

repudiation of the leading position that Egypt had held in the national-liberation struggle since the July 1952 revolution.[138]

The Soviet government responded officially on March 31, 1976.[139] In a note handed to the Ministry of Foreign Affairs, it said "this unjustified step" was part of "a noisy anti-Soviet campaign" that is trying to distort "all that the Soviet Union has done and is still doing for the well-being of the Egyptian people." It called attention to Nasir's interest "on more than one occasion" in a Soviet-Egyptian treaty; to the USSR's unstinting help in 1956, in 1967, and in 1973; and to the USSR's extensive economic and military assistance. Quoting Nasir to the effect that "We are fully aware that Egypt would not have been able to solve a single complex problem, whether economic or political, had it not been for the support of the Soviet Union," the note charged that the "abandonment of the policy of cooperation with the Soviet Union by the Egyptian leadership, as well as its abandonment of the principles of the Soviet-Egyptian treaty, has accelerated since the end of 1973." It accused the Egyptian leadership of making "unilateral deals . . . behind the backs of the other Arab countries," of removing "Egypt from the forefront of the struggle for the liberation of the occupied Arab territories," of distorting the nature of Soviet-Egyptian relations, and of misleading "its own people and public opinion with regard to finances and loans between the Soviet Union and Egypt." The note maintained that the Soviet side has shown "understanding for the recent Egyptian government's request regarding easier conditions for repayments and showed readiness to solve this problem in the interest of both sides," as well as "special readiness to positively solve the question of exporting spare parts and repairing the Soviet-made military equipment in Egypt."

In the weeks that followed, the Soviet media amplified these points, emphasizing that Sadat's abrogation of the treaty "serves only the enemies of the Egyptian and other Arab people" and that "hopes that foreign monopolies will help Egypt to overcome its economic difficulties are founded on sand."[140] Of Mubarak's mission to Peking, they observed that "the thirty engines in question are undoubtedly insufficient for the hundreds of planes

[138] *Pravda*, March 20, 1976.
[139] FBIS/USSR, April 1, 1976, pp. F1-F4.
[140] *Izvestiia*, April 4, 1976.

which Egypt obtained from the Soviet Union;"[141] and that the "main purpose of the visit was a Chinese-Egyptian military agreement," which reflects a rapprochement predicated on a mutual anti-Soviet attitude.

In late April, with the sending of War Minister General Muhammad al-Gamasi to Moscow to represent Egypt at the funeral of Soviet Defense Minister Andrei Grechko, Cairo struck its first conciliatory note since the termination of the treaty. The signing of the trade protocol for 1976 on April 28 showed that each party wanted to limit the latest deterioration in relations. And on May 1, Sadat declared in his May Day speech, "We do not at all wish to engage in or escalate a fight with the Soviet Union, for we appreciate what it provided for us and are also aware of what we in turn gave it."[142]

In the post-October War period the fluctuations in the Soviet-Egyptian relationship, though often severe, stayed within the limits of toleration. One crude measure of this approximate symmetry of controlled tension may be seen in a comparison of the Soviet-Egyptian interactions during two equal time frames: on one hand, the period from the expulsion of Soviet military personnel in July 1972 to the end of the October War; on the other, the period from the immediate post-October War days to early 1975 (see Table One).

Table One

	From USSR to EGYPT Time Frames		From EGYPT to USSR Time Frames	
	7/72-10/73	11/73-1/75	7/72-10/73	11/73-1/75
Political missions	2	5	6	5
Military missions[a]	1	0	3	0
Economic missions	0	3	2	3
Cultural-scientific missions	15	14	13	11

[a] In a number of instances, military missions, having been sent with political missions, do not show up on the chart.

[141] FBIS/USSR, April 22, 1976, p. F2.
[142] FBIS/Egypt, May 3, 1976, p. D11.

In the fifteen months prior to the October War, the Egyptians sent six political missions to the Soviet Union, the Soviets only two to Egypt; three military missions were sent to one from the USSR; and two economic missions to none from Moscow. The flow of missions was strongly from Cairo to Moscow. Egypt was the supplicant but not the subordinate. It bargained, successfully, for the means to make war a viable option. By contrast, the post-October period was characterized by a fundamental reciprocity, and the level of interaction was sustained. The important factor was not the tension but the continuing discussion and exchange in the political, economic, and cultural-scientific areas. Neither side wanted to disrupt the relationship or curtail levels of activity, even in a period of intense disagreement.

Chapter Ten

CURRENTS OF INFLUENCE

THE Egyptian connection has been Moscow's costliest in the Third World—and its most valuable. Despite the frustrations, the risks, and the disappointments attending relations with Cairo, Moscow generally encouraged Egyptian leaders to follow their own bent, because their course complemented its strategic objectives in the Middle East—and several times it intervened to save them from certain defeat. That the USSR has only a few tangibles to show for its efforts since 1967 has nurtured the comforting conjecture in the West that the game has not been worth the candle, that the Soviet gains, actual or prospective, did not justify the outlay. But in diplomacy there is no way of putting a price on achievement: too much depends on the value assigned it by the buyer—and of this we know precious little. However, by giving Egyptian leaders the military option and protecting them from the consequences of flawed policies, we see that the Soviet Union was the beneficiary of an Arab nationalism that weakened America's position and alliances in a region of continuing, albeit changing, strategic importance; that it was instrumental in inflaming the Arab-Israeli conflict; that it was in a position to play on other local animosities and encourage regional propensities toward self-assertiveness and anti-Westernism; and that it was able to advance its imperial goals. Not a bad haul; indeed, a very good one.

Involvement begat commitments. The frequent difficulties, irregular dividends, and occasional losses notwithstanding, Moscow persisted, drawn on by the prospect of strategic gains. The alternative—to reduce inputs and pare policy objectives to modest dimensions—seems never to have been seriously considered. Soviet leaders restored Egypt's military capabilities after the 1967 defeat; they backed the war of attrition in 1969–1970, committing sizable forces outside of the Soviet bloc for the first time; they endured expulsion in July 1972, even turning it to some advantage in dealings with a Washington preoccupied with superpower relationships and electoral politics; in October 1973 they squandered their credit with the United States to uphold Egypt; and in the post-October period they viewed Sadat's turn toward the United States from a long-term perspective, as in 1972, rather than from any narrow view of costs and benefits.

Over a period of more than twenty years Soviet leaders have had numerous opportunities to reverse or fundamentally modify their Egyptian policy. That they chose not to means that on balance they have been satisfied with the benefits. The considerations shaping Soviet decisions are secreted in the interstices of the Kremlin. Suffice it to say the motivations were many. Like players at a gambling table, some decisionmakers were attracted by the prospect of quick gain; some played for prestige—to enhance their internal role and the image they wanted elites in target countries to hold of them; others started as cautious risk-takers, but once in the game had to raise their stakes to preserve their position and vindicate their having agreed to play at all; others, having gone along to oblige a political benefactor, dared not desist and be thought disloyal or fainthearted. Many, having committed themselves to a forward policy in the Middle East, could not turn back.

The record of Soviet-Egyptian relations suggests that the Soviet Union has had limited influence on key Egyptian decisions. Yet Moscow continues to give support and to do so on a substantial scale. The reasons may be applicable to donors in general: a donor derives more benefit from the broad consequences of a donee's policy that it favors than from the immediate results of its input.

The Soviet objective was to maintain as close a relationship with the Egyptian leaders as they were prepared to accept and for as long as they pursued options whose basic thrust was congenial to Soviet interests in the area. The USSR was not responsible for the post-World War II polarization of the Arab world or for the genesis of the Arab-Israeli conflict, but it has been the principal beneficiary. Strife was the motive force that brought Moscow into the Middle East; aid was the manna that nourished its imperial expansion. The U.S.-Soviet bilateral talks on the Middle East that began in late 1969 marked the first recognition of the USSR as a coming member of the Board of Directors of the region. No Metternichian schemes can prevent this development.

Only the imperial nature of Soviet aims can account for Moscow's lack of interest in any settlement of the Arab-Israeli conflict on terms other than those set by Cairo (and Damascus). Its open partisanship assures a residual belligerence and irreconcilability that guarantee Egyptian military dependence. There is no justification for the ingenuous argument that the Soviet leadership prefers peace so that it can more productively utilize its scarce resources at home: not only does the Soviet military as a matter of policy keep enormous stocks of weaponry in reserve— hence the minimal drain on the Soviet economy of arms shipments to Egypt and other Arab countries—but one cannot discuss economic considerations when the price tag is so relatively small and in an area where political and strategic considerations are so obviously controlling. There is no evidence of any agonizing Soviet reappraisal of policy toward Egypt. The USSR has expressed far less displeasure with Egyptian policy than Egypt has with Soviet policy. The reasons are clear. Irrespective of the ups-and-downs in their relationship since 1972, the USSR retains a presence in Egypt: militarily, it remains the principal quartermaster (directly or through third parties) for the Egyptian army, and no matter how much Sadat or his successors would prefer to diversify, it will very likely continue in this role for some time to come; economically, it is heavily engaged in Egypt's industrial sector, to a far greater extent than any other great power,[1] and its assistance in economic planning and technological transfers remains important. Yet aside from this presence and Egypt's military dependence, the advantages Moscow derives are from the consequences of Sadat's policies and from the constraints on them inhering in Egypt's relations with the Arab world, and not from any strings it can pull in Cairo. Recognizing the arbitrary nature of Egyptian politics and the virtual impossibility of institutionalizing its influence through indigenous interest groups, the Soviet leadership works primarily within a government-to-government

[1] The Egyptian minister of manpower, writing in *TRUD*, said Egypt had benefited from Soviet economic assistance on 140 projects, 80 of which have been completed and 30 of which are industrial and engineering projects. FBIS/USSR, January 29, 1975, p. F3. See also *Pravda*, January 9, 1975; BBC/ME/W816/A1/2-3 (March 4, 1975); and Yaacov Ro'i and David Ronel, *The Soviet Economic Presence in Egypt and Its Political Implications* (Jerusalem: The Soviet and East European Research Centre, Research Paper No. 9, September 1974).

Also, two years after the October War, the first stage of the Nag Hammadi aluminum complex in upper Egypt was completed, with Soviet economic and technical assistance. FBIS/Egypt, November 6, 1975, p. F7.

framework. Stripped of illusions and devoid of trust, the Soviet-Egyptian relationship feeds on tactical necessities. The Soviets and Egyptians have been likened to two men sitting across a table genially smiling as they lie through their teeth to each other. Guile and calculation predominate, whether in discussing the Aswan Dam, with the Soviets belittling the ecological and engineering problems the Egyptians know to be serious but choose to ignore because of the hard choices they might have to make, or in discussing Egypt's diversion of cotton sales to world markets to take advantage of higher world market prices at the expense of honoring contractual commitments, or in arranging for arms shipments, which Moscow delivers willy-nilly for cash, some directly, others through Arab third parties.

The benefits to Egypt have been incalculable. The Soviet connection enabled it to recover from 1967, surmount 1970, and prepare for 1973. Egypt's remarkable comeback would have been impossible without Soviet assistance and involvement. But if "to sup with the Devil you need a long spoon," then it can be said that Nasir and Sadat had it, for they were nourished by the Soviet Union without falling under its influence. And the Soviet Union, despite political frictions and Egyptian arms indebtedness that exceeded six billion dollars by 1975, kept the provisions coming in one way or another, making possible the policies that were determined in Cairo.

On the domestic front neither political nor economic nor social practices and priorities were determined according to Soviet preferences. Egypt's preponderant foreign trade with the Soviet bloc, for example, was a function of Soviet credits and willingness to accept repayment in goods that could not be marketed in hard currency areas, and that were of marginal utility to the Soviet economy. Far from feeling compelled to balance the accounts, whenever possible Egypt kept cash crops such as cotton and rice out of bilateral accounts with the USSR. The brutal economic truth is that Egypt has little else to offer. Its main hope for the immediate future is Western investment and the letters of credit still doled out sparingly by the Arab oil magnates. Egypt's economy is in dire condition. The Soviet assistance that helps keep it going has not been sufficient to generate any significant new economic development since the mid-1960s.

Soviet policy has adjusted to Egyptian domestic politics more often than Egyptian policy has yielded to Soviet preferences.

There is no evidence that Moscow has been able to mobilize or strengthen the position of Egyptian officials or interest groups disposed to accommodate to Soviet desires. Egypt followed Moscow on Czechoslovakia, disarmament, European security, and the German question, only because these issues were of no consequence to it. Moscow's leverage on issues of importance to Egyptian leaders has at best been marginal once Cairo resolved upon a course of action. Gratitude for Soviet support has not carried with it any willingness to tolerate Soviet interference in Egyptian decision-making on key issues. In a word, Moscow has never attained with Egypt the sort of relationship that it has with the East European members of the Warsaw Pact. An observer once said, "the Soviet Union wants its client states to be strong enough to stand on their own, but weak enough to take orders." Throughout much of the period examined, Egypt was not strong enough to stand on its own, but was strong enough to refuse to take orders. On no major issue in Soviet-Egyptian relations was Moscow able to make Egypt do something against its will, although it was occasionally able to restrain what Egypt did or wanted to do.

These general conclusions are derived from analysis of the main issue areas that defined the Soviet-Egyptian relationship in the 1967–1975 period (Appendix 1). They tend to be confirmed by the results obtained from testing the hypotheses that were postulated at the beginning of this study. In practice, these formal intellectual constructs proved too restrictive for the reality they imperfectly help to illumine. They were refuted more than confirmed. Yet even in the noncorroboration of several widely accepted theoretical propositions, there is some yield for an assessment of the Soviet-Egyptian influence relationship and for narrowing the choice of approaches for operationalizing the concept of influence.

First, there is no demonstrable correlation between intensified interactions and influence. Increased trade or inputs of economic assistance might have improved the milieu within which influence is exercised, but the increase did not bring Moscow favorable outcomes in key issue areas. Egypt's exports to the Soviet bloc rose quickly after 1967: they passed the fifty-percent level in 1970 and approached the sixty-percent level by 1971–1972, the years in which tensions between Cairo and Moscow became serious; and at the end of 1973 more than half of Egypt's total medium and long-term indebtedness was to the Soviet bloc. Yet this did not improve Moscow's leverage over Egypt after the October War, nor did it impair Sadat's diplomatic flexibility to anywhere near the extent that Arab world constraints did. The absence of any apparent correlation between the expansion of trade or economic assistance, on the one hand, and the outcome of issue areas, on the other, is evident also in the lack of concordance between the signing of economic agreements and the tension in the issue areas. Economic inputs do not automatically bring political concessions; indeed, they did not even bring agreement on economic issues that cost Egypt little but that were high on the Soviet list of priorities.

Thus, during the peak years of Soviet aid, Moscow did everything it could to capture the Egyptian civil aviation market. In October 1968, at the time Egyptair was putting its first American-built Boeing 707s into operation, the Soviet minister of civil aviation pressed the Egyptian ministry to purchase Soviet jets, offering bargain basement terms. He finally obtained Egyptian approval in September 1971, in what may have been a friendly gesture made in expectation of an influx of new weapons, for the purchase of twelve planes. The contract, which was not signed until the fall of 1972, stipulated delivery of eight TU-154 passenger planes, the first three to be delivered in June 1973, the remainder over the next nine months, with the price of three returned prop-driven Ilyushin-18s and three Antonovs to be deducted from the cost of the new aircraft. There were rumors in Cairo that Sadat had intervened personally, overriding the continuing opposition within the Ministry of Aviation to the purchase, in order to help repair relations damaged by the expulsion of Soviet military personnel several months earlier. At the same time, Egyptair purchased an additional four Boeing 707s. The first TU-154 was handed over after the October War. A crash occurred during a familiarization flight in July 1974, at the height of post-October Soviet-Egyptian tensions, and led the Egyptian government to reconsider its decision. In February 1975, after indefinite postponement of Brezhnev's visit, it canceled the deal and returned the fleet of seven TU-154s.[2]

Second, an extensive presence is no assurance of influence. Even during the heyday of their military and economic presence, the

[2] FBIS/Egypt, February 18, 1975, p. D11; *The Guardian*, March 22, 1975.

Soviets had limited ability to effect desired outcomes of key decisions in foreign policy or for that matter in the spheres into which Soviet inputs flowed: for example, despite the extensive Soviet presence, Moscow played no direct role in Cairo's decisions to start the war of attrition or the October War; nor, despite much fanfare, did Nasir or Sadat really shake up Egyptian economic ministries, practices, or priorities, in line with Soviet suggestions. A presence is important in assuring access to decision-makers, but access, taken by itself, is no guarantee of influence. The easy entrée of the Soviet ambassador to Egyptian leaders was a perquisite granted by Nasir and Sadat in recognition of Soviet services; it was not a badge of intimacy or a sign, as it would have been in another age, of behind-the-scenes manipulation by an imperial procurator. The absence of credible instruments of direct control vitiates the patron's prospects for exercising influence.

Third, the hypothesis that the recipient of the greater number of visits will exercise asymmetrical influence over the sender is not confirmed, though it can have some utility (see sections 4 and 8 of Appendix 2), depending on how the data are aggregated. One thing is certain: aggregation on a per annum basis is too detached from context to be useful—it serves the tabulator's need but not the analyst's. The effect of aggregating missions is to subsume particularity into mass, to ignore distinctions for uniformity. The Soviet-Egyptian record suggests that missions should be differentiated as to kind and importance (Appendix 3); that of all the missions, the political missions will correlate most directly with agreement or disagreement, with cooperation or conflict; that the number of military missions is generally too few to be a meaningful gauge—usually because they are included in and counted as part of political missions; and that economic or cultural-scientific missions show an approximate symmetry, irrespective of political tensions, eliminating their utility for the assessment of influence relationships. Between a superpower and a nonaligned Third World country, the economic and the cultural-scientific interactions tend to be the most impervious to the disappointments and disagreements that beset the political relationship, and thus perhaps by mutual consent act as stabilizers to prevent the oscillation from going too far and undermining the entire relationship in a period of flux.

The importance of a visit is best determined by political context, the delegation's composition, the content of the joint communiqué, and the commentaries in the media. Divorced from context, symmetries can prove misleading. For example, according to the central assumption of communications flow theory, little influence is presumed to have been exercised by the Soviet Union or Egypt during the Nasir period (1967–1970), since there was an essential symmetry in the missions exchanged (Appendix 3). Indeed, since the Soviet Union sent five military missions and received only one from Egypt in return, one could, by reductio ad absurdum, contend that as the recipient of the preponderant number of military missions Egypt was the benefactor and the USSR the dependent. Table Two shows a basic symmetry in the

Table Two

Exchange of Missions

Time Frame	From USSR to EGYPT				From EGYPT to USSR			
	Political	*Military*	*Economic*	*Scientific/ Cultural*	*Political*	*Military*	*Economic*	*Scientific/ Cultural*
May 1971- July 1972	5	2	5	12	6	2	3	10
July 1972- September 1973	1	1	0	16	6	3	3	13

number of visits exchanged during the period from the signing of the Soviet-Egyptian Treaty of Friendship and Cooperation in May 1971 to the termination of the Soviet military presence in Egypt in July 1972. This reciprocity extends to all categories of missions. But the symmetry is formal only. On closer examination, the composition of the political missions exchanged shows a gross asymmetry of status: three of the six Egyptian visits to the USSR during the May 1971–July 1972 period were made by President Sadat; on the other hand, of the five Soviet visits to Egypt only the first (Podgornyi in May 1971) was made by a political counterpart of Sadat, the others being of lesser rank in the Soviet hierarchy. As the recipient of significantly higher-ranking visits, the Soviet Union would ordinarily be presumed to be the influencer, the dominant party in the relationship. Yet the end result of Sadat's succession of visits was the forced Soviet military exodus from Egypt. Dependence on Soviet arms had brought him to Moscow in October 1971, February 1972, and April 1972; but dependence does not necessarily beget subservience.

From the termination of the Soviet military presence in July 1972 to the start of the war in October 1973, the Egyptians sent by far the greater number of political, military, and economic missions to the USSR. Yet it would be incorrect to presuppose that the data demonstrate the preeminence of Soviet influence over Egypt during this period. It is, of course, possible to argue that Moscow wanted Sadat to go to war and pushed him to it. This would fulfill the needs of data in search of a theory, but it would contravene reality as we have been able to reconstruct it (after all, a Moscow that actually wanted war could have been more forthcoming with weaponry and not insisted on payment).

The utility of visits as a variable improves when periodicity is tied to issue areas and joint communiqués. Compiling missions in this way exposes the shortcomings of the assumption that the principal recipient of visits will be the influencer. During the June 1967 to June 1975 period, about seventy-five percent (twenty-two out of twenty-nine) of all Soviet political missions and about seventy percent (twenty-seven out of forty) of all the Egyptian political missions and about sixty-four percent (eighteen out of twenty-eight) of the joint communiqués clustered around six of the issue areas, namely, #4) the start of the war of attrition; #5) Nasir's inability to cope with Israeli deep penetration raids and his need for direct Soviet military involvement; #7) the 1971 Treaty of Friendship and Cooperation; #9) the expulsion of the Soviet military personnel; #10) the October War; and #11) the deferral of the reconvocation of the Geneva conference (see Appendices 2 and 3).

From December 1968 to June 1969, when Moscow and Cairo were arguing the case for the war of attrition, the Soviet Union sent four political missions to Egypt's one, and the two joint communiqués issued during this period were signed in Cairo. This suggests that Moscow was trying to dissuade Cairo, that in this instance the recipient of the most missions, i.e. Egypt, was indeed the influencer, in conformity with the theory. Six months later Nasir urgently needed help. The near symmetry of missions during that period provides no clue to the influence that Egypt was exercising. Later, between Nasir's death and the ratification of the 1971 treaty, the unprecedented round of consultations—six communiqués and twelves visits (six each way)—signified tentative probing and tough bargaining between equals: Sadat was militarily dependent, but not without political leverage. In the events leading up to the 1972 expulsion and the October War, Egypt turns out to have been the party principally shaping the outcome of the issue areas, even though it sent the disproportionately larger number of delegations and from October 1971 to January 1974 all the joint communiqués were signed in Moscow. Sadat went to Moscow on a number of occasions (see Appendix 2, #9 and #10), clearly as a supplicant, yet this did not prevent him from initiating policies that showed him to be very much his own man. During the post-October War period, when Egypt held the veto on whether or not to go to Geneva, the general symmetry of missions and communiqués gave no indication of the independence of Egypt.

The other hypotheses—propositions concerning the diminution of the political uses of aid over time and the attempt to correlate the sophistication of weaponry delivered—remain unverifiable because of deficient data. The weapons problem is complicated: data on the withholding of spare parts and on promises of future deliveries are impossible to obtain; also, a country, such as Egypt, which can readily acquire replacements from other Arab countries that buy from the USSR, has an unusual ability to withstand a Soviet slowdown or embargo on new shipments. Hypothesis-testing is destined to remain a highly uncertain exercise as long as the data essential for their confirmation or falsifiability are inadequate or are not compiled in a form appropriate for the task.

Finally, at the heart of the Egyptian-Soviet relationship is a fundamental asymmetry in aims and accomplishments. Cairo has sought from Moscow the military, economic, and diplomatic support that would enable it to turn the Arab-Israeli struggle to its advantage—whether militarily or diplomatically. While binding Moscow, it has tried over the years to neutralize or even reduce U.S. support for Israel. Moscow, on the other hand, has sought since 1967 to maintain a major presence in Egypt, not principally with the expectation of turning it onto a "socialist" or incipiently Communist path, but in order to acquire strategic advantages relative to its geopolitical rivalry with the United States. By provisioning that major Arab state (and others as well) with enough weapons to resist settling with Israel on disadvantageous or intolerable terms, Moscow has been responsibile for accelerating the Middle East arms race and raising the level of tension, albeit within bounds that it hoped to be able to control. In sum, the Soviet purpose, for reasons of its regional and global strategy, has been to perpetuate regional tension without letting it get out of hand. Its overall policy was against war but not in favor of peace, at least not on terms that the local contestants would accept in the absence of a superpower fiat. And if wars did erupt, reasoned Moscow, they might create difficulties, but they would not threaten vital Soviet security interests and hence could be tolerated.

From this asymmetry of goals has flowed an asymmetry of accomplishments. At no time was this more dramatically evident than in Sadat's decision to go to war in October 1973. Sadat accepted Soviet advice on how to use the military hardware, but he did not look to Moscow to develop a foreign policy for Egypt's new strategic situation. Arms were the price Moscow paid for undermining the U.S. position in the Middle East and for the rental of strategically valuable real estate. Somewhat untidily, they also opened options to Egypt that were sometimes uncongenial to larger Soviet aims. At the very least, they meant that Moscow was confronted with the task of reconciling its quest for improving relations with the United States with its policy of aggravating regional tensions, which, it must be noted, were there to begin with. The resulting "contradictions," the "givens" of international politics, remain unresolved and a source of dilemmas. But they are accepted by Moscow as inherent in the nature of change, even though the changes themselves often run counter to the short-term state interests of the Soviet Union.

The influence relationship between a superpower and a Third World country being asymmetrical, a superpower, though unable to impose its preference on the domestic or foreign policy behavior of the client, may nonetheless be quite satisfied with the relationship because of the accretion of regional and global advantages that it sees as stemming from facilitating a client's general policy orientation. In this study we have called this phenomenon strategic context.

Presumably, Moscow judges the successes and failures of its different policies in different ways. For the Western analyst it is essential to avoid oversimplified judgments of Soviet policy that are based only on what the USSR has accomplished in the bilateral relationship with the Third World client and that do not consider the broader consequences of the relationship for Soviet policy. A failure to see the forest for the trees is serious. The dimension of strategic context helps to explain why superpowers persist in giving aid to client states in the face of continued failures to bring about changes in their behavior. Indeed, it is very likely that the elites in superpowers show little inclination to curtail the indiscriminate quest for influence in the Third World for a combination of similar reasons: the competition among key bureaucracies for power, a larger share of scarce resources, and vindication of a certain line of policy; a leadership's image of the behavior befitting a global power; a continued fascination with the mystique of shaping events and trends in the Third World; and the rational dimensions of the geo-strategic arguments.

The substantive evaluation of the Soviet-Egyptian influence relationship completed, there remains the need for conclusions on the general theme of operationalizing the concept of influence. The challenge for analysts of foreign policy lies not in assessing the Soviet Union's power or presence, both of which are fairly straightforward computational exercises, but in determining the extent and nature of the influence it has with client states in the Third World.

The first prerequisite for any influence analysis is to identify the instances of tension and the kinds of problems that exist between the two parties, and then to trace and study their fluctuations and intensity. This can be accomplished by a systematically chronological and micro-historical examination of all interactions that take place between countries A and B and of the responses of each to these interactions. In the process, most of the important issue areas troubling the relationship will become evident. Once identified, these instances of variance become the focal points for detailed case studies that illumine and define the influence relationship itself. The outcomes of these different issue areas provide the basis for the evaluation of influence.

During the 1967 to 1975 period, there were eleven issue areas that could be researched with the data that were available and appropriate for use (Appendix 1). Some of these (for example, #1, #2, and #6) were short-lived; others (for example, #7 and #11) festered on, exacerbating tensions and giving the lie to the hoary belief that material inputs and political support necessarily build influence. Their clinical examination revealed that small and medium powers have far more control over their domestic and foreign policies than is usually appreciated and that a presence, though a precondition for influence, is neither a measure nor an indicator of it. Influence is a complex phenomenon but not an undeterminable one. Except in rare instances of continued ambiguity, the influencer and the influencee emerged fairly clearly.

Second, the proper study of the Soviet-Egyptian influence relationship demands at least as much attention to Egypt and Egyptian politics as to the Soviet Union and Soviet policy. Perhaps more. Close study of the developments, interactions, and prominent issue areas provides the analyst of Soviet foreign policy with a knowledge of the domestic politics of the Third World country and, through this, the necessary appreciation of how the interplay between domestic and external considerations shapes and steels responses to the pressures from the superpower. It enhances his understanding of the limitations on a superpower's leverage and the reasons a small power can withstand pressures. In a word, it goes a long way toward explaining why dependency seldom leads to compliance. Failure to give domestic determinants their just due inevitably results in distortion of the USSR's actual leverage and in underestimation of the extent to which it must cope with a dearth of options, uncertainty over how to proceed in the face of stern resistance to Soviet preferences, and anxiety over the potential capriciousness of the client. The analysis of the Soviet-Egyptian influence relationship in 1969, during the incipient stage of the war of attrition; in May 1971, when the Soviet-Egyptian Treaty of Friendship and Cooperation was signed; and in October 1973, at the time of the Fourth Arab-Israeli War, would have suffered had not due attention been paid to the domestic factors that shaped Egyptian policy.

The reasons for the difficulty in pressuring a client are several: the inability of the superpower to project its military power directly into the client's political system; the absence of manipulative links to indigenous elites that are able and willing to topple the existing government and assume power on the bayonets of a superpower; and each superpower's concern lest an open intervention on its part prompt the adversary to make a countervailing response that could escalate out of all proportion to the potential gains.

There is a growing realization that non-coercive diplomacy is the only way to cultivate closer relations with nonaligned Third World countries, who remain fearful of any signs of superpower interventionism. The marginality of these countries to the superpower's essential security disposes it toward toleration of rebuffs and setbacks. Aware of the limits of their own influence in Third World countries, the policymaking elites in a superpower are nevertheless prone to exaggerate that of their adversary. Utterly fascinated by each other, the leaders of the Soviet Union and the United States tend to slight the element of choice available to countries such as Egypt, largely oblivious of the paradoxical fact that decolonization and nonalignment, and the constraints imposed on the superpowers by nuclear deterrence, have done more to change the character of international politics and decrease superpower options in the Third World than all of their ponderous maneuvers vis-à-vis each other to gain the upper hand.

Third, the collection and proper use of relevant data are essential for a more precise evaluation of an influence relationship. These data are joint communiqués, editorials in elite newspapers and journals, official speeches, and exchanges of political missions. When analyzed in combination and supplemented by the irregularly available but highly pertinent political and military information, they provide the empirical referents for securing a "fix" on the influence relationship. It is essential to compare these data—particularly the thematic content analyses of joint communiqués—over a period of time (Appendix 4). Working within a contextual framework turns up much to illumine the influence relationship.

Fourth, an influence relationship may sometimes be ambiguous and therefore be difficult to treat methodologically. By way of illustration, we shall take two different types of circumstances: one in which the superpower sought to restrain the client by depriving it of the means of pursuing an avowedly preferred policy; and another in which it counseled restraint but, because of other considerations, ultimately enabled the client to exercise an option contrary to what the superpower wanted.

In the first situation, the Soviet decision to curtail arms shipments to Egypt in December 1971 was alleged by Sadat to have been the reason that he could not make 1971 "the year of decision" and go to war, as he had repeatedly promised. If, as I believe, Moscow, by withholding arms, prevented Sadat from starting hostilities, this would certainly be an example of Soviet influence over Egyptian behavior. Of course the question can be asked, did Sadat really contemplate war at the time or did he use the Soviet Union as a scapegoat for his lack of action. This speculation, by minimizing the importance of the Soviet role as well as the internal opposition Sadat risked at a time when his own position was weak, gives rise to an ambiguity. But in the absence of conclusive information, it must be considered.

In the second situation, in 1973 the Soviet leadership was counseling the Egyptians against war but at the same time was supplying the arms that very quickly made possible the option of war. Moscow may have given the arms for reasons quite apart from any desire to encourage the military option, namely, because of Sadat's renewal in December 1972 of the five-year agreement under which the Soviet navy used Egyptian port facilities; the receipt from Arab sources of payments for Egypt's weapons at a time when Moscow was in need of hard currency; and the Soviet leaders' low opinion of Egyptian military ability and resolve. An explanation along these lines does not ignore the extent to which the Soviet leadership made possible the Egyptian decision to go to war in October 1973; but it does make clear that there were many considerations that went into the initial decision to agree to the Egyptian requests for arms and that though none of these was a desire to encourage Egypt to go to war, once Moscow did perceive Sadat's real intent, probably in late spring and early summer, it could not suddenly cut down on the arms flow.

In the two cases noted above, subsequent developments brought the USSR consequences clearly unwanted and unanticipated: the first resulted in the July 1972 expulsion of Soviet military personnel; the second, in the October War, which affected the course of Soviet-American relations. We find, then, that it is easy both to overestimate the extent to which Soviet inputs into Egypt bring influence and to underestimate the profound constraints on Soviet influence inherent in the institutions, practices, and political climate of this target country. Though "dependent," Egypt has been capable of undertaking independent foreign policy initiatives, at times to the detriment of the immediate interests of the Soviet Union. The party to be influenced may turn out in the end to be the one that holds the whiphand.

Finally, this study hopes to have demonstrated that though influence relationships are complex, variable, and occasionally ambiguous, the existing data do provide analysts of foreign policy with the means for more precise assessments. The Soviet experience with Egypt is not atypical. It has counterparts elsewhere in the Third World. From India to Cuba, from Indonesia to Syria, from Iraq to Ghana, the Soviets have invested heavily to establish a presence, but they have seldom, and even then only briefly, acquired direct influence over the institutions, policies, or elites of the putative puppets. More than two decades after the start of direct Soviet involvement in the Third World the time has come to utilize the relevant data for taking a critical look at what influence the Soviets have actually wielded and the benefits they have personally derived as a consequence of their assorted programs and policies. In-depth studies of the Soviet influence relationship with other Third World countries are feasible. They can provide the basis for an informed, rational, far-sighted approach to the very real problem of coping with the Soviet challenge in the Third World, and elsewhere, in the years ahead.

Appendices

Appendix One

Key Event / Issue Area	Date	Egypt's Behavior/Position	Soviet Behavior/Position	Policy Initiator	Who Benefits	Influencer
1. Egypt's effort to recover from the June War and avoid being pressured into a settlement with Israel	Post-June 10, 1967	Is defeated by Israel Remains extremely vulnerable	Undertakes massive and rapid rearmament of Egypt Convenes emergency session of U.N. General Assembly in an attempt to pressure a repeat of 1956 Israeli withdrawal	Soviet Union	Egypt's recovery starts USSR expands its presence USSR's support enables Egypt to refuse a settlement with Israel	Soviet Union
2. A Soviet-American initiative at the United Nations to persuade both parties to the Middle East conflict to agree to a compromise settlement	July 10-20, 1967	Nasir meets with Soviet deputy foreign minister in Cairo, but refuses to accept the Soviet case for a political settlement	Works with the United States to devise a draft resolution acceptable to Egypt and Israel Tries to convince Nasir to agree to the compromise superpower proposal	Soviet Union (and the United States)	Egypt adheres to its own position	Egypt
3. Adoption of U.N. General Assembly Resolution 242	November 22, 1967	Demands a return to status quo ante Presses for U.N. action against Israel	Favors acceptance of Resolution 242, which is somewhat less than a call for a total Israeli withdrawal	Soviet Union and Egypt both played an active role in the United Nations	Egypt has a resolution that can be interpreted to suit its needs and aims	Egypt

4. Start of the War of Attrition	March-June 1969	Breaks the truce and resumes heavy fighting along the canal Draws the super-powers into an ominous confron-tation	Egypt	Calls for a polit-ical settlement Criticizes Arab groups who contend Arab forces are strong enough to achieve a military victory Consults with U.S. about the basis for a settle-ment	Egypt	Nasir offsets sagging domestic image and the effect of student unrest Nasir preempts the role of militant leader from Palestine Libera-tion Organization and Fedayeen guerrillas Nasir carries USSR along with his policy	Egypt
5. Egypt's inability to cope with Israeli deep penetration raids, and Nasir's quest for a direct Soviet military intervention	January 1970	Nasir flies secret-ly to Moscow to ask for help		Agrees to send missile crews, pilots, and air defense teams to protect Egypt's heartland	Egypt	Egypt gains greater commitment from the USSR USSR acquires additional military bases	Egypt
6. Cease-fire along the Suez Canal	August 7, 1970	Agrees to a three-month cease-fire, thus implicitly acknowledging the failure of the War of Attrition Nasir cracks down on Pales-tinian organiza-tions, terminating their broadcasting privileges		Favors the cease-fire	Egypt (in support of U.S. cease-fire plan)	Egypt gains a respite The USSR is enabled to defuse a dangerous situation	Egypt

Key Event/ Issue Area	Date	Egypt's Behavior/Position	Soviet Behavior/Position	Policy Initiator	Who Benefits	Influencer
7. Soviet-Egyptian Treaty of Friendship and Cooperation	May 27, 1971	Sadat purges his domestic opponents some of whom are known to favor closer ties with the Soviet Union and considers the Rogers Plan for an interim settlement and reopening of the canal	Is uneasy over developments in Egypt Soviet President Podgornyi arrives on May 25, with a top level government, party, and military delegation, to discuss Soviet-Egyptian relations in the light of Sadat's purge	Soviet Union	Sadat obtains formalization and expansion of Soviet military commitment, and Soviet assurance of non-interference in Egypt's domestic policies The USSR seeks to institutionalize its presence in Egypt and lessen the likelihood of a resurgence of U.S. activity in Egypt	Egypt (though the USSR was the apparent influencer)
8. Difficulties stemming from the Indo-Pakistani War	December 1971	Defers resumption of hostilities against Israel	Diverts to India arms promised Egypt Withdraws missile crews and planes from the defense of Aswan Dam, supposedly to reinforce India, and cautions Sadat against starting a war	Soviet Union	The USSR assures itself against possible military involvement at a time when it is involved in the crisis on the Indian sub-continent	Soviet Union

		Egypt	Egypt	Egypt
9. Expulsion of Soviet military personnel	July 17, 1972	Orders the 15,000 Soviet military advisers and troops to leave Egypt	Withdraws its military personnel, thus sharply diminishing its presence in Egypt	Sadat retains support of the Army and gains popularity among Egyptians
10. The Fourth Arab-Israeli War (the October War)	October 6, 1973	Launches an attack across the Suez Canal to retake Sinai (while Syria strikes in the Golan Heights) Reinforces its military initiative with an Arab oil boycott organized by Egypt and Saudi Arabia	Airlifts arms and supplies to Egypt (and Syria) within seventy-two hours after the outbreak of hostilities Prevents the U.N. Security Council from acting during early stages of the fighting when Egypt (and Syria) was gaining ground	Egypt regains the eastern bank of the Suez Canal Sadat forces the United States to take an active role in seeking a Middle East settlement Sadat's position internally and in the Arab world is enormously enhanced
11. Deferral of the reconvening of the Geneva conference	December 23, 1973–March 30, 1975	Opposes a reconvening of the Geneva conference, preferring Kissinger's step-by-step approach In late March 1975 formally calls for a return to Geneva, but does not press the matter	Calls for a return to Geneva, maintaining that only there could an overall settlement be negotiated	Egypt is the prime beneficiary from piecemeal, step-by-step disengagement agreements

Appendix Two

Date	Issue Areas	Influencer	*Joint Communiqués	Political Missions Related to Issue Areas	
				USSR → Egypt	Egypt → USSR
1. post-June 10, 1967	Egyptian Recovery	Soviet Union	1. June 24, 1967 (Cairo)	1	2
2. July 10-20, 1967	U.S.-Soviet Discussion of a Political Settlement	Egypt		1	0
3. November 22, 1967	Resolution 242	Egypt	*2. January 13, 1968 (Cairo) *3. July 10, 1968 (Moscow)	0	0
4. March-June 1969	Start of the War of Attrition	Egypt	4. December 24, 1968 (Cairo) 5. June 13, 1969 (Cairo)	4	1
5. January 1970	Egypt's Quest for Direct Soviet Military Involvement	Egypt	6. December 12, 1969 (Moscow)	5	5
6. August 7, 1970	Cease-fire Agreement	Egypt	7. July 17, 1970 (Moscow) *8. October 3, 1970 (Cairo) *9. December 20, 1970 (Cairo) *10. December 26, 1970 (Moscow) *11. January 19, 1971 (Cairo) *12. April 20, 1971 (Moscow)	0	1

7. May 27, 1971	Soviet-Egyptian Treaty	Egypt	13. May 27, 1971 (Cairo) 14. July 4, 1971 (Moscow) 15. July 30, 1971 (Cairo)	6	6
8. December 1971	Difficulties Stemming From Indo-Pakistani War	Soviet Union	16. October 13, 1971 (Moscow)	0	1
9. July 17, 1972	Expulsion of Soviet Military Personnel	Egypt	17. February 4, 1972 (Moscow) 18. April 29, 1972 (Moscow) 19. July 14, 1972 (Moscow) 20. October 18, 1972 (Moscow)	2	6
10. October 6, 1973	The Fourth Arab-Israeli War	Egypt	21. February 10, 1973 (Moscow) 22. May 29, 1973 (Moscow)	1	4
11. December 22, 1973-March 31, 1975	Deferral of the Reconvening of the Geneva Conference	Egypt	23. January 24, 1974 (Moscow) 24. March 5, 1974 (Cairo) 25. October 18, 1974 (Moscow) 26. December 30, 1974 (Moscow) 27. February 4, 1975 (Cairo) 28. April 22, 1975 (Moscow)	4	5

*For reference purposes all the communiqués are listed in chronological order. Those that do not relate directly to specific issue areas are marked with an asterisk.

Appendix Three
EXCHANGE OF MISSIONS

	Political		Military		Economic		Cultural-Scientific	
	USSR to Egypt	Egypt to USSR	USSR to Egypt	Egypt to USSR	USSR to Egypt	Egypt to USSR	USSR to Egypt	Egypt to USSR
June-December								
1967	2	3	2	1	0	1	1	0
1968	2	3	2	0	4	1	3	3
1969	5	6	0	0	1	4	4	2
1970	6	6	1	0	2	2	12	9
1971	4	6	0	1	4	3	13	10
1972	2	6	2	2	2	2	12	13
1973	4	4	1	2	0	1	11	8
1974	3	5	0	0	3	3	14	11
January-June								
1975	1	1	0	0	3	2	2	1
Total	29	40	8	6	19	19	72	56

COMMUNIQUÉS (1968-1975)

1. Date	January 13, 1968
2. Place	Cairo
3. Head of Delegation	Kirill T. Mazurov
4. Duration	January 7-13
5. Major Focus	a) Bilateral Relations
	b) "The withdrawal of the Israeli forces from all the occupied territory back to the 5 June 1967 lines"
6. Level of Agreement	Mazurov holds "detailed, friendly" discussions with Nasir.
7. Commitments	"The possibilities of increasing cooperation in all fields . . ." were discussed. [This formulation signified that neither the USSR nor Egypt got all it wanted.]
8. Overall Assessment	a) No mention of appreciation for Soviet aid implied a certain coolness (Brezhnev had been expected).
	b) There was no mention of the Palestinians or "imperialism," i.e. the United States.
	c) There was no mention of Resolution 242.
	d) There was no mention of socialism or party-to-party ties.
9. Differences from Previous Communiqué	[This is the first communiqué in this study that was subjected to a thematic content analysis.]

1. Date	July 10, 1968
2. Place	Moscow
3. Head of Delegation	Nasir
4. Duration of Visit	July 4-10
5. Major Focus	a) Middle East
	b) Global issues: Vietnam, disarmament, NPT, anti-colonialism, European security, etc.
	c) CPSU/ASU ties
	d) Imperialism
6. Level of Agreement	a) "Frank views" are exchanged on several matters connected with "the development of comprehensive cooperation" between the USSR and Egypt on the Middle East situation.
	b) Both sides agree on the need to settle the crisis in accordance with U.N. Security Council Resolution 242, though they do differ on a number of points.
	c) Both sides stress the importance of strengthening government-to-government contacts in all fields and welcome "the establishment and the development of friendly contacts between the CPSU and the ASU in the UAR."
7. Commitments	a) Soviet Union offers and "will continue to offer . . . various kinds of political and economic support, as well as assistance in enhancing [Egypt's] defense ability."

Appendix Four (continued)

8. Overall Assessment	a) The formation of an anti-imperialist front acquired importance.
	b) Both sides made concessions (see below) in this far-ranging communiqué.
9. Differences from Previous Communiqué	a) Nasir expresses "deep gratitude" for Soviet political, economic, and military support.
	b) The USSR does not call for Israel's withdrawal from all Arab territory.
	c) It says that peace requires "heeding the legitimate rights" of the Arab people in Palestine.
	d) Party-to-party contacts are established.
	e) Socialism is mentioned.
	f) Resolution 242 is specifically mentioned.

1. Date	December 24, 1968
2. Place	Cairo
3. Head of Delegation	Gromyko
4. Duration	December 21-24
5. Major Focus	Bilateral relations
6. Level of Agreement	The two sides demand that Israel withdraw "from all territory" that it occupied in 1967.
7. Commitments	The USSR "once again declares its complete support" of Egypt.
8. Overall Assessment	a) Each side said it "appreciates" the steps taken by the other, but neither specifically expressed full approval of these steps.
	b) Moscow leaned somewhat toward Cairo's position.
9. Differences from Previous Communiqué	a) There is no mention of the Palestinians, imperialism, or socialism.
	b) Egypt does not express gratitude for Soviet aid.

1. Date	June 13, 1969
2. Place	Cairo
3. Head of Delegation	Gromyko
4. Duration	June 10-13
5. Major Focus	Bilateral relations
6. Level of Agreement	a) The same as in December 1968
	b) Both sides say a peaceful settlement requires implementation "of all parts and provisions" (i.e. implying but not mentioning a solution of Palestinian problem) of Resolution 242.
7. Commitments	No change
8. Overall Assessment	No change
9. Differences from Previous Communiqué	No change

1. Date	December 12, 1969
2. Place	Moscow
3. Head of Delegation	Sadat (as personal representative of Nasir and member of the ASU Executive Committee)
4. Duration	December 9-12
5. Major Focus	a) Bilateral relations
	b) Special attention devoted to "the present international situation" [i.e. the War of Attrition] . . . which "calls for urgent and constructive steps. . . . ."
6. Level of Agreement	a) The "serious danger to peace and security" is caused by Israel's aggression, which is supported by "imperialist forces, the United States in the first place."
	b) The two sides stress the "importance" of closer governmental and party ties.
7. Commitments	The two sides "agreed on practical steps to further develop" their "all-round cooperation."
8. Overall Assessment	Notwithstanding persisting political differences, the two sides expanded their cooperation in various fields.
9. Differences from Previous Communiqué	a) The U.S. is mentioned by name as the main force behind Israel.
	b) The need for closer party ties was stressed.
	c) The two sides agreed to rally "all progressive forces" against imperialism.
	d) They mentioned the "Arab people of Palestine" again.
	e) Their call for "practical steps" signified renewed attention to military assistance.

---

1. Date	July 17, 1970
2. Place	Moscow
3. Head of Delegation	Nasir
4. Duration	June 29-July 17
5. Major Focus	"Great attention was paid" to the "further development of all-round cooperation" between the Soviet Union and Egypt, to the situation in the Middle East, and to "other international problems of mutual interest."
6. Level of Agreement	a) The two sides "confirmed their similarity (*Pravda* used the word "identicality") of views "on the Middle East."
	b) Israel is called upon to withdraw from all Arab lands.
	c) Solidarity with the Arab people of Palestine is expressed.
7. Commitments	a) The two sides discuss "further steps" to achieve a "political settlement."
	b) The USSR reaffirms its readiness "to continue supporting the just struggle of the Arab peoples . . . and give them the necessary assistance in this."

357

8. *Overall Assessment*	a) The Rogers Plan, though not mentioned by name, was the main topic of discussion.
	b) The attention to the Palestinians was minimal.
9. *Differences from Previous Communiqué*	a) There is a stress on global issues of interest to the USSR.
	b) Nasir "expressed profound gratitude for the all-round assistance" of the USSR and for its "decisive support" against Israel.
	c) Brezhnev accepts an invitation to visit Egypt.

1. *Date*	October 3, 1970
2. *Place*	Cairo
3. *Head of Delegation*	Kosygin
4. *Duration*	September 29-October 3
5. *Major Focus*	Bilateral relations
6. *Level of Agreement*	Nasir's death led both sides to emphasize the need to strengthen Soviet-Egyptian friendship.
7. *Commitments*	No change
8. *Overall Assessment*	Kosygin sized up the new leadership and counseled caution.
9. *Differences from Previous Communiqué*	Coming so soon after Nasir's funeral, the communiqué does not deal with any specific issues.

1. *Date*	December 20, 1970
2. *Place*	Cairo
3. *Head of Delegation*	Ponomarev
4. *Duration*	December 10-20
5. *Major Focus*	a) CPSU/ASU ties
	b) International problems, "including the people's struggle in Asia, Africa and Latin America against imperialism"
6. *Level of Agreement*	a) Any settlement is to be based on Resolution 242, with due regard for the "legitimate rights" of the Palestinians.
	b) Both sides agree on the need to secure progress "without delay."
7. *Commitments*	CPSU delegation promises continued Soviet support, citing the Warsaw Pact statement of December 2, 1970.
8. *Overall Assessment*	a) CPSU delegation "expressed satisfaction" with ASU's determination to follow Nasir's "progressive line."
	b) It expressed satisfaction with Egypt's efforts for peace and "for avoiding resumption of military operations in the Middle East."
	c) The ASU expressed "profound gratitude to the CPSU and the Soviet Union generally for their comprehensive aid. . . ."
9. *Differences from Previous Communiqué*	No change from July 17, 1970.

1. Date	December 26, 1970
2. Place	Moscow
3. Head of Delegation	Ali Sabri
4. Duration	December 20-26
5. Major Focus	Bilateral relations
6. Level of Agreement	a) There is a call for closer party-to-party contacts.
	b) A peaceful settlement is considered possible "by full implementation" of Resolution 242, including regard for the just rights of the Palestinians.
	c) The two sides note that Israel could not pursue its policy without "constant" U.S. support.
7. Commitments	a) New agreements are reached "on a further development of trade and economic cooperation."
	b) The USSR promises "further aid and support" for the struggle to liberate the "occupied territories."
8. Overall Assessment	The concentration on economic issues and new Soviet commitments in the economic field suggested some difficulties on military matters.
9. Differences from Previous Communiqué	No change

1. Date	January 19, 1971
2. Place	Cairo
3. Head of Delegation	Podgornyi
4. Duration	January 13-19
5. Major Focus	a) Bilateral relations
	b) Economic issues
6. Level of Agreement	a) The two sides note "with satisfaction" the "friendly ties in the political, economic, defense and other fields."
7. Commitments	a) The USSR agrees to provide "all possible assistance in the electrification of rural areas, in the reclamation of new lands and in other fields as well."
	b) USSR gives assurance that it "will further support" Egypt's efforts to regain its lands.
8. Overall Assessment	a) The Soviet delegation was heavily economic in character. It came to celebrate the completion of the Aswan High Dam.
	b) Egypt expressed "its high appreciation and its gratitude" for Soviet support against Israel.
	c) It also expressed "profound gratitude" for Soviet aid in building the Aswan Dam.
9. Differences from Previous Communiqué	a) Sadat is invited to visit the USSR.
	b) Cooperation in the field of defense is specifically mentioned.

1. Date	April 20, 1971
2. Place	Moscow
3. Head of Delegation	Mahmud Riyad
4. Duration	April 15-20

Appendix Four (continued)

5. Major Focus	a) Bilateral relations
	b) The Middle East
6. Level of Agreement	a) "The talks brought out a full identity of views on all questions discussed."
	b) Attitude on Resolution 242 and the Palestinians is same as December 26, 1970.
7. Commitments	No change
8. Overall Assessment	a) The need for regular contacts and consultations was stressed.
	b) Egypt noted its positive reply to Jarring's memorandum of February 8, 1971.
9. Differences from Previous Communiqué	a) No gratitude is expressed for Soviet aid.
	b) Military matters are not mentioned.

1. Date	May 27, 1971
2. Place	Cairo
3. Head of Delegation	Podgornyi
4. Duration	May 25-28
5. Major Focus	Bilateral relations
6. Level of Agreement	a) No change regarding Resolution 242 and the Palestinians
	b) "Agreement was reached on practical and specific measures for implementation of the 1971 party contacts programs."
7. Commitments	A 15-year Treaty of Friendship and Cooperation is signed. The USSR affirms that it "will continue in the future to extend its comprehensive aid and support" to Egypt and other Arab states in their "just struggle against the Israeli aggression."
8. Overall Assessment	The treaty marked a new stage in the Soviet-Egyptian relationship, especially Articles 8 and 9, which have military and security implications.
9. Differences from Previous Communiqué	a) The military and political relationship is formalized.
	b) Sadat "expressed profound gratitude to the Soviet Union for its aid and support."

1. Date	July 4, 1971
2. Place	Moscow
3. Head of Delegation	Mahmud Riyad
4. Duration	June 29-July 4
5. Major Focus	Bilateral relations to exchange instruments of ratification of the May 1971 treaty
6. Level of Agreement	No change
7. Commitments	No change
8. Overall Assessment	No change
9. Differences from Previous Communiqué	a) While noting that the treaty facilitates "a further invigoration of relations between the two countries in the political, economic, and cultural fields, no specific mention is made of the defense field.

b) The problem of reopening the Suez Canal is singled out for attention: it cannot be solved in isolation from other problems, including the withdrawal of Israeli forces back to the June 5, 1967 lines.

c) There is no mention of Egypt's gratitude for Soviet aid.

1. Date	July 30, 1971
2. Place	Cairo
3. Head of Delegation	Ponomarev
4. Duration	July 20-30
5. Major Focus	A party-to-party visit, with the CPSU attending the second ASU National Congress
6. Level of Agreement	No change
7. Commitments	No change
8. Overall Assessment	The USSR was disappointed by Egypt's position on the attempted Communist coup in the Sudan.
9. Differences from Previous Communiqué	a) The ASU expresses gratitude for Soviet aid "in all fields." b) The two sides agree that "hostility toward communism is detrimental" to the liberation of Arab peoples and creates divisions in the struggle against Israel.

1. Date	October 13, 1971
2. Place	Moscow
3. Head of Delegation	Sadat
4. Duration	October 11-13
5. Major Focus	a) Bilateral relations b) The Middle East c) Global issues
6. Level of Agreement	The description of the talks as having been held "in a spirit of frankness" suggests that there were serious disagreements, notwithstanding the satisfaction expressed by the two sides with the development of ties under the 1971 treaty.
7. Commitments	No change
8. Overall Assessment	a) Soviet side noted with satisfaction Egypt's position with regard to a peaceful settlement of the Middle East crisis, through Jarring, and in accordance with Resolution 242. b) Moscow was angry at manifestations of anti-Soviet sentiment, which it attributed to Egypt's actions.
9. Differences from Previous Communiqué	a) The two sides "agreed specifically on measures aimed at further strengthening the military might of Egypt." b) Sadat notes that Egypt will "build a new life through a socialist reconstruction of society," using the experience of the USSR and relying on its assistance.

c) Sadat "highly commented on the great assistance" given by the USSR and stressed that "the
attempts to spread anti-communism and anti-
Sovietism" were detrimental to the Arab struggle.

---

1. Date	February 4, 1972
2. Place	Moscow
3. Head of Delegation	Sadat
4. Duration	February 2-4
5. Major Focus	The Middle East
6. Level of Agreement	No change on political questions pertaining to the Middle East
7. Commitments	The sides "again considered measures" for a further strengthening of Egypt's defense capacity "and outlined a number of concrete steps in this direction."
8. Overall Assessment	Sadat's principal concern was to clarify Soviet plans for building up Egypt's military capability.
9. Differences from Previous Communiqué	a) Sadat "expressed his heartfelt gratitude" for Soviet aid.
	b) Sadat invites Brezhnev to visit Egypt.

---

1. Date	April 29, 1972
2. Place	Moscow
3. Head of Delegation	Sadat
4. Duration	April 27-29
5. Major Focus	a) Bilateral relations
	b) The Middle East
6. Level of Agreement	a) Both sides "discussed" (apparently without any agreement) a wide range of questions pertaining to "the situation now taking shape in the Middle East area . . ." (in his speeches, Sadat used the term "frankness" in describing the discussions).
	b) The USSR agrees that the Arab states "have every reason to use other means [i.e. military force] to regain" their lands.
7. Commitments	No change: Moscow expresses "full support" for Arab efforts, though "the sides found it necessary to study again in a spirit of fraternal cooperation measures" for increasing the military potential of Egypt.
8. Overall Assessment	The circumstances of the visit, which came less than two months after the previous one by Sadat, were unusual.
9. Differences from Previous Communiqué	a) The inclusion of the phrase "to use other means" is regarded by the Arabs as the green light for war, if necessary.
	b) Sadat "expressed gratitude to the Soviet Union for its constant support"; but he does not mention the word "aid," and the phrasing is lukewarm.

1. Date	July 14, 1972
2. Place	Moscow
3. Head of Delegation	Sidqi
4. Duration	July 13-14
5. Major Focus	Bilateral relations
6. Level of Agreement	a) No change from Sadat's visit in late April
	b) USSR agrees that "in conditions of Israel's stubborn rejection of a just political settlement" the Arab states "have every reason to use all means at their disposal for the liberation of Arab territories seized by Israel in 1967 and ensuring the legitimate rights" of the Arab people of Palestine.
7. Commitments	No change from previous communiqué
8. Overall Assessment	The brevity of Sidqi's visit suggested tension and disagreement.
9. Differences from Previous Communiqué	The mention of economic cooperation serves to highlight the absence of any mention of military cooperation or of Soviet efforts to increase Egypt's defense capability.

1. Date	October 18, 1972
2. Place	Moscow
3. Head of Delegation	Sidqi
4. Duration	October 16-18
5. Major Focus	Bilateral relations
6. Level of Agreement	a) The talks were held "in an atmosphere of frankness," indicating serious disagreements (probably over arms deliveries).
	b) No change in other respects
7. Commitments	No change from previous communiqué: Both sides reaffirm the importance of the 1971 treaty.
8. Overall Assessment	This was the first high-ranking Egyptian delegation to visit the Soviet Union since the expulsion of Soviet military personnel the previous July.
9. Differences from Previous Communiqué	a) Egypt "expressed its gratitude" for Soviet help in "developing its economy, strengthening its military potential, and in other fields."
	b) The commitment of the two sides "to the principles of socialism" is noted.

1. Date	February 10, 1973
2. Place	Moscow
3. Head of Delegation	Hafiz Isma'il
4. Duration	February 7 to 10
5. Major Focus	The Middle East
6. Level of Agreement	a) "The two sides pointed out that the tense situation fraught with great dangers . . . still prevails. . . ."
	b) The USSR again upholds the right of the Arab states "to use any form of struggle in liberating their occupied territories."

7. *Commitments*	The Soviet side affirms "its continued political and economic support and its backing for the Egyptian military capabilities" in accordance with the 1971 treaty.
8. *Overall Assessment*	Many of the strains occasioned by the expulsion of the Soviet military personnel in July 1972 appeared to have ended.
9. *Differences from Previous Communiqué*	a) Egypt rejects "any plans for a settlement on the basis of the so-called partial settlement."
	b) It does not express any gratitude for Soviet support or aid.
	c) The two sides stress the importance of the 1971 treaty and the need "for a decisive checking of any attempts aimed at weakening the Soviet-Egyptian relationship."
	d) There is again reference to Soviet assistance in building up Egypt's military potential.

1. Date	May 29, 1973
2. Place	Moscow
3. Head of Delegation	Zayyat
4. Duration	May 27-29
5. Major Focus	The Middle East, especially as it relates to the upcoming debate in the Security Council
6. Level of Agreement	No change from the February communiqué
7. Commitments	No change
8. Overall Assessment	The two sides concentrated on diplomatic strategy relating to the UN Security Council debate of the Middle East crisis.
9. Differences from Previous Communiqué	The two sides call for a full Israeli withdrawal from "all the Arab territories occupied in 1967" and for a guaranteeing of the legitimate rights of the Palestinian Arab people as in previous communiqués; but they do not specifically mention Resolution 242.

1. Date	January 24, 1974
2. Place	Moscow
3. Head of Delegation	Fahmi
4. Duration	January 21-24
5. Major Focus	a) Bilateral relations
	b) The Middle East situation
6. Level of Agreement	a) The two sides note that their cooperation "is not based on transient interests but on the long-term principled bases" which are set forth in the 1971 treaty.
	b) They agree that "the holding of the Conference in Geneva is considered a great step in the direction of restoring the situation in the Middle East to normal."
	c) They "stressed that the separation agreement is positive and important," and that a final settle-

<table>
<tr><td></td><td>ment must be based on the full implementation of Resolution 242 of 22 November 1967 and Resolution 338 of 22 October 1973.
d) They agreed that the Palestinian problem "can not be discussed and solved without the representatives of the Arab People of Palestine."</td></tr>
<tr><td>7. Commitments</td><td>None are mentioned.</td></tr>
<tr><td>8. Overall Assessment</td><td>This first high-level Soviet-Egyptian exchange of missions after the October War was intended by Egypt to ease the tensions that had arisen during and after the war.</td></tr>
<tr><td>9. Differences from Previous Communiqué</td><td>The Soviet Union does not reaffirm its support for Egypt's position.</td></tr>
</table>

<table>
<tr><td>1. Date</td><td>March 5, 1974</td></tr>
<tr><td>2. Place</td><td>Cairo</td></tr>
<tr><td>3. Head of Delegation</td><td>Gromyko</td></tr>
<tr><td>4. Duration</td><td>March 1-5</td></tr>
<tr><td>5. Major Focus</td><td>a) Bilateral relations
b) The Middle East situation</td></tr>
<tr><td>6. Level of Agreement</td><td>No change from the previous communiqué</td></tr>
<tr><td>7. Commitments</td><td>None are mentioned.</td></tr>
<tr><td>8. Overall Assessment</td><td>a) There were "detailed debates" of Middle East issues, suggesting continued differences.
b) The discussions dealt primarily with the disengagement talks and the bargaining strategy for dealing with Israel.
c) As in January, this communiqué made no allusion to military questions and contained no Egyptian expression of gratitude for Soviet support or aid.</td></tr>
<tr><td>9. Differences from Previous Communiqué</td><td>a) Gromyko received PLO Chairman Yasir Arafat.
b) Egypt "received with appreciation the Soviet Union's preparedness in principle to participate in the repair work connected with the Suez Canal."
c) Sadat invites Brezhnev to visit Egypt.</td></tr>
</table>

<table>
<tr><td>1. Date</td><td>December 30, 1974</td></tr>
<tr><td>2. Place</td><td>Moscow</td></tr>
<tr><td>3. Head of Delegation</td><td>Fahmi</td></tr>
<tr><td>4. Duration</td><td>December 28-30</td></tr>
<tr><td>5. Major Focus</td><td>a) Bilateral relations
b) The Middle East situation, especially the question of the resumption of the Geneva Conference</td></tr>
<tr><td>6. Level of Agreement</td><td>The two sides "firmly" come out for the resumption of the Geneva Conference</td></tr>
<tr><td>7. Commitments</td><td>None are mentioned.</td></tr>
<tr><td>8. Overall Assessment</td><td>The announcement that Brezhnev had postponed his visit to Egypt was made separately: it was not part of the communiqué.</td></tr>
<tr><td>9. Differences from Previous Communiqué</td><td>No issues other than that of the Geneva Conference are mentioned.</td></tr>
</table>

Appendix Four (continued)

1. Date	February 5, 1975
2. Place	Cairo
3. Head of Delegation	Gromyko
4. Duration	February 3-5
5. Major Focus	Bilateral relations
6. Level of Agreement	The two sides call for the immediate resumption of the Geneva Conference and for guaranteeing the Palestinians their "national rights, including their right to self-determination and the establishment of their national entity."
7. Commitments	a) The USSR "declared its determination to continue giving aid and support in all fields. . . ." b) New consular, economic, and cultural-scientific agreements were signed.
8. Overall Assessment	The attention to economic and political issues highlighted the continued difficulty over arms shipments.
9. Differences from Previous Communiqué	A decision is made to come out officially in favor of national self-determination for the Palestinian Arab People.

1. Date	April 22, 1975
2. Place	Moscow
3. Head of Delegation	Fahmi
4. Duration	April 19-22
5. Major Focus	a) Bilateral relations b) The Middle East situation
6. Level of Agreement	No change
7. Commitments	No change
8. Overall Assessment	The contrast remained between the seeming accord in their expressed agreement to press for resumption of the Geneva Conference "at the earliest date" and the actual foot-dragging by the Egyptians.
9. Differences from Previous Communiqué	For the first time, the two sides uphold, in a communiqué, the right of the Palestinians "to set up their own state."

Selected Bibliography

THIS study of Soviet-Egyptian relations owes a heavy debt to two sources that provided invaluable primary materials on a day-to-day basis: the Foreign Broadcast Information Service (FBIS), published in Washington, D.C., and the BBC Summary of World Broadcasts. The main Soviet sources used were the newspapers, *Pravda* and *Izvestiia*, and the journals, *Kommunist, Mirovaia ekonomika i mezhdunarodnye otnosheniia, New Times,* and *International Affairs*. The Current Digest of the Soviet Press translated materials from a wide range of Soviet newspapers. The key Egyptian sources were *Al-Ahram* and the *Cairo Press Review*, a daily translation of the Egyptian press published by the Middle East News Agency. Also useful was *Arab Report and Record* (London).

BOOKS

Akademiia nauk SSR. Institut mirovoi ekonomiki i mezhdunarodnykh otnoshenii. *Mezhdunarodnyi ezhegodnik: politika i ekonomika,* 1968–1974. Moscow: Gospolitizdat, 1968 to 1974, respectively.

Beliaev, I. P. and E. M. Primakov, *Egipet: vremia prezidenta Nasera.* Moscow: Mysl, 1974.

Ben-Porat, Y., et al. *Kippur.* Tel-Aviv: Special Edition Publishers, 1974.

Blishchenko, I. P. and V. D. Kudriavtsev, *Agressiia Izrailia i mezhdunarodnoye pravo.* Moscow: Izdatel'stvo "Mezhdunarodnye otnosheniia," 1970.

Confino, Michael, and Shimon Shamir (eds.). *The U.S.S.R. and the Middle East.* New York: John Wiley and Sons, 1973.

Copeland, Miles. *The Game of Nations: The Amorality of Power Politics.* London: Weidenfeld and Nicolson, 1969.

Dekmejian, R. Hrair. *Egypt Under Nasir: A Study in Political Dynamics.* New York: State University of New York Press, 1971.

Demchenko, P. *Arabskii vostok i chas ispytanii.* Moscow: Gospolitizdat, 1967.

Dishon, Daniel (ed.). *Middle East Record, Volume Three: 1967.* Jerusalem: Israel Universities Press, 1971.

———. *Middle East Record, Volume Four: 1968.* Jerusalem: Israel Universities Press, 1973.

El-Rayyes, Riad N., and Dunia Nahas (eds.). *The October War.* Beirut: An-Nahar Report Books, 1974.

Evron, Yair. *The Middle East: Nations, Superpowers and Wars.* New York: Praeger Publishers, 1973.

Freedman, Robert O. *Soviet Policy Toward the Middle East Since 1970.* New York: Praeger Publishers, 1975.

Glassman, Jon D. *Arms for the Arabs: The Soviet Union and War in the Middle East.* Baltimore: The Johns Hopkins University Press, 1975.

Golan, Galia. *Yom Kippur and After: The Soviet Union and the Middle East Crisis.* Cambridge: Cambridge University Press, 1976.

Golan, Matti. *The Secret Conversations of Henry Kissinger: Step-by-Step Diplomacy in the Middle East.* New York: Quadrangle Books, 1976.

Heikal, Mohamed. *The Road to Ramadan.* London: Collins, 1975.

Herzog, Chaim. *The War of Atonement: October, 1973.* Boston: Little, Brown and Company, 1975.

Hunter, Robert E. *The Soviet Dilemma in the Middle East, Part I: Problems of Commitment.* London: The Institute for Strategic Studies, September 1969, Adelphi Paper No. 55.

Insight Team of the Sunday *Times. Insight on the Middle East War.* London: André Deutsch, 1974.

Kalb, Marvin, and Bernard Kalb. *Kissinger.* Boston: Little, Brown, 1974.

Kerr, Malcolm H. *The Arab Cold War: Gamal 'Abd al-Nasir and His Rivals 1958–1970.* New York: Oxford University Press, 1971. 3rd ed.

Kohler, Foy S., Leon Gouré, and Mose L. Harvey. *The Soviet Union and the October 1973 Middle East War: The Implications for Detente.* Coral Gables, Florida: Center for Advanced Studies, University of Miami, 1974.

Lall, Arthur. *The UN and the Middle East Crisis, 1967.* New York: Columbia University Press, 1968.

Laqueur, Walter. *The Struggle for the Middle East: The Soviet*

Union in the Mediterranean, 1958–1968. New York: Macmillan, 1969.

———. *Confrontation: The Middle East and World Politics.* New York: Quadrangle, 1974.

Lenczowski, George. *Soviet Advances in the Middle East.* Washington, D.C.: American Enterprise Institute, 1972.

Matar, Fuad. *Russya al-nasiriyya wa Misr al-misriyya,* Vol. 2. Beirut: Al-Nahar Publications, 1972.

MccGwire, Michael (ed.). *Soviet Naval Developments: Capability and Context.* New York: Praeger Publishers, 1973.

MccGwire, Michael, Ken Booth, and John McDonnell (eds.). *Soviet Naval Policy: Objectives and Constraints.* New York: Praeger Publishers, 1975.

Mirskii, G. I. *Armiia i politika v stranakh Azii i Afriki.* Moscow, Nauka, 1970.

Monroe, Elizabeth, and A. H. Farrar-Hockley. *The Arab-Israel War, October 1973: Background and Events.* London: International Institute for Strategic Studies, 1974/1975. Adelphi Paper No. 111.

O'Ballance, Edgar. *The Third Arab-Israeli War.* London: Faber and Faber, 1972.

———. *The Electronic War in the Middle East, 1968–1970.* Hamden, Conn.: The Shoe String Press, 1974.

Pennar, Jaan. *The U.S.S.R. and the Arabs: The Ideological Dimension 1917–1972.* New York: Crane, Russak and Company, 1973.

Perlmutter, Amos. *Egypt: The Praetorian State.* New Brunswick, N.J.: Transaction Books, 1974.

Ro'i, Yaacov. *From Encroachment to Involvement: A Documentary Study of Soviet Policy in the Middle East, 1945–1973.* New York: John Wiley and Sons, 1974.

Sadat, Anwar El. *Speeches by President Anwar El Sadat, September 1970–March 1971.* Cairo: Ministry of Information, 1971.

Smolansky, Oles. *The Soviet Union and the Arab East under Khrushchev.* Lewisburg, Penna.: Bucknell University Press, 1974.

Whetten, Lawrence. *The Canal War: Four Power Conflict in the Middle East.* Cambridge: The MIT Press, 1974.

Yodfat, Aryeh. *Arab Politics in the Soviet Mirror.* Tel-Aviv: Israel Universities Press, 1973.

ARTICLES

Andreasyan, Ruben, "Middle East: The Oil Factor," *New Times,* No. 45-46 (November 1973), 18-20.

Ashkar, Riad, "The Syrian and Egyptian Campaigns," *Journal of Palestine Studies,* 3, No. 2 (Winter 1974), 15-33.

Ballis, William B., "Soviet Foreign Policy Toward Developing States: The Case of Egypt," *Studies on the Soviet Union,* 7, No. 3 (1968), 1-30.

Bell, Coral, "The October Middle East War: A Case Study in Crisis Management During Detente," *International Affairs,* 50, No. 4 (October 1974), 531-543.

Belyaev, I., "Ways of Ending the Middle East Crisis," *International Affairs,* No. 10 (October 1968), 25-28.

―――, "Dragged-Out Middle East Conflict: Who Stands to Gain?," *International Affairs,* No. 9 (September 1969), 67-70.

―――, "The Middle East in Contemporary World Affairs," *Journal of Palestine Studies,* 2, No. 4 (Summer 1973), 13-24.

Belyaev, Igor, and Evgeny Primakov, "The Situation in the Arab World," *New Times,* No. 39 (September 27, 1967), 8-11.

―――, "Kogda voina stoit u poroga," *Za rubezhom,* No. 27 (June 30–July 6, 1967), 6-7.

Brown, G. M., "The Consequences of Yom Kippur: Some Preliminary Notes," *Australian Outlook,* 28, No. 2 (August 1974), 196-204.

Campbell, John C., "Is America's Lone Hand Played Out?," *New Middle East,* No. 36 (September 1971), 11-15.

Demchenko, P., "Blizhnii Vostok mezhdu voinoi i mirom," *Mirovaia ekonomika i mezhdunarodnye otnosheniia,* No. 6 (June 1968), 77-80.

―――, "Egypt Today," *International Affairs,* No. 6 (June 1973), 72-76.

―――, "The Middle East: From War to Peace," *International Affairs,* No. 5 (May 1974), 66-69.

Dimant-Kass, Ilana, "*Pravda* and *Trud*: Divergent Soviet Attitudes Toward the Middle East," *Soviet Union,* 1, Part 1 (1974), 1-31.

―――, "The Soviet Military and Soviet Policy in the Middle East, 1970–73," *Soviet Studies,* 26, No. 4 (October 1974), 502-521.

Dmitriev, E., "Soviet-Arab Friendship: A New Stage," *International Affairs*, No. 8 (August 1971), 66-68.

―――, "Problema likvidatsii ochaga voennoi opasnosti na Blizhnem Vostoke," *Kommunist*, No. 4 (March 1973), 103-112.

―――, "Middle East: Dangerous Tension Must Go," *International Affairs*, No. 7 (July 1973), 27-32.

Eran, Oded, and Jerome E. Singer, "Soviet Policy Towards the Arab World 1955-71," *Survey*, 17, No. 4 (Autumn 1971), 10-29.

Evron, Yair, "Moscow Moves Closer to Delhi: What Will It Mean for Egypt?" *New Middle East*, No. 40 (January 1972), 15-17.

Frankel, Jonathan, "The Anti-Zionist Press Campaigns in the USSR 1969–1971: An Internal Dialogue?," *Soviet Jewish Affairs*, No. 3 (May 1972), 3-26.

Freedman, Robert O., "Soviet Policy Toward Sadat's Egypt," *Naval War College Review*, 26, No. 3 (November–December 1973), 63-79.

Golan, Galia, "Soviet Aims and the Middle East War," *Survival*, 16, No. 3 (May–June 1974), 106-114.

Griffith, William, "The Fourth Middle East War, the Energy Crisis and U.S. Policy," *Orbis*, 17, No. 4 (Winter 1974), 1161-1188.

Hottinger, Arnold, "The Great Powers and the Middle East," in William E. Griffith (ed.), *The World and the Great-Power Triangles* (Cambridge: The MIT Press, 1975), pp. 99-184.

Hunt, Kenneth, "The Middle East Conflict 1973: The Military Lessons," *Survival*, 16, No. 1 (January–February 1974), 4-7.

Kapeliuk, Amnon, "The Egyptian-Russian Conflict," *New Outlook*, 15, No. 7 (September 1972), 8-18.

Kerr, Malcolm H., "Soviet Influence in Egypt, 1967–73," in Alvin Z. Rubinstein (ed.), *Soviet and Chinese Influence in the Third World* (New York: Praeger Publishers, 1975), pp. 88-108.

Kimche, Jon, "Sadat and the Russians: Why . . . and What Next?," *Midstream*, 18, No. 9 (November 1972), 12-21.

―――, "New Soviet Moves in the Middle East," *Midstream*, 18, No. 4 (April 1972), 3-11.

―――, "Fall 1973: The Soviet-Arab Scenario," *Midstream*, 19, No. 10 (December 1973), 9-22.

―――, "The Riddle of Sadat," *Midstream*, 20, No. 4 (April 1974), 7-28.

Kimche, Jon, "The Making of a Myth: Unwarranted Lessons of the October War," *Midstream*, 20, No. 7 (May 1974), 3-12.

——, "Where Does Sadat Stand?," *Midstream*, 21, No. 3 (March 1975), 51-57.

Kolcum, Edward H., "Soviets Accelerating Mideast Drive," *Aviation Week and Space Technology*, 92, No. 20 (May 18, 1970), 14-18.

Kudryavtsev, V., "The Middle East Knot," *International Affairs*, No. 9 (September 1967), 29-34.

——, "Egypt's Ill-Wishers Rebuffed," *New Times*, No. 20 (May 1972), 10-11.

Laqueur, Walter, "Russia Enters the Middle East," *Foreign Affairs*, 47, No. 2 (January 1969), 296-308.

——, "Russians vs. Arabs: The Age of Disenchantment," *Commentary*, 53, No. 4 (April 1972), 60-66.

——, "On the Soviet Departure from Egypt," *Commentary*, 54, No. 6 (December 1972), 61-68.

Lewis, Bernard, "The Great Powers, the Arabs and the Israelis," *Foreign Affairs*, 47, No. 1 (July 1969), 642-652.

McDermott, A., "Sadat and the Soviet Union," *The World Today*, 28, No. 9 (September 1972), 404-410.

——, "A Russian Withdrawal; or Divorce, Egyptian Style," *New Middle East*, No. 47 (August 1972), 4-6.

Menaul, Stewart, "Reflections on the Middle East War 6–24 October 1973," in *Defence Yearbook 1974* (London: Brassey's Naval and Shipping Annual Ltd., 1974), pp. 149-161.

Mirskii, G., "Obedinennaia Arabskaia Respublika v god tiazhelykh ispytanii," *Mezhdunarodnyi ezhegodnik: politika i ekonomika 1968* (Moscow: Gospolitizdat, 1968), pp. 220-224.

——, " 'Novaia revoliutsiia' v OAR," *Mirovaia ekonomika i mezhdunarodnye otnosheniia*, No. 1 (January 1969), 38-48.

Morison, David L., "Middle East: The Soviet Entanglement," *Mizan*, 11, No. 3 (May–June 1969), 165-173.

Nes, D., "The Soviets and the Middle East," *Military Review*, 52, No. 9 (September 1972), 40-49.

O'Ballance, Edgar, "Problems of the Egyptian Phoenix," *The Army Quarterly and Defence Journal*, 102, No. 4 (July 1972), 451-457.

Ofer, Gus, "The Economic Burden of Soviet Involvement in the Middle East," *Soviet Studies*, 24, No. 3 (January 1973), 329-347.

Pajak, Roger, "Soviet Arms and Egypt," *Survival*, 17, No. 4 (July–August 1975), 165-173.

Pennar, Jaan, "Moscow and Socialism in Egypt," *Problems of Communism*, 15, No. 5 (September–October 1966), 41-47.

———, "The Arabs, Marxism and Moscow: A Historical Survey," *The Middle East Journal*, 22, No. 4 (Autumn 1968), 433-447.

Petrov, P., "Step Towards Arab Unity," *New Times*, No. 35 (September 1971), 20-22.

———, "The Soviet Union and Arab Countries," *International Affairs*, No. 11 (November 1972), 22-29.

Primakov, E., "Cairo Conspiracy Trial," *New Times*, No. 7 (February 21, 1968), 15-16.

———, "Peace Prospects in the Middle East," *International Affairs*, No. 2 (February 1969), 49-50.

———, "Why the Canal Must Be Reopened: A Soviet View," *New Middle East*, No. 46 (July 1972), 7-8.

———, "The Fourth Arab-Israeli War," *World Marxist Review*, 16, No. 12 (December 1973), 52-60.

———, "Blizhnevostochnyi krizis v 1973g." in *Mezhdunarodnyi ezhegodnik: politika i ekonomika 1973* (Moscow: Gospolitizdat, 1974), pp. 220-232.

Ra'anan, Uri, "The USSR and the Middle East: Some Reflections on the Soviet Decision Making Process," *Orbis*, 17, No. 3 (Fall 1973), 946-977.

———, "Soviet Global Policy and the Middle East," *Naval War College Review*, 24, No. 1 (September 1971), 19-29.

Rejwan, Nissim, "Nasserism: The Decline and Fall of a Radical Arab Ideology," *New Outlook*, 16, No. 6 (July–August 1973), 28-37.

Rodolpho, Claudine, "Le conflit israélo-arabe en 1968: Quelques aspects de la diplomatie arabe," *Orient*, 12, No. 47-48 (1968), 249-260.

Rubinstein, Alvin Z., "Moscow and Cairo: Currents of Influence," *Problems of Communism*, 23, No. 4 (July–August 1974), 17-28.

———, "U.S. Specialists' Perceptions of Soviet Policy Toward the Third World," *Canadian-American Slavic Studies*, 6, No. 1 (Spring 1972), 93-107.

Rumiantsev, V., "Arabskii Vostok na novom puti," *Kommunist*, No. 16 (November 1969), 90-101.

Sadat, Anwar El, "Where Egypt Stands," *Foreign Affairs*, 51, No. 1 (October 1972), 114-123.

Safran, Nadav, "The War and the Future of the Arab-Israeli Conflict," *Foreign Affairs*, 52, No. 2 (January 1974), 215-236.

———, "Engagement in the Middle East," *Foreign Affairs*, 53, No. 1 (October 1974), 45-63.

———, "The Soviet-Egyptian Treaty—As Seen From Washington," *New Middle East*, No. 36 (July 1971), 10-13.

Singh, K. R., "The Soviet-UAR Relations," *India Quarterly*, 25, No. 2 (April–June 1969), 139-152.

Smart, Ian, "The Super-Powers and the Middle East," *The World Today*, 30, No. 1 (January 1974), 4-15.

Smolansky, Oles M., "The Soviet Setback in the Middle East," *Current History*, 64, No. 377 (January 1973), 17-20.

Smolansky, Oles, and Bettie Smolansky, "Soviet Policy in Egypt: An Assessment," *Middle East Forum*, 48, No. 2 (Summer 1972), 19-28.

Strategic Survey 1973 (London: IISS, 1974), pp. 1-55.

Tolkunov, L., "Blizhnii Vostok: istoki krizisa i puti ego uregulirovaniia," *Kommunist*, No. 13 (September 1974), 97-105.

Tueni, Ghassan, "After October: Military Conflict and Political Change in the Middle East," *Journal of Palestine Studies*, 3, No. 4 (Summer 1974), 114-130.

Vatikiotis, P. J., "Egypt's Politics of Conspiracy," *Survey*, 18, No. 2 (Spring 1972), 83-99.

Vladimirov, V., "A Peaceful Settlement for the Middle East," *International Affairs*, No. 11 (November 1974), 111-113.

Volskii, D., "Istoki i uroki izrail'skoi agressii," *Mirovaia ekonomika i mezhdunarodnye otnosheniia*, No. 8 (1967), 16-27.

Volsky, D., "Middle East Prospects," *New Times*, No. 44 (October 29, 1971), 7-9.

———, "Soviet-American Relations and the Third World," *New Times*, No. 36 (September 1973), 4-6.

———, "Support the Arab Peoples Can Count On," *New Times*, No. 18-19 (May 1974), 18-19.

Weinland, R., "The Changing Mission of the Soviet Navy," *Survival*, 14, No. 3 (May–June 1972), 129-133.

Yodfat, A. Y., "Arms and Influence in Egypt: The Record of Soviet Military Assistance since June 1967," *New Middle East*, No. 10 (July 1969), 27-32.

Index

'Abd al-Latif al-Baghdadi, 178, 181
'Abd al-Nasir, Gamal: diplomacy of,
  3–7, 18–19, 24–25, 39–41, 49, 53,
  61–62, 73, 79–80, 88, 91–92,
  108–9, 116–17; domestic reforms of,
  18, 23–24, 34–35, 49–53, 71–72;
  foreign policy of, 63–65, 77–79,
  80–83, 91, 95–96, 102–3, 113,
  120–23, 127–28, 210, 212; health,
  65, 92–93, 127; leadership position
  of, 71–73, 75–76, 93–95, 101–3,
  107–8, 127–28; personnel changes
  of, 34–35, 47–51, 93–95; relations
  with Arab states, 25–26, 61, 73, 78,
  91–92, 102–3, 120–22; relations
  with the Soviet Union, 7, 30, 37,
  46–49, 62–65, 77–79, 88, 100,
  109–10, 210, 327; relations with the
  U.S., 98, 116–17, 122, 135; visits
  to the Soviet Union, 7, 59, 64, 65,
  107–9, 118, 149n
'Abd al-Quddus, Ihsan, 142, 184, 187,
  204, 207–8, 216, 222, 224, 243; on
  Egyptian-Soviet relations, 94n,
  209–10, 228, 298–99; Soviet
  criticism of, 207–8, 231
Abdullah, Isma'il Sabri, 150–51
Abû al-Nasr, Abd al-Karim, 194
Abu an-Nur, 'Abd al-Muhsin, 106–7,
  131, 146
Afghanistan, 4
aid, role in influencebuilding of,
  XVII–XVIII, XXIII, 5, 7, 18, 45–46,
  63–65, 119, 134, 185–86, 209–10,
  335, 339
Al-Ahram, 19, 41, 45, 67, 75, 78,
  79, 80, 86, 94, 99, 102, 130, 171, 174,
  182, 184, 202
Al-Fatah, 102, 121
Algeria, 19, 22, 24, 25, 97, 102, 120
'Ali, Ahmad Isma'il, 93, 213, 216,
  224–25, 227, 246
'Amir, 'Abd al-Hakim, 36–37, 131
Andropov, Iurii V., 17n, 213
Arab Communist Parties, 6, 7,
  21–22, 32, 154–56, 175, 206
Arab diplomacy, 243, 273–74; in

October War, 266–67; policy on
  Israel, 25–38, 312–13. *See also*
  Arab relations; Egyptian-Arab
  relations; oil diplomacy;
  Soviet-Arab relations
Arab-Israeli conflict: effect of
  superpower politics on, 90, 115–16,
  122–23, 140, 160–62, 164–65,
  168–70, 175, 177, 179–80, 183–85,
  204–5, 210, 225, 230–35, 244,
  272–77, 280–81, 291; Four Power
  role in, 76, 78–82, 84, 97, 111, 117,
  132; internationalization of, 53–54,
  108, 115–16, 140–41, 165, 169,
  210, 283–85; U.N. role in, 37–42,
  53–55, 67–69, 71, 76, 82, 140, 162,
  202, 231, 244. *See also* Arab-Israeli
  Wars; Geneva Conference; Middle
  East arms control proposals; Middle
  East arms race; Separation of
  Forces Agreement; settlement
  initiatives; settlement proposals;
  Sinai Agreement; United Nations
Arab-Israeli War (1948–49), 55–56
Arab-Israeli Wars. *See* June War;
  October War; Suez War; War of
  Attrition
Arab relations, 91–92, 120–21,
  163–64, 202, 238–44; Federation
  of Arab Republics, 145, 156, 158;
  Khartoum Conference, 38, 41,
  53; Rabat Summit Meetings, 91,
  102, 315. *See also* Egyptian-Arab
  relations
Arab Socialist Union (ASU), 20, 22,
  33, 35, 46, 51, 145, 157, 319–20;
  leadership of, 47–49, 62, 93–95,
  131, 219–22. *See also* Sabri, Ali
Arafat, Yasir, 61, 249, 313, 315
Arbatov, G. A., 278
arms control. *See* Middle East arms
  control
arms race. *See* Middle East arms race
Asad, Hafiz al-, 156, 187, 209, 238–39,
  244; diplomacy of, 263–64;
  relations with Egypt, 238–39,
  244, 246, 263–64, 289

375

Library of Congress Cataloging in Publication Data

Rubinstein, Alvin Z
    Red star on the Nile.

    (A Foreign Policy Research Institute book)
    Bibliography: p.
    Includes index.
        1. Egypt—Foreign relations—Russia.   2. Russia—
    Foreign relations—Egypt.   I. Title.
    DS63.2.R9R8   327.62'047   76-3021
    ISBN 0-691-07581-6
    ISBN 0-691-10048-9 pbk.